Key Contested Issues in Criminology and Criminal Justice

Key Contested Issues in Criminology and Criminal Justice addresses the key issues within criminology and criminal justice that are strongly contested among scholars in the field.

Covering 18 different themes, the book identifies the ways in which different issues are contested and demonstrates how biopsychosocial concepts and methods can inform most of them. It is divided into four broad sections. The first section examines philosophical issues such as the value of philosophy in criminology/criminal justice, the role of ideology in our disciplines, and the issues of human nature and free will versus determinism. The second section explains the biopsychosocial perspective that provides the framework used in exploring the various issues. It explores the possibility of integrating the natural sciences with criminology, behavioral and molecular genetics, evolutionary theory, and neuroscience. It also considers issues related to child maltreatment, brain development, and the role of rationality vis-à-vis emotion in decision-making. The third section examines crime causation and contains chapters on social learning versus control theories, radical/critical theories, the relationship between intelligence and criminal behavior, issues of socioeconomic status (SES), poverty, and crime, and whether religion is a barrier or bridge to antisocial behavior. The final section looks at four issues in criminal justice: the police abolition movement, the nature of punishment and its justifications by the criminal justice system, and issues in sentencing and the death penalty.

Key Contested Issues in Criminology and Criminal Justice will be of value to students and scholars in criminology and criminal justice, as well as to criminal justice practitioners.

Anthony Walsh is an emeritus professor at Boise State University, from which he retired at age 77 after 34 years of service. He has worked as a marine, police officer, and adult probation officer and entered academia at the ripe old age of 43. He has published 57 books and over 150 articles/book chapters/encyclopedia entries. He has received lifetime achievement awards from the Biosocial Criminology Association (2014) and the Biopsychosocial Division of the American Society of Criminology (2019).

Crime Science Series
Edited by: **Richard Wortley**, *University College London*

Crime science is a new way of thinking about and responding to the problem of crime in society. The distinctive nature of crime science is captured in the name.

First, crime science is about crime. Instead of the usual focus in criminology on the characteristics of the criminal offender, crime science is concerned with the characteristics of the criminal event. The analysis shifts from the distant causes of criminality – biological makeup, upbringing, social disadvantage and the like – to the near causes of crime. Crime scientists are interested in why, where, when and how particular crimes occur. They examine trends and patterns in crime in order to devise immediate and practical strategies to disrupt these patterns.

Second, crime science is about science. Many traditional responses to crime control are unsystematic, reactive, and populist, too often based on untested assumptions about what works. In contrast crime science advocates an evidence-based, problem-solving approach to crime control. Adopting the scientific method, crime scientists collect data on crime, generate hypotheses about observed crime trends, devise interventions to respond to crime problems, and test the adequacy of those interventions.

Crime science is utilitarian in its orientation and multidisciplinary in its foundations. Crime scientists actively engage with front-line criminal justice practitioners to reduce crime by making it more difficult for individuals to offend, and making it more likely that they will be detected if they do offend. To achieve these objectives, crime science draws on disciplines from both the social and physical sciences, including criminology, sociology, psychology, geography, economics, architecture, industrial design, epidemiology, computer science, mathematics, engineering, and biology.

Crime Science
Modern Technologies to Combat Crime
Lisa Stolzenberg & Stewart J. D'Alessio

Key Contested Issues in Criminology and Criminal Justice
A Biopsychosocial Perspective
Anthony Walsh

For more information about this series, please visit: www.routledge.com/criminology/series/CSCIS

Key Contested Issues in Criminology and Criminal Justice

A Biopsychosocial Perspective

Anthony Walsh

Routledge
Taylor & Francis Group
LONDON AND NEW YORK

Designed cover image: nevodka, Getty Images

First published 2026
by Routledge
4 Park Square, Milton Park, Abingdon, Oxon OX14 4RN

and by Routledge
605 Third Avenue, New York, NY 10158

Routledge is an imprint of the Taylor & Francis Group, an informa business

British Library Cataloguing-in-Publication Data
A catalogue record for this book is available from the British Library

ISBN: 978-1-041-11980-7 (hbk)
ISBN: 978-1-041-11978-4 (pbk)
ISBN: 978-1-003-66249-5 (ebk)

DOI: 10.4324/9781003662495

Typeset in Sabon
by KnowledgeWorks Global Ltd.

Contents

Preface x
Acknowledgements xviii

SECTION 1
Philosophical Issues 1

1 **Philosophy in Criminology/Criminal Justice** 3

The Value of Philosophy 3
Ontology and Epistemology 4
Moral Relativism 7
Reductionism and Holism 8
Essentialism 11

2 **Ideology and Criminology** 14

Criminology's Achilles' Heel 14
Temperament and Ideology 16
Visions of Social Reality 17
The Locus of Control 19
The Locus of Control Among Criminologists 21

3 **Human Nature and Criminology** 25

Is There a Human Nature? 25
The Blank-Slate View 28
The Ancient Seeds of Human Nature 31
Good and Evil are Both Driven by Selfishness 33

4 **The Issue of Free Will Versus Determinism** 37

Do Humans Have Free Will? 37
Free Will as Quantitative 39

Neuro-Determinism 39
Compatibilism 41
Free Will and Rationality 43
Emotion and Crime 46

SECTION 2
Biopsychosocial Issues 49

5 **Integrating the Natural Sciences with Criminology** 51

Tinbergen's Four Questions 51
Criminology and Evolutionary Biology 52
Sexuality and Criminality 54
Cheater Theory 56
Conditional Adaptation Theory 58

6 **Behavioral and Molecular Genetics** 62

Genes and "Genetic Determinism" 62
Behavioral Genetics 63
Shared and Non-Shared Environment 65
Gene-Environment Interaction and Gene-Environment Correlation 66
Molecular Genetics 68
Serotonin Polymorphisms and Criminal Behavior 69
Dopamine Polymorphisms and Criminal Behavior 71
The Differential Susceptibility Hypothesis 72

7 **The Human Brain** 75

The Wonders of the Human Brain 75
Brain Communication: Neurotransmitters 77
Glutamate and Gamma-Aminobutyric Acid 78
Getting Connected: Synaptogenesis 79
Hormones: Testosterone 80
Hormones: Cortisol 81
The Triple Imbalance Hypothesis and Aggression 81
Reinforcement Sensitivity Theory 82

8 **Childhood Maltreatment and Brain Development** 87

Evolutionary Developmental Biology and the Brain 87
The Nurturing Experience 89

Maltreatment and Early Brain Development 91
Experience-Expected and Experience-Dependent Brain Development 93
Maltreatment and Antisocial Behavior 94
Epigenetics 96

9 Rationality or Emotion: Which One Drives the Bus? 99

The Enlightenment and Rationality 99
Primary and Secondary Emotions 100
The Autonomic Nervous System and Conscience 101
Empathy and Callous-Unemotionality 105
Low Fear 107

SECTION 3
Issues of Crime Causation 111

10 Social Learning Versus Social and Self-Control Theories 113

Broad Assumptions of the Theories 113
Differential Association Theory 114
Akers' Social Learning Theory 115
The Neglect of Individual Differences 117
Social Control/Bonding Theory 118
Self-Control Theory 120
Child Effects and Genetics 122

11 Radical/Critical Idealism Versus Orthodox Realism 124

The Radical/Critical Perspective and the Nature of Crime 124
The Ontological Status of Crime 125
Labeling Theory 128
Romanticizing Criminals 130
Left Realism 131
The Square of Crime and Crime Prevention 133

12 What is Intelligence and How is it Related to Crime? 136

What is Intelligence? 136
Neurobiology and Intelligence 139
Intelligence and Crime 141
Intellectual Imbalance and Crime 143

Factors Mediating the IQ/Crime Relationship 143
Offending Among High-IQ People 145

13 Issues Related to Socioeconomic Status, Poverty, and Crime 147

Socioeconomic Status 147
IQ and SES 148
Environmental Effects on IQ 150
Temperament and SES 153
Poverty and SES 154
Poverty and Crime 155
The War on Poverty and Other Anti-Poverty Programs 157

14 Religion: Barrier or Bridge to Antisocial Behavior? 159

Religion: The Moral Institution 159
Religion as a Bridge to Antisocial Behavior 161
Religion as a Barrier to Antisocial Behavior 164
Religion and Self-Control 167

SECTION 4
Issues in Criminal Justice 171

15 Abolish the Police: Why or Why Not? 173

Do the Police Prevent Crime? 173
The Effects of De-Policing 176
Is There a War on the Police? 177
Police Shootings of Blacks and Crime Statistics 179
Police Shootings and Race-Differentiated Crime Levels 180
Circumstances in Which Officers Are Justified in Using Lethal Force 182
Shootings by Black Police Officers 184

16 Issues in Criminal Punishment 186

Consequentialism and Punishment Justification 186
Non-Consequentialism and Retribution 188
Rejecting Punishment 189
Punishment as an Evolutionary Adaptation 192
Detecting Cheats in Cooperative Groups 193
Forgiveness Strategies 195

17 **Issues in Criminal Sentencing** 197

Race and Criminal Sentencing 197
Is Criminal History a Proxy for Race? 199
Criminal Sentencing and Gender 201
Sentencing Guidelines 203
Presentence Investigation Reports 206

18 **The Death Penalty Issue** 209

The Death Penalty and Public Opinion 209
Interpreting Death Penalty Studies 210
Race and the Death Penalty 211
The Death Penalty and Victim Race 213
Women and the Death Penalty 217
Life Without the Possibility of Parole (LWOP) 218

Bibliography 221
Index 260

Preface

This book is divided into four broad sections. The first section examines philosophical issues such as the value of philosophy in criminology/criminal justice, the role of ideology in our disciplines, and the issues of human nature and free will versus determinism. The second section explains the biopsychosocial perspective that provides the framework I use to examine the various issues. It explores the possibility of integrating the natural sciences with criminology, behavioral and molecular genetics, evolutionary theory, and neuroscience. It also considers issues related to child maltreatment, brain development, and the role of rationality vis-à-vis emotion in decision-making. The third section examines crime causation and contains chapters on social learning versus control theories, radical/critical theories, the relationship between intelligence and criminal behavior, issues of socioeconomic status (SES), poverty, and crime, and whether religion is a barrier or bridge to antisocial behavior. The final section looks at four issues in criminal justice: the police abolition movement, the nature of punishment and its justifications by the criminal justice system, and issues in sentencing and the death penalty.

Few criminologists doubt that their discipline is rife with doctrinal differences in many key issues. There are debates in the physical and natural sciences on issues, but they are quickly resolved when new technologies, experiments, and observations become available. The most well-known examples are the battle between the geocentric and heliocentric models of the solar system in the 16th and 17th centuries and the eternal static versus Big Bang theories of the universe in the 20th century. There were many skeptics of the new theories, but they prevailed with virtually unanimous agreement as new evidence was discovered. No scientist today holds a geocentric view, and perhaps only a handful of physicists dispute the Big Bang theory. This is because those in the physical and natural sciences follow the evidence wherever it points while remaining open to revisions as new evidence is found.

This is not the case in criminology. Many criminologists cannot even agree on the fundamental metaphysical foundations of the plethora of contending theories in the discipline such as reductionism, holism, or emergence, free will versus determinism, nominalism versus realism, whether humans have a nature, or whether many of its key concepts such as socioeconomic status or poverty are achieved or ascribed. Many decline to even consider new technologies, experiments, and observations because they may subvert their favored theories. They are like the many academicians whom Copernicus described as stubbornly refusing to look through his telescope. Cesare Cremonini, a colleague of Copernicus, did look through the telescope but complained it gave him a headache and wanted nothing more to do with it. Many criminologists likewise complain that the technologies, methods, and theories of the biological sciences that biopsychosocial criminologists have imported make them reach for the aspirin bottle.

Perhaps the situation is such because criminology deals with the illicit behavior of individuals, and some loathe to make moral judgments about it. Of course, the technologies, methods, and theories of the biological sciences focus on individuals' genes, brains, hormones, and physiologies, and this can lead to invidious comparisons, and lead many to fear that environmental effects are being ignored, and that all illicit behavior will be attributed to the "defective" genes and brains. Nothing could be further from the truth. Biopsychosocial criminologists examine how biological variables are affected by the environments in which people find themselves. The more they learn, the more they realize just how important the environment is to understanding human behavior. No biological system, from the immune system to our genes and brains, is unaffected by environmental circumstances.

The first chapter focuses on philosophical issues. If we think philosophy is unimportant in criminology, we are reminded that many of the finest minds in physics are immersed in philosophy. Philosophy provides unity and systematizes a body of science that results from the critical examination of personal convictions, prejudices, and beliefs. It organizes our thoughts and guides us to examine the assumptions and methods we apply to our inquiries and to ponder the nature of truth and reality. As with any other domain of inquiry, the philosophy of criminology seeks to expose the practices and assumptions underlying inquiries the discipline makes and offers critiques to enhance the ability to improve its understanding of the phenomena it claims as its domain. Philosophy asks us to contemplate the abstractions and concepts we work with, which are usually, consciously or otherwise, taken for granted.

Chapter 2 examines ideology, which has been called criminology's Achilles' Heel. As in many other areas of sociopolitical life, the fault line in criminology lies between the liberal and conservative positions. This line is present, subtly hidden or in plain view, in all the key issues fought about in criminology and criminal justice. Surveys of American criminologists regarding favored causes of crime and favored theories find that ideology—conservative, moderate, liberal, or radical—best predicts the favored cause or theory. Much of this disagreement is traced to the locus of control (internal or external) that conservatives and liberals have. Criminologists with an internal locus of control favor individual-level causes of crime (e.g., lack of empathy) and theories of crime (e.g., self-control). Those with an external locus of control favor external causes of crime (e.g., poverty) and theories of crime (e.g., social learning).

The chapter examines the temperamental basis of ideology noted long ago by Plato and reinforced by modern genetics and neuroscience.

Chapter 3 explores whether human beings have an innate nature. Social scientists on the left tend to think human nature is a blank slate at birth and is formed de novo by engagement with culture. Those on the right believe that it is innate, that culture builds upon a Darwinian universal nature forged by natural selection, and that to claim otherwise discontents us from the lessons of the past. We examine the ancient hominin seeds of human nature and the basic drives of our behavior in terms of the social instincts of status-seeking, nepotism, and reciprocal altruism, and their strong opponent, our egalitarian instinct. We also look at selfishness as both good and bad. It was the position of the iconic founding fathers of sociology—Durkheim, Marx, and Weber—who all insisted that selfishness was an innate part of human nature.

Chapter 4 delves into the perennial issue of free will versus determinism. This is an important issue when considering the level of responsibility we attribute to criminals. The question is almost insoluble if we view it in dichotomous terms, either libertarian free will or hard determinism. Libertarians see humans as practically free of all externalities, such that whatever situation we are in and whatever choices we make, they could have been otherwise. Hard determinists maintain that human choice is completely determined by genetics and developmental experiences and could not be otherwise. Compatibilism is a middle ground that avers that there is some causal space for free choice. I argue that free will is a quantitative rather than a qualitative trait, unevenly distributed, and that we need both free will and determinism to understand human behavior.

Chapter 5 investigates the possibility of integrating criminology with the natural sciences. It explores Tinbergen's famous "four questions," which maintain that to understand human behavior, we must examine all levels of explanation from its distal evolutionary history to its most proximate causal mechanisms—phylogeny, function, ontogeny, and cause. This chapter primarily examines phylogeny and what evolutionary theory offers criminology. The genome is the molecular archive of millions of years of selective elimination and retention of alleles that contributed to all living organisms' twin goals—survival and reproductive success. It informs us why we have the traits we have as a result of pursuing those goals. Evolutionary theories of exploitative behavior thus focus on sexuality, particularly mating versus parenting effort. Antisocial behavior is identified with behaviors that promote mating effort, and prosocial behavior is identified with behaviors that promote parenting effort.

Chapter 6 investigates behavioral and molecular genetics, emphasizing that there is no such thing as "genetic determinism." All behavior results from genetic traits interacting with the environment. We explore the concepts of heritability, shared and nonshared environment, gene-environment interaction (G*x*E), and gene-environment correlation (rGE). Heritability quantifies the proportion of variance in traits or behaviors attributable to genes in each population. It does not tell us which genes; we need molecular genetics to do that. Important polymorphisms of the dopaminergic and serotonergic systems related to criminal behavior and the differential susceptibility hypothesis are explored. All modern genetic studies emphasize the crucial role of the environment in determining the extent to which genes are expressed. It cannot be said enough: the more we learn about genetics, the more we learn how important the environment is.

Chapter 7 explores the role of the brain, evolution's magnum opus, in explaining criminal behavior. It examines crucial brain areas such as the limbic system and prefrontal cortex, certain neurotransmitters and hormones, particularly testosterone/cortisol ratios, and the process of synaptogenesis. We note that the experiences that infants and toddlers have are of utmost importance in determining which synapses are retained or pruned. We then explore the triple imbalance hypothesis, a neuro-evolutionary theory that proposes that an imbalance of the serotonergic system and cortisol/testosterone levels leads to reactive aggression. Finally, the neuro-genetic reinforcement sensitivity theory of approach/avoidance behavior is addressed. This theory focuses on three interacting systems: the behavioral approach system (or activating BAS), the behavioral inhibition system (BIS), and the fight, flight, or freeze system (FFFS).

Chapter 8 examines the interaction between the processes of phylogeny and ontogeny, what the species' evolution "expects" from developmental experiences. The brain is an organ of adaptation exquisitely calibrated to its environment. Evidence has shown that cranial capacity increases most rapidly in colder parts of the globe, in areas with greater population density, and where food procurement is problematic. This led to a conflict between the obstetric and postural requirements of ancestral females, requiring human infants to be born at earlier stages of gestation. This necessitated a continuous symbiotic relationship between mother and child for extended periods. We look at the effects of breastfeeding and the accompanying tactile stimulation on brain development, and at the adverse effects of maltreatment on the brain and how this is more common among children living in a single-parent household, followed by a discussion of experience-expected and experience-dependent brain development and antisocial behavior. We conclude with a discussion of how the level of maternal care affects the epigenetic regulation of genes.

Chapter 9 examines the relative importance of rationality and emotion in driving human behavior. We saw in Chapter 2 that neuroscience has shown that decision-making is based primarily on emotional rather than rational information processing. Criminology has focused on antisocial behavior-promoting emotions and ignored prosocial behavior-promoting emotions. We examine primary and secondary emotions with an emphasis on the social emotion of empathy. High empathy and fear levels have been called the natural enemies of crime. Empathy is other-oriented and prevents one from committing acts injurious to others; fear is self-oriented and prevents one from committing acts injurious to others out of fear of negative consequences for oneself. We delve into the role of the autonomic nervous system (ANS) in the development of conscience via classical conditioning. Psychopaths and chronic criminals know what is right and wrong but have poorly integrated rational and emotional systems that do not activate the appropriate emotions, leading them to behave according to the call of immediate self-gratification. Finally, we examine the role of callous-unemotionality and low fear in producing antisocial behavior.

Chapter 10 begins the section that examines theories and conditions relating to crime causation. It is by no means exhaustive; it only involves the two criminological traditions that form the primary fault line between individual-level theories of crime causation: social learning and control theories. Both theory types emphasize learning, but because they hold different views about human nature, they disagree about what is learned. Social learning theories maintain that people are basically good and must learn to be antisocial; control theories argue that people are basically selfish and must learn to be prosocial. We examine and critique differential association, social learning, and social and self-control theories from a biopsychosocial perspective. Social learning theory must address the question of why some individuals are more likely than others to respond to negative life experiences with antisocial behavior and why they are more likely to self-select into deviant peer groups. Control theories must address genetic and child effects on self-control.

Chapter 11 examines the radical/critical tradition in criminology, which is concerned with the larger structural forces at work in society. It has a strong leftist orientation and has the goal of achieving a socialist society because it places the problem of crime at the feet of capitalism. Radical/critical criminologists deny the ontological reality of crime, claiming that it is merely a social construct, and deny the distinction between *mala in se* and *mala prohibita* crimes. Any attempt to look at anything but structural forces is viewed as the "psychopathologizing" of criminals, who are often romanticized as fighters against capitalist oppression or simply as nothing more than victims of an unjust system. Various branches of this perspective, such as labeling theory, left-idealism, and left-realism, are examined. Left-realism, while still socialist, realizes the reality of crime and that both criminals and victims are found in the same neighborhoods. A core concept of left realist criminology is the "square of crime," which is a difficult idea to grasp; even its formulator said he doesn't understand it!

Chapter 12 examines intelligence, as measured by IQ, and its relationship to antisocial behavior. Some scholars find intelligence to be ill-defined, controversial, and a reification of a mathematical correlation. Physicists cannot define energy other than its ability to perform work, but they can measure it in many ways as it moves physical objects around. We can also think of intelligence similarly: operationalized mental energy that moves the concepts in our minds around to find adaptive solutions to life's problems. All of life can be seen as an intelligence test because it predicts so much of what we may achieve in it. We explore the genetics and neurobiology of intelligence, followed by an examination of the relationship between IQ and criminal behavior and between crime-related factors such as education, poverty, and employment status. Huge national samples from Scandinavian countries find that IQ is a strong and consistent correlate of criminal offending. We also look at intellectual imbalance (performance IQ–verbal IQ discrepancy), factors that mediate the IQ-offending relationship, the differential detection hypothesis, and offending among high-IQ people.

Chapter 13 considers socioeconomic status (SES), a central concept in the social sciences often used as an independent variable in criminology studies. It is rarely treated as a dependent variable with its causes; it is not simply an ascribed status, as many seem to treat it. Numerous studies have found that children with high IQs achieve higher SES than their parents. However, the environments that parents provide affect IQ independent of the genes they provide. We look at environmental effects on IQ through the lens of the Flynn Effect. This is followed by discussions of environmental factors that lead to lower cognitive functioning in children, such as child maltreatment, maternal ingestion of teratogenic substances while pregnant, and environmental lead. The role of temperament and personality in SES achievement is also addressed. Poverty and SES are related, but they are not synonymous. We consider various models of poverty causation—demographic, cultural, and behavioral, all of which play some part. We then examine whether poverty causes crime, crime causes poverty, or some third set of variables causes both. Finally, the various federal programs designed to reduce poverty and their effects are examined.

Chapter 14 explores a neglected area in criminology—religion. Because religion is society's moral institution that binds people with a core of common beliefs and is a source of unity, stability, and informal social control, it is assumed to be a barrier to antisocial behavior. However, some people, led by the New Atheist movement, maintain that religion is a source of intolerance and violence and, therefore, more of a bridge to antisocial behavior than a barrier. Criminologists on the "bridge" side of the debate emphasize that murder rates are much higher in Central and South American countries that are high in religious belief than in the more secularized countries of Europe and North America, but they suffer from the ecological fallacy. Those on the "barrier" side emphasize cross-sectional, longitudinal, meta-analytical, and experimental studies that show frequent church attendance is the best barrier society has against antisocial behavior because it fosters charitable giving, volunteering, attachment to prosocial others, and self-control.

Chapter 15 is the first of four chapters that shift gears to criminal justice issues. The first issue is the police abolition/defunding issue pressed by the Black Lives Matter (BLM) movement. We examine the effects of defunding the police and less proactive policing during 2020. We saw the largest one-year increase in murders on record from 2019 to 2020, and the number of arrests nationwide plummeted by 24% in 2020 from 2019. When examining police shootings by race in terms of the BLM narrative, it's all about racist cops hunting down innocent Black males. We look at this by asking if an officer is more likely to shoot if the subject is Black than if he is White, *given* a confrontation in which the officer would be justified in using lethal force. Many studies find that situational factors determine an officer's decision to shoot. One study found that Black suspects were almost nine times more likely to be in potentially deadly confrontations with police than White suspects and 10 times more likely to be armed. It is also found that Black officers are just over twice as likely to shoot a suspect of any race/ethnicity as White officers.

Chapter 16 looks at punishment issues. Arguments for and against punishment often engage with the concepts of free will and determinism. Justifications of criminal justice punishment—deterrence, incapacitation, rehabilitation, and retribution—ebb and flow in primacy according to the ideology of the times. The first three justifications are consequentialist, justified by the hoped-for positive consequences that are presumed to flow from them. Retribution is a deontological position because it justifies punishment based on its intrinsic moral worth, regardless of any benefits that may flow from its application. All justifications contain free will assumptions. Immanuel Kant is the best-known defender of retributive justice based on his concept of the categorical imperative. Other scholars believe that free will is an illusion and want to abolish punishment as such, but others are not necessarily opposed to incapacitation and prefer the medical term "isolation." We examine evolutionary theories that stress the adaptive significance of punishment and that retributive emotions reflect compassion for a victim's (or survivor's) pain and distress and a virtuous expression of solidarity. We conclude with a discussion of the value of forgiveness strategies.

Chapter 17 engages sentencing issues. There are such issues, but none are as controversial as the relationship between race and sentencing. Most studies show that Black defendants are punished more severely than White defendants. Most, but not all, studies show that this is accounted for by Blacks having committed more serious crimes and having greater criminal histories. To the extent that Blacks exceed Whites in offending, the use of criminal history will produce disparate sentencing, disfavoring Blacks. This has led some to argue that because criminal history overlaps with race, it has become a proxy for race and should, therefore, not be considered in sentencing. However, such an omission undermines the idea of individualized justice if crime seriousness were the only sentencing concern. We then look at sentencing disparity between men and women, which almost invariably shows that, controlling for legally relevant variables, males are punished more severely. This is usually explained by the "chivalry hypothesis." Finally, we look at gender differences in sex offenses, serial killing, and sentencing, followed by discussions of sentencing guidelines and presentence investigation reports.

Chapter 18 looks at the death penalty, the most controversial issue in criminal justice. The USA is the only Western nation that retains the death penalty, and a favorable public opinion of it appears to be why. Death penalty studies have more than a tint of advocacy to them; it has been shown how opposite findings can be derived from the same data sets. Some have looked at claims of racial bias by comparing percentages of total racial populations with those executed or on death row rather than comparing the percentages of each race eligible for the death penalty. There is a growing consensus that while Blacks are overrepresented among those sentenced to death relative to their share of the US population, they are underrepresented based on their convictions for murder. With the evidence now showing that Blacks are less likely to receive a death sentence than Whites, the race issue has become victim-centered rather than defendant-centered, with those murdering Whites, regardless of the defendant's race, more likely to receive a death sentence. White victim homicides show a greater percentage of aggravated circumstances that increase the likelihood of a death sentence. The chapter concludes with brief discussions of women and the death penalty and life without the possibility of parole (LWOP) sentences.

Acknowledgements

I would first like to thank executive editor Morwenna Scott for her faith in this project. Thanks also for the commitment of her very able assistant (Lauren Powell) and the production team (Knowledgeworks, and in particular Prasanna Pattnayak) and indexer (Tom Norton). This wonderful group of professionals has done everything to make this book as presentable as possible and has kept up a most useful dialogue between author, publisher, and reviewers. The whole Routledge group is a pleasure to work with. The copy editor (Sandra Stafford) spotted every errant comma, dangling participle, missing reference, and misspelled word in the manuscript, for which we are truly thankful, and our production editor (Curtis Hill) made sure everything went quickly and smoothly thereafter.

I would also like to acknowledge the kind words and suggestions of those who reviewed this project. I have endeavored to respond to those suggestions and believe I have adequately done so. Any errors or misinformation that lie lurking somewhere in these pages, however, are entirely our responsibility. I thank God for giving me the time and inclination to write, and the love and support of my soulmate, Grace Jean, aka "Grace the face." Grace is drop-dead gorgeous and the pleasantest of people, as all who know her will attest. Grace's love and support have sustained me so long that life without her is unimaginable. Being married to Gracie is a perpetual pleasure that has never faded, and she is priceless! Szeretlek szépségem.

Section 1

Philosophical Issues

1 Philosophy in Criminology/ Criminal Justice

The Value of Philosophy

Criminologists consider themselves empirical scientists concerned with collecting and analyzing data rather than armchair speculators, so they might be tempted to believe that philosophy is a waste of time. However, they would be mistaken because the finest minds in physics, the "big guns" of science, were steeped in philosophy. Howard (2005: 34) writes of Albert Einstein, the greatest of all scientists: "Einstein's philosophical habit of mind, cultivated by undergraduate training and lifelong dialogue, had a profound effect on the way he did physics." Einstein believed that all scientists should cultivate a philosophical frame of mind or rest content to be outhouse counters unable to see the forest for the trees: "So many people today—and even professional scientists—seem to me like somebody who has seen thousands of trees but has never seen a forest. ... [P]hilosophical insight is ... the mark of distinction between a mere artisan or specialist and a real seeker after truth" (in Howard, 2005: 34). Galison (2008: 122) writes of another Nobel laureate, Niels Bohr: "historians of physics have made much of the way Niels Bohr used the ideas, directly and indirectly, of Søren Kierkegaard as he formulated his principle of complementarity." Yet another Nobel laureate, Werner Heisenberg, lectured extensively on Immanuel Kant's ontology and epistemology and used it as an aid when interpreting quantum phenomena (Camilleri, 2005).

Nobel laureate Bertrand Russell considered philosophy to be critical to all sciences because: "The knowledge it aims at is the kind of knowledge which gives unity and system to the body of the sciences, and the kind which results from a critical examination of our convictions, prejudices, and beliefs" (1988: 18). Philosophy organizes our thoughts and guides us to examine the assumptions and methods that we apply to our inquiries and to ponder the nature of truth and reality. As with any other domain of inquiry, the philosophy of criminology seeks to lay bare the practices and assumptions underlying the inquiries the discipline makes and offers critiques to enhance the ability to improve its understanding of the phenomena it claims as its domain. Philosophy asks criminologists to contemplate the abstractions and concepts they work with, which are usually, consciously or otherwise, taken for granted.

DOI: 10.4324/9781003662495-2

Williams and Arrigo (2006: 15) maintain that "criminology proper has mostly failed to contemplate let alone critically examine its conceptual underpinnings, that is, the philosophical cornerstones that support its purpose and potential." I think we can agree that criminologists do not spend much time pondering the ontological and epistemological assumptions upon which the discipline rests such as the concepts of human nature, justice, free will, determinism, rationality, emotion, punishment, the nature of reality, determinism, essentialism, realism, reductionism, nominalism, and so forth. Criminologists must do this because: "Criminology is fundamentally wedded to philosophy in countless ways, and the crossroads for criminology and philosophy are ripe for exposition and assimilation by scholars in both camps" (Williams & Arrigo, 2006: 2). Because it is in the grip of ideology which is all too often the "silent partner" in criminological work, many of the concepts and philosophical assumptions in criminology engage seemingly dichotomous either/or positions that appear to be irreconcilable but may not be.

Ontology and Epistemology

Philosophy explores the fundamental categories of existence and reality and thus takes up the slack in areas where science cannot go. It tries to come to grips with the nature of being and reality in a branch of metaphysics known as ontology, the "study of being." Ontology asks significant questions such as: Why is there something rather than nothing?, Does God exist?, Does life have meaning?, and so forth. We cannot know the nature of the circumstances that triggered the Big Bang or why we have evolved brains that equip us with a capacity far beyond what is needed for survival and reproduction. Physics can tell us how the universe evolved after it arrived, but it cannot tell us how or why it is here. Evolutionary biology and neuroscience can inform us how a bigger brain evolved and how it works, but not how we have been gifted with a forward-looking consciousness. Science cannot answer these existential questions, so we turn to philosophy (and theology). Of course, we can ignore such questions and say they are just brute facts, but that would make us Einstein's mere artisans or specialists and not "seekers after truth."

The above questions are metaphysical, but ontology is not concerned only with metaphysics. It is also concerned with what exists in the world we can acquire knowledge about, although whether or not something "really" exists can be a bone of contention. Epistemology explores how we can know and reason about existence and reality, how we acquire knowledge about those things, and the reliability of our knowledge claims. Every discipline has its ontology and epistemology in which its practitioners assert the reality of the things they study and how they explore them, rather than asserting general statements about reality and knowing as philosophers do. A discipline's ontology informs its scholars of the fundamental categories of reality within its domain, and its epistemology defines its investigatory techniques and how they should discover more knowledge about them.

Nominalism and realism are separate ontologies with meaning for the fate of social science categories such as society, social class, and criminality, and arguments about reductionism and essentialism. If we use scientific methodology to explore some phenomenon, then it would seem to follow that its ontological status is a given, but nominalists might disagree. Nominalism maintains that the conceptual categories by which we organize the phenomena we investigate do not correspond to any inherent structure of the phenomena but are just products of the human mind. They do not deny that criminals exist, for instance, but would contest the universality of the descriptor "criminal" they would contest because for them, there is no universal "criminal-ness"; there are only particular criminals. The individual specimen is a *subject* with material substance; the *predicate* "criminal" has no substance and is simply a descriptor used to place him or her into some convenient category.

Nominalists thus draw a sharp line between the concrete and the abstract and maintain that only particulars we can see, feel, and touch are real, but universals—as unseen properties—are not, and to view them as such is to reify them. The abstraction "criminality" is instantiated only in particular criminals in the phenomenal world; it does not exist independently in some noumenal world. Extreme nominalists even reject the notion of the commonality of subjects or objects selected by a name (e.g., human, female, large, automobile). For them, all subjects or objects named are unique representations of the world, and the terms indicative of a universal nature (humanness, femaleness, largeness, automobile-ness) have no meaning. Nominalists disdain nomothetic (quantitative generalizing) accounts and embrace ideographic (qualitative specificity). Postmodern and certain radical criminology theories are opposed to objectivism and realism, although there is a tendency to reify certain concepts such as patriarchy and capitalism.

The opposite of nominalism is realism. Realists claim the reality of abstract universals and the usefulness of generalities. Realists maintain that to make use of universals such as humanness, we ignore individual differences such as gender, color, age, and so on, and *abstract* from all instances what they have in common; that is, their humanity. Both Plato and Aristotle were realists about universals, although their ideas about them are radically different. Plato's universals are his archetypal Forms, his "perfect" humanness, redness, triangle-ness, justice, etc. The Forms were the ultimate reality and existed in the noumenal world before any material manifestation in the phenomenal world. This form of realism tends to be paired with an idealist rather than a materialist epistemology. Materialists can be, and most often are, realists about universals, but in the Aristotelian rather than Platonic sense. In Aristotle's view, universals exist, but only become real when instantiated in the observable. Put otherwise, Plato's universals existed before any human being; Aristotle's universal abstractions such as humanness, femaleness, and intelligence are qualities we ascribe to humans, and thus human beings must exist before we can realistically talk about things that describe them.

Aristotle's view is necessary if we are to talk about the world rationality. We cannot see or touch abstractions such as intelligence, empathy, happiness, or criminality. Still, they can be measured in various ways and we can note how variation in them has meaningful effects on people's lives.

The notion of "society" is central to the social sciences although no one has gazed upon that abstraction, but if we deny the reality of social facts, we risk becoming extreme eliminative reductionists. Most theories in the social/behavioral sciences have ontological commitments to abstractions, the existence of which nominalists deny. If things marked off by a common kind have nothing that is universally true about them save the name they are given, nomothetic social science with its talk of universal abstractions such as human nature, social class, status groups, and culture is dead and what remains is only a series of atomized individual biographies.

One of the central concepts of physics—the law of the conservation of energy—also deals with abstraction, but physicists do not worry about it. Nobel laureate Richard Feynman informs us that: "It is important to realize that in physics today, we have no knowledge of what energy 'is'" (Hecht, 2008: 88). We can't touch, smell, or weigh energy; it is an intangible only observed and defined as "the capacity to do work." It is operationalized and quantified by measures such as joules, calories, and kilowatts, from which we can make useful predictions. Measured abstractions in the social/behavioral sciences also lead to useful knowledge and predictions.

Critical realism is a middle ground between nominalism and realism. It is a philosophy that claims the possibility of gaining mind-independent knowledge of the world as it is. It does, however, hold that science is fallible and our perceptions of reality are functions of the mind, and consequently, that we must always critically reflect on our perceptions. This position is akin to Kant's phenomenal/noumenal distinction without the skepticism that the noumenal world is forever lost to us. Critical realism maintains that science can progressively close the gap between our views of the world and reality itself; that is, the chasm between the phenomenal and the noumenal can be bridged incrementally as scientists interpret and reinterpret their data. This is the "realism" in critical realism, the "critical" element lies in the belief that nothing should go unchallenged; if it is not challenged, no reinterpretation is possible and no progress is made.

Critical realism reminds us that our theories are maps of reality, not reality itself. When we look at maps, we see a representation of the terrain, not the terrain itself. Likewise, when we devise experiments and surveys, we construct an artificially closed world to isolate regularities between and among variables that we rarely can directly observe in the more chaotic open world. However, just like maps, experiments and surveys help to get us where we want to go and give us an idea of what it will be like when we arrive. Thus, critical realism is ontologically realist (it affirms a mind-independent world) and epistemologically fallibilistic (no theory or model of the world can ever be rationally justified conclusively) (Walsh & Wright, 2015).

Moral Relativism

The concepts of crime, criminal law, and punishment are fundamentally about moral injunctions stating that we should not treat others in ways we don't want to be treated. Moral or ethical values are "ought" propositions; that is, one ought to do this or ought not to do that because it is morally right or wrong and for no other reason. This is a statement avering universal moral truths, but some hold that morality is relative to time, place, or person. For instance, Zhang (2013: 149) asserts: "There is nothing absolutely right or wrong, because different people have different views of the same social fact, and the different views are formed with different references." The reductio ad absurdum of this position is that murder, rape, robbery, and sundry other harms are never absolutely wrong simply because perpetrators may believe otherwise.

Moral relativism thus asserts that we do not have an objective basis by which to make judgments of right and wrong because they depend on one's culture or on whom you ask. Seunebae Park declares that "moral truths do not exist because moral properties do not inhabit the universe" (2014: 51). He is a nominalist because moral properties do not have material properties, so for him, they cannot possibly be real. Park also notes: "Relativism asserts that cultural approval is what makes an action right. ... I insist that the relativist belief stands that we are right about the morality of a certain action as we appeal to the culture which commends it" (2014: 46). Such thinking leads to an unqualified tolerance of all practices and no meaningful way to morally judge them. While cultural relativism is useful for cross-cultural comparisons, it does not mean we should adopt moral relativism to deny universal standards of human decency and say with Park that "cultural approval is what makes an action right." To do so implies that some people are less entitled to human rights simply because they live in cultures that disdain human rights. Relativism about mundane things is fine, but not when it engages beliefs about how we should treat others.

Certain practices are inherently evil, and the litmus test for deciding if a practice is evil is to ask if any sane person would want to be victimized by it. Those who criticize the Holocaust, honor killings, infanticide, or any other obnoxious practice have no defensible grounds to do so from a relativist position. Andrei Cornea (2012: 41) maintains that if there are no absolute universal standards of moral decency the rulings of the International Courts should be disposed of:

> In order to enjoy moral and judicial legitimacy, their standards of justice must be either those of a universal culture or, at least, of a better culture than the one whose members were put on trial. But since there is neither a universal culture nor a better culture than another, as the relativist creed proclaims, none of these rulings can be legitimate and right. So they have to be disposed of.

Without a common standard for deciding among conflicting moral beliefs, discussions of morality are relegated to non-normative descriptive discourse, which is intellectual laziness hiding behind a mask of cultural tolerance. Burke (2009: 287) notes that moral relativism is central to postmodernism which is dear to many in the social sciences, including criminology:

> The relativism implied by postmodernism thus denies the possibility of truth, and hence of justice, in anything other than a purely subjective form, which inevitably consigns us to the prospect of conflict. ... Postmodernism therefore appears contemptuous of the possibility of developing an objective normative (moral) order which human beings can translate into enforceable norms or laws.

Research has shown that people who endorse moral relativism most strongly score higher on personality traits associated with immoral behavior. Lauren Collier-Spruel et al. (2019: 772) reviewed the literature on this issue, concluding: "Research utilizing these scales [moral relativism scales] presents a particularly negative picture of relativism, suggesting that moral relativists have higher levels of psychopathic traits and are more inclined toward immoral intentions as well as diverse types of immoral behavior." This does not mean that relativists are psychopaths; it only means they score higher on psychopathic traits than non-relativists.

Reductionism and Holism

Reductionism is a boo word in much of criminology where only social facts such as social class, poverty, and neighborhoods matter. Crime is viewed in some theories as socially constructed and the product of reactions to these social facts. Going beyond them to identify individual differences that explain variation in these reactions is dismissed as reductionism. However, reductionism only entails taking causal explanations from fuzzier levels to a deeper, more precise level so that fuzzy explanations may become less so. Thomas Nagel points out that: "non-reductionist accounts simply *describe* phenomena while reductionist accounts *explain* them" (Rose, 1999: 915), and Steven Pinker (2002: 72) describes the differences between reductionist and non-reductionist explanation as "the difference between stamp collecting and detective work, between slinging around jargon and offering insight, between saying something just is and explaining why it had to be that way as opposed to some other way." Lower-level explanations often absorb the explanatory power of broad demographic categories and add extra explanatory power to them.

To explain something rather than simply to describe it, we must discover its causes, and to do this, we must look at its constituent parts. Reductionism and determinism are thus joined at the hip because the reductionist goal of explanation is intimately tied to the determinist goal of prediction. The utility of any explanation is gauged by its predictive power. Emile Durkheim (2005: 35) believed that to unlock the mysteries of social facts we have to unlock the parts that constitute them:

> Although sociology is defined as the science of society, in reality it cannot deal with human groups, which are the immediate concern of his research, without in the end tackling the individual, the ultimate element of which these groups are composed ... It is impossible to explain the whole without explaining the parts.

Fear of reductionism infected even the natural sciences in the past and was seen as a threat to a young discipline's autonomy. Edward Wilson (1990) coined the term "antidiscipline" to describe the relationship between a young science and its older adjacent science. A tension exists between the two sciences as the younger science attempts to define discipline boundaries by identifying its appropriate level of analysis. As practitioners of the younger science feel less threatened, they begin to absorb the ideas and theories of the adjacent mature science. After a period of creative interplay, the younger science became complementary with its former antidiscipline and, as a result, made huge gains in theoretical and methodological sophistication, which it could not have if it had not shaken itself free of its anxieties and insecurities about status and territory.

This process was first evidenced in chemistry as it debated the intrusion of physics and its atomic theory in the 19th century. Chemist Benjamin Brodie believed that any reference to atoms was reductionist because chemical compounds were *sui generis* entities possessing emergent properties not predictable *a priori* from their constituent parts (Coffey, 2008). Chemists who subscribed to Bodie's concerns changed their minds when "the deductive power of the atomic theory [became] evident ... the atomic theory now enabled definite predictions and detailed explanations to be made. The experimental and deductive aspects of chemistry were cohering at last" (Knight, 1992: 124). Likewise, Joseph Woodger (1948) argued that biology has a characteristic way of thinking that is not reducible to physics and chemistry. Yet only five years later, Watson, Crick, and Wilkins won the Nobel Prize for decoding the "language of life" by discovering the chemistry and atomic structure of the DNA molecule.

Many scholars in the social sciences today have problems with more advanced disciplines. The psychology of the first part of the 20th century tended to disdain biology, as witnessed by Zing Kuo's assertion that psychology "needs the concept of heredity as much or as little as the concept of God" (Degler, 1991: 155–159). However, Christopher Peterson notes that most modern psychologists have surrendered their opposition to biology, their erstwhile antidiscipline: "Most contemporary psychologists prefer to regard people as biopsychosocial beings, believing that people and their behavior are best explained in terms of relevant biological mechanisms, psychological processes, and social influences" (1997: 20). Many modern criminologists, especially radical/critical criminologists, still refuse the notion that people are "biopsychosocial beings" because they view the intrusion of biology as "biopathologization" (Carrier & Walby, 2014: 3).

Such fears are allayed when it is realized that reductionist science does not entail the elimination of higher-level explanations. Eliminative reductionism is the notion that higher-level phenomena are explained wholly by lower-level properties and that higher-level properties have no causal impact independent of their parts. Cell biologists are aware that, at some level, they are dealing with atoms and seek to understand their function in the cell (in protein folding, for instance). They also know that there are properties of the cell that cannot be deduced from atoms *a priori*, that they require functional explanations of the whole cell, and how that cell fits into a network of other cells to form the living organism. There are multiple layers of complexity going from dead atoms to living creatures. Science requires both holistic and reductionist accounts that complement and do not exclude one another. Natural scientists recognize this, and useful observations, hypotheses, and theories proceed in both reductionist and holistic directions, from sub-atomic particles to the cosmos in physics and from the plant microbiome to ecological systems in biology.

Daniel Dennett (1995: 82) calls eliminative reductionism "bad" or "greedy" reductionism, which is the practice of skipping over several layers of complexity in a rush to fasten everything to a supposed solid foundation. He also opined that antireductionists seek "skyhooks" without foundations to lift them out of scientific difficulty. Dennett's "good reductionism" is "the commitment to non-question-begging science" (1995: 82). Science has progressed most rapidly when it has taken the whole thing apart to examine its parts. When it has done this, it has gained a better understanding of the wholes they constitute. As Matt Ridley (2003: 163) notes, "Reductionism takes nothing from the whole; it adds new layers of wonder to the experience." Reductionist science means examining phenomena at a deeper level; it is not about eliminating higher-level explanations. Meaning is most often found at higher levels of explanation, but higher-level analyses must be consistent with what is known at lower levels. Thus, complaints about reductionism should be met with Dennett's mocking reply: "That's such a quaint, old-fashioned complaint! What on earth did you have in mind?" (1995: 81).

However, holistic accounts may be more coherent and satisfying than reductionist accounts. Phenomena may be *explained* in their fine details by reductionism, but they find their *significance* in more holistic regions. We must be careful not to lose meaning as an essential component of understanding behavior by overemphasizing reductionist explanations. Propositions about entities such as neurons and genes do not contain terms that define the most meaningful aspects of the human condition, such as love, justice, and morality. For instance, neuroscientists have scanned the brains of people in love and discovered that love has a distinctive neurobiological substrate in the chemical soup and electrical sparks that light up the brain's pleasure centers (Shih et al. 2022). We can describe the roles of testosterone, dopamine, and serotonin in producing the feeling of love, but they are not love; they are the tools love makes use of. Brain scans describe what happens neurologically when we fall in love, but such reductionism does not even come close to explaining why Jack fell for Jill.

Emergentism is a concept that unites reductionism and holism, and "is the position that certain higher-level properties display a kind of metaphysical autonomy from the lower-level properties in which they are grounded" (Taylor, 2022: 302). Emergence is a self-organizing process that produces qualitative "novelties" that cannot be fully expressed as the sums of the quantitative properties of the constituent parts. Corning (2002: 26) notes that reductionism used to mean an understanding of the parts that comprise the whole, but modern reductionists "speak of parts and their 'interactions.'" Corning (2002: 26) maintains that by analyzing interactions among parts and the environments in which these parts operate, we are thereby analyzing emergent wholes or systems: "The 'whole' is not something that floats on top of it all." Emergentism also advocates for the concept of downward causation (Walker & Cloete, 2023). An example of top-down causation would be Jack's explanation of why he fell for Jill. He would appeal to her beauty, lovely smile, and sweet character, and when he perceived and thought about them, his brain responded and released the chemicals associated with love. Stated otherwise, the content of Jack's mind, relative to Jill, determined his brain's activity; his brain activity did not determine the content of his mind alone.

Essentialism

Essentialism is another dismissive term in social science. There are different varieties of essentialism, but its enemies tend to attack only extreme versions, such as Platonic essences tied to his perfect, changeless, and eternal Forms. For instance, Naomi Zack alleges that people who believe in the reality of race: "to this day assume the following (1) races are made up of individuals sharing the same essence; (2) each race is sharply discontinuous from all others" (2002: 63). Laypersons do tend to see sharp boundaries in things such as race, but I doubt that Zack has heard a biologist claim that racial groups share a common "essence" or that racial boundaries are "sharply discontinuous"; if they were we would call them species, but even species are not *sharply* discontinuous. Sayer (1997: 462) notes that defining essentialism this way constructs a straw man that "helps to load the dice against essentialism."

Essentialism is best exemplified by the Aristotelian notion that any given subject or object has necessary, unalterable attributes indispensable to them such that any entity lacking those properties cannot be included in the category. Such properties are universal in every entity that belongs to a particular classification and are not idiosyncratic or context-dependent. Aristotle distinguishes between *per se* and *per accidens* properties of an entity. A *per se* property is an essential inherent property that an entity possesses and cannot lose and remain what it is; a *per accidens* property is a non-essential property that an entity may not have that does not change its nature. For instance, a water molecule must have two hydrogen atoms and one oxygen atom; without either, there is no water. The atomic structure H_2O is the *per se* property of water; its manifestations as a liquid, solid, or gas are *per accidens* changes resulting from its *per se* property interacting with the ambient temperature. Likewise, a person can be male, female, intersex, tall or short, Black or White, saint or sinner, or anything else in his or her *per accidens* properties and still be nothing other than *per se* human. What counts as an essential property does not have to be both necessary and sufficient for defining a kind, but it must be necessary. As Oderberg (2011: 89) notes about definitions of natural kinds, "That definitions range from partly accurate to completely accurate does not militate against the fact that achieving any degree of accuracy in definitions requires attending to characteristics of the object to be defined."

There has been a recent resurgence of Aristotelian essentialism in biology (Rieppel, 2010; Williams, 2011). Denis Walsh (2006: 442) maintains that modern evolutionary biology is an Aristotelian essentialist science:

> Evolutionary developmental biologists deploy their conception of organisms' natures in ways that are remarkably similar to the ways in which Aristotle deployed the concept of an organism's nature—viz. to explain: (i) the presence of features (ii) recurrence of traits and (iii) the resemblance among organisms.

Darwin destroyed the idea that natural entities possess a Platonic unchanging essence that makes them eternally what they are. Today, biologists discuss natural kinds that they identify by DNA analyses. This kind of essentialism is called "origin essentialism," which, according to Williams (2011: 154),

> is a matter of standing in a specific historical relation, perhaps to an ancestor. An animal that does not stand in this historical relation is not a member of the kind. ... The essence of a natural kind is a set of (relational or intrinsic) properties.

Essences are thus relational properties that biological entities of a kind take with them into all possible worlds. Natural selection assures continuous change and speciation over the vastness of evolutionary time. However, this does not refute accurate categorizations of biological kinds that are not contingent on idiosyncratic interpretations because they are as they are now and will be so for a very long time.

Charges of essentialism in social science rarely engage the arguments made by biologists, and use the epithet "essentialism" when confronted with statements of generality they find offensive. Those who charge others with essentialism tend to see it as homogenizing the class of subjects being discussed. However, as Newman and Knobe (2019: 591) point out, "One important function of essentialism (if not the most important function) is that it provides a basis for categorization." Categorizing individuals by sex, race, criminal status, SES, etc. for study purposes homogenizes them only with respect to the category of interest, and doing so is not to deny that they differ along many other dimensions. Anti-essentialists often even attack generalities as essentialism, but searching for generalities, patterns, similarities, and differences is a goal of science. They fail to note the distinction between Aristotle's *per se* and *per accidens* essentialism and attack Plato's changeless essences. Essentialist thinking is necessary for scientific classification, which can only be done by sorting things according to what distinguishes them from all things they are not.

2 Ideology and Criminology

Criminology's Achilles' Heel

Criminology is plagued by ideological fractures that impede progress in understanding the phenomenon of crime (Cullen, 2005; Walsh & Wright, 2015; Williams & Robinson, 2004; Wright & Cullen, 2012). Chris Eskridge opines that many criminological theories contain "a pinch of science (and often bad science at that) and a pound of ideology" (2005: 304). The primary fault line in criminology, as well as in the social sciences in general, is the liberal-conservative or left-right division. The line can, of course, be drawn in a more nuanced fashion along a continuum of positions and hybrids. For the sake of expediency and simplicity, I will ignore the nuances, edit out the qualifiers, and stick with the liberal-conservative divide because most people in the United States view ideology in terms of this bipolar distinction (Jost, 2006). Ideology has closer connections to the social sciences than to the natural sciences because social science investigates topics that are more closely related to human concerns.

Gunnar Myrdal noted the influence of ideology in the social sciences over 80 years ago. He wrote:

> The place of the individual scientist along the scale of radicalism-conservatism has always had strong influences on both the selection of research problems and the conclusions drawn from research. In a sense, it is the master scale of biases in social science.
>
> (Myrdal, 1944: 1038)

To the extent that Myrdal's statement rings true, it does not bode well for the advancement of criminology because ideology is radically at odds with science. Science describes and clarifies the objective world, while ideology prescribes and distorts it. Indeed, ideology insinuates itself into so much criminological theory and research that Walsh and Ellis (2004) have called it the "Achilles' Heel" of criminology, and we all know what became of Achilles.

DOI: 10.4324/9781003662495-3

Prominent criminologists John Wright and Francis Cullen decry the grip of ideology in their discipline, calling it a new style of scientific repression that hinders progress. They remark:

> This form of repression is internal to academic disciplines in that it restricts scientific inquiry by imposing rigid ideological boundaries about certain topics and it requires scholars to self-censor their own work. Of course, when science is repressed, either directly through the State or indirectly through threat of disciplinary excommunication, knowledge suffers. Moreover, science itself takes on an entirely political meaning—one that advocates for certain causes and for specific groups and one that marshals resources when those causes or groups are subject to criticism.
>
> (Wright & Cullen, 2012: 238)

Because the term "ideology" has a plethora of definitions and has attracted pejorative connotations, some have dismissed it in favor of terms such as "worldview", "philosophy", or "belief system". However, they seem to be distinctions without a difference, and "ideology" is still the term of choice in social science discourse. By ideology, I mean an integrated and consistent pattern of emotionally felt thoughts, beliefs, and values about the "ought" of sociopolitical reality. Ideologies organize and control these beliefs and values into a patterned way of thinking that simplifies things and are consistent and coherent by those who hold them. People tend to adopt consistent positions toward issues, resulting in the crystallization of opinions, attitudes, and values into an ideology by which they evaluate issues encountered through a kind of subconscious "factor analysis" that reduces them to broad, manageable value choices (Federico & Schneider, 2007). Such clustering allows for a degree of attitude consistency and reduces cognitive dissonance. Attitudes thus tend to crystallize and become relatively unresponsive to contrary opinions. Ideology is something embedded in the everyday habits of thought that shape each person's taken-for-granted "common-sense" vision of reality.

Although there are some inconsistencies or gray areas in any ideology, we almost invariably see the same people with shared moral representations of red or blue truth on opposite sides of the barrier on a host of moral/ethical, social, economic, and political issues such as abortion, the death penalty, immigration, gay rights versus religious liberty, law and order, taxes, welfare, and so on that polarize the modern American cultural landscape. Peterson, Smith, and Hibbing (2020: 600) note that while sociopolitical ideologies are highly stable across the course of people's life spans, "on those occasions when political attitudes do shift across the life span, liberals are more likely to become conservatives than conservatives are to become liberals." Ideology is thus a relatively fixed philosophical worldview that often imposes radically alternative meanings on the same set of facts. Different worldviews lead their adherents to interpret social facts in ways commensurate with their ideologies and to advocate for policies that are responsive to them.

Temperament and Ideology

I used the words "emotionally felt" in my definition of ideology. However, most people like to think that their worldviews (we rarely want to think of them as ideologies) are based on sound reasoning and not about emotion—that's for those irrational folks on the opposite side of the barrier! However, the 19th-century English poet and philosopher Samuel Taylor Coleridge believed that all humans are temperamentally destined to follow the ideological path of one of the two great pillars of Western thought: the idealist Plato or the realist Aristotle:

> Every man is born an Aristotelian or a Platonist. I do not think it possible that anyone born an Aristotelian can become a Platonist; and I am sure that no born Platonist can ever change into an Aristotelian. They are two classes of man, beside which it is next to impossible to conceive a third. The one considers reason a quality or attribute; the other considers it a power.
>
> (Porteous, 1934: 97)

Plato and Aristotle have long been considered the intellectual archetypes of liberal and conservative modes of thought, respectively (Herman, 2014; Popper, 1971). When examining the same set of facts, Aristotle and Plato differed on almost every issue relevant to the major social institutions, from the family to the government (Walsh, 2023). Herman (2014: 412) considered the tension between these two modes of thought as "a battle for the heart of Western civilization. … The creative drive of Western civilization had arisen not from a reconciliation of the two halves but from a constant alert tension between them."

As much as we might want to deny the notion that temperament, and by extension, emotion, intrudes into our scholarly work, William James avers that it inevitably does so and that its grip is stronger than that of our vaunted reason. Offended scholars may discount emotion's subconscious role in their work. But James notes:

> Yet his temperament really gives him a stronger bias than any of his more strictly objective premises. It loads the evidence for him one way or the other, making for a more sentimental or a more hard-hearted view of the universe, just as this fact or that principle would.
>
> (1988: 488–489)

James gains strong support from neuroscience, a discipline that has long held that rationality plays the handmaiden to emotion: "Neuroscientific studies have proven that most decision-making is based primarily on emotional and not rational processing of information" (Alsharif, Salleh, & Baharun, 2021, p. 72).

Emotions are birthed in the evolutionarily ancient limbic system, which predates the evolution of the "rational" prefrontal lobes by at least a million years (Suwa et al., 2009). As Douglas Massey (2002: 15) notes: "Emotionality clearly preceded rationality in evolutionary sequence, and as rationality developed it did not replace emotionality as the basis for human interaction. Rather, rational abilities were gradually added to preexisting and simultaneously developing emotional capacities." Moreover, as with Coleridge, James, and modern neuroscience, Jonathan Haidt (2001: 819) notes the primacy of emotion over rationality: "It comes first in phylogeny, it emerges first in ontogeny, it is triggered more quickly in real-time judgments, and it is more powerful and irrevocable [than rationality] when the two systems yield conflicting judgments." Otherwise put, what we "feel" about an issue often trumps an objective rational evaluation of it because emotions choose for the brain what sensory information to pay attention to and how to process it (Polanía, Burdakov, & Hare, 2024). If emotional differences did not strongly influence the ideologies individuals embrace, we would not see such eminently reasonable thinkers as Plato and Aristotle and their ideological counterparts throughout history differing so widely on important economic, social, and political issues.

However, there is no clear delineation between the brain regions that underly emotion and cognition; the brain is a fully integrated system. Certain areas of the "rational" prefrontal cortex have important functions concerning emotions, and the hippocampus, a key component of the "emotional" limbic system, is crucial in memory storage and retrieval (Phelps, Lempert, & Sokol-Hessner, 2014). Neuroscience research has demonstrated that emotion and cognition are integrated in the lateral prefrontal cortex, which weighs cognitive/affective motivational input from their respective brain areas to guide a person's responses to stimuli (Pessoa et al., 2019). Emotion and reason always operate in complementary fashion, with reason sometimes stronger and emotion sometimes stronger, but when they conflict, the more ancient system of responding will triumph (Etkin, Egner, & Kalisch, 2011). The more urgent a person considers an issue or decision, the more it will engage emotions.

Visions of Social Reality

Like the Plato/Aristotle division, the eminent African American economist and philosopher Thomas Sowell's (1987) concepts of constrained and unconstrained visions. These visions are another way of describing the liberal (unconstrained) and conservative (constrained) ideologies. Like Coleridge's and Herman's Plato/Aristotle division, Sowell proposes that the left-right division is universal and that these two contrasting visions have shaped human thought throughout history. They have been in constant conflict with each other because they imply radically different ways of thinking about everything of economic, political, or social importance. These visions are the intuitive temperament-based feelings different people have about human nature; either it is "perfectible" under the right social circumstances determined by the elite philosopher-kings, as with Plato, or it is merely "improvable" through individual effort, as with Aristotle. Sowell uses the terms "gut level" and "instinct" to describe how these visions, consciously or subconsciously, intrude into human thinking: "It is what we sense or feel *before* we have constructed any systematic reasoning that could be called a theory, much less deduced any specific consequences as hypotheses to be tested against evidence" (1987, p. 14). Sowell clearly believes that emotion eclipses rationality.

The constrained vision says, "This is how the world *is*," and the unconstrained vision says, "This is how the world *should be*." Sowell examined the American and French Revolutions as examples driven by constrained and unconstrained visions, respectively. The first was built on existing foundations, while the latter was undergirded by the Platonic utopian notion of sweeping away everything associated with the *ancien régime* and starting anew. Thus, the two visions ask different questions: "While believers in the unconstrained vision seek the special causes of war, poverty, and crime, believers in the constrained vision seek the special causes of peace, wealth, or a law-abiding society" (Sowell, 1987, p. 31). This implies that unconstrained visionaries believe that crime, war, and poverty are deviations from the norm. If this is so, they need to explain why good people often find themselves in such conditions. Constrained visionaries see crime, war, and poverty as historically normal and inevitable, albeit regrettable, and believe that what we must understand are the conditions that foster well-ordered societies, peace, and wealth.

When addressing social problems, constrained visionaries tend to think of trade-offs, while unconstrained visionaries think of solutions. Constrained and unconstrained visionaries will thus have different policy recommendations that they consider fair and just for dealing with these problems. However, the concepts of fairness and justice are saturated with contradictory notions; we all praise them but differ on when their promise is fulfilled. For Sowell, unconstrained visionaries tend to define fairness in terms of equality (equal outcomes regardless of contribution: "To each according to his need") and constrained visionaries define fairness in terms of merit (outcomes equal to contribution: "From each according to his ability"). The major fault line in criminology lies in these visions. Theories broadly classified as social learning theories view crime as caused primarily by a malevolent social structure, and theories classified as social control theories see crime as inevitable unless steps are taken to prevent it by prosocial parenting that leads to self-regulation.

Several studies have found the heritability of the liberalism-conservativism continuum to range between 0.40 and the mid-0.50s (Bell et al., 2018; Dawes & Weinschenk, 2020; Wajzer & Dragan, 2021) and neuroscientists are finding that political orientation is correlated with variant brain structures (Funk et al., 2013; Kim et al., 2020). Of course, geneticists do not expect to find genes coding for liberal or conservative proteins while rummaging among our chromosomes, nor do neuroscientists expect to find color-coded ideology clusters of neurons embedded in their MRI images. Ideologies are shaped by genes and environments working synergistically in the processes of gene-environment interaction and evocative and active gene-environment correlation. Gene-environment processes guide and shape environmental experiences in ways that increase the likelihood of people developing traits, attitudes, and values that paint how they perceive their worlds in colors most congenial to their temperament (Olson, Vernon, & Harris, 2001; Smith et al., 2011). The result of these processes is to reinforce people's propensities to seek out only information (liberals only getting their news and views from MSNBC or CNN and or conservatives from Fox News or OAN) that conforms and confirms their biases, thus further cyclically reinforcing them.

The Locus of Control

One of the major reasons why liberals and conservatives differ in how they interpret the world revolves around the locus of control. Loci of control lie on a continuum from internal to external:

> An internal locus of control reflects the perception that reinforcements are principally caused by an individual's behavior or characteristics. In contrast, an external locus of control reflects the perception that reinforcements are triggered by factors external to the individual, such as chance, fate or other people.
>
> (Farnier et al., 2021: 3514)

Thus, people with an internal locus of control interpret most of their life experiences as contingent on their actions, and those with an external locus of control view them as contingent upon factors outside their control, such as powerful others, luck, or fate.

It is well established that criminals, in general, are strongly on the external side of the locus of control continuum (Fontao & Ross, 2021; Nwankwo et al., 2018), although the literature is silent on high-status white-collar offenders, whom I suspect mostly have an internal locus of control. To illustrate the external locus of control existing among most offenders, Boyd Sharp (2006: 3) cites a *Calvin and Hobbes* cartoon in which Calvin says this:

> I have concluded that nothing bad I do is my fault ... I'm a helpless victim of countless bad influences. An unwholesome culture panders to my undeveloped values, and it pushes me into misbehavior. I take no responsibility for my behavior. I'm an innocent pawn of society.

Sharp's point is that most criminals think like Calvin in the context of a society where many people prefer to claim victimhood rather than personal responsibility (McDonald's made me fat, the Marlboro man made me smoke, etc.). Criminals are eager to accept authoritative statements by criminologists emphasizing external causes of their behavior (in effect, removing responsibility from them for their behavior), and defense lawyers are equally quick to argue them in court. All of this reinforces an external locus of control and patterns of criminal denial (correctional personnel call this "stinkin' thinkin'") that treatment providers find inimical to their rehabilitative goal (Sharp, 2006; Stohr & Walsh, 2025). Attributing blame to others for offending or viewing oneself as a victim of society's supposed malevolence toward them is hardly conducive to behavioral self-change and is a form of learned helplessness. The prerequisite of positive self-change is accepting responsibility for one's actions. However, because criminals tend not to believe their behavior is a source for altering the positive or negative reinforcements they receive, they do not concede the point.

There is no consensus on whether the locus of control is a stable personality trait or a state that fluctuates according to environmental circumstances. Various studies have provided heritability values for the locus of control construct between 0.30 and 0.56 (Mosing et al., 2012; Xue et al., 2020), and thus there is a small to moderate genetic influence. However, the highest heritability coefficients are typically found in advantaged (in SES terms) environments because they are where genes may reach their optimal potential, so the question becomes, does an individual's locus of control cause their life circumstances, or is their locus of control formed in response to those circumstances? It could be that a tendency toward one form of locus of control or the other leads to a continuing spiral of successes or failures depending on the strength of a person's genetic tendency. A person's tendency may have been weak, and what it ultimately became was largely the learned outcome of their successes or failures.

People in advantaged environments probably believe they have more freedom of personal choice than people in disadvantaged environments. This may account for the consistent finding that belief in personal autonomy is related to happiness:

> Happy individuals also score high on measures of internality, i.e., a tendency to attribute outcomes to oneself rather than to external causes. Happy people perceive a high degree of control and tend to believe that they have choice in their activities.
>
> (Csikszentmihalyi & Wong, 2014: 197)

On the other hand, in people inhabiting disadvantaged environments where happiness is a luxury, the conditions they find themselves in swamp any positive effects of genes for prosocial traits while giving easy play to traits associated with criminal offending (Peñaherrera-Aguirre, Dunkel, & Sarraf, 2021). This is doubtless the reason that most criminals are found in disadvantaged environments and why their locus of control is external.

The Locus of Control Among Criminologists

However, we are concerned with those who evaluate criminals' behavior and attribute causes to it, not with criminals themselves; that is, criminologists' locus of control. No one doubts that conservatives and liberals focus on different causes of crime. Orlando Patterson (1998: ix) asserts that conservatives believe that only "the proximate internal cultural and behavioral factors are important ('So stop whining and pull up your socks, man!')," and "liberals and mechanistic radicals" believe that "only the proximate and external factors are worth considering ('Stop blaming the victim, racist'!). These causal attributions reflect differences in locus of control and suggest that they may differ according to a person's ideology.

Indeed, the locus of control literature consistently finds such a liberal/conservative divide (Hannikainen et al., 2017; Tyler, Heffernan, & Fortune, 2020). Conservatives tend to attribute the locus of control to internal dispositional factors; liberals tend to attribute the locus of control to factors external to individuals. Sweetser (2014: 1183) notes: "The results indicate supporters for the two major parties are wired differently, in line with previous findings about ideology. Democrats were driven by an external locus of control and Republicans by an internal locus." Clarkson et al. (2015, p. 8250) also note the different causal attribution proclivities of conservatives and liberals:

> The possibility that conservatives and liberals differ in their freewill beliefs would be consistent with the attributional proclivities of conservatives and liberals. Specifically, conservatives tend to attribute causality to internal or dispositional factors (e.g., personal effort and control), whereas liberals tend to attribute causality to external factors (e.g., systemic or sociocultural forces).

These two loci of control are revealed in a Cato Institute nationwide poll of American adults about attitudes about the sources of wealth and poverty. Among its many findings, the poll found: "When asked the top three reasons people become wealthy, strong liberals selected family connections (48%), inheritance (40%), and luck (31%). In contrast, strong conservatives selected hard work and grit (62%), ambition (47%), self-discipline (45%), and risk-taking (36%)" (Ekins, 2019: 17). Strong liberals also said that the top causes of poverty are discrimination (51%), an unfair economic system (48%), and lack of educational opportunities (48%); strong conservatives say that the problems are poor life choices (60%), lack of work ethic (52%), breakdown of families (47%), and drugs and alcohol (47%) (Ekins, 2019: 20–21). Furthermore, strong conservatives are almost twice as likely (61%) to reject the idea that "powerful others" direct their lives than strong liberals (34%) (p. 25). However, liberals and conservatives who hold their respective ideologies less strongly converge on the issue, with 53% of conservatives and 47% of liberals rejecting the idea (Ekins, 2019: 26).

These attributions of loci of control reflect differing *general* liberal or conservative views of the internal or external contributions to wealth and poverty, and their disagreement on these issues rests primarily on where they place the emphasis. Whether a person is wealthy, poverty-stricken, or somewhere in between reflects a complicated mixture of internal dispositions and external circumstances. A person's success may have been determined by conscientious application to that endeavor, but it may owe something to external circumstances. However, even the most self-controlled and conscientious of people with a strong internal locus of control may sink into poverty due to circumstances beyond their control, such as a recession, job loss, an accident, or protracted illness. Conversely, some who lack self-control and conscientiousness and have an external locus of control may be wealthy due to family connections or luck. Still others are doubtless poor despite the opportunities they may have had because they lack self-control and conscientiousness, and have an external locus of control. Of course, no one is in complete control of their lives, and only in the rarest circumstances are people's lives completely determined by external factors.

The liberal external locus of control leads them to believe that external circumstances control criminals' lives and will explain their behavior by emphasizing those circumstances. Conversely, the conservative internal locus of control leads us to assume they will think that criminals are responsible for their behavior and that to claim otherwise is to deprive them of their agency. These attributions of blame were showcased in Cooper, Walsh, and Ellis's (2010) survey of 3,970 criminologists who attended the 2007 American Society of Criminology conference (less than a third responded). Respondents were asked about their sociopolitical political orientation (conservative, moderate, liberal, and radical) and to rank from a list of 23 alleged causes of crime presented in the literature what they considered the most important causes of "serious and persistent crime" on a scale ranging from 0 ("not important") to 9 ("extremely important"). Consistent with loci of control differences on causal attributions, conservatives and moderates favored individual-level explanations most strongly, and liberals and radicals favored external explanations most strongly. The top three causal factors selected by conservatives were (in order) "Lack of empathy and concern for others," "Impulsiveness and risk-taking tendencies," and "Unstable family life." The top three selected by moderates were "Lack of empathy and concern for others," "Poor discipline practices," and "Unstable family life." The top three liberal factors were: "Unfair economic system," "Lack of educational opportunities," and "Peer influences." For radicals, the top three causal factors were: "Unfair economic system," "Bias in law enforcement," and "Lack of educational opportunities."

Thus, it is evident that conservative and moderate criminologists lean toward an internal locus of control, and liberal and radical criminologists lean toward an external locus of control. It must be noted, however, that the disagreement is where the emphasis is placed rather than a complete denial of the causes favored by their ideological counterparts. After all, conservatives and moderates selected "unstable family life" (an external cause) as their third most important cause, and individual factors were not absent from the responses of liberals or even from the radicals. For instance, all ideological categories considered the individual-level "lack of empathy and concern for others" as important by assigning a score greater than 5 to it, and all ideological categories likewise considered the external factor of "peer influences" to be important according to the same criterion.

The surveyed criminologists were also asked to name the theory they believed has the most empirical support in explaining serious and persistent crime. No fewer than 24 theories were listed, and the results differed significantly by ideology ($\chi^2 = 134.6$, $p < 0.001$). Previous iterations of this study in 1987 identified 15 theories (Ellis & Hoffman, 1990), and 23 theories were listed in the 1997 iteration (Walsh & Ellis, 2004). In both these prior studies, ideology was also the best predictor of the causes selected. Such a surfeit of theories is indicative of theoretical fragmentation in criminology and a selective ideology-based interpretation of the literature since there can only be one theory with the most empirical support in explaining serious and persistent crime. A discipline with such an excess of theories can also be assumed to lack scientific rigor.

No one likes to be called an ideologue held captive to ideological beliefs that dominate their views since these terms are considered derogatory extra-scientific terms. The label would be particularly offensive when applied to those who take pride in participating in a scientific enterprise, including criminologists. Nevertheless, we all inescapably have our ideologies that serve as subconscious roadmaps of the cultural terrain by which we navigate the bumpy and pot-holed roads of sociopolitical conflict. It does not matter if our maps conceal more of the terrain as they reveal because they are at least useful in arranging the furniture of our minds. Possessing a roadmap is thus almost inevitable for everyone since roadmaps contain and organize the beliefs and values needed to help guide meaningful human actions.

When people are tasked with making important decisions, they make them according to their roadmaps, and the direction the map points to is believed to be the correct route to their destination. It is the nature of beliefs that they are not doubted, so when politicians or criminal justice administrators must decide what crime prevention and treatment policies to adopt, their beliefs must be considered true since they would hardly advocate for policies based on beliefs they doubt. As Boyd (2012, p. 55) puts it: "If a proposition is to be applied to action, it has to be embraced, or believed without reservation. There is no room for doubt, which can only paralyze action." If it is believed that "nothing works" in terms of criminal rehabilitation, then all that remains is to set criminals apart from society and build more prisons. If it is more optimistically believed that some rehabilitative programs work for some people some of the time, then efforts will be made to implement them.

However, this position should only be adopted by people who must act on their beliefs, in which case the taken-for-granted representations of their ideology are useful to their decision-making, regardless of the degree to which they are true or false. The situation is very different when it comes to science. In theorizing the causes of crime, beliefs taken as fixed and true in the same way block the road to progress. Favored theories must never be held as articles of faith, and criminologists must consider their current beliefs to be fallible and open to revision or even discarded. If they do not, the discipline will slowly die (Cullen, 2011), and the study of criminal behavior will be forfeited to other disciplines such as psychology, genetics, and neurobiology. As Boyd (2012: 55) notes: "But the scientific spirit requires a man to be at all times ready to dump his whole cart-load of beliefs, the moment experience is against them. The desire to learn forbids him to be perfectly cocksure that he knows already." This is the spirit of science: go where the facts lead, but because criminology is infected by ideology, many criminologists find it emotionally difficult to do. However, they must do so because science is obliged to "tell it like it is," not how we would like it to be.

3 Human Nature and Criminology

Is There a Human Nature?

All sciences must explore and evaluate theories relevant to the nature of the phenomena they investigate—in this case, human nature—but many criminologists appear reluctant to do so in the belief it is socially constructed. Nevertheless, all criminological theories contain at least an implicit theory of human nature, and even those that deny human nature cannot help making assumptions that imply one. Social policies and recommendations regarding the crime problem, or any other social problem, are unavoidably based on conscious or subconscious anticipations about how people will react to threats and incentives. A policymaker or recommender with a Platonic unconstrained vision will anticipate differently from an Aristotelian constrained visionary. Crime prevention policies are often based on data produced by criminologists, so it would be socially beneficial for criminologists to strive to understand the human nature that underlies all aspects of social life. As Gerhard Lenski notes:

> Human nature is an extraordinarily complex combination of elements, some that are shared with all other species, some that are shared with some others but not all, and still others that are unique and peculiar to *Homo sapiens*. To deny or ignore any part of this rich heritage in constructing social science theories is to deny or ignore elements of the rich world that are altogether fundamental to understanding human life.
>
> (2005: 46)

But is there a human nature? I assume that most people would reply affirmatively to this question, but some in the social sciences deny it, perhaps on essentialist grounds. Critical criminologist Jenny Francis, for instance, notes that human nature is largely ignored in social science and rightly so "because nature is constructed as that which cannot be produced" (2013: 510). I confess that I am at a loss to decipher what that means, but she also says that the concept of human nature leads us to think of ourselves as separate from other

DOI: 10.4324/9781003662495-4

species, and that leads us to harm them. London, Troshynski, and Panos, (2021: 4) also deny human nature:

> This article contends that this construct known as "human nature" does not exist. At the same time, we assert that using the legal system to counteract a presumed fallen nature justifies those with privilege and power in dominating those without privilege and power.

Thus, in common with Francis, they deny human nature because it allegedly grants us leave to harm others, such as by imprisoning criminals. To claim that human nature does not exist is a path of least resistance because to take that path is to be relieved of the burden of pondering what it may be.

Biosocial criminologists Maestripieri and Boutwell (2022: 7) have a quite different take, pointing out that human nature is not a controversial concept in the natural sciences:

> Human nature simply refers to the neurological, cognitive, and psychological adaptations and tendencies characteristic of the species Homo sapiens. Unless one objects to the notion that human beings are one among many other biological species, and that every species shows species-typical psychological and behavioral adaptations (so that there is also a cat nature, a dog nature, a chimpanzee nature, etc.), there is nothing intrinsically controversial about human nature.

Maestripieri and Boutwell note that everything in nature, from acorns to zebras, has a nature (a set of defining characteristics) that sets it apart from everything else that is not it (*pace* Francis) and that their natures have been forged by natural selection. Thus, for the biologist, human nature is the sum of human adaptations accumulated over millions of years of evolution: "Human nature may be defined as our collection of adaptations" (Kennair, 2002: 27). Edouard Machery offers a similar view: "Human nature is the set of properties that humans tend to possess as a result of the evolution of their species" (2008: 323). To describe the nature of any living thing, we list its adaptive features and note those that are unique (or quantitatively enhanced) that differentiate it from everything else it is not. Karl Marx famously wrote that the quintessential defining feature of humans is their ability to create their environments rather than simply adapting to them (Sayers, 2005). The most salient features that enable us to do this include complex cultures, language, a large brain relative to body size, intelligence, self-consciousness, foresight, agency, spirituality, a theory of mind, and moral sensibility. The sum of these and other features constitutes human nature even if none are separately necessary, nor jointly sufficient, to define it.

Some of these attributes are not unique to humans, but their quantitative enhancement among humans is exponential. Humans are unique, but they are not uniquely unique. Every animal species is unique in some way. The information for the design and expression of human features is in our human DNA. Since all humans belong to a single species, they must "share all cognitive and psychological characteristics" (McCrae & Terracciano 2005: 559). This observation is supported by several cross-cultural studies involving thousands of subjects from every inhabited continent and at least 50 cultures, which exhibit numerous social, cultural, economic, religious, and political differences (Costa, Terracciano, & McCrae, 2001; McCrae & Terracciano, 2005; Schmitt et al., 2008). These studies confirm that the same personality profiles are present in all cultures and correlate with the same behavioral practices. These species-typical psychological regularities imply a universal human nature, even if different payoffs associated with those psychological profiles are determined by ecology and culture.

In our discussion of essentialism in Chapter 1, Williams (2011: 154) noted that a biological kind

> is a matter of standing in a specific historical relation, perhaps to an ancestor. An animal that does not stand in this historical relation is not a member of the kind. ... The essence of a natural kind is a set of (relational or intrinsic) properties.

Although natural selection assures continuous change and speciation over the vastness of evolutionary time, this does not contradict accurate categorizations of biological kinds and their natures because they have been what they are now and will be for a very long time. The idea that living entities have unchanging essences that make them *eternally* what they are, however, does not prevent biologists from talking about natural kinds that they can identify given sufficient DNA material. All human behavior rests on an evolved nature packaged in our universally shared genes and specific cultures in interaction. This is known as the dual inheritance theory (Richerson, Boyd, & Henrich, 2010) or gene-culture coevolution (Walsh & Yun, 2016). This model maintains that genes affect the direction of cultural evolution, and culture creates situations in which genes are selected for adaptive utility in their current environment.

Since Charles Darwin's *On the Origin of Species*, we have expected fuzzy boundaries around biology's taxonomies, such that no sharp dividing lines between species exist. Species change across evolutionary time; thus, we may rule out any constellation of features as *timelessly* necessary and sufficient for membership in any species. If we rewind the evolutionary clock to the Big Bang some 13.8 billion years ago, everything in the universe that has since evolved was once pure energy from which the fermions and bosons formed, which, in turn, formed into neutrons and protons. This all occurred within seconds, but it wasn't until about 380,000 years later that the universe had cooled enough to allow electrons to establish orbitals around protons and neutrons to form atoms. Stars coalesced from hydrogen and helium atoms, and when they did, they forged the heavier elements in their fiery furnaces. After a few million years, the largest stars went supernova and spewed those elements into space (Cassé, 2003). Thus, even atoms evolved. We, and everything else on earth, are composed of these elements; as Carl Sagan famously informed us—we are all "made of star stuff" (1980: 233). Then somehow the chemistry of these lifeless elements produced the first living organism and began the process of biological evolution that eventually led to millions of different species, including *Homo sapiens*. Thus, no life form can be essentialist in the Platonic sense that things have always existed as they now are. As Lisa Gannett (2010: 367) declares, we can rule out the strong essentialist "*really* real" philosophical concept of human nature while safely adopting the "merely real" of the biologist.

The Blank-Slate View

Those who deny human nature believe that the human mind is a *tabula rasa*, a blank slate, at birth, and that culture is an autonomous realm of reality having an arbitrary and almost limitlessly variable character. For left-leaning thinkers from Plato to Marx, this view fits their utopian visions of secular salvation, but if there is such a thing as human nature, it serves to constrain those visions. This is why the "war on human nature" has been waged by utopian dreamers and why the 18th-century blank slate/noble savage view of humans is still popular among left-leaning scholars (Pinker, 2002). The blank slate view is a totalitarian dream, as Mao Zedong knew. In a speech before the 1958 Supreme State Conference, he said: "With blank paper many things can be done. You can write on it or draw designs. Blank paper is best for writing on" (Gregor, 2017: 39). If humans are blank slates, dictators can inscribe anything they like on their minds. Political leaders such as Mao and his fellow tyrants murdered over 100 million people in the belief that they could take blank organisms and turn them into the "new Soviet, Chinese, or Cambodian man" (van den Berghe, 1990: 179).

No one denies that our natures are shaped differently in different cultural environments, but human nature is not formed de novo by culture; rather, it is expressed differently across cultures. As anthropologist Donald Brown wrote: "Whatever the motive may be for resisting the idea that there is a human nature whose features shape culture and society, its intellectual foundations have all but collapsed" (1990: 144). Humanity's universal nature and its diverse culturally specific natures are not mutually exclusive since cultural nature flows from humanity's evolved nature. As Jerome Barkow (1992: 635) reminds us, "psychology underlies culture and society, and biological evolution underlies psychology."

Emile Durkheim accepted this notion in his concept of *Homo duplex*, that is, humans are beings of two natures, biological and social. As Jonathan Fish (2013: 339) explains: "*Homo duplex* is Durkheim's depiction of humans as rooted in two interacting aspects of their being: insatiable egoistic desires and appetites which are, in turn, constrained by socially generated normative moral concerns." Durkheim viewed these two natures as contending opposites, but I see them as complementary, with our cultural nature being the polished product of our evolved nature. They are opposites in the sense that the Freudian concepts of the id (Durkheim's "insatiable egoistic desires and appetites") and the superego (Durkheim's constraining social norms) are opposites at the individual level, but both are required to form the finished product, the ego. Culture completes what biology started.

Durkheim's *Homo duplex* concept is criticized by those who subscribe to the *tabula rasa* doctrine because they believe that humans have no nature, only a culture. For them, humans are almost infinitely malleable and capable of constructing any imaginable set of cultural practices because the *tabula* is *rasa*. Anyone who believes that culture is an autonomous causal agent would be obliged to accept the culture of David Buss's counterfactual Bongo-Bongo tribe:

> They live in peace and harmony and don't get into social conflicts; sex roles are reversed, with women being masculine and aggressive, men being feminine; husbands don't care if their wives have sex with other men, and women don't care if their husbands give the bulk of the meat from the hunt to their lovers; they lack envy, jealousy, and avarice; men find older women who are grandmothers to be more sexually attractive than young women; they lack status hierarchies and are perfectly egalitarian; and they channel acts of altruism as much toward other people's children as their own.
>
> (2001: 973)

This caricature of the blank-slate view of human nature is not entirely new. Margaret Mead's anthropological work in Samoa and New Guinea in the 1930s made equally outlandish claims, such as the lack of sexual jealousy, sex role reversal, and several other claims about the supposed cultural practices existing in those cultures. Given what she purported to find among these cultures, Mead wrote: "We are forced to conclude that human nature is almost unbelievably malleable, responding accurately and contrastingly to cultural conditions" (1935: 289). Even though later studies of the same cultures showed her claims to be completely baseless, and despite Mead's later repudiation of her early claims, her early work is still quoted approvingly in some sociology and anthropology intro textbooks (see Walsh & Vaske, 2015, for an evaluation of Mead's early work and how it was highly touted in social science circles).

Buss concocted his Bongo-Bongo culture to show that human nature constrains what is possible and that such a culture could not exist. This is not to claim that human nature is not malleable because malleability is part of the definition of human nature, but not malleable to this extent. Human nature is historically and culturally malleable and is expressed contingently. Hunter-gatherers, agrarians, and industrial and post-industrial workers living in different times and cultures express their natures in different ways. However, these expressions are variations of a common theme, and nature limits how far the theme can be stretched. Former cultural determinist Melford Spiro realized this after studying cultures worldwide. As a cultural anthropologist, Spiro began his career interested in cultural uniqueness, novelty, and relativism, but he later perceived the similarities underlying the differences. This led him

> to the conclusion that I could not make sense of my findings so long as I continued to operate within the postulates of strong cultural determinism and relativism. I could see no way of accounting for [my findings] short of postulating a pancultural human nature.
>
> (Spiro, 1999: 8)

To claim that human nature is constructed anew in each culture disconnects us from the lessons of history and cuts us off from the ideas of the ages. It would mean that humans inhabiting different cultures and living in different times had nothing in common except their naked appearance with people living in other cultures and times. If humans in all cultures and at all times did not have the same hopes, aspirations, character traits, emotions, feelings, goals, needs, and moral strengths and weaknesses as humans do today, we could not fathom the wisdom bequeathed to us by the past. But as Peter Grosvenor tells us, we can: "It is the existence of perennial traits that enable us to understand, for example, the motivations of characters in the plays of Shakespeare or Sophocles, even though they were written in times radically different from our own" (2002: 434). Sun Tzu's *The Art of War*, written in China in the 5th century BC, is required reading in military academies and is widely read in business schools for advice on tactics and negotiating techniques to this day. We appreciate the lessons of Plato's allegories as though written by a modern English-speaking philosopher, and the lessons of ancient religious leaders still resonate with billions. Ideas bequeathed to us by these ancients are just as potent and relevant today as they were in their times and cultures because we share their human nature. David Hume said of this common understanding across time and place:

> It is universally acknowledged that there is a great uniformity among the actions of men, in all nations and ages, and human nature remains still the same in its principles and operations. ... would you know the sentiments, inclinations and course of life of the Greeks and Romans? Study well the temper and actions of the French and English.
>
> (Trigg, 1999: 83)

The Ancient Seeds of Human Nature

Do humans acquire a sense of morality by cultivating natural inclinations toward morality or by imposing rules on naturally selfish humans lacking natural inclinations toward morality? In the first instance, all we need to imbibe moral rules is to avoid the corruption of distorting environments, and the seeds of our natures will bloom like roses in an English garden. In the second instance, learning moral rules requires avoiding corrupting environments and restraining, sometimes forcibly, the self-seeking seeds of our nature. These contrasting positions were most forcefully put in Western philosophy by the dovish Jean-Jacques Rousseau in the first instance and by the hawkish Thomas Hobbes in the second. We see so much evil in the world driven by self-seeking motives, but also a lot more goodness in the world driven by empathetic regard for the well-being of others. How can evolutionary logic reconcile the simultaneous existence of good and evil in the human behavioral repertoire?

We might begin with Jerome Barkow's (1992) triad of social instincts—status-seeking, nepotism, and reciprocal altruism—the most salient features of human nature, to understand both good and bad behavior. As with every functional trait of every animal, the story begins with the central concerns of survival and reproduction. In our earliest primate times, our ancestors lived in dominance hierarchies with resource-rich ecological niches where high-status males enjoyed disproportionate access to resources and mating opportunities, and used their status and resources to favor close kin and high-status peers, thus enabling mutually advantageous alliances to maintain the hierarchy (Gavrilets, 2012). Humans are reciprocal altruists with all conspecifics, but favoring kin (nepotism) is beneficial for reproductive success because kin pass on many of the same genes shared with the altruist. The evolutionary benefits of high status are apparent. High status relieves males of the burden of competing with others for resources because it simultaneously draws females to those who have it and leads males of lower status to defer. The mating advantages these individuals enjoyed enabled genes underlying status-seeking to be perpetuated down the generations. Individuals not disposed to seek status would leave so few descendants that such a tendency would be largely eliminated from the gene pool.

Humans thus have an evolved motivation to strive for their best interests, but we also have a strong egalitarian instinct. Before children can articulate any moral reasoning for it, the first moral statement they typically utter is "That's not fair!" How do they arrive at that conclusion, and why is it so compelling? When Hominins branched off from the ancestral line to become foraging nomads during the Pliocene-Pleistocene epoch, they faced a different ecology that demanded the evolution of strong norms of reciprocal altruism. Life may have been "nasty, brutish, and short," but transitioning from tree-dwelling and abundant resources to roaming the savannah and foraging for scarce resources evoked different behaviors and emotions. Several scholars

(Gavrilets, 2012; Rogers, Deshpande, & Feldman 2011) have argued that the nomadic lifestyle characterized by uncertain prospects of obtaining survival resources generated the evolution of our egalitarian instinct. Foraging, hunting, and gathering demanded group-wide cooperation, where behavior that subverted reciprocity could not be tolerated. Scarce resources had to be distributed fairly lest the group fall into disputes and fracture. In such a group, sharing resources would occur under the vigilant eyes of all almost as soon as they were obtained. Perceptions of unequal distribution would have produced immediate emotional reactions that would have discouraged cheaters. Of course, hunter-gatherer bands would have had leaders who doubtless benefited from that role, and their leadership role would be a function of their personal qualities—skilled hunter, fighter, strategist, speaker, leader, etc.—rather than of some artificial process of ascription.

Adkins and Guo (2008) provide a model of the shifting role of genes in status attainment across different levels of cultural development. Using data from the Standard Cross-Cultural Sample of the Ethnographic Atlas, they show that the influence of genes on status attainment describes a reverse J pattern across the expanse of human phylogeny. Status differences among hunter-gatherers were a function of individual traits:

> With each generation, status assortment begins on a fairly level playing field and proceeds on the basis of ability and luck. Thus, the genome → ability and ability → status relationship is apt to be relatively strong as all society members develop in largely the same environment.
>
> (Adkins & Guo, 2008: 248)

With the development of agriculture, resources became more abundant and reliable, leading to task specialization, private property, inheritance mechanisms, and wealth accumulation. Agriculture generated larger settled populations and the need for protection against other large populations. Protecting common group interests demanded effective leaders possessing the qualities of pre-hominid troop leaders who could form kin-based coalitions that demanded resources be allocated to them and their allies commensurate with their status. Agrarian societies thus ushered in the reemergence of ancient nepotism and dominating leadership styles.

Because of the nature of farming, there was less opportunity to form oppositional coalitions, resource allocation was delayed, and no longer under the watchful eye of all. Thus, the genome → ability → status relationship weakens as agrarian cultures become more entrenched, and only the most talented can rise above their birth station. In such cultures, status had little to do with individual traits and everything to do with transmitted patterns of hereditary privilege (chiefs, aristocrats, royalty) to which other group members had to defer. Societies characterized by huge inequalities between elites and commoners have a drastic reduction in the genome → ability and ability → status relationships. With the emergence of capitalism and democracy, the genome → ability and ability → status relationship became strong again, although not as strong as in hunter-gatherer societies. Modern societies thus contain individuals with an evolutionary history that has provided them with traits at odds with each other. The most ancient traits of status and nepotism evolved in our pre-hominid history but were blunted by necessity during our species' history as foragers and hunter-gatherers in which reciprocal altruism was a survival imperative.

Good and Evil are Both Driven by Selfishness

Philosophers have long debated whether human nature is good, bad, or selfish. Selfishness implies neither good nor bad if we disregard the negative connotation it has acquired. Jean-Jacques Rousseau believed that: "'Man is naturally good'; he becomes bad chiefly through social institutions that restrain or corrupt his tendencies to natural behavior" (Durant & Durant 1967: 29). For Rousseau, humans have an innate drive aimed at satisfying *amour de soi*, but this self-love becomes *amour proper* (pride, vanity) when people congregate in societies and begin to compare themselves to others in terms of superiority and inferiority and compete for resources (Velkley, 2002). However, Rousseau never explained how the sum of good individuals created malevolent social institutions. In the state of nature, Rousseau imagined man as a "Noble Savage" living in peace and harmony, while for Thomas Hobbes, life in a state of nature was "Brutal, nasty, and short." Who got it right? Yaldir and Der (2016: 277) opine that:

> [Rousseau's] optimism about the nature of men in the state of nature makes it hard for one to make sense of why the society should be established in the first place. If men live in harmony with nature, it seems that they do not necessarily need a society to live in. In that respect, Hobbes does a better job. Since men face a state of chaos and violence in the state of nature, this requires the transition to civil life where they can enjoy peace as well as protection. Hobbes fills in the gaps that Rousseau leaves blank.

The founding fathers of sociology—Durkheim, Marx, and Weber—recognized that each new generation of humans is a recurrent invasion of self-centered beings who would remain so without civilizing society; thus, they would agree with Hobbes. Durkheim noted that the insatiability of human appetites would lead to criminal tendencies unless society provided a preventative moral discipline. Marx and Engels wrote that they were "well aware that egoism, just as much as selfishness, *is* in definite circumstances a necessary form of self-assertion for individuals" (Replogle 1990: 695). Max Weber "quite unmistakably regards personal self-interest as innate and universal among humans. ... "Personal self-interest is already fixed by genetic inheritance in all human individuals and needs no further fixing there by external imposition" (Wallace, 1990: 209). Inborn selfishness is vital for newborns during their helpless years. Babies cannot be concerned with their mothers' sleep requirements; if they are hungry or uncomfortable, they scream for attention; they *must* be utterly self-absorbed and indifferent to the concerns of others, and there can be no other way. It is this necessary self-centeredness that must be contained by the later realization that our wants and needs are inextricably tied to the wants and needs of others, and this results in socially useful selfishness. This is Freud's famous (1961: 80) socialization dictum: "Where id was, there shall ego be."

Plato's allegory of the Ring of Gyges reveals how important it is for socialization to rein in natural egoism. Gyges was a good young shepherd who found a gold ring in a cave that made him invisible when he turned it. Realizing the possibilities this opened for him, he went to the royal court, seduced the queen, murdered the king, and became the king. The point of the allegory is that, given the gift of invisibility, no one would be able to resist the temptation to act unjustly:

> No man can be imagined to be of such an iron nature that he would stand fast in justice. No man would keep his hands off what is not his own when he could safely take what he liked out of the market or go into houses and lie with anyone at his pleasure, to kill or release from prison whom he would, and in all respects be like a God among men.
>
> (Plato, 1960: 44)

Plato thought we would be slaves of our passions without the stern gaze of others and fear of their opprobrium, and that invisibility is the only difference between the just and the unjust. Gyges reverted to his egoistic id when invisibility rendered his socialization irrelevant, and engaged in the wanton pursuit of status and resources. This is not to say that invisibility would turn us all into Gyges-like characters.

In many respects, Rousseau and Hobbes were both right, but Hobbes was more so. The difference is that Rousseau saw a naturally good nature marred by society, while Hobbes saw society as restraining a naturally selfish nature. Evolutionary theorists view selfishness as good rather than bad and as the basis for social cooperation. As Edward O. Wilson remarks:

> Human beings appear to be sufficiently selfish and calculating to be capable of infinitely greater harmony and social homeostasis. This statement is not self-contradictory. True selfishness, if obedient to the other constraints of mammalian biology, is the key to a nearly perfect social contract.
>
> (1978: 157)

Wilson's point is that self-interest is the root of altruistic moral conduct—its necessary emotional scaffold. This sounds counterintuitive to anyone not acquainted with evolutionary logic because such people think of selfishness and altruism as opposites. Laypersons think of selfishness as a concern exclusively with one's interests, even at the cost of others, but only callous, unemotional psychopaths behave this way. Behaving this way may be self-serving in the short term (securing immediate rewards), but it is self-destructive in the long run because there are social and legal costs associated with unbridled selfishness.

Because humans are reciprocal altruists, they are selectively altruistic toward those who, by definition, reciprocate. This is reflected in the adage: "Those who give, get." People who habitually fail to reciprocate are most unlikely to enjoy good relationships with their fellow humans, which is hardly indicative of rational concern for their long-term self-interest. Few people want anything to do with such a person; he or she will end life bitter and lonely, but we all love altruists and want to be part of their lives. Stellar, Feinberg, and Keltner's (2014) experimental studies show that unbridled egoists are unlikely to receive help from others, even in times of great need—you reap what you sow. Altruism is ultimately driven by concerns for the self, although its self-serving nature is rarely consciously perceived and eventually becomes habitual. We benefit ourselves (inwardly or outwardly, immediately or in the future) by being habitually agreeable and cooperative with others and showing genuine concern for them. Humans are adapted to act in their best interests, but their goals are best realized by embracing altruism, being friendly, helpful, sharing, cooperative, trustworthy, and reliable. Giving one's money, time, and effort to help others leads to more health and happiness (Crocker, Canevello, & Brown, 2017). This is what Wilson meant by selfishness as "obedient to the other constraints of mammalian biology."

Altruists recoup the costs of extending benefits and cooperation to others many times over, so while altruism is ultimately self-serving, this does not diminish its value to its beneficiaries. Consider the value of selfishness in your intimate relationships. Jesus commanded us: "You shall love your neighbor as yourself." Jesus took it for granted that we love ourselves; the problem is extending that love to others. Jesus did not consider the love of oneself to be a bad thing, for if it were, loving others would also be a bad thing. You can only love others if you first love yourself. I courted, married, and stayed with my wife because of the self-centered pleasures and satisfactions I receive from being with her, and I know she loves me just as selfishly. My relationship with her is guided by the saying, "Happy wife, happy life." This little aphorism makes it plain that her happiness makes me happy; if that makes me "selfish," then I don't want it any other way, and neither does she. How would she feel if I told her that although I feel no pleasure in her company, I stay with her because I pity her and feel obliged to seek her happiness, however painful it may be for me? I know how I would feel if she said that to me.

In short, I believe that criminology needs a theory of human nature that encompasses all disciplines involved with human behavior. Without a foundational understanding of human nature, criminology lacks a fundamental understanding of the reasons behind criminal behavior and how we can effectively respond to it in our theories. Neither can it expect to reconcile key issues that separate ideological camps without one. We must strive for consensus on contending issues such as to what extent criminals are responsible for their actions. Do we learn to be bad (social learning theories) or to be good (bonding and self-control theories)? Is behavior more strongly driven by rationality or emotion? Do we have free will? Why is the urge to punish so strong? Does poverty cause crime, or crime cause poverty, or does something else cause both? No scientific discipline moves forward without a consensus or near consensus about the nature of the phenomena it investigates; why should criminology expect to do so?

4 The Issue of Free Will Versus Determinism

Do Humans Have Free Will?

Almost 50 years ago, Stephen Shafer (1976: 481) noted, "The problem of man's free will is critically important to criminological views, despite its almost insoluble nature and the inordinate Sisyphean intellectual labor required even to take sides in the centuries-old dispute." Like Sisyphus rolling his boulder up the mountain, just when philosophers think they've got this notorious issue nailed, it rolls back down again. Witness psychologist B.F. Skinner's insistence that we don't have free will but keep pretending that we do, and existentialist philosopher J.P. Sartre's insistence that we have free will but keep pretending that we don't. These are extreme positions; either we are completely determined or free, and neither position offers space for the other. Of course, there are many nuances and qualifiers in both positions that we cannot entertain here. Nevertheless, the issue is important for those contemplating attributions of responsibility for human behavior. Differences of opinion on this issue partially form one's attitudes about punishment, sentencing practices, and the prison abolition movement.

The extreme positions on the issue are libertarian free will and hard determinism. Libertarian free will posits the ability to choose a course of action independent of, or even in defiance of, any external or internal influences, an undetermined *causa sui*. This kind of free will implicitly assumes freedom from all externalities, but our subjective sense of self and patterns of reasoning and desiring are never wholly our own. They are not entirely self-generated phenomena, nor can they be, for we cannot detach ourselves from all externalities and remain functioning human beings. Rather, our self-identities and patterns of reasoning and desiring are continually constituted and modified by their ongoing engagement with other people, our culture, and our world. The well-known line "No man is an island" emphasizes how human beings are inextricably connected and how important the connection is for our well-being and survival. While I think it necessary to believe that humans make their own history, they do not make it from cloth they wove themselves.

Belief in libertarian free will leads to the unpredictability of behavior since if people can choose any possible behavior in any situation, we would have no

DOI: 10.4324/9781003662495-5

basis for making predictions in our relationships. Modern libertarians base their notions of unpredictability on Heisenberg's quantum mechanical principle of uncertainty (Schuster, 2009). Quantum phenomena are "free" in that they are random and unpredictable before observations, but this tells us nothing about human behavior. If free will is taken to mean action without a cause, all human actions would be unpredictable, and chaos would reign. The firing of neurons without reference to what is occurring in the world outside one's addled brain is one of the defining features of unmedicated schizophrenia, and I assume that being in that sad condition is not your idea of freedom. As Max Weber said, this kind of "freedom" is "the privilege of the insane" (Eliaeson, 2002: 35).

On the other hand, hard determinism is all about externalities. It maintains that one's choice of action in any situation results from a sequence of external causes channeled through one's genetic makeup, developmental experiences, and the current situation such that one cannot do other than what one does. The volitional actor is completely removed from consideration in this view. The sticking point is that hard determinists believe that free will requires determinism to be false, but it does not. Science demonstrates conclusively that determinism is true; therefore, they say, science proves we do not have free will. This does not commit us to hard determinism since we can cause our actions. If we are not responsible for our behavior, praise and blame are pointless. Why give medals to brave soldiers or praise and admiration to creative scientists, writers, and artists, and why blame and punish criminals for their actions if they could not have done otherwise? Certainly, what people do, commendable or decried, has a long causal chain traceable to a complex mixture of their genomes, brains, developmental experiences, and the situations they find themselves in. However, these are the hands dealt to us, and we must play them the best we can. Some of us get royal flushes; others do no better than a pair of twos, but the choices we make given the hands we are dealt make them praiseworthy or blameworthy. After all, praiseworthy achievements result from goal-directed activities that might well have failed since they are by no means predetermined.

It may be that soft determinism is necessary for free will because if I did not think that what we do produces meaningful consequences, why would we do anything? All rational action, coaching, training, and guidance are deterministic in that they are designed to cause desired effects. We debate, educate, counsel, and write under the assumption that we can change the minds of others, whom we assume are free to accept or reject what we propose. Without a belief in human agency—our ability to shape our worlds—our minds would be imprisoned in the deadly *Que sera, sera* fatalism. If human action is solely the result of outside determinative forces, desires and motives should translate into action with the well-lubricated ease of a fine engine, but they do not. Choices are burdensome; they must be made against the pull of impulse, habit, sloth, and the presence of alternative options. We all make bad choices we recognize as such only in hindsight, when all we can do is resolve not to make them again. Perhaps that is what free will is: the ability to make good and bad choices and learn from them. Even as we acknowledge that factors impinging on our life choices have significance, they are still subject to our appraisal of how to deal with them constructively.

Free Will as Quantitative

Neuroscientist Bjorn Brembs (2011: 933) views free will as a quantitative trait with some having more of it than others: "A scientific concept of free will cannot be a qualitative concept. The question is not any more 'do we have free will?' [but rather] 'how much free will do we have?'" Viewing free will as a quantitative concept distributed on a continuum, rather than a qualitative binary either/or thing, it is logical to assume that we become increasingly freer of external constraints as we move from childhood to old age. Being freer of external constraints means we can live progressively more, following the proclivities of our natures infused with the wisdom of age. However, free will is constrained or enabled by one's temperament, upbringing, knowledge, conscience, physical and cognitive abilities and disabilities, the size of one's bank account, and the constraints imposed on one by others. The free will of a millionaire is quantitatively far greater than that of someone born into poverty and with limited cognitive ability. Does that mean that a rich, well-educated man—as a possessor of greater ability to exercise his agency—may be held more responsible for criminal acts than the poor man? It would seem to follow logically if we assume, as does the law, that people freely choose their behavior and are therefore held responsible.

A concept associated with free will is the locus of control discussed in Chapter 2. Individuals with a deterministic worldview tend to have an external locus of control, and those with a free-will worldview tend to have an internal locus of control (Hannikainen et al., 2017). Rigoni and his colleagues found that undermining free will beliefs degrades self-control and leads to antisocial tendencies: "Feelings of responsibility and accountability promote socially desirable actions, such as altruism and impulse control, and thus undermining free will could act as a catalyst for impulsive behavior ('I could not do otherwise!')" (2012: 1483). Of course, this does not "prove" that free will is true, it only suggests that if one believes it is true, one will tend to have more prosocial attitudes such as hard work, ambition, and self-discipline, attitudes that lead to success in life.

Neuro-Determinism

Francis Crick provides the quintessential neuro-determinism statement:

> You, your joys and your sorrows, your memories and your ambitions, your sense of personal identity and free will, are in fact no more than the behavior of a vast assembly of nerve cells and their associated molecules. Who you are is nothing but a pack of neurons.
>
> (1994: 3)

Hawking and Mlodinow likewise assert: "It is hard to imagine how free will can operate if our behavior is determined by physical law, so it seems that we are no more than biological machines and that free will is just an illusion" (2010: 32). Crick, and Hawking and Mlodinow, take a hard determinist line that when we sense we are making "free" choices our inflated self-images delude us and that in actuality we interact with the world as biological machines destined to behave in a preprogrammed way by genetic hardware and environmental software. Thus, when we believe we are making volitional choices, it is simply a matter of becoming consciously aware of what the programmed brain has already decided we should do, and we deceive ourselves when we think that our free intentions initiated those choices.

Neuro-determinists often refer to experiments showing that the brain registers decisions to make simple movements, such as pressing buttons, before subjects consciously decide to act. For example, Libet and his colleagues (1985) had subjects perform simple physical tasks with EEG electrodes attached to their scalps while seated in front of an oscilloscope. A clock with a fast-circulating dot was created on the oscilloscope's screen. Subjects were asked to move a finger or raise an arm whenever they felt the urge and to report the dot's position on the screen when they became conscious of the decision to do so. Subjects' reports and oscilloscope readings indicated that unconscious brain activity was observable as EEG signals about 500 milliseconds before they reported conscious awareness of their urge to move. This led Greene and Cohen (2004: 1784) to state: "Free will as we ordinarily understand it is an illusion generated by our cognitive architecture."

However, perhaps we have subconscious neural substrates that serve as ideomotor reflexive readiness potentials behind urges we are told to expect. Iain McGilchrist says that "it is only a problem if one imagines that, for me to decide something, I have to have willed it with the conscious part of my mind. Perhaps my unconscious is every bit as much 'me'" (2009: 187). After all, we do not make conscious decisions to put one foot in front of the other when we walk, but our decision to walk from one place to another is ours nonetheless. We have a mechanism designed to enable us to act without conscious deliberation: the autonomic nervous system. If someone throws a rock at you, there is no time for conscious deliberation; you duck. You don't perceive the threat and chew it over in your mind before deciding that it is a good idea to duck.

In other experiments, Libet instructed subjects to stop their intended actions when they became aware of the urge to carry them out. Subjects had a window of about 150 milliseconds to veto subconscious urges. Libet notes: "It is proposed that conscious will can function in a permissive fashion, either to permit or to prevent the motor implementation of the intention to act that arises unconsciously" (1985: 529). He called this abortive process "free won't." We exercise "free won't" in our conscious minds every time we abort an automatic subconscious unhealthy or illicit urge because it is the process of exercising self-control over our immediate desires. To interpret

Libet's findings to mean that we are automatons ignores that when important decisions are made in everyday life, they are never as simple as "When will I move my finger or raise my arm?" You don't automatically act when deciding things that have a major impact on your life, such as buying a house, quitting a job, or getting a divorce. These decisions require conscious, rational thought. Conscious thought enables you to mentally simulate alternative possibilities of action and the possible consequences of each alternative. Perhaps free will is desiring (willing) something and then consciously deciding if that's really what you should do, and if it is, how you should do it. Libet did not interpret his results in a deterministic fashion. Indeed, he was a firm believer in free will and says as much:

> My conclusion about free will, one genuinely free in the non-determined sense, is then that its existence is at least as good, if not a better, scientific option than is its denial by determinist theory. ... We would not need to view ourselves as machines that act in a manner completely controlled by the known physical laws.
>
> (Libet, 1999: 56–57)

Alan Felthous (2008: 23) suggests that the way around the free will-determinism debate is to discard the prefix "free" and focus on "will," which is simply the intentional faculty: "Through motivation and decision the will settles upon and then implements an action." The notion that will initiate movement toward desired goals was the position of philosopher Arthur Schopenhauer, who notes: "Man can do what he wills, but he cannot will what he wills" (Clark, 2007: 96). In other words, absent constraints, we are free to do whatever our will desires, but we are not free to choose what we desire because our natures dictate that. To say that we can "will" absolutely anything, even things contrary to our nature, is to think of human actions as entirely capricious. Conscious choices are driven by subconscious desires forged by our nature and the learned habits of experience. These things lead us to will (desire) certain things and courses of action over others. This view makes a real practical difference when applied to meaningful choices that people make when multiple desires meet multiple options vying for supremacy.

Compatibilism

Compatibilism is a position that asserts that free will and determinism can coexist. Pockett (2007: 282) notes: "Many, or even most, present-day philosophers are so-called compatibilists." Most of us interpret the conduct of self and others in compatibilist terms. We attribute conscious intentions to free will but explain motives and behavior by assuming they are the products of genetics and developmental experience. Compatibilism does not demand from free will what free will libertarians demand from it. It acknowledges that while humans are never free of external influences, human actions are free within that causal space because external influences are influences that incline us toward one choice rather than another without necessitating it. This soft determinism does not deny that human events have a chain of prior events leading to them. However, as long as we are free from external coercion, we can decide how to respond to those events positively or negatively. We can ask how free a person is in circumstance X, or how determined a person is in circumstance Y.

Compatibilism may be analogized with Niels Bohr's principle of complementarity—the wave/particle dual nature of light. There was initial resistance to this counterintuitive duality since they reasoned that natural phenomena cannot be two things at once, but as it became more empirically endorsed it led to modern quantum theory. Albert Einstein and Leopold Infeld had the following to say about this supposed conundrum:

> But what is light really? Is it a wave or a shower of photons? ... It seems as though we must use sometimes the one theory and sometimes the other, while at times we may use either. We are faced with a new kind of difficulty. We have two contradictory pictures of reality; separately neither of them fully explains the phenomena of light, but together they do.
>
> (Einstein & Infeld, 1938: 262–263)

Compatibilists maintain that human behavior exhibits this same complementarity. If we substitute human action for light, and free will and determinism for waves and particles, we can also conclude that neither free will nor hard determinism alone can explain human behavior; we need both to do so. Although voluntary actions and inclinations may be initiated by free will, they proceed from a web of influences we may not be consciously aware of. Just as there is no paradox in the wave/particle duality of light, there should be no paradox in viewing humans as both free agents and determined. While our innate dispositions may not be subject to our voluntary control, and neither are the environments and situations we find ourselves in, our actions within them can be. This kind of soft determinism—a psychological "uncertainty principle"—gives us the only free will worth having. Free will allows us to follow the reasoned appetitive dictates of our nature, but it also places on our shoulders the responsibility of owning our actions. We are not morally responsible for illicit feelings and desires that may intrude on us, but we are for whatever action we take in response. This differentiates freedom of action from freedom of will

The criminal justice systems of all Western societies are compatibilist. They assume that human beings behave in a free-willed fashion and hold criminals responsible for their actions yet leave space for a variety of mitigating factors (mental illness, self-defense, coercion, etc.) that remove them from the purview of complete responsibility when sentencing them for their crimes. However, the law still assumes that if criminals, absent any mitigating factors, will their actions and could just as easily willed otherwise, they would be fully responsible for their criminal choices, regardless of their social and physical environmental circumstances. The legal practice of punishing criminals relies on the premise that criminals know right from wrong, have freedom of choice, choose to exercise it to harm others, and are thus justly punished. The criminal justice system also assumes that its intervention will become part of a criminal's determinative consciousness that will modify his or her future behavior.

Some scholars strongly dispute the legal system's free will assumptions. Greg Caruso (2021: 123) is skeptical of individual responsibility, and claims, "free will skepticism maintains that criminals are not morally responsible for their actions in the basic desert sense." Free will skepticism is the basis for scholars' calls to abolish prisons and punishment, as we will see later. Scholars such as this are heirs to lawyer Clarence Darrow's statement that a criminal acts when committing a crime "only in the sense that he acts, when cut, by bleeding" (Walsh, 1981: 70). To believe this is to remove all agency from criminals and thus to remove all responsibility. Left realist criminologist Steven Box voices a more reasonable position. He asserts that although people choose to act criminally, "their choices make them responsible, but the conditions [in which they live] make their choices comprehensible" (1987: 29). Robert Agnew (2013: 87) asks, "is it appropriate to hold individuals accountable for their agentic behavior when the ability and inclination to exercise agency may be determined by forces beyond their control?" He replies:

> I would respond by stating that while individuals *may* have no control over those factors that contribute to the exercise of agency, agency still involves the ability to make and act on choices that are not fully determined by forces beyond the individual's control. Agentic individuals therefore have the ability—to varying degrees—to choose crime or conventional behavior. As such, they still bear some responsibility for their behavior.
>
> (Agnew, 2013: 87)

Free Will and Rationality

George Botescu (2022: 596) views free will as intertwined with rationality: "Free will and implicit freedom of will are the expression of the rationality of the human being and reflect one of the ontological sides of the idea of freedom." Rationality, free will, and hedonism were the basis for the classical theorists of crime and penology hedonistic calculus. Rational behavior may be succinctly defined as behavior that is consistent with logic. People are said to behave rationally when we observe a logical fit between the goals they strive for and the means used to achieve them (regardless of whether or not they achieve them). For classical theorists such as Cesare Beccaria and Jeremy Bentham, the goal of human rationality is self-interest, and self-interest, as we view it, governs our behavior, whether in conforming or deviant directions. Hedonism is a doctrine whose central idea is that happiness (pleasure) is the main goal of life. All other life goals are seen only as instrumentally desirable; that is, desirable if they achieve pleasure or avoid pain. Thus, for classical theorists, hedonism is the greatest single motivator of human action. For classical criminologists and modern rational choice theorists, criminals employ this calculus when deciding to behave criminally.

We must understand rationality and its limits to understand criminal offending and devise effective ways to deter it. Rationality is a desirable quality assumed to be inherent in human beings. Although rationality is defined somewhat differently in different disciplines, the basic notion is that rationality is the state of having good sense and sound judgment. Good sense and sound judgment are said to be present when we base our choices on the evidence before us at any given time and if we revise our reasoning (and hence our behavior) as new evidence arises. Rationality should not be confused with morality because rationality's goal is self-interest and self-interest governs all human behavior whether in conforming or deviant directions. The behavior of criminals is commonly seen as irrational. However, crime is rational (at least in the short run) if criminals employ reason and act purposely to gain desired ends. Some individuals choose to offend and others do not because they have different subjective expectations about the risks and rewards involved. If criminals view the probability of arrest as sufficiently high, they may rationally decide that the potential benefits of committing the crime are not worth the risk. Rationality is thus the quality of cost/benefit thinking and behaving consistent with logic and reason such that one's reality is an ordered and intelligible system for achieving goals and solving problems.

The notion of human rationality in criminology owes much to Max Weber's two broad types of rationality: *Zweckrationalitat* ("purpose" or "instrumental" rationality) and *Wertrationalitat* ("value" rationality). *Zweckrationalitat* is a self-serving means-ends rationality Weber assumed to be innate: "Personal self-interest is already fixed by genetic inheritance in all human individuals and needs no further fixing there by external imposition" (Wallace, 1990: 209). In other words, Weber agreed with classical scholars that rationality is a part of human nature pressed into service to meet goals that serve the interests of maximizing pleasure and minimizing pain. *Wertrationalitat* is rationality related to a value such as honor or duty to some revered entity (e.g., one's nation, group, or God) or idea (e.g., patriotism, ideology, or religion) that may appear to others as antithetical to instrumental rationality. For instance, Catholic priests taking vows of poverty, obedience, and chastity are denying themselves the opportunity to gain material wealth, a degree of personal autonomy, and sexual pleasure to serve God. Likewise, jihadists who blow themselves up along with innocent men, women, and children, are denying themselves life in the belief that they are serving Allah. *Zweckrationalitat* thus points us to reasoned means of attaining a goal, and

Wertrationalitat defines those means and goals in terms of the norms and values we have internalized.

A rational decision is one reasoned to be optimal for achieving a goal, but rationality is subjective (personal and biased) and bounded (it has limits). Given that it is subjective and bounded, unwanted outcomes can result from rational strategies. This is because we do not all make the same calculations or arrive at the same plan when pursuing the same goals. We all contemplate our anticipated actions with less-than-perfect knowledge, different mindsets, and different reasoning abilities. In other words, we may think we are behaving in ways that best serve our self-interest, but our behavior may bring unwanted results because we are ignorant of some things and misinterpret others. We strive to order our decisions relating to our self-interest with limited knowledge and understanding regarding the possible outcomes of a particular course of action. All people have mental models of the world and behave rationally concerning them, even if others might consider their behavior irrational. Criminals behave rationally from their private models of reality and "are generally doing the best they can within the limits of time, resources, and information available to them. This is why we characterize their decision making as rational, albeit in a limited way" (Clarke & Cornish, 2001: 25).

It is assumed that everyone agrees that all humans of sound mind are rational in the classical sense of wanting to maximize their pleasure and minimize pain. However, we need to know the factors that affect offenders' rationality but do not affect nonoffenders' rationality, or vice versa. That is, what leads criminals to decide, quite rationally, that increasing their pleasure means immediate gratification (a robbery target, a drug fix now, a sex partner for tonight) and minimizing their pain (lack of funds, boredom, or drug craving) are best met by criminal means and others decide, just as rationally, that their needs are best met by delaying gratification, getting an education or training, getting a good job, getting married, and settling down? In other words, what concerns criminologists most are the factors that lead people to exercise the rationality they have in common in radically different ways.

It would seem that the typical criminal's rationality is severely bounded. We continually see more than two-thirds of released criminals going back to prison, and that is hardly maximizing pleasure and minimizing pain (Stohr & Walsh, 2025). Criminals are rational from their limited point of view and they weigh costs and benefits. But like the rest of us, criminals are not walking calculating machines who routinely take time to weigh the pros and cons of their every move. As van den Haag (2003: 247) put it: "Law abiding people habitually ignore criminal opportunities. Law breakers habitually discount the risk of punishment. Neither calculates." On the other hand, Loughran et al. (2016) found that adolescents seriously involved in crime act under anticipated rewards and costs of offending and rationally reallocate their time in response to expected changes in the costs and benefits of their activities. They also found that the anticipated rewards of their behavior carry more weight than the potential costs. After all, the rewards of criminal acts generally follow quickly while the costs may or may not follow, and if they do, it occurs much later. Because rational choice theory grants offenders the dignity of possessing agency, just as nonoffenders purposely weigh options before deciding on a course of action, so do offenders. Therefore, "He or she can be held responsible for that choice and can be legitimately punished" (Clarke & Cornish, 2001: 25).

Emotion and Crime

It is surely not good enough to say that crime is a rational choice made by someone who could have chosen otherwise. Of course, an offender "wanted" ("free" willed) to commit the criminal act and did so, but this is hardly an explanation. We would like to know what differentiates criminals who decide to lead a life of crime and have no intention of pursuing a straight life from non-criminals, or one-time criminals from chronic criminals. One factor absent from rational choice theory is emotion. As we shall see later, there is an abundance of studies showing that emotion is stronger than rationality in human decision-making. Merton's anomie/strain theory avers that crime is an alternative way to achieve monetary success. Yet the meager monetary gains and dismal long-term consequences of a criminal lifestyle suggest different motivations. Studies of street criminals (Katz, 1988; De Haan & Vos, 2003) paint a picture of "unreasonable" individuals seduced by a life of action who value their "badass" reputations more than monetary success, and Albert Cohen's (1955) view of delinquents as being motivated by short-run hedonism, which is expressive, malicious, and destructive rather than instrumental.

There must be something that makes crime appealing for its own sake independent of any extrinsic rewards that may accrue. Chronic criminals are certainly motivated by the need for fast cash to feed their "every night is party night" lifestyles, but interviews with criminals find that the internal rewards of committing expressive crimes are powerful motivators (Wood, et al., 1997). As Jock Young (2003: 391) put it: "The sensual nature of crime, the adrenaline rushes of edgework—voluntary illicit risk-taking and the dialectic of fear and pleasure ... all point to a wide swath of crime that is expressive rather than narrowly instrumental." Jack Katz (1988: 235) notes that hardened criminals leave it to others to think about costs and benefits: "The hardman triumphs, after all, by inducing others to calculate the costs and benefits." Incentives and disincentives to law-abiding or criminal behavior are perceived differently due to ingrained habits forged by genes and developmental experiences. That is, stable individual differences are linked to proximal situations when a person decides to act.

Emotional edgework is not devoid of cost-benefit considerations, however, and thus not bare of all rationality. For instance, the notorious 1930s bank robber Willie Sutton relished the visceral rush of crime. When asked why he robbed banks he replied: "Because I enjoyed it. I was more alive when I was inside a bank, robbing it, than at any other time in my life," but he would also sometimes answer "Because that's where the money is" (Sutton & Linn, 1976: 120). Sutton was thus rewarded emotionally and financially, as are street robbers by their adrenaline rush and monetary gains. What is missing from these accounts of "hot" emotions motivating crime are the "quiet" moral emotions of empathy, guilt, and shame that prevent it. Criminologists should ponder if it would be more productive to focus on how people develop positive emotions rather than only on negative ones. Glen Walters (2015: 8) states: "Once the moral emotions are eliminated, we are left with the utilitarian decision to commit or not commit a crime. Thus, dampening relevant moral emotions with proactive criminal thinking leads to a situation where rational choice is less than optimal."

Section 2

Biopsychosocial Issues

5 Integrating the Natural Sciences with Criminology

Tinbergen's Four Questions

According to Matthews and Turkheimer (2021), no single discipline is sufficient to explain the complexities of human behavior. This observation is consistent with Nobel laureate ethologist Nikolas Tinbergen's (1963) famous four questions. Tinbergen maintains that to understand the behavior of any animal, including humans, we must examine levels of explanation, ranging from its distal evolutionary history to its most proximate causal mechanisms. Tinbergen's first question asks: What is the current adaptive function (adaptive significance) of this behavior, and how does it contribute to the conscious and subconscious concerns of all living organisms—survival and reproductive success? The second is: What is the phylogenetic history of the behavior, and how did it come to have its current form? The third question is ontogenetic: How do genes and environments interact in individual developmental history to produce this behavior? The fourth is causation: It asks what causal mechanisms trigger the behavior. The first two questions engage ultimate-level issues, and the last two engage proximate-level issues. Bateson and Laland (2013: 712) note: "Tinbergen's framework has attracted little criticism, and has stood the test of time." Of course, no one carries out research mindful of all levels since these questions have been parceled out to different disciplines, but they all complement one another, and no level should contradict the others.

Zhuravel and Kurumisawa (2020: 373) note: "By its nature criminology has multidisciplinary inter-scientific connections with a variety of branches of knowledge. ... related to technical and natural sciences. ... [but it is not] a complex of any constituent parts of various sciences, but [a] deep synthesis." As Francis Cullen (2011: 311) remarked in his Sutherland Address to the American Society of Criminology, "[W]e can no longer pretend that biology is not intimately implicated in human behavior and thus in criminal behavior." The only interdisciplinary perspective in criminology that takes Cullen seriously was called the "biosocial" perspective but today, many criminologists refer to it as the "biopsychosocial" perspective adding "psycho" when it became a division of the American Society of Criminology. Biosocial

DOI: 10.4324/9781003662495-7

criminology, of course, always included psychological traits. The "social" syllable was always part of criminology, as was the "psycho" syllable. The "bio" syllable in the word encompasses five interrelated areas: evolutionary biology, physiology, molecular genetics, behavioral genetics, and neurobiology (Barnes & Boutwell, 2015). These disciplines encompass all Tinbergen's levels of explanation of non-trivial behavior from its distal evolutionary history to the individual's developmental history to the most proximate causal mechanisms. From the biopsychosocial perspective, these causal mechanisms include everything from neurons to neighborhoods, and it recognizes that the genome and the brain are systems that are reactive to environmental experiences.

Some criminologists (e.g., Cooper, Walsh, & Ellis, 2010; Wright & Boisvert, 2009) consider the movement from a strictly sociological orientation in criminology to a biopsychosocial one a Kuhnian paradigm shift. However, Rocque and Posick (2017: 290) maintain that "biosocial criminology is not a paradigm shift, but rather should be considered as 'normal science,' in which the existing paradigm is pushed, expanded, and molded in new directions." Rocque and Posick may be right, and if they are, it would reduce or eliminate much of the animosity between traditional and biopsychosocial criminologists. Many sociologists, particularly younger ones who have grown up with genomics and the "age of the brain," are conversant with the role played by biology in understanding human behavior. Even sociology's flagship journal, the *American Journal of Sociology*, devoted an entire issue to genetics in 2008, as did *The Sociological Review* in 2016, although some articles were skeptical. Also, note the statement of prominent behavioral geneticists Turkheimer and Harden (2014: 180) that behavioral genetics "is ordinary social science. ...We argue, therefore, that biosocial and social criminology are already partners in the quest to answer criminological questions; both bring different strengths and weaknesses, both also complement one another very well." And as E.O. Wilson opines (1998: 205), "the social sciences are intrinsically compatible with the natural sciences. The two great branches of learning will benefit to the extent that their modes of causal explanation are made consistent." Add to this Nichole Rafter's (2004: 736) argument that, "today biological explanations are again gaining credibility and are joining forces with sociological explanations in ways that may soon make them equal partners." We will examine this partnership in evolutionary biology in terms of the first two of Tinbergen's four questions: function and phylogeny.

Criminology and Evolutionary Biology

Tinbergen's function and phylogeny have to do with evolutionary processes, and as Theodosius Dobzhansky wrote more than 50 years ago: "Nothing in biology makes sense except in the light of evolution" (1973: 125). If nothing makes sense in biology except in the light of evolution, then nothing about the behavior of any animate organism, including that of humans, makes sense. Evolutionary processes order the material of the universe, from atoms in the inanimate material world to behavior in the animate world. Plomin et al. (2003: 533) assert that organisms' behavior is the primary driving force of evolution: "The behavioral genomic level of analysis may be the most appropriate level of understanding for evolution because the functioning of the whole organism drives evolution. That is, behavior is often the cutting edge of natural selection." However, it is not the behavior evoked by an environmental challenge per se that creates new trait variants via natural selection, it is the *consequences* of that behavior. A behavior must have adaptive consequences if the genes underlying the behavior are to be selected.

Charles Darwin called the selective process *natural selection* because it was nature that "selected" the adaptive genetic variants that fit the environments organisms found themselves inhabiting at the time. Evolution can be succinctly defined as changes in a species' gene pool over time achieved by the selective retention or elimination of alleles. Natural selection does not induce genetic variation; it is a winnowing process that reacts to environmental conditions by preserving favorable genetic variants and eliminating deleterious variants. The sub-discipline that seeks to integrate evolutionary biology with other disciplines is evolutionary psychology. As Klasios (2019: 30) explains, "One of the virtues of evolutionary psychology is its aspiration to integrate relevant theoretical insights and empirical findings from the evolutionary sciences, natural sciences, and social sciences."

The great value of evolutionary theory is that it explains why we see consistent behavioral patterns among humans across diverse times and cultures. In every society across geographic space and time, men are more violent than women, youth are more unruly than adults, and there is a sex-based division of labor. Sociocultural forces cannot explain such remarkable consistency in these observed patterns. We would expect more variation in these patterns across the various cultures if sociocultural factors were the cause. We would expect to see somewhere and/or at some time a society in which it is the norm that women aggress at similar rates to men, where adolescents are better behaved than adults, and where women are the primary resource acquirers and men stay at home to raise the children, but we do not. The only thing cultures across the globe share that could explain these consistent behavioral patterns is that people in all cultures across time and space share a common evolutionary history and, thus, a common nature.

The genome is the molecular archive of millions of years of selective elimination and retention of alleles that contributed to all living organisms' twin goals—survival and reproductive success. Evolutionary psychologists view crime as normal behavior (albeit morally regrettable) committed by normal individuals engaged in normal social processes. If it is "normal" in this sense, it follows that the potential for criminal behavior must be in all humans. Thus, it must have conferred some adaptive advantage on our distant ancestors. But how can such heterogeneous acts as murder, theft, rape, robbery, and assault be viewed as adaptations when they are maladaptive in modern societies? Because a specific behavior may be maladaptive, it does not mean that the mechanisms underlying it were not evolved adaptations. Modern environments are so radically different from the environments in which *Homo sapiens* evolved that many traits that had adaptive value at the time may not be adaptive today. It is the behavioral *traits* underlying criminal behavior, not a specific criminal act, that are the functional adaptations: "Genes do not code themselves for jimmying a lock or stealing a car ... the genome does not waste precious DNA encoding the specifics" (Rowe, 1996: 285).

Sexuality and Criminality

The powerful logic of evolution helps illuminate the ultimate reasons why these traits exist, not the proximate motivation for executing them. Evolution is morally blind; it selects traits and behaviors that enhance fitness regardless of how repugnant they may be. Certain psychological traits and behaviors we now associate with criminal personalities were doubtless adaptive in primitive hunter-gatherer bands. Judith Harris (1998: 299–300) speculates on the adaptive benefits of those traits for leaders of hunter/gatherer bands:

> Almost all the characteristics of the "born criminal" would be, in watered-down form, useful to a male in a hunter-gatherer society and useful in his group. His lack of fear, desire for excitement, and impulsiveness made him a formidable weapon against rival groups. His aggressiveness, strength, and lack of compassion enable him to dominate his groupmates and give him first shot at hunter-gatherer perks.

These "first-shot" perks such a man would have acquired are those most relevant to survival and reproductive success—resources and women. His valued status marked him as a good protector and would have provided him plentiful resources, making him most attractive to women (Xygalatas et al., 2021). He would have thus left more offspring than other group members, passing the genes associated with his traits down to subsequent generations. Those psychological and behavioral traits were selected for retention because they provided ancestral possessors survival and reproductive advantages regardless of whether they are associated with criminality today. Although these traits were favored by natural selection to facilitate mating effort, they are also useful in the pursuit of non-sexual resources via illegitimate means. Being highly aggressive and impulsive in social relationships may have been adaptive for males in our evolutionary past, but are now detrimental because they can easily lead to reactive violence.

Criminal behavior may be viewed as a means of obtaining reproductively relevant resources at minimal cost by exploiting others' weaknesses. This exploitive strategy is conditional because although preparedness to engage in it is universal, it is employed only when environmental conditions are conducive. There are differences in people's perceptions of the conditions in which the emergence of exploitative behavior is deemed advantageous. Whether such behavior is manifested depends on relevant environmental triggers interacting with individual differences in relevant traits (e.g., self-control, intelligence, moral conscience, etc.) and constraining cultural practices. These thresholds are not fixed and can shift in response to changes in the sociocultural environment, such as perceptions related to opportunities and the probability of punishment. This is the social part of the biopsychosocial whole.

All evolutionary theories of crime focus on sexual behavior as their key factor because it is how genes are passed down the generations. These theories identify two strategies that any animal species can follow to maximize reproductive success: *parenting effort* and *mating effort* and the attitudes and behaviors associated with them. Mating effort is the proportion of reproductive effort invested in obtaining sexual partners, and parenting effort is the proportion invested in caring for offspring. Valentova et al. (2020) examined reproductive effort, trait sociosexuality (differences in people's attitudes about unrestricted sex), and the dark triad (Machiavellianism, narcissism, and psychopathy) among 1,110 heterosexual men and women from Brazil and the Czech Republic. They found that mating effort was the highest among manipulative, self-centered individuals and that parenting effort characterized those who endorsed sexual commitment and higher degrees of empathy. They found the largest differences in sociosexuality and dark triad traits were between their high-mating/low-parenting subjects and lowest among their low-mating/high-parenting subjects. They describe the characteristics of those following each strategy: "Focus on mating is thus higher among self-centric individuals pursuing interpersonal manipulation, while individuals endorsing sexual commitment with higher empathy and affinity with children pursue a parenting strategy" (2020: 1).

Of course, both sexes engage in mating and parenting strategies and a mixed mating strategy at various times in their lives, but mating effort is more typical of males because male reproductive success increases proportionate to the number of females to whom they have sexual access; thus, they have an evolved propensity to seek multiple partners (Schacht & Kramer, 2019). Parenting effort is more typical of females because female investment requires enormous time and energy in gestating, lactating, and child care. In contrast, the only *obligatory* male investment is the time and energy spent copulating. The reproductive success of ancestral females rested mainly on their ability to secure mates to assist them in raising offspring in exchange for exclusive sexual access, and females evolved to be more sexually discriminating. The inherent conflict between the reckless and indiscriminate male mating strategy and the careful and discriminating female strategy drove the evolution of traits in males, such as aggressiveness and, relative to females, lower levels of empathy and constraint that help males overcome both male competitors and female reluctance. Conversely, female-centered parenting effort drove the selection of higher levels of traits such as empathy and self-control. David

Rowe (2002: 62–63) provides a sketch of the traits useful to mating effort that can be co-opted to support criminal behavior:

> A strong sexual drive and attraction to novelty of new sexual partners is clearly one component of mating effort. An ability to appear charming and superficially interested in women while courting them would be useful. The emotional attachment, however, must be an insincere one, to prevent emotional bonding to a girlfriend or spouse. The cad may be aggressive, to coerce sex from partly willing partners and to deter rival men. He feels little remorse about lying or cheating. Impulsivity could be advantageous in a cad because mating decisions must be made quickly and without prolonged deliberation; the unconscious aim is many partners, not a high-quality partner.

The reverse is also true—traits that facilitate parenting effort underlie other forms of prosocial activity: "Crime can be identified with the behaviors that tend to promote mating effort and non-crime with those that tend to promote parenting effort" (Rowe, 1996: 270). This identifies the ultimate reasons why females everywhere and always have lower levels of crime and other forms of antisocial behavior (Campbell, Muncer, & Bibel, 2001; Ellis, Beaver, & Wright; 2009; Walsh & Vaske, 2015).

Cheater Theory

The cheater (or "cad vs. dad") theory is an evolutionary theory emphasizing the asymmetry between male and female reproductive strategies. An emphasis on mating effort often relies on cheating strategies and is employed primarily by competitively disadvantaged males. As Linda Mealey (1995: 527) remarks, males "who are the least likely to out compete other males in a status hierarchy... are the ones most likely to adopt a cheating strategy." Sexual coercion, and criminality in general, are more likely to be evoked when males perceive themselves to be competitively disadvantaged in obtaining and retaining desirable mates. Criminologists have always known that violence and other forms of antisocial behavior are most prevalent in low socioeconomic environments; evolutionary theory provides them with an ultimate-level explanation for why. Natural selection has equipped humans to respond to inequality and expectations of a short life to take risks in male–male competitions that frequently result in violence. Violence is a contingent response to environmental conditions; it is pathological from a moral point of view but not from the point of view of evolutionary biology.

Empirical research supports the notion that an excessive concentration on mating effort is linked to criminal behavior. A review of 51 studies relating the number of sex partners to criminal behavior found 50 of them to be positive. Another review of 31 studies found that the earlier the age of onset of sexual behavior, the greater the criminal activity in all 31 (Ellis & Walsh,

2000). A British cohort study found that the most antisocial 10% of males in the cohort fathered 27% of the children (Jaffee et al., 2003). Elijah Anderson's seminal *Code of the Streets* tells us that sexuality is a major concern of "street family" (competitively disadvantaged) males in the inner-city, where access to females is "taken quite seriously as a measure of the boy's worth;" a young male's "primary goal is to find as many willing females as possible. The more 'pussy' he gets, the more esteem accrues to him" (1999: 150). Yao et al.'s (2014) longitudinal study of almost five million Swedes found strong associations between criminality and sexuality. Convicted criminals had more children, more sexual partners, were less often married, and had more sexually transmitted diseases than non-offenders. The number of children criminals had resulted from them having children with multiple partners, indicative of mating effort. However, they had fewer children with each partner than non-offenders, which is indicative of low parenting effort. The more criminal convictions a person had the stronger the relationship between mating effort and criminality was.

Tielbeek et al. (2018) also provided evidence for the common genetic origin of traits linked to sexuality and antisocial behavior using genetic data from sample sizes ranging from 31,968 to 318,863 to estimate genetic correlations (rg) between measures of reproductive effort and antisocial behavior. Genetic correlations measure the overlap between the two phenotypic traits due to genetic influences such as brown eyes and dark hair or in this instance, reproductive effort and antisocial behavior. Tielbeek et al. conclude:

> Our genetic correlation analyses demonstrate that alleles associated with higher reproductive output (i.e., faster life history styles) were positively correlated [rg = 0.50] with alleles associated with antisocial behaviour, whereas alleles associated with giving birth later in life were negatively associated with alleles linked to antisocial behaviour [rg = −0.64].
>
> (2018: 468)

In other words, 50% (rg = 0.50) of the genetic influence on mating effort is identical to the alleles associated with antisocial behavior, and 64% of the variance associated with parenting effort is negatively related to alleles associated with antisocial behavior (rg = −0.64).

Because reciprocity occurs among groups of cooperators, it creates fertile niches for noncooperators to exploit others by signaling their cooperation and failing to follow through (Roach & Pease, 2013). Countless men have persuaded countless women with promises of love and marriage in exchange for sex and then reneged. In this tit-for-tat world, most women, like most men, have learned to expect reciprocity in their social relationships. We have seen that traits naturally selected for mating effort prove useful in the pursuit of illegal goals, and the more antisocial the person, the more likely they are to cheat in their relationships. Criminal behavior may thus be viewed as an extreme form of defaulting on the rules of cooperation. However, cheating comes at a cost because non-reciprocators are not welcome in social groups, so before deciding to cheat or not, individuals must weigh its costs and benefits. Cheating is rational (albeit immoral and self-defeating in the long run) when the perceived immediate benefits outweigh the costs.

However, if cheating is rational, how did cooperation become predominant in social species? Cheating proves rational only in circumstances of limited interaction and communication. Frequent interaction and communication breeds trust and bonding, and cheating becomes a less rational strategy because cooperators remember and retaliate against those who have cheated them. Chronic cheaters have their reputations, relationships, and lives shattered and are set apart from the rest of us in jails and prisons. Ultimately, cooperation is the logical strategy for social species because each player reaps what they have sown.

Yet we continue to see cheating behavior despite threats of exposure and retaliation. We do so because exposure and retaliation are threats only if cheats must operate within the same environment where their reputation is known. Cheats can move from location to location, victimizing a series of others unaware of their reputation. This is the pattern of many criminals who move from place to place, job to job, and relationship to relationship, leaving a trail of misery behind them before their reputation catches up. This is why cheaters are more likely to prosper in large cities in modern societies than in small traditional communities where the threat of exposure and retaliation is great (Wiebe, 2012). Of course, group stability and cultural dynamics must be considered. Even in communities containing large numbers of chronic criminals, there must be some meager level of group loyalty and cooperation.

Conditional Adaptation Theory

A second evolutionary theory is conditional adaptation theory (CAT). Whereas the cheater theory emphasizes the function and phylogeny of traits involved in antisocial behavior—how they developed and how they presently function in terms of pro- or antisocial behavior—CAT places more emphasis on ontogeny. That is, how people adjust their developmental trajectories in response to environmental factors such as the level of attachment they had with parents in early life. These adjustments are accomplished by neurochemical systems and gene pathways reflecting children's sensitivity to their immediate environments. The theory avers that childhood is a sensitive period in which future reproductive strategies are calibrated by stressors relating to interpersonal relationships, with being raised in a single-parent home being the primary stressor. The absence of a father at home is linked with the acceleration of the onset of puberty and early sexual activity (Dinh, Haselton, & Gangestad, 2022; Pham et al. 2022). Children subliminally monitor their environments and will tend to adopt an unrestricted sexual strategy in their reproductive years if they perceive interpersonal relationships to be ephemeral, unreliable, and emotionally unrewarding. Conversely, children who experience stable pair bonding and secure parental attachment will tend to adopt a sexually restricted strategy. Neither strategy is, of course, consciously chosen but rather flows from subconscious expectations based on early experiences of interpersonal relationships. These conditional adaptations "result from specialized evolved mechanisms that detect features in the early environment and set development on a course to make the individual as fit as possible in future environments" (Karasewich & Kuhlmeier, 2020: 10).

CAT makes predictions about women's involvement in antisocial behavior as well as men's and posits a whore vs. Madonna dichotomy to define female strategies. If female assessment of interpersonal relationships has led them to view men as "cads," they will not expect long-term male investment, and tend to enter menarche early and emphasize their sexuality to procure short-term investment from a variety of males. If females have come to view men as "dads" they will emphasize chastity and fidelity, thus maximizing the probability of securing long-term paternal investment (Anderson, 2019). These are features of the environment that have proven reliable over evolutionary time in predicting the nature of the social world children inherit, and these ontogenetic pathways reliably match the phylogenetic features of the species' evolution.

However, because the traits underlying the respective strategies are heritable, individuals may vary in their susceptibility to adopt a particular sexual strategy for genetic reasons rather than early childhood experiences (Belsky, 1999). The short-term relationships observed among sexually unrestricted females may thus be a consequence of their genetically influenced strategy. Children receive genes as well as environments from their parents, and the similarity of sexual strategies between parents and their offspring may be a case of gene-environment interaction or gene-environment correlation rather than purely environmental or purely genetic.

Conditional adaptations reflect systematic contingent strategies that enable individuals to function competently in different environments. Applying CAT to criminal behavior, we note that natural selection has equipped humans to respond to high levels of inequality and expectations of a short life to take risks in male-male competitions that frequently result in violence. Violence is a contingent response to environmental conditions; it is morally pathological, but it is not pathological according to evolutionary biology. It is frequently noted that impulsiveness and discounting the future are maladaptive; that is, they are poor ways of adjusting to the conditions one finds oneself in. However, Wilson and Daly (1997: 1271) suggest that discounting the future "may be a 'rational' response to information that indicates an uncertain or low probability of surviving to reap delayed benefits, for example, and 'reckless' risk taking can be optimal when the expected profits from safer courses of action are negligible." In other words, when the young perceive little opportunity for legitimate success and when many people they know in their neighborhoods die at an early age, living for the present and engaging in risky violence to obtain resources makes evolutionary sense. Wilson and Daly assert that natural selection has designed humans to compete for the status and resources necessary for survival and reproductive success using whatever means are available to them in their present environments.

Wilson and Daly tested their assumption with homicide, income inequality, and life expectancy data from 77 neighborhoods in Chicago for the years 1988 through 1995. They hypothesized that neighborhoods with the lowest income levels and the shortest life expectancies (excluding homicides) would have the highest homicide rates. Life expectancy (homicide mortality statistically removed) ranged from an average of 54.3 years in the poorest neighborhood to an average of 77.4 years in the wealthiest, and the attending homicide rates ranged from 1.3 per 100,000 in the wealthiest neighborhood to 156 in the poorest, a huge 120-fold difference. Wilson and Daly appeal to evolutionary logic to interpret these data, viewing them as reflecting escalations of risky competitive tactics that make sense from an evolutionary point of view, given the conditions in which people in disadvantaged and disorganized neighborhoods live. In harsh and unpredictable environments, investing effort toward gaining immediate rewards that discount future consequences may be a more successful strategy than long-term investments that pay off gradually (Mogilski et al., 2020). As an old saying goes, "If you ain't got nothin', you got nothin' to lose." Of course, just because a behavior is understandable when viewed through an evolutionary lens, it does not make it morally right or excusable.

CAT underlines the notion that there is no "best" strategy for achieving evolutionarily relevant goals. As Boyce and Ellis (2005: 289; internal references omitted) maintain:

> Over the last 2 decades, theory and research in evolutionary biology has begun to acknowledge that, in most species, single "best" strategies for survival and reproduction are unlikely to evolve. This is because the best strategy varies as a function of the physical, economic, and social parameters of one's environment, and thus a strategy that promotes success in some environmental contexts may lead to failure in others. Selection pressures therefore tend to favor adaptive phenotypic plasticity, the capacity of a single genotype to produce a range of phenotypes—manifested in morphology, physiology, and/or behavior in response to particular ecological conditions that recurrently influenced fitness during a species' evolutionary history.

French priest and scientist Pierre Teilhard de Chardin notes the power of evolutionary theory:

> Is evolution a theory, a system, or a hypothesis? It is much more—it is a general postulate to which all theories, all hypotheses, all systems must henceforward bow and which they must satisfy in order to be thinkable

> and true. Evolution is a light which illuminates all facts, a trajectory which all lines of thought must follow—this is what evolution is.
>
> (Baedke et al., 2024: 337)

As useful as evolutionary theory is, it only pertains to ultimate level "why" explanations and tells us nothing about proximate level "how" questions. To explore such questions, we must engage with ontogeny and causal mechanisms since we do not all experience the same developmental pathways, and even if we did, genetic variations lead people to respond differently to similar experiences.

6 Behavioral and Molecular Genetics

Genes and "Genetic Determinism"

Francis Galton coined the phrase "nature and nurture" in 1874 and ignited hostilities between so-called hereditarians and environmentalists that continue in some circles today, albeit one that is petering out as we learn more about the interaction between nature and nurture. The biggest holdout is sociology since it has always considered itself a purely environmentalist "social factist" discipline and has a fractious relationship with genetics. For instance, Peter Bearman provides three reasons some fellow sociologists fear genetics (although he doesn't necessarily endorse them):

> The first concern that sociologists have is. ... it serves to legitimate existing arrangements. The second concern is that [it] runs the risk of distorting the sociological project. The third concern ... is that the focus on the supposed genetics of behavior is a eugenicist project in (not so veiled) disguise.
>
> (2008: vi)

Considering the many statements quoted in the previous chapter to the effect that biological and sociological explanations are becoming partners, an article by sociologists Mills and Tropf (2020) touting sociogenomics is most welcome. They write: "We show how genetics can be introduced to understand a myriad of topics such as fertility, educational attainment, intergenerational social mobility, well-being, addiction, risky behavior, and longevity." They also note, however, "Although models of gene-environment interaction and correlation mirror agency and structure models in sociology, genetics is yet to be fully discovered by this discipline" (2020: 553). This chapter focuses on these models and engages Tinbergen's proximate developmental and causation questions, which are addressed by behavioral and molecular genetics.

We can dispel the notion of genetic determinism that is still held by some (e.g., Peters, 2014). Genes and environments are jointly responsible for all human characteristics. Genetic mutations create variations that are either adaptive or not, but the environment determines the winners and losers.

DOI: 10.4324/9781003662495-8

The direction of evolution is thus determined by the environment that selects the advantageous variants the genome throws out. Asking whether genes or environment is most important for a given trait is just as nonsensical as asking whether height or width is most important to the area of a rectangle because without height and width together, there is no rectangle. Genes only determine what proteins are manufactured; these proteins *influence* how our personalities develop and how we behave, but they do not *cause* our personalities or behavior independently of environmental input. Genes incline us in one way or another, but they do not determine that direction. By various neurohormonal routes, genes *facilitate* our behavioral responses to environmental challenges only in a probabilistic fashion, and DNA is certainly not destiny. As Matt Ridley notes about the role of genes and fears of genetic determinism:

> Genes are not puppet masters, nor blueprints. ... They are both the cause and consequence of our actions. Somehow the adherents of the 'nurture' side of the argument have scared themselves silly at the power and inevitability of genes and missed the greatest lesson of all: the genes are on our side.
>
> (Ridley, 2003: 6)

Genes are indeed "on our side" because the genome is a reactive system, not a controlling one. It reacts to the environment by activating genetic transcription mechanisms that lead to brain activity, enabling us to respond to environmental conditions in adaptive ways. As Moczek (2012: 109) maintains, "Rather than causing or controlling development, genes enable it to take place." Nature and nurture constitute a seamless whole. Indeed, genetic research has provided us more insight into the role played by the environment in producing our personalities and behavior than pure environmentalism ever did. The dean of behavioral genetics Robert Plomin remarks: "It is ironic that, after a century of environmentalism, genetic research provided the strongest evidence for the importance of the environment; previous environmental research was confounded because it ignored genetics" (2023: 77). And environmentalists can find further heart in Baker, Bezdjian, and Raine's (2006: 44) statement, "the more we know about the genetics of behavior, the more important the environment appears to be."

Behavioral Genetics

Personality traits and behavioral patterns lie on continua along which different people fall. Behavioral genetics seeks to determine the genetic and environmental sources of variation. Two methodologies are used in this endeavor: adoption and twin studies. Adoption studies are "natural experiments" that randomize either genes or environments. To the extent that traits and behaviors of monozygotic (MZ) twins adopted into different families are correlated, the similarity is a straightforward indication of the effects of shared genes since they were reared apart. Conversely, trait correlations between adopted children and non-adopted siblings are straightforward measures of shared environment effects because they share no common genes. However, because of the rarity of MZ twins adopted apart, the workhorse of behavioral genetics is twin studies of reared-together MZ and same-sex dizygotic (DZ) twins reared together to determine the heritability of a trait or behavior.

Heritability (h^2) is a quantification ranging between 0 and 1 of the extent to which variance in a trait is attributable to genes in a particular population at a given time. Under the assumption of additive genetic effects (the effect of individual genes summed over all loci), because MZ twins share 100% of their genes and DZ twins share an average of 50%, the correlations between MZ twin pairs should theoretically be double those of DZ twins. If genes did not contribute to variance in a trait, it would be logically and empirically impossible to calculate heritability coefficients. Heritability is the proportion of variance in a trait attributable to *actualized* genetic potential in a population; we cannot infer from it what the unactualized potential may be. Turkheimer presents his three laws of behavioral genetics:

> First Law. All human behavioral traits are heritable. Second Law. The effect of being raised in the same family is smaller than the effect of genes. Third Law. A substantial portion of the variation in complex human behavioral traits is not accounted for by the effects of genes or families.
>
> (Turkheimer, 2000:160)

The second and third laws refer to shared and non-shared environments, respectively.

Turkheimer's claim that all cognitive, behavioral, and personality traits are heritable, that is, $h^2 \neq 0$ for any trait or behavior, was vindicated by a massive meta-analysis of 2,748 twin studies published over 50 years containing over 14.5 million twin pairs from 39 countries, showed that all the human traits are heritable (Polderman et al., 2015). Heritability is a *population* statistic that apportions trait variance averaged into genetic and environmental sources; it says nothing about a particular person. Heritability values thus depend on population-specific factors such as environmental quality and the allele frequency associated with the variable of interest in the population. The most important thing to note about behavioral genetic analyses is that they are about *variations* in traits or behaviors in a particular population, environment, and time. Variation does not inform us which genes influence our traits or behaviors; it only tells us the extent to which people in a specified population vary concerning them. Heritability does not reveal the proportion of a trait in a specific individual that is genetically caused and what proportion is environmentally caused. A heritability of 0.50 for a trait or behavior does not mean that 50% is genetically caused in an individual. It means that 50% of the *variance* in the trait or behavior is attributed to genetic variation averaged across all subjects in the studied population.

Turkheimer (2000: 162) notes that purely environmental research could only achieve the same level of precision as behavior genetics if we were to "have 'identical environmental twins' whose experiences were exactly the same, moment by moment, and another variety who shared exactly but randomly 50% of their experiences." Of course, there are no such "mono- or di-enviro" twins, but we don't need them because heritability also informs us of the environmental contribution to human traits and behavior. Personality traits, cognitive abilities, and behavioral differences among individuals arise from only two sources: genes and environments. Heritability is thus a measure of environmental effects because $1.0 - h^2$ = environmental effects.

Shared and Non-Shared Environment

Environmental effects on traits and behavior are divided into shared (c^2) and non-shared (e^2) components. Shared influences are those experiences that make people like one another; nonshared influences are experiences that may make them different. Shared environments are everything twins have in common, such as socioeconomic status (SES) of rearing and neighborhoods; non-shared environments are unique to each twin, such as different friends and experiences. It is often found that shared childhood environmental effects on cognitive and personality traits disappear almost completely in adulthood, meaning that the environments that shape these traits are specific to individuals rather than shared with siblings. A meta-analysis of 28,709 sibling pairs in 103 twin and adoption studies of aggressive and non-aggressive forms of antisocial behavior found that genetic influences on these two forms were 65% and 48%, respectively. Shared environmental effects were 5% and 18%, respectively, and non-shared environmental effects were 30% and 34%, respectively (Burt, 2009).

The small effects of shared environments appeared counterintuitive to Burt and Simons:

> Indeed, the conclusion from many of these heritability studies that little—if any—of the variance in criminal behavior is due to shared environments, often interpreted to include parenting and community factors, contradicts a wealth of research conducted during the past century as well as the major theories of crime.
>
> (2014: 224)

However, behavioral genetic studies showing the low effects of shared environments only reveal that parental effects on personality and cognitive traits that made siblings somewhat similar when they shared a home failed to survive the period of common rearing. This is certainly not to say that parents or neighborhoods do not affect the *mean* level of these traits. The weak effects of shared environments mean they have few *similar* effects on adult siblings, not that they have had *no* effect. Environmental factors can have large effects on phenotypic traits and behaviors without affecting trait *variance*, which can remain stable even as the mean level of a variable rises, falls, or remains constant.

Heritability is higher in advantaged than disadvantaged environments because advantaged environments bring out the best in the genetic material. Advantaged environments provide inhabitants with a greater range of opportunities to seek out environments consistent with their genetic dispositions, leading to more genetically influenced behaviors and, thus, greater heritability (Selita & Kovas, 2019). Disadvantaged environments strongly influence behavior. Genetic influences will be masked, and genes associated with prosocial traits will have scant opportunity to express themselves. However, such environments are conducive to the expression of genes related to antisocial traits because antisocial behavior is the "natural" default option among poorly socialized individuals, which helps to explain the cross-generational stability of antisocial behavior (Erath, El-Sheikh, & Cummings, 2009).

Gene-Environment Interaction and Gene-Environment Correlation

Gene-environment interaction (G*x*E) and correlation (rGE) emphasize the inseparability of genes and environments and that developmental and behavioral outcomes can only be predicted by genes and environments in tandem. People are differentially sensitive to identical environmental influences and respond to them differently: "The heat that melts the butter hardens the egg" (Nettler, 1984: 295). Some people are genetically more likely to take advantage of opportunities for antisocial behavior than others, and prosocial people will be attracted to different careers based on their personalities. Extraverted and sensation-seeking prosocial individuals will be attracted to exciting, action-filled careers, while introverts will be attracted to safer occupations.

There are three kinds of rGE: passive, evocative, and active. Passive rGE is the correlation between a child's genotype and its environment. It is called "passive" because the correlation is the product of its parents' genotypes and the environments they provide, not the product of anything the child does. Children who inherit genes from prosocial parents of high intelligence will doubtless find themselves in an environment where prosocial and intellectual activities are modeled, encouraged, and reinforced, and the opposite is true for children who receive genes from antisocial parents of lower intelligence.

Evocative rGE refers to how others in children's environment (parents, siblings, teachers, peers) react to them based on their behavior. The behavior of others towards the child is often more a function of the child's evocative behavior as it is of the behavioral style of those who react to it. The behavior and personality traits children present to others increase or decrease the probability of evoking certain responses from others. Regardless of the parents' or teacher's supervisory style, an ill-behaved, bad-tempered, and disrespectful child will evoke fewer positive responses than a well-behaved, easy-tempered, and respectful child. Meta-analyses of parenting have shown that parenting styles are mostly driven by children's genetically influenced characteristics (Avinun & Knafo, 2014). Children with bad temperaments may evoke punitive reactions from others that exacerbate their antisocial personality and drive them to seek out peers similarly predisposed, further reinforcing their antisocial tendencies. Evocative rGE thus magnifies differences among phenotypes.

Active rGE is based on the notion that people seek out environments compatible with their genetic dispositions. That is, our genes nudge us toward features of the social world we find rewarding within the range of cultural freedom and constraints. In active rGE, genes guide the selection of environments, which then loop back to shape and reinforce further expression of genetic dispositions. Active rGE gains more explanatory power as individuals mature and take greater control of their lives. This is consistent with several studies that find that MZ twins *reared apart* have similar personalities and construct their lives almost as similarly as MZ twins reared together, and MZ twins *reared apart* are more similar in personality and select more similar environments than DZ twins *reared together* (Bouchard & McGue, 2003).

The rGE concept emphasizes that people don't find themselves in criminogenic environments by happenstance (Moffitt & Beckley, 2015). Children who find themselves in bad neighborhoods and abusive families have inherited trait dispositions from parents (passive rGE) that may lead them to perpetuate those criminogenic environments. The family environment is itself partly due to parental genes, as Plomin and Von Stumm (2021: 50–51) point out:

> Forty years of quantitative genetic research on GE correlation has revealed that most environmental measures widely used in the behavioural sciences show substantial genetic influence, about 25% heritability on average and correlations between environmental measures and behavioural traits are substantially mediated genetically, about 50% on average.

These environmental measures exacerbate criminogenic tendencies, but without behavioral genetic study designs, we cannot know their unique causal contribution unless we can rule out self-selection into them.

Because genes influence differential *exposure* to environmental risks via active rGE and differential *susceptibility* to them via G*x*E, both processes always operate simultaneously. Adults self-select into different environments based on their genetically driven preferences, and thus will be more susceptible to their influence (G*x*E) than those who find themselves there coincidentally. In addition to furthering our understanding of the role of genes in behavior, the concepts of G*x*E and rGE have yielded enormous benefits to our understanding of the environment's role in shaping behavior. The power of active rGE is evident from changing heritability patterns with age. Genes remain constant, but the environments we select give them expression. Heritability increases for our personality traits and cognitive ability from childhood to adulthood because as twins age, they have more non-shared experiences, with DZ twins becoming considerably less similar than MZ twins. Correlations between DZ pairs on those traits and abilities shrink more than MZ correlations as they gain the freedom to construct their environments. Increases in heritability with age reflect the increasing ability of MZ twins to fashion their lives consistent with their identical genomes and the increasing ability of DZ twins to construct their personalities and lives differently consistent with their different genomes (Tuvblad & Baker, 2011).

Molecular Genetics

Molecular genetics studies trait variation at the molecular level. Any two randomly chosen humans differ only in about 0.01% of their DNA, yet 0.01% of approximately 3 billion base pairs yield 3 million differences (Nurk et al., 2022). While many base-pair differences have little or no effect on phenotypic differences, Bonham, Warshauer-Baker, and Collins (2005: 12) state that "about 200,000 common variants are responsible for the genetic components of the differences in health, behavior, and other human traits." These gene variants are called genetic polymorphisms. A gene is a segment of DNA containing instructions for making a specific protein. The gene is polymorphic if more than one allele occupies the same locus of a coding region, and it is these variations that lead to the diversity of human physical, psychological, and behavioral traits. Most polymorphisms do not change a protein molecule's function, while others change a gene's expression, leading to the formation of variant proteins that alter physiological responses to certain stimuli. Single-nucleotide polymorphisms (SNPs) are the most prevalent polymorphisms. More than 14 million SNPs have been found in the human genome (Jin et al., 2018). As the term indicates, a difference in just one nucleotide differentiates one allele from another in a SNP.

A SNP of interest to criminologists is the $Val^{158}Met$ polymorphism of the enzyme catechol-O-methyltransferase (COMT) that affects the breakdown of dopamine (DA). This occurs when guanine (G) is replaced by adenine (A) in the COMT enzyme, resulting in methionine (Met) rather than valine (Val). The Met allele slows the degradation of DA and thus increases its availability in the prefrontal cortex. Hence, the Val variant, particularly Val-Val homozygotes, should be more antisocial because the rapid catabolizing of DA suggests they should be addictive pleasure-seekers to raise DA levels. Yacubian et al. (2007) monitored activity in the prefrontal cortex and ventral striatum (a reward-related area) using fMRI and found that Val-Val subjects showed high levels of activity in the ventral striatum in anticipation of rewards, Met-Met subjects showed blunted activity in anticipation, and Val-Met heterozygotes showed intermediate activity. The Val allele is frequently associated with conditions such as conduct disorder and with an increased risk of aggressive behavior in males with ADHD (Caspi et al., 2008). On the other hand, schizophrenic men with the Met allele have an elevated risk of violent behavior (Singh et al., 2012). This is understandable since unmedicated ADHD is a condition with low DA activity and unmedicated schizophrenia is a condition with high DA activity.

One of the goals of molecular genetics is to match SNP heritability with quantitative heritability, but SNP data have only been able to match it for various traits between 15% and 37% (Forero, Pereira-Morales, & Gonzalez, 2017). However, Plomin and Von Stumm (2021: 50) are confident that:

> The missing heritability gap will be narrowed with bigger and better genome-wide association studies and with whole-genome sequencing that assesses all DNA differences in the genome rather than several hundred thousand SNPs assessed in current studies. The only way is up for the predictive power of polygenic scores.

These are known as Genome-Wide Polygenic scores (GPSs). GPSs are premised on the heritable traits resulting from the aggregated influence of thousands of common and rare SNPs. A single SNP may account for no more than 0.001% of the variance in a trait but aggregating the effects of millions of SNPs into GPSs allows the identification of individuals by their genetic propensity for traits of interest.

Plomin and Von Stumm (2021) maintain that unlike purely environmental measures in which the causal directions are rarely clear, with GPS data, the causal direction is entirely unambiguous:

> Polygenic score predictions are correlations, and correlations do not necessarily imply causation. However, polygenic scores have a unique causal status among predictors in one important sense: correlations between polygenic scores and traits can only be interpreted in one direction causally. That is, there can be no backward causation.
>
> (Plomin and Von Stumm, 2021: 50)

Finding the missing heritability is further complicated, however, in that each genetic variant may affect more than one trait in a pleiotropic fashion, that is, the proportion of variance that two separate traits share due to shared alleles.

Serotonin Polymorphisms and Criminal Behavior

The second type of polymorphism is VNTRs (variable number of tandem repeats), which refers to the length of contiguous nucleotide bases on the number of repeats. For instance, the nucleotide base sequence TTA may be repeated two to eleven times in different alleles. Serotonergic and dopaminergic polymorphisms are the most studied in criminology, largely because they influence avoidance (punishment sensitivity) and approach (reward sensitivity) behaviors, respectively (Iofrida, Palumbo, & Pellegrini, 2014). Serotonin (5-HT) plays a major role in the brain by maintaining a balance between excitatory and inhibitory neurotransmitters. After a neurotransmitter activates a neuron, it is almost instantaneously taken back into the presynaptic knob to avoid signaling confusion, and any 5-HT that is not taken up is degraded by the enzyme monoamine oxidase A (MAOA).

The MAOA gene is a VNTR polymorphism that repeats two to five times. The two and three-repeat versions result in low activity (MAOA-L), and the four and five-repeat variants result in high (MAOA-H) activity. Low serotonergic functioning is consistently related to impulsivity, a strong correlate of criminal behavior (McDermott et al., 2009; Watts & McNulty, 2016). It is also a strong correlate of negative emotionality and low serotonergic functioning "may be a heritable diathesis for a personality style involving high levels of negative affect and low levels of constraint, which generates in turn a vulnerability to criminal behavior" (Caspi, et al., 1994: 188). Brain imaging studies have shown that MAOA-L males show higher activity in the amygdala (an area linked with emotion) and lower activity in prefrontal areas during emotional arousal than MAOA-H males (McDermott et al., 2009).

The landmark G*x*E study of MAOA is that of Caspi et al. (2002), who looked at the effects of officially verified child maltreatment and MAOA activity on antisocial outcomes, including verified convictions for violent crimes by the age of 26. There were no main effects for MAOA but strong G*x*E effects. Maltreated males with the MAOA-L variant constituted only 12% of the cohort but were responsible for 44% of its convictions for violent offenses. Comparing these males with MAOA-H/non-maltreated males with a conviction revealed an odds ratio of 9.8. The two groups did not differ significantly with regard to the version of the MAOA allele they carried, thus ruling out evocative rGE effects. In other words, low MAOA activity did not contribute to child maltreatment via children's evocative behavior.

A meta-analysis of MAOA-maltreatment studies concluded that the interaction between MAOA and maltreatment is a significant predictor of antisocial behavior (Kim-Cohen et al., 2006). Another meta-analysis concluded: "Across 20 male cohorts, early adversity presaged antisocial outcomes more strongly for low, relative to high, activity MAOA genotype" (Byrd & Manuck (2014: 9). Kolla and Bortolato (2020) note that neuroimaging studies have shown that MAOA-L individuals exhibit abnormalities in cortico-amygdaloid connectivity, diminished PFC activity during inhibitory control tasks, and heightened limbic responsiveness to emotional arousal. A study by Fritz et al. (2021) looked at both MAOA and Val-Val variants together with childhood maltreatment and found that a combination of MAOA-L and the COMT Val-Val polymorphism increased levels of reactive and appetitive aggression in forensic psychiatric patients.

Dopamine Polymorphisms and Criminal Behavior

The dopaminergic system is involved in motivated reward behavior. Its "approach" function is effectively opposed to the serotonergic "avoid" function. DA signaling is regulated by VNTR genes involved in its synthesis, transport, reception, and degradation. The 7-repeat (7R) allele of the D4 receptor gene (DRD4) receives the most attention in studies of antisocial behavior because it underlies novelty-seeking and sensation-seeking behaviors. These adventurous traits are evident in population migration patterns studied by Ding et al. (2002), who report a correlation of 0.85 between the population prevalence of the 7R allele and the geographic distance from the parent population among 39 ethnic groups. Groups that have remained in the same region for the last 30,000 years, such as the Han Chinese and Yemeni Jews, have almost zero 7R alleles, while six South American native tribes have an average of 63%, over three times the global average.

The 7R allele is a young variant that arose approximately 40,000 years ago. It was probably favored by natural selection among migrating populations because individuals who had it were able to function better in new environments that posed novel risks (Kitayama et al., 2016). Charles Darwin noted over 150 years ago: "Restless men ... emigrate to newly settled countries, where they prove useful pioneers" (1981: 172). Harpending and Cochran (2002: 12) note:

> It is probably no accident that two of the best known ethnographies of the 20th century are titled "The Harmless People," about the !Kung who have few or no 7R alleles, and the "Fierce People," about the Yanomamo with a high frequency of 7R.

The dopamine D2 receptor gene (DRD2) is also highly polymorphic, with primary attention focused on the A1 allele. Individuals who are homozygous for the A2 allele (A2/A2) have receptors with the highest binding potential for DA, and A1/A1 homozygotes have the lowest binding potential (Hirvonen et al., 2004). The A1 allele is the risk allele because it "is a contributor to the reward deficiency syndrome, which typifies people who need high levels of excitement and stimulation to activate their reward system in the same capacity as those with normally functioning reward systems" (DeLisi et al., 2009: 1189).

The DA transporter gene DAT1 is another important VNTR dopaminergic gene. It largely determines the magnitude and duration of synaptic DA signaling by transporting DA back into the presynaptic knob for repackaging after exciting downstream neurons. DAT1 contains 7 and 11 repeats, with the 9R and 10R repeats being the most common (Guo et al., 2007). As with the degradation process of the VAL-VAL COMPT polymorphism, the 10R evidences a more efficient reuptake of DA than the 9R, which implies less DA available for activation (Miller-Butterworth et al., 2008). Because

DA activates pleasure centers in the brain, a too-rapid clearing of DA leads people with the 10R to seek more experiences that activate DA to experience normal levels of pleasure. Pleasure (legal or illegal) raises DA levels easier with less behavioral activity for people with slower reuptake.

In addition to examining G*x*E effects, it is important to consider the interaction of genes (G*x*G) relevant to criminal behavior. A G*x*G study by Watts and McNulty (2016) examined DAT1 and MAOA, which catabolizes both DA and 5-HT. They divided their sample into three groups: carriers of MAOA-L and 10R-allele DAT1 homozygotes: carriers of MAOA-L only, DAT1-10R homozygotes only, and those that carried neither allele. They concluded:

> [R]esults reveal that males who carry the 2R or 3R alleles of MAOA and are homozygous for the 10R allele of DAT1 are more likely to have lower levels of self-control and in turn engage in more criminal behaviors when they experience a PPCR [poor parent-child relationship] than their counterparts who do not carry either of these plasticity alleles.
>
> (Watts and McNulty, 484)

Both G*x*E and G*x*G studies thus clearly emphasize the crucial role of the environment. Yun, Cheong, and Walsh's (2011: 252) study of the DAT1 polymorphism, family adversity, and self-selection in delinquent peer networks found that the relationship between the DAT1 10R and delinquency held only among those from high-risk families. They concluded: "In short, our study reaffirms that genetic predisposition prompts adolescents to self-select themselves into delinquent peer networks (active rGE), and this effect on self-selection is conditioned by family environment (G*x*E)."

The Differential Susceptibility Hypothesis

The search for the causal effects of G*x*E and G*x*G is compromised because a putative risk allele in one environment may be protective in another. A strong reward drive in a supportive environment may result in prosocial risk-taking and personal success; the same drive in a non-supportive environment may result in antisocial risk-taking and personal failure. In other words, some individuals are more negatively impacted by poor environments than others, but more positively by positive environments. This is known as the "differential susceptibility hypothesis (DSH)," or the "orchid–dandelion hypothesis." Dandelion children, like dandelions, can bloom in many different environments, are resilient, and can survive and even thrive in adverse environmental circumstances. Orchid children, like orchids, thrive only in conditions of support and nurture, and if they do, like the flower, they will be "beautiful" and flourishing human beings. On the other hand, if they are neglected, like orchids, they will wither. Fox and

Beevers (2016: 1657) explain why this pattern undermines the search for genetic main effects:

> The essence of the differential susceptibility hypothesis (DSH) is that with similar group sizes of more and less susceptible individuals there will be no main genetic effect. Instead, there will be a crossover interaction with susceptible individuals doing worse in adverse environments but better in supportive environments than less susceptible individuals. This pattern does of course undermine large-scale genome-wide association studies (GWAS) that look only for main genetic effects.

The DSH model suggests that "plasticity factors" should replace "risk factors" on the genetic diathesis side of the diathesis-stress model equation (Ellis et al., 2011). Variation in environmental sensitivity is underpinned by DA and 5-HT brain circuitry that governs sensitivity to reward and punishment (Belsky, Zhang, & Sayler, 2022). The 5-HT transporter (5-HTT) gene cycles serotonin from the synaptic cleft back to the presynaptic neuron, terminating its effects. Variants of the 5-HTT gene promoter, 5-HTTLPR ("serotonin transporter linked polymorphous region"), provide different expression levels. The 5-HTTLPR has short (s) and long (L) versions. The s variant reduces gene expression, resulting in less efficient transporter function, thus allowing serotonin to remain in the synaptic gap longer, where it gets degraded by enzymes, resulting in a net reduction of serotonin. Carriers of the s allele (particularly s/s homozygotes) are more affected by negative environmental experiences but also more by positive environmental experiences (Hankin et al., 2011). That is, carriers of the s allele suffer more from negative experiences than L carriers but benefit more from positive experiences.

The differential susceptibility hypothesis is highlighted in East Asian vs. European susceptibility to mental and behavioral problems. About 75% of people of East Asian origin carry at least one s allele compared with about 44% of Europeans (Chiao & Blizinsky, 2010). However, fewer East Asians than Europeans are diagnosed with depression and anxiety disorders, for which the s allele is a strong marker (Mrazek et al., 2013), and East Asians are almost invariably found to be less crime-prone than people of European or African origin (Ellis, Beaver, & Wright, 2009; Walsh & Yun, 2018). One answer to why a risk allele in one culture is protective in another is that historically high levels of pathogen-borne diseases imposed selective pressures on cultural practices that resulted in a behavioral "immune system" (Murray, Trudeau & Schaller, 2011). A study of over 100,000 individuals from 68 countries found that individualism/collectivism scores were strongly associated (r = -.0.69) with a historically high prevalence of pathogens in their cultures (Fincher et al., 2008).

Collectivist cultures stress interdependence, group obligations, and reliance on the group for social support, whereas individualistic cultures emphasize independence and self-reliance. It has been suggested that the s allele drove the selection for collectivist personalities, leading Chiao and Blizinsky (2010: 531) to propose that collectivist values that serve an anti-pathogen function also serve an anti-psychopathology function: "Collectivist cultural values serve an adaptive function by reducing the probability of environmental stress, a known catalyst for negative affect, thus leading to genetic selection of the s allele within collectivist cultures." Chiao and Blizinsky found a correlation of 0.70 between the prevalence of the s allele and collectivism over 29 countries and note:

> Emphasizing social norms that increase social harmony and encourage giving social support to others, collectivism serves an "anti-psychopathology" function by creating an ecological niche that lowers the prevalence of chronic life stress, protecting genetically susceptible individuals from environmental pathogens known to trigger negative emotions and psychopathology.
>
> (2010: 536)

7 The Human Brain

The Wonders of the Human Brain

The human brain is evolution's magnum opus. Although we might describe its physicality as a mere 3-pound lump of tofu-like tissue encased in a skull, it is the most awe-inspiring entity in the universe. Nobel Laureate physicist Sir Roger Penrose wrote of its wonder: "If you look at the entire physical cosmos, our brains are a tiny, tiny, part of it. But they're the most perfectly organized part. Compared to the complexity of a brain, a galaxy is just an inert lump" (Holt, 2012: 178). Likewise, neuroscientist Roger Sperry wrote: "In the human head there are forces within forces within forces, as in no other cubic half-foot of the universe we know" (Walsh & Bolen, 2012: 1). Within the soup and sparks of this enchanted loom our genetic dispositions and environmental experiences are integrated and become one as they are captured in its circuitry. The brain comprises only 2% of body mass, but 50 to 60% of our genes are involved in building it, and it consumes a voracious 20% of the body's energy resources (Mitchell, 2007). The brain is built by genes, but the building is more complex than the builder. There are too few genes to specify brain functioning, which involves trillions of connections wired together by experience. Han et al. (2022: 2) inform us that while genetic processes shape the basic structure and function of the brain:

> ... in the whole life cycle, the addition of various stimulation from the environment and the interaction with genes form a precise neural circuit structure with complexity far exceeding the content of genomic information, in which highly ordered neuronal activities are the basis of advanced brain function.

The brain is almost endlessly divisible, and thus we can only briefly discuss major areas associated with behavior, editing out all the qualifiers and nuances found in neuroscience. The limbic system is a set of structures above the brainstem and beneath the cerebral cortex. It has several functions, but we are concerned only with its emotional response function governed by the amygdala, hippocampus, and anterior cingulate cortex (ACC). The amygdalae

DOI: 10.4324/9781003662495-9

are almond-shaped groups of nuclei that abut the hippocampus. Its primary function is the storage of memories associated with a range of emotions, particularly fear, and is the center of threat interpretation and response. The hippocampus specializes in storing and processing visual and spatial memories of events. Connections between the amygdala and the hippocampus help to focus the brain on what it has learned regarding responses to emotional stimuli that have aroused it in the past, thus regulating it with memories of prior experiences. Ling, Umbach, and Raine (2019: 631) note that while "reduced amygdala volume in adulthood has been associated with increased aggressive and psychopathic characteristics from childhood to early adulthood, it is also associated with increased risk for future antisocial and psychopathic behavior."

Parts of the ACC serve as processing stations for stimuli arriving from other brain areas and assigning appropriate controls. Among its functions is "its role in fundamental cognitive processes, including motivation, decision making, learning, cost-benefit calculation, as well as conflict and error monitoring" (Apps, Rushworth, & Chang, 2016: 692). It is a key area for motivating and regulating behavior through cognitive and affective mechanisms. Sandwiched between the emotional limbic system and the rational prefrontal cortex (PFC), it is ideally situated for this. According to Tancredi (2005: 36), the ACC "provides for civilized discourse, conflict resolution, and fundamental human socialization."

The neocortex is the "rational brain" and defines the human species more distinctly than anything else; "the human cerebral cortex is the organ that enabled abstract thinking and the creation of civilization ..." (Kolk & Rakic, 2022: 41). The most important part of the cerebral cortex is the prefrontal cortex (PFC), "the most uniquely human of all brain structures" (Goldberg, 2001: 2). The PFC is the seat of our higher-order cognitive functions and continues to develop into adulthood. As the site of abstract reasoning, language, foresight, and judgments, it allows us to recognize and respond in socially acceptable ways to feelings and urges from the limbic system. Raine (2008: 324) suggests that the "prefrontal cortex acts as an 'emergency brake' on runaway emotions generated by limbic structures." The PFC occupies about one-third of the cerebral cortex and has extensive connections with limbic system structures. Tracing the integrity of pathways from the PFC to the limbic system via brain imaging reveals much about the brain functioning of serious criminals (Wolf et al., 2015). Because of its many connections with other areas, the PFC plays a major integrative and supervisory role in the brain. It is vital to forming moral judgments, mediating affect, and social cognition. The PFC can perform all these tasks because it is not concerned with mundane tasks involved in sensory processing and concentrates on sorting and making sense of input from other brain areas (Shimamura, 2000). Many criminals have disruptions in brain regions that underly cognitive control such as the anterior cingulate, the amygdala, areas of the PFC, and certain other areas (Schiffer et al., 2014).

Brain Communication: Neurotransmitters

The brain contains about 100 billion neurons that communicate by converting environmental information into electrochemical impulses that process it and facilitate a response. The neuron body contains the nucleus, where most of the neurotransmitters that will eventually be released at the synapse are synthesized. Each neuron has one axon and numerous dendrites. Axons are coated with a cholesterol myelin sheath that acts like insulation around electrical wiring, amplifies nerve impulses, and protects axons from short-circuiting. Myelinated axons (the brain's white matter) transmit impulses 100 times faster than unmyelinated axons (gray matter) (Fields, 2014). Dendrites are small projections from the cell body that serve as receivers of electric impulses (both excitatory and inhibitory) from neighboring neurons, which pass their information along the axon if excitatory impulses exceed inhibitory impulses via charged atoms that pass in and out of the permeable membrane until they reach the axon's presynaptic knob. The message is then changed from electrical to chemical.

The chemical messengers are the neurotransmitters stored in vesicles that open up and spill into the synaptic cleft (gap) between sending and receiving axons. The cleft is approximately 3,000 times smaller than the width of a human hair (Binotti, Jahn, & Pérez-Lara, 2021). When they cross the synaptic cleft to postsynaptic receptor sites, the message is translated back into electrical form for further excitation or inhibition. A neuron can make thousands of synaptic connections with other neurons, and their number is astronomical: "The human brain has 10^{15} connections and around 100 billion neurons, so roughly as many stars as there are in the Milky Way" (DeWeerdt, 2019: 6). Neurotransmitters remain in the gap for 1/500 of a second; the excess is pumped back up into the presynaptic knob or degraded by enzymes, thus terminating the signal.

We have already addressed the two major neurotransmitters implicated in antisocial behavior—dopamine and serotonin—so they will not be discussed here. There are other important transmitters, among which is norepinephrine (NE). NE is a major mobilizer of action and functions as both a neurotransmitter and a hormone. As a transmitter, NE is primarily produced in an area of the brainstem known as the locus coeruleus. As a hormone, it is synthesized and released by the kidney's adrenal medulla into the bloodstream. Likewise, epinephrine is produced by the adrenal medulla and functions as a hormone, but small amounts are synthesized in the brain and act as a neurotransmitter. NE is synthesized from dopamine (DA) in a series of enzymatic steps. NE is an energizing chemical that mobilizes the body for action by increasing arousal, alertness, and vigilance and aids in the formation and retrieval of memory. Because it increases heart rate and blood pressure, and triggers the release of energizing glucose, excess amounts can trigger restlessness and anxiety in the absence of an overt threat (Terbeck et al., 2016).

Like its DA precursor, NE is an important mood regulator and is the neurotransmitter released in the "fight-or-flight" fear, stress, and panic responses. Situations that activate the locus coeruleus also activate the sympathetic branch of the autonomic nervous system (ANS). Thus, the locus coeruleus mobilizes the brain for action, while the ANS mobilizes the body. The sympathetic branch of the ANS is driven primarily by epinephrine. Both compounds are thus structurally related and differ in that epinephrine has a methyl group of atoms, while NE contains just a hydrogen atom at that same locus. While NE is specific in its action, epinephrine has more wide-ranging effects. NE is continuously released in the brain at low levels, but epinephrine is only released when the organism faces acute stress.

NE is related to criminal behavior, especially in males with attention-deficit/hyperactivity disorder (ADHD). Gottfredson and Hirschi's (1990) low self-control is the "powerhouse" theory of traditional criminology, which DeLisi (2011: 103) calls the "T-rex of criminology." Eme (2015: 446) adds: "If the brain-based disorder of low self-control is the T-Rex of criminology, then ADHD is the T-Rex of the brain-based disorder of low self-control." For instance, using the Swedish National Patient Register and the Swedish National Crime Register of males born between 1986 and 1997 (n = 635,391), Ångström et al. (2024) assessed violent and nonviolent criminal convictions among ADHD patients and controls over seven years. There were 27,103 males in the data with ADHD. The cumulative incidence of nonviolent criminal convictions was 54.2% for ADHD males and 19.0% for non-ADHD males. For violent criminal convictions, it was 28.3% versus 5.5% for ADHD and non-ADHD males, respectively. The hyperactivity, inattention, and impulsivity of people with ADHD mean that they have under-aroused brains. Maintaining awareness of what is happening in the world and self-control requires the coordination of cortical and subcortical functioning. Psychopharmacological drugs are the mainstay of ADHD treatment because they act either as stimulants or dual DA and NE reuptake inhibitors, thus increasing their availability and the patient's attention and self-control.

Glutamate and Gamma-Aminobutyric Acid

Glutamate and gamma-aminobutyric acid (GABA) are the most common neurotransmitters, with about half of synapses using glutamate and between 30 and 40% using GABA. Glutamate is an excitatory transmitter, and GABA is an inhibitory transmitter. Both transmitters work in tandem to control many processes, including the brain's overall excitation level. The abundance of glutamate reflects widespread effects on the brain's functioning and behavior. It has been most researched in the areas of learning and memory, and glutamate dysfunction has also been extensively studied in schizophrenia and mood disorders (Machado-Vieira, Manji, & Zarate, 2009). GABA's abundance also indicates that it serves many functions, not least of which is its guardian role in preventing random action potentials (electrical signals that activate neurons) that could have negative behavioral effects. Many forms of substance abuse affect the normal balance of glutamate and GABA. GABA reduces anxiety and can facilitate aggression for people prone to such behavior when they are under the influence of alcohol or tranquilizer drugs due to the reduction of the fear of the consequences (Miczek, Fish, & De Bold, 2003).

Although alcohol is ultimately a brain-numbing depressant, at low dosages it is a stimulant. It also reduces anxiety and fear by increasing GABA levels and enhancing binding to its receptors. When inhibitory GABA occupies a receptor, it reduces a neuron's electrical activity. The effect of alcohol-enhanced GABA expression is "reduced anxiety about the consequences of aggressive behavior" (Martin 2004: 143). This reduced anxiety may embolden drinkers to commit antisocial acts, particularly acts of violence. Alcohol ingestion also inhibits the release of glutamate, which accounts for the inhibition of cognitive and motor skills and the sedative effects of alcohol. Allostatic adjustments to GABA receptors in response to excessive activation over time involve reducing the number of functional GABA receptors, resulting in lessened ability of the GABAergic system to counteract glutamatergic excitation of neurons, thus disturbing the normal balance between excitation and inhibition of the central nervous system.

Getting Connected: Synaptogenesis

Synaptogenesis refers to the process of organizing the brain's wiring patterns by forming connections between communicating neurons. Synaptogenesis is a lifelong process, but infancy is a critical developmental period characterized by a unique sensitivity to social influences. These periods enable the tuning of brain systems vital for successful navigation through life. During the first few months of life (fetal and neonatal), there is an explosion of synapses as dendrites proliferate and send out their tentacles to hook up with any available mate and glial cells wrap around neuronal axons to begin the myelination process. The lower brain regions of the spinal column and limbic system are the first to be myelinated; higher brain regions such as the PFC are not fully myelinated until early adulthood (Sowell, Thompson, & Toga., 2004). A human infant may create two million synaptic connections a second at its peak (U.S. Department of Health and Human Services, 2009). Most synapses will not survive the competition for synaptic space and will be pruned, but others will develop more permanent relationships and strengthen. The pruning process retains connections with adaptive purpose and eliminates those without according to the "use it or lose it" principle. Although the brain creates and eliminates synapses throughout life, creation exceeds elimination in the first two years, after which creation and elimination are roughly balanced until adolescence, when elimination exceeds creation (Bonnycastle, Davenport, & Cousin, 2021).

Just as the species' genome evolved in geological time by the selective elimination or retention of genes, individual brains evolve in somatic time by the selective elimination or retention of synapses. The more enriched the environment, the more synapses are created, and the more brain plasticity is promoted (Han et al., 2022). Adaptive behaviors within a given environment are what evoke synaptic selective pressures. Synapse retention is a use-dependent process, with only those connections that exchange information most frequently and strongly being preserved. Experiences with strong emotional content are accompanied by strong electrochemical impulses that become more sensitive and responsive to similar stimuli latency in the future (Shi, et al., 2004). Frequently activated neurons are primed to fire at lower stimulus thresholds once neurological tracks have been laid down. This is analogous to establishing a trail in the wilderness; the more often a trail is trodden, the more distinct it becomes from its surroundings and the easier it is to follow. Like people, synapses like to follow well-trodden trails. This process is summed up in the pithy adage: "The neurons that fire together, wire together; those that don't, won't" (Penn, 2001: 339).

Hormones: Testosterone

Neurotransmitters and hormones are chemical signaling molecules, but the dividing line between them can be blurry because the central nervous system (neurotransmitters) and endocrine system (hormones) act synchronously. Hormones such as epinephrine, vasopressin, and oxytocin can function both as hormones and neurotransmitters. Neurotransmitters send their signals electrically from neuron to neuron along specified pathways in milliseconds and may be voluntary (concentrating on a task) or involuntary (perceiving a reward or threat). Hormones released from glands are carried slowly around the body by blood to distant cells and are secreted involuntarily.

Testosterone (T) is involved in many things, including the masculinization of the XY fetus's brain and sex organs and the development of secondary sex characteristics at puberty. The production of T is controlled by the hypothalamus and pituitary gland, which send hormonal messages to the testes to manufacture it when needed. Up to 98% of T circulating in the bloodstream is bound to sex hormone-binding globulin (SHBG), leaving only about 2% biologically active, or "free" to bind to an androgen receptor to exert its effects. Although base levels of T vary greatly, young adult males have almost 18 times more circulating T and much less SHBG, so the bioavailable T in males is at least 30 times that of females (Garrett, 2009).

T is associated with male-typical behaviors, particularly aggression (Grotzinger et al., 2018). It does not cause aggression; it only facilitates it. T levels rise and fall in different environmental contexts consistent with biopsychosocial reciprocal models (Mazur, 2023). Batrinos (2012: 563) notes that the power of T is attenuated in man relative to other animals: "However, it still manifests itself in various intensities and forms from thoughts, anger, verbal aggressiveness, competition, dominance behavior, to physical violence." Booth et al. (2006: 170) view T's behavioral role as facilitating dominance/status: "In humans ... higher testosterone is associated with a type of dominance that sometimes entails aggression."

Hormones: Cortisol

While T is a key anabolic hormone (it produces reactions that build new molecules and stores energy), cortisol (CRT) is a catabolic hormone (it releases energy to break down complex organic molecules into simpler substances) secreted by the adrenal cortex in response to stress. Anabolic reactions require catabolic reactions to drive them, so they comprise an integrated metabolic system. The production of CRT is governed by the hypothalamic-pituitary-adrenal (HPA) axis. The HPA axis responds to stressful situations with the hypothalamus feeding various chemical messages to the pituitary gland, leading to further chemicals that stimulate the adrenal glands to release CRT. The HPA axis response is far slower than the ANS response and lasts longer because its impact on the brain occurs through changes in gene expression (Gunnar & Quevedo, 2007). It is activated in situations that require prolonged thought and series of responses rather than the ANS's visceral immediacy (van Voorhees & Scarpa, 2004). The release of CRT is part of the general adaptive response to stress, mobilizing and focusing the mind and body for action. However, chronic stress may lead to hypocortisolism, which suggests an adaptive allostatic downregulation to frequent stressful encounters.

The Triple Imbalance Hypothesis and Aggression

The influence of T on behavior depends on the CRT response to stress. High T levels suppress the release of CRT, and high levels of CRT suppress T levels: "Thus, within the dual-hormone hypothesis, individuals will be more likely to engage in antisocial and aggressive behavior when they have high levels of testosterone and low levels of cortisol" (Cooke et al., 2020: 1476). A high T/CRT ratio is likely to result in aggressive responses to stress among people with increased sensitivity to reward, and a low T/CRT ratio is more likely to result in avoidance behavior (Batrinos, 2012). Based on experimental data from neurobiological research, it has been hypothesized that reactive aggression ensues from an imbalance in three neurohormonal systems: the subcortical, the cortical-subcortical, and the cortical. This has been termed the triple imbalance hypothesis (TIH). The subcortical imbalance hypothesis avers that aggression is motivated by the imbalance between T (high) and CRT (low). A high T/CRT ratio is associated with significantly increased activation of the hypothalamus and amygdala, vital components of the subcortical reactive stress circuit. Terburg, Morgan, and van Honk (2009: 217) observe: "High testosterone/low cortisol ratios seem to predict approach motivation/reward sensitivity. In these motivational stances, individuals are more likely to confront threat, which could result in aggressive behavior."

The cortical-subcortical imbalance hypothesis posits that high T tends to decrease the coupling of the cortical-subcortical regions and impedes information transfer between the orbitofrontal cortex (OFC) and the amygdala. The OFC guides and monitors fear-generated responses from the amygdala. Communication deficits in either the cortical or subcortical systems may result in high levels of reactive aggression (Mehta & Beer, 2009). Much of the evidence from imaging studies of OFC-amygdala disconnectedness comes from studies of patients with intermittent explosive disorder (IED) who show exaggerated amygdala reactivity and diminished OFC activation relative to controls when presented with images of angry faces (Coccaro et al., 2007).

The cortical imbalance hypothesis centers on left/right frontal cortex imbalance and serotonergic activity. Left-side dominance is associated with approach behavior and right-side dominance with avoidance behavior (Schutter et al., 2008), and anger predicts increased left and decreased right frontal activity (Hewig et al., 2006). Studies such as these led Von Honk et al. (2010: 86) to propose that extreme left-side imbalance indicates "a state of readiness to respond to social threat with anger and aggression rather than fear and submission." It has also been proposed that low serotonergic functioning promotes reactive aggression in individuals with high T/CRT ratios because low serotonin is associated with impulsiveness (Dolan, Anderson & Deakin, 2001). T modulates serotonergic receptor activity in ways that can result in aggression by influencing serotonin functioning in the OFC and enhancing amygdala reactivity to threat cues (Mehta & Beer, 2009).

Reinforcement Sensitivity Theory

A key neurobiological theory of approach/avoidance behavior for biopsychosocial criminologists is the reinforcement sensitivity theory (RST). RST is psychology's premier theory of personality and has been put forward as a possible metatheory for biosocial criminology (Walsh, 2019). In 1789, British lawyer and philosopher Jeremy Bentham wrote: "Nature has placed mankind under the governance of two sovereign masters, *pain* and *pleasure*. It is for them alone to point out what we ought to do, as well as to determine what we shall do" (Bentham, 1948: 125). While this design feature is an adaption for the individual it can be socially maladaptive if immediate concerns for gratification are placed above maintaining social harmony and a person seeks "money without work, sex without courtship, and revenge without court delays" (Gottfredson & Hirschi, 1990: 89). In seeking individual hedonism, we must consider the pains and pleasures of others and the pains we might endure in the pursuit. This consideration is the calculus half in Bentham's hedonistic calculus, and RST is a theory that provides "a scientific theory of the hedonistic calculus" (Corr, 2008: 17).

Bentham was not the first to recognize the hedonistic tug-of-war people have with themselves. Plato's (1960) tripartite model of the soul (psyche) is an approach-avoidance model of balancing behavior told in the form of his allegory of the chariot. The soul consists of the appetitive, rational, and spirited souls. The appetitive soul motivates us to seek the pleasures necessary to sustain individual life and is analogous to the Freudian id. The rational soul thinks and urges us to make wise decisions when pursuing goals (Freud's ego), and the spirited soul (Freud's superego) values virtue, which, in the good and wise person, emotionally enforces the dictates of the rational soul. In Plato's allegory, the charioteer represents the rational soul (the PFC) fighting to control the emotional white horse and the appetitive black horse (limbic system urges). The black and white horses pull in opposite directions, the white horse toward virtuous behavior and the black horse toward unabashed hedonism.

Plato realized that both black and white horses and the charioteer are needed to move the chariot forward because each has strengths and weaknesses. Both horses must be harnessed as a cooperative team. The white horse has an innate affinity for the charioteer's commands, but the black horse requires the whip to move it in the right direction. If the black horse proves too strong for the charioteer, it will be able to enlist the emotional energy of the white horse to achieve its lust for pleasure. If the white horse dominates, the individual will have an anxious but virtuous life. Balancing the three parts of the psyche is the key to a happy and successful prosocial life.

Evolutionary views of human nature are that we are designed to follow Bentham's "sovereign masters" of pleasure and pain and that we engage in an internal hedonic tug-of-war as we approach potentially rewarding opportunities while avoiding potentially punishing consequences. RST avers that almost all reward-seeking involves approaching incentives while avoiding threats, "and that personality reflects inter-individual variation in sensitivity to these reinforcing stimuli" (Smillie, 2008, p. 360). Thus, RST emphasizes that different personalities reflect the variety of perceptions and evaluations of stimuli that people make, and that motivation and emotion regulation must be considered to understand behavior.

RST posits three interacting systems of emotional/behavioral regulation located within different brain circuits and associated with neurotransmitters that move us to maximize fitness-enhancing rewards and minimize fitness-threatening pains. The first is the *behavioral activating* system, or behavioral approach system (BAS). The BAS heeds only the pleasure principle and evolved to motivate us to seek evolutionarily relevant pleasures (food, water, sex) necessary for life's continuance. It thus "represents a general domain approach mechanism designed to solve the important evolutionary adaptive problem of attaining critical resources, such as food, water, sex, and social status" (Krupić, Gračanin, & Corr, 2016: 223). However, it is easily hijacked for the pursuit of evolutionarily novel pleasures and may lead to addictive behavior and criminality (Walsh & Bolen, 2012).

The BAS is sensitive to both conditioned and unconditioned appetitive stimuli. It is primarily located in neural structures responsible for processing reward, namely the dopaminergic system consisting of structures such as the nucleus accumbens and the ventral pallidum, and with various PFC areas (Barrós-Loscertales et al., 2010). The limbic structures provide the reward via dopamine surges, and the PFC structures provide its evaluations. Dopamine surges promote efforts to obtain future rewards (Peters, Cheer, & Tonini, 2021). As nature's built-in reward system, it makes us feel good when we do things that contribute to survival and reproduction, such as eating, drinking, and sexual activity, and is thus a pleasant addition to our adaptations. However, we must ensure that we do not exceed appropriate boundaries and seek our pleasures in impulsive and antisocial ways.

Counteracting the BAS is the behavioral inhibition system (BIS). The BIS is oriented to threatening stimuli and avoidance behavior. It involves conditioning to punishment cues, striving for the ideal between desire and prudence, and it is the emotional component of the moral and social mores people have (or should have) internalized (Rogers, 2011). RST maintains that the BIS evolved once humans had mastered challenges presented by the physical environment (acquiring food, avoiding predators, and building shelter), and were presented with the problem of navigating complex human interaction in ever-larger social groups. The BIS is thus a system of self-control necessary for social life, which Wright, Boisvert & Dietrich et al. (2009, p. 83) note "involves a complex, dynamic balancing of limbic and cortical functioning." Chen (2020) found that active criminals (compared to college students) showed poor fear conditioning, and this lower fear was associated with low BIS functioning.

The BIS is associated with serotonin and limbic system structures, such as the hippocampus, amygdala, and anterior cingulate cortex, that feed their memory circuits into the PFC (Hughes et al., 2012). Serotonin is critically involved in emotion regulation, and there are associations between low serotonin and low self-control (DeWall, Finkel, & Denson, 2011). Serotonin improves emotion regulation, and its depletion in the orbitofrontal cortex results in poor emotion regulation and disinhibition (Pourhamzeh et al., 2022). However, highlighting the complexities involved in neuroscience, serotonin receptors are also expressed throughout the dopaminergic system and modulate dopamine release, and certain serotonin receptors can potentiate dopamine release and support reinforcement (Peters, Cheer, & Tonini, 2021).

The third system is the fight-flee-freeze (FFFS); a reflexive visceral warning system. We sometimes encounter danger when pursuing rewards when there is no time to think about options and our senses tell us to fight, flee, or freeze. The FFFS "mediates responses to aversive stimuli, and its neurobiology consists of input from the periaqueductal gray, the medial hypothalamus, the amygdala, the anterior cingulate cortex, and the ventral stream of [the] prefrontal cortex" (Lopez-Vergara et al., 2012: 131). The periaqueductal gray plays a role in autonomic nervous system (ANS) regulation, and the arousal of the sympathetic branch of the ANS stimulates the release of norepinephrine and epinephrine to energize fighting and fleeing behavior. Depending on subconscious subjective evaluations, an aroused FFFS state may be characterized by fear and flight, while a state of identical valence may lead to anger and aggression.

The FFFS mediates reactions to all aversive stimuli, whether unconditioned or conditioned, whereas the BIS is responsive to stimuli associated only with conditioned stimuli. The activation of both systems involves the amygdala (anxiety, fear) and hippocampus (memories of similar situations), suggesting that they comprise a single integrated behavioral inhibition system (Corr, 2013). The BIS is activated by the joint activation of the BAS and FFFS, which involves conflicting approach-avoidance stimuli. The BIS is thus a system of conflict detection and resolution that inhibits behavior until either the BAS or FFFS is most strongly engaged, but it always tries to arrive at the most prudent response. The BIS triggers anxiety, but in cases in which people possess relatives unresponsive ANSs and thus lack anxiety when confronted with conflicting motivational goals (reward desire versus aversive cues), antisocial behavior may ensue. However, the BAS is the preeminent system because goal-seeking entails a wider set of tactics and strategies. As Corr (2008, p. 19) maintains, "the BAS entails a much more flexible repertoire of behaviours and planning processing than either the FFFS or BIS."

The majority of our rewards are natural (unconditioned) and evoke natural responses such as salivation, consumption, and sexual arousal (unconditioned responses) and thus constitute classical conditioning. They become embedded in operant conditioning circumstances as rewards are actively sought. Depending on their rewarding or punishing consequences, they guide future approach/avoidance behavior (Day & Carelli, 2007). Although natural rewards are life-sustaining, compulsively seeking these rewards drastically alters brain circuits that regulate the ability to guide behavior. Most people balance conflicting interests because their reward and punishment systems are balanced. However, persistent offenders have difficulty balancing their behavior because they have a strong BAS, a weak BIS, and/or a hypoactive FFFS. The BIS and the FFFS can be likened to brakes that slow us down in pursuit of pleasures. Problems with either the accelerator or the brakes may lead to a "craving brain" and a multitude of physical, social, moral, and legal difficulties, such as criminality and addiction to gambling, food, sex, alcohol, and drugs (Walsh, Johnson & Bolen, 2012).

Neuroscience provides hard evidence, but we must tread carefully when interpreting this evidence because neuroscience is the brain trying to understand itself. Neuroscientists know how difficult their subject is, as evidenced by their aphorism: "If the brain were so simple that we could understand it, we would be so simple that we couldn't." However, there is much well-replicated research showing that the brain is a marvelously plastic organ calibrated to environmental experiences. Brain-based theories such as RST and the TIH reveal that some people may be congenitally more prone to criminality and addiction because of imbalances in brain areas vital to self-control. However, the extent to which these imbalances are affected by experience is an open question, but without a doubt, they are. Early nurturing and loving experiences during childhood appear to be crucial factors in developing healthy brains.

8 Childhood Maltreatment and Brain Development

Evolutionary Developmental Biology and the Brain

Evolutionary developmental biology ("evo-devo") attempts to synthesize Tinbergen's four-pronged approach to behavior. It investigates how ancient phylogenetic developmental pathways contribute to the ontogeny of human behavioral traits and the causal mechanisms by which they do. Evo-devo tries "to unravel the interaction between these two processes – evolution and development" (Ploeger & Galis, 2021:1211) and enlists the help of all the natural and behavioral sciences in this endeavor. Criminologists, of course, are interested in developmental experiences linked with antisocial behavior. We begin with the neotenous human brain.

Our hominin ancestors on the African savanna couldn't outfight or outrun predators or prey, so they had to outwit them. As they got smarter, they were able to devise more efficient hunting methods and tools, which provided them with more protein and fat to build bigger brains, which made them even smarter. It was not only ecological challenges that led to bigger brains. Studies of hominin crania dating back 1.9 million years have shown that cranial capacity increases most rapidly in colder areas of the globe, in areas with greater population density, and where food procurement was most problematic (Ash & Gallup, 2007; Kanazawa, 2008). Both latitude ($r = 0.61$) and population density ($r = 0.79$) are strongly related to cranial size, which led Bailey and Geary (2009: 77) to conclude that the burden of natural selection has moved from "climactic and ecological to social." Food procurement is more problematic in colder climates, necessitating more future-oriented thinking, and the more people there are in the social group the greater the number of social relationships there are to navigate. In navigating those relationships, humans slowly developed a theory of mind—the capacity to reason about the mental states of others.

Greater intelligence requires greater brain mass, which requires bigger skulls to house it. About two million years separate *Australopithecus afarenis* and *Homo sapiens*, and during this period hominin cranial capacity has increased from an average of 450cc to 1350cc, which is warp speed on an evolutionary time scale (Adolphs, 2009). To appreciate human brain

DOI: 10.4324/9781003662495-10

size, we look to the encephalization quotient, which measures actual brain size relative to the expected brain size for a given mammalian body size. González-Forero (2024: 1325) notes that "adult brain size evolves from being ancestrally slightly over four times larger than expected to being about six times larger than expected."

The brain is thus an organ of adaptation exquisitely calibrated to its environment. Gene-culture coevolution creates vast opportunities for genetic changes, and the more culture changes the greater the genomic changes (Walsh & Yun, 2016). Hawks et al. (2007) found that the rate of change in the human genome has been 100 times greater over the last 40,000 years than during the 1.8 million-year-long Pleistocene. They attributed this rapid genomic evolution to the challenges posed by living in ever larger groups: "The rapid cultural evolution during the Late Pleistocene created vastly more opportunities for further genetic changes, not fewer, as new avenues emerged for communication, social interaction, and creativity" (2007: 20757). It is a mathematical truism that genetic mutations, either positive, negative, or neutral, arise more frequently in large populations than in smaller ones. The combination of ecological, social, and cultural pressures, such as moving from tree-based to savanna life, becoming more carnivorous, and developing agriculture, led to the enlargement of hominin brains and greater intelligence. A larger brain provides more room for more experiences to be encoded and more associations to be made among them (Kanazawa, 2012).

However, increasing cranial size placed great birthing burdens on our ancestral females. The human birth canal cannot accommodate birthing infants whose brains are 60% of their adult weight, as in newborn macaques, or even 45%, as in newborn chimpanzees (Hublin & Coqueugniot, 2006). The Australopithecine female pelvis was probably shaped to accommodate upright posture and bipedalism (which has the effect of narrowing the birth canal) more than to accommodate increased infant skull size, precipitating a conflict between obstetric and postural requirements of ancestral females (Van As, Fieggen, & Tobias, 2007). The obstetric/posture conflict was partially solved by selection for larger pelvises in human females relative to males. There is a greater sex difference in the human pelvis than in any other species, and human females still have greater difficulty giving birth than any other species (Parente, Bergqvist, Soares, & Filho, 2011). The continuation of this trajectory would have produced extremely bow-legged females, so thankfully, an alternative strategy worked out better: having infants born at ever earlier stages of development as cerebral mass increased. Human infants experience 25% brain growth inside the womb (*uterogestation*) and 75% outside (*exterogestation*) (Perry, 2002). The high degree of developmental retardation of the human brain assures a greater role for the extra-uterine environment in its development than is true of any other species.

Strong selection pressures for neurohormonal mechanisms designed to ensure the young are nurtured for an extended period are expected in species burdened with extremely helpless young such as ours: "The co-evolution of the family and the brain, building on the maternal/offspring attachments of our mammalian ancestors, involved profound adaptations in the hominid biology" (Papero et al., 2018: 22). As evolutionary anthropologist Ashley Montagu pointed out long ago, this has necessitated "a continuing symbiotic relationship between mother and child during the exterogestation period designed to endure in an unbroken continuum until the infant's brain weight has more than doubled." He expands on this, stating that love is the cement of this symbiotic relationship:

> It is, in a very real and not in the least paradoxical sense, it is even more necessary to love than it is to live, for without love there can be no healthy growth or development, no real life. The neotenous principle for human beings—indeed, the evolutionary imperative—is to live as if to live and love were one.
>
> (Montagu, 1981: 93)

The Nurturing Experience

Montagu's "symbiotic relationship between mother and child" is most salient in infancy and best exemplified behaviorally at this stage by breastfeeding (Yurdakök, 2014). Lawrence and Lawrence (2011: 267) note: "Human milk provides substantial nutritional, cognitive, emotional, and immunologic benefits for the infant." Although a newborn's immune system cannot battle all antigens in its environment, it will receive a 100% safe vaccine in high-octane colostrum if breastfed. After a few days of feasting on this super-food, the infant gets 10 to 14 days of transitional milk (a blend of colostrum and thinner breast milk), and after that, regular breastmilk which contains many chemical compounds important for brain development.

The cognitive effects of breastfeeding are typically assessed via IQ scores. Kim et al. (2017) found that children who were ever breastfed scored significantly higher on learning skills such as speaking, reading, writing, spelling, and mathematics than children who were never breastfed after controlling for various gestational and SES variables. A Spanish cohort study (Julvez et al., 2014) found that children who never breastfed had a mean IQ of 98 and that children who were breastfed longer than six months had a mean of 108. After adjusting for SES, maternal education, smoking, and infant birth weight, the 10-point advantage diminished to a 7.5-point advantage. However, such studies rarely have access to mothers' IQs because there is a positive relationship between mothers' IQs and the probability of breastfeeding, we may be witnessing a genetic effect on children's IQ rather than a breastfeeding effect.

Kramer, et al. (2008) addressed this concern with a randomized experimental design in a study of 13,889 Belarusian breastfeeding mothers, a random half of whom were given incentives to prolong breastfeeding while the other half were not. When the children were assessed six years later, it was found that children breastfed for more than 6 months had a mean IQ almost six points higher than the control group children. The experimental research design allowed them to assess breastfeeding effects on IQ without concerns about biasing confounds. Similarly, a study of 3,000 British and New Zealand children born in the early 1970s and IQ-tested in the 1990s found that subjects who were breastfed scored on average 6 to 7 points higher on IQ tests than non-breastfed subjects (Caspi, et al., 2007). Adjusting for relevant covariates, Herba et al. (2013: 332) compared exclusively breastfed, breastfed and bottle-fed, and bottle-fed only infants and found: "Exclusive breastfeeding was associated with more optimal brain development compared with babies who were bottle-fed or never breastfed."

However, breastfeeding might exert its effects through physical and emotional contact between mother and infant more than its nutrition effects (Wallenborn et al., 2021). Yurdakök (2014: 8) remarks:

> Healthy development of the neural systems which allows optimal social and emotional functioning depends upon attentive, nurturing caregiving in early life. ... Skin-to-skin contact should be facilitated, supported, and encouraged as early and often as possible to initiate attachment relationships for appropriate synaptic formation and brain development and to prevent maltreatment.

The tactile stimulation and mother/infant gaze are significantly elevated during breastfeeding and positively influence the child's emotional development. Breastfeeding combines the panoply of sight, sound, smell, touch, and the tangible evidence in the mother's arms that affirms her womanhood and stimulates the release of oxytocin (the "cuddle chemical"), which intensifies the warm feeling that is released in a felicitous feedback loop. Oxytocin is also conveyed to infants through breast milk and skin contact (UvnäsMoberg et al., 2020). Lactating mothers show significantly fewer stress responses to infant stimuli, as determined by skin conductance and cardiac response measures, than non-lactating mothers, and the oxytocin-generated sense of emotional warmness motivates a significantly greater desire to pick up their infants in response to infant-presented stimuli (Herba et al. 2013).

Breastfeeding and the accompanying tactile stimulation are experience-expected features of brain development since it was the only way of feeding hominin infants during the vast majority of our evolution. As an experience-expected feature, the failure of the infant to experience it may be seen as the deprivation of important brain development input. Whether the nutritional or emotional aspects of breastfeeding or a combination of both confer developmental benefits, the benefits exist. Unfortunately, the literature consistently shows a marked downward gradient in the rates of breastfeeding as maternal IQ and SES fall. A random sample of 10,519 mothers in California found that the odds of breastfeeding of women in the highest income category was 3.65 times greater than for women in the lowest income category

(Heck, et al., 2006). Children of lower SES women are more likely to be deprived of important experience-expected input.

Maltreatment and Early Brain Development

Neotenous development provides humans more time to adapt to sociocultural environments that are continually in flux and thus many windows of opportunity for those adequately nurtured. However, it also provides windows of vulnerability for those that are not. What if infants and children do not experience Montagu's "continuing symbiotic relationship" but rather experience abuse and neglect instead? Tottenham (2020: 351) points out:

> The link between adverse caregiving and brain development is not unique to humans, and animal models have established that the link is causal. However, humans do stand out, perhaps more than any other species, as a result of their neotenous brain development.

Social scientists have long known that childhood abuse and neglect can have negative behavioral consequences later in life, but they do not address the brain mechanisms that give rise to them. If negative early experiences constitute an elevated risk for antisocial behavior, it must do so by altering brain functions. If children's brain wiring is established by experience-expected nurturing, they will be disposed to view the world positively. However, if their brains were wired by maltreatment, later experiences, even those viewed as neutral by most people, are likely to be diverted onto a neurological track that signals hostility. As Firestone, Firestone, and Catlett (2013, p. 14) note:

> We are just as capable of adapting to unhealthy environments and pathological caretakers. The resulting adaptations may help us to survive a traumatic childhood but impede healthy development later in life. ... Because the first few years of life are a period of exuberant brain development, early experience has a disproportionate impact on the development of neural systems.

As Belsky (2024: 7) states:

> The fundamental point to be made is whether genes related to prosocial or antisocial behavior, for example, become phenotypically expressed, such that their latent potential becomes manifest, depends on whether the environment in which the child develops "enables" or "disables" such expression.

Maltreatment in all forms and poor child development outcomes are more likely to occur in female-headed low-SES households (Cicchetti et al., 2016).

The optimal developmental and socialization experiences for children virtually require the presence of a biological father, which leads to willing conformity and cooperation with the appropriate authority figures, good psychological adjustment, and fewer internalizing and externalizing problems (Cheung et al., 2018). Based on 10 years of data from National Health Interview Surveys, Sullins (2021:184) remarks: "This evidence strongly supports the claim that maximum child development occurs only in the persistent care of both of the child's own biological parents." Sullins is supported by a Swedish study of 986,342 children that found that children living in a single-parent household had a greatly elevated risk of many psychiatric issues, suicide or attempted suicide, crime, and drug and alcohol addiction (Weitoft et al., 2003).

The Centers for Disease Control and Prevention (2022) tells us that in 2019, just over 40% of children born in America were born out of wedlock, but to focus on this problem, according to James Q. Wilson, "is to risk being called a racist, unless you quickly add that families are not important to children, in which case you may be called either a progressive or a fool" (2000: 107). However, progressive African American activists Cosby and Poussaint join Wilson in noting: "A house without a father is a challenge. A neighborhood without fathers is a catastrophe" (2007: 3). Kruk highlights the criminogenic consequences of growing up in fatherless homes:

> Eighty-five percent of youth in prison have an absent father, 71% of high school dropouts are fatherless, 90% of homeless and runaway children have an absent father, and fatherless children and youth exhibit higher levels of depression and suicide, delinquency, promiscuity and teen pregnancy, behavioral problems and illicit and licit substance abuse, diminished self-concepts, and are more likely to be victims of exploitation and abuse.
>
> (2012: 49)

However, having a criminal, abusive, or substance-abusing man in the home, particularly a live-in boyfriend, is highly undesirable, as decades of data from the National Incidence Study of Child Abuse and Neglect have shown. Based on the fourth study in this series, Sedlak et al. (2010: 14) noted:

> Compared to children living with married biological parents, those whose single parent had a live-in partner had more than 8 times the rate of maltreatment overall, over 10 times the rate of abuse, and nearly 8 times the rate of neglect.

The result of this maltreatment and neglect in many fatherless homes is evident from crime data. McLaughlin and Mackey (2008) examined non-marital births and violent crime in all 50 states and the District of Columbia from 1980 to 2004. They found that non-marital birth rates explained 48.7%

of the variance in violent crime, and for a generation lag of 20 years, the explained variance was 65.1%. A study by Mackey and Immerman (2007: 128) found that:

> Taking the US as a unit, from 1951 to 2003 (or 53 years or n = 53), the correlation between out-of-wedlock births and rates of violent crime was significant. ... Over 75% of the variability in rates of violent crime can be explained by differential rates of out-of-wedlock births.

Similarly, Errol, Madsen, and Moslehi's examination of crime rates in 16 advanced countries over 200 hundred years found: "Our results suggest that family structure, measured by divorce rates and out-of-wedlock births, is a significantly positive determinant of violent crime, property crime, assaults, homicide and robbery over the past two centuries" (2021: 535).

Experience-Expected and Experience-Dependent Brain Development

The brain is always a work in progress and depends significantly on environmental input. Neuroscientists distinguish between two brain developmental processes: experience-expected and experience-dependent (McLaughlin, Weissman, & Bitrán, 2019). Experience-expected phenomena are analogous to a smartphone received directly from the factory containing all the information needed to work. Experience-dependent phenomena are analogous to all the apps its owner downloads onto it. The distinction between experience-dependent and experience-expected development is best illustrated by language. The *capacity* for language is an entirely genetic, hard-wired, experience-expected species-wide capacity that is not learned in the traditional sense but is absorbed as if by osmosis. The language(s) a person speaks is entirely cultural; that is, "downloaded" in an experience-dependent fashion. The experience-expected nature of language explains why children acquire language effortlessly, but struggle when learning evolutionary novel things such as calculus.

The experience-expected notion of brain development maintains that to develop normally, the brain "expects" to encounter when neurobiological circuitry is especially responsive to experience. These experiences include sensory and perceptual experiences such as seeing, hearing, and being held and nurtured by a sensitive and responsive caregiver during critical periods of infant life. In all but the rarest of instances, all human brains are exposed to sight and speech, but many are not blessed with sensitive and responsive caregivers. Natural selection moves population traits towards genetic fixity (genetic variability is eliminated) the more important a feature becomes to survival. Although experience-expected mechanisms are hard-wired, they require specific environmental experiences to trigger them. In other words, there is an evolved neural readiness during "critical" or "sensitive" developmental periods to incorporate environmental information vital to organisms that cannot be left to the vagaries of learning. Natural selection has recognized that certain processes, such as sight, speech, depth perception, affectionate bonds, mobility, and sexual maturation, are vital and has provided mechanisms designed to take advantage of experiences occurring naturally within the normal range of human environments. Pre-experiential brain organization frames or orients our experiences so that we will respond consistently and stereotypically to them (Geary, 2005). Maturational processes will always occur "as expected" in genetically normal individuals born into the normal range of human environments. If individuals experience gross departures from these species-expected environments, there are many negative outcomes (Twardosz & Lutzker, 2010).

Experience-dependent mechanisms reflect the brain's plasticity as experiences are *physically* captured during an organism's life, particularly during its early life (Gunnar & Quevedo, 2007). As Koukkou and Lehmann (2006, p. 47) explain: "experience-dependent plasticity refers to the learning and memory mechanisms that extract personal meaning out of the interaction of individuals with their environment and that lead to the genesis of the neuronal networks that represent autobiographical memory." Individuals will thus vary in the efficiency of their brain functioning as their genes interact with their environments to construct their brain's wiring patterns. Depue and Collins (1999, p. 507) emphasize that: "experience-dependent processes are central to understanding personality as a dynamic developmental construct that involves the collaboration of genetic and environmental influences across the lifespan."

As we have seen, brain plasticity is greatest in infancy and early childhood, but maintained to a lesser degree across the lifespan as the brain is continually shaped and reshaped. As Perry and Pollard (1998, p. 36) point out: "Experience in adults *alters* the *organized* brain, but in infants and children it *organizes* the *developing* brain." Brains organized by stressful and traumatic events tend to relay future events along the same pathways laid out by early events because pathways laid down early in life are more resistant to elimination than pathways laid down later. As Kolb and Gibb (2011: 272) remark: "There is little doubt that the parent–child relationships are critical and that they play a key role in brain development. Differences in the pattern of early maternal-infant interactions can initiate long-term developmental effects that persist into adulthood."

Maltreatment and Antisocial Behavior

Stress is an inevitable part of life; it energizes and focuses us, and without it, we would be impeded in our ability to cope with life's challenges. Adults who experienced average stress levels during childhood likely possess brains better calibrated to navigate the travails of life than those who were protected from almost all stress (Rudland, Golding, & Wilkinson, 2020). While moderate stress is functional, the toxic protracted stress of abuse and maltreatment damages vital brain areas responsible for memory storage and behavioral regulation, such as the amygdala, hippocampus, and PFC (Narvaez & Vaydich, 2008). Frequent activation of stress response mechanisms during childhood may lead to dysregulation (such as sending wrongly perceived information to the amygdala) and several psychological, emotional, and behavioral problems (Mainali, Rai, & Rutkofsky, 2020).

The stress response is mediated by two interrelated systems controlled by the hypothalamus: the ANS and the hypothalamic-pituitary-adrenal (HPA) axis. When an organism perceives a threat to its well-being, the hypothalamus—the center of the endocrine world—directs the ANS to mobilize the body for vigorous action aided by pumping out epinephrine. When the organism perceives the threat is over, the ANS restores the body to homeostasis. Because the HPA axis response occurs through changes in gene expression, it is slower than the ANS response and lasts longer (Gunnar & Quevedo, 2007). The HPA axis is activated in situations that call for prolonged rumination rather than the visceral immediacy of the ANS's preparation for fight or flight in the face of imminent threat. The HPA axis response begins with the hypothalamus feeding various chemical messages to the pituitary gland, which leads to further chemical products that stimulate the adrenal glands to release cortisol. Cortisol energizes coping mechanisms by increasing vigilance and activity and is functional within the normal range.

However, frequent HPA axis arousal may lead to dysregulation of arousal mechanisms. Upward dysregulation results in the overproduction of cortisol (hypercortisolism), which leads to anxiety and depressive disorders, and is most likely to be found in maltreated females because females activate more neural systems associated with emotional stress and encoding it into long-term memory than males (Van Voorhees & Scarpa, 2004). Females will thus have emotional experiences more readily available for rumination than males, and pondering those experiences increases their valence over time. Males can develop hypercortisolism also, but females are more likely to under similar circumstances. Hypercortisolism suggests a failure of the system to adjust to chronic environmental stressors and leads to internalizing problems such as chronic depression and post-traumatic stress disorder.

On the other hand, hypocortisolism suggests an adaptive downward adjustment to chronic stress and leads to externalizing problems. It is adaptive because frequent stressful encounters habituate the HPA axis to them and consequently, it does not react to further encounters as it had previously (Haller, 2018). Habituation means that both the HPA axis and ANS response have become dulled. Hypocortisolism is linked to the early onset of aggressive antisocial behavior (McBurnett et al., 2000), to criminal behavior in general (Ellis, 2005) and is more likely to be found in maltreated males (van Goozen, et al., 2007). O'Leary, Loney, and Eckel (2007) found that males high in psychopathic traits lacked stress-induced increases in cortisol compared to other males. Blunted arousal means low levels of anxiety and fear, which is useful for those committing or contemplating committing a crime (Haller, 2018).

Hypocortisolism is an example of allostasis; the body's attainment of equilibrium by *altering* the acceptable range of physiological set-points to adapt to extreme acute or chronic stress rather than returning them to their previous state, as in homeostasis. According to Goldstein and Kopin (2007: 111): "Adaptations involving allostasis to cope with real, simulated, or imagined challenges are determined by genetic, developmental, and previous experiential factors. While they may be effective for a short interval, over time the alterations may have cumulative adverse effects." Meaney (2010: 63) notes hypocortisolism may be adaptive: "Environmental adversity decreases parental investment in the offspring and thus alters phenotypic development. And there is evidence that these phenotypic effects are adaptive with adverse settings." Children subconsciously use parental signals to forecast the type of environments they are likely to encounter in their later years (good or bad), and their development will be biased in the forecasted direction via neurophysiological modifications.

Epigenetics

In the past, the genome was considered a static "blueprint" with one-to-one mapping from gene to phenotype. We now view it as a recipe from which the phenotype forms from the genetic recipe and the environment in which it is "baked." Evo-devo does not see development as merely a readout of a genetic blueprint, but rather as the evolution of the phenotype through heritable changes in development (Moczek 2012; Müller, 2020; Nuño de la Rosa & Müller, 2024). The circumstances people face, particularly in early life, can affect the genome by altering gene transcription without altering DNA sequences. This leads to epigenetics, described as "any process that alters gene activity without changing the DNA sequence" (Weinhold, 2006: 163). Epigenetic modifications affect the ability of the DNA code to be read by rendering it accessible or inaccessible (O'Donnell & Meaney, 2020). Many genes of interest to criminologists are regulated by signals from environmental events, "which may be internal or external to the organism, e.g., a change in the availability of glucose, an electrical impulse, or a social interaction" (Meaney, 2010: 50). Epigenetics thus emphasizes the permeable boundaries between the biological and the social.

The epigenetic regulation of genetic activity involves two main processes: DNA methylation and histone acetylation. Methylation may be permanent, retained during cell replication, and passed on to offspring, while acetylation is transient. DNA methylation is a process by which DNA methyltransferase attaches a methyl group of atoms to a cytosine base and prevents protein synthesis. The enzyme RNA polymerase (RNAP) copies the DNA sequence of a protein by running up the DNA strand. However, if it encounters a methyl group on the strand it can go no further and the protein cannot be made. Acetylation involves histone acetyltransferases transferring an acetyl group of atoms that bind to the amino acid lysine tail of the histone, which reduces lysine's electrostatic attraction to the DNA's negatively charged phosphate backbone. The reduced charge loosens the chromatin enabling RNAP to read the gene code more readily. After transcription, another group of enzymes called histone deacetylases removes the acetyl atoms, reinstating the electrostatic attraction and repressing chromatin activity.

Epigenetics reveals how early-life experiences, particularly nurturing, affect gene expression in the brain. Early studies linking methylation to maternal care were done with rodents, with nurturing indexed by the level of pup licking and grooming (LG) and arch-back nursing (ABN) (Weaver et al., 2004). Pups receiving high LG/ABN showed better responses to stress and were more socially adept than pups receiving low levels of LG/ABN. A portion of the pups from each strain was cross fostered (high LG/ABN mothers fostering pups born to low LG/ABN mothers and vice versa) to determine how much of the pup's behaviors were attributable to genes versus nurturing. High LG/ABN led to similar epigenetic modifications in pups, regardless of whether they were the mothers' offspring or cross-fostered. These modifications resulted in stable behavioral differences in adulthood between the high and low-nurtured pups.

Low-nurtured pups showed high methylation of the glucocorticoid receptor (GR) gene in the hippocampus. The hippocampus modulates hypothalamic-pituitary-adrenal (HPA) axis functioning. The GR gene is naturally heavily methylated and inactive at birth. In highly nurtured pups, the GR gene gradually demethylates (replacing the methyl group with a hydrogen atom) and becomes active. Methylated receptors are inoperable, while unmethylated genes produce more receptors, resulting in better feedback control of the stress response. Poorly nurtured pups retained a high level of methylation and responded to stress with anxiety and fear, but in a world of cats and other dangers, it pays to be hypervigilant. The early environment teaches lessons about the world we will inhabit that are captured in our genomes and brains.

Significant epigenetic effects have been observed in orphanage-raised children who typically have low levels of nurturing. Naumova, et al. (2012) comparing children raised since birth in Russian orphanages with children raised by both biological parents, found that the orphanage-raised children had greater methylation of the HPA. They noted, "the presence and level of maternal care are highly responsible for the epigenetic regulation of genes involved in the control of the hypothalamic-pituitary-adrenal system" (Naumova, et al., 2012: 8). Likewise, Wismer-Fries et al. (2005) compared Romanian children raised in orphanages for an average of 16.6 months before being fostered into American families with a matched control group of children reared by both biological parents. The foster children showed significantly lower levels of vasopressin and oxytocin (hormones that help to regulate the HPA) than controls. This suggests epigenetic down-regulation of neuropeptide receptors in response to 16+ months of deprivation of attachment experiences (Schury & Kolassa, 2012).

Cicchetti et al. (2016) examined methylation patterns among school-aged low-income maltreated (n = 298) and non-maltreated (n = 250) children. All maltreated children had Child Protective Services (CPS) documented maltreatment (neglect, emotional, physical, or sexual abuse) experiences while non-maltreated children showed no history of maltreatment in CPS records. Only 17.1% of the mothers of maltreated children were married. The researchers found significant differences between the maltreated and non-maltreated children in methylation at multiple sites across the epigenome implicated in a wide variety of physical and mental health problems. Yurdakök (2014) remarks that methylation of the brain-derived neurotrophic factor (BDNF) gene, essential for synaptic plasticity, may account for the profound effects of childhood maltreatment. BDNF plays a vital role in neuronal growth, maturation, and maintenance, especially in neurons in the PFC. Maltreated children have elevated levels of BDNF gene methylation in the PFC compared to non-maltreated children. Methylated genes are identified by determining the amount of 5-methylcytosine they contain (Khodadadi et al., 2021). Boyce and Kobor (2015: 16) describe the overall message from epigenetics: "The adversities inherent within environments of poverty, neglect and trauma are transduced into molecular events controlling the expression of neuroregulatory genes, which in turn guide brain development, calibrate stress reactivity, and influence lifelong risks of psychopathology and other morbidities."

9 Rationality or Emotion: Which One Drives the Bus?

The Enlightenment and Rationality

If 100 criminologists were asked to boil down to a minimum of two individual-level causes they believed to be the most important in explaining the causes of criminal behavior, there would doubtless be a wide range of answers. Some would apply to rationality (purposeful choices, monetary gain, low cognitive abilities, etc.) and others to emotionality (low empathy, low fear, low self-control, etc.). However, almost all extant criminological theories pay little attention to the impact of positive emotions on their subject matter. Emotion is largely left to biopsychosocial theorists who engage with neurobiology and physiology. Although emotion has not been central to criminological theorizing, Walsh and Vaske (2015: 168) boiled them down to what they call "the natural enemies of crime": high fear and high empathy. Of course, these are preventative of crime, but their opposites—low fear and low empathy—are the "natural friends" of crime. They explain why these emotions prevent involvement in crime:

> Empathy is other-oriented and prevents one from committing acts injurious to others because one has an emotional and cognitive investment in the well-being of others. Fear is self-oriented and prevents one from committing acts injurious to others out of fear of the consequences to oneself. Many other prosocial tendencies flow from these two basic foundations, such as a strong conscience, altruism, self-control, and agreeableness.
>
> (Walsh & Vaske, 2015: 168)

To the extent that this assertion is empirically supported, emotions drive the behavioral bus. The idea that emotion may trump rationality in driving the behavioral bus is an affront to the Enlightenment idea that humans are rational animals. According to Immanuel Kant, emotions are "pathological," or as Gottfried Leibniz described them, "confused passions," (Solomon, 1977: 41). Most criminological theories assume that rationality is the primary guide of human behavior, which leads to an image of Mr. Spock-like

DOI: 10.4324/9781003662495-11

humans devoid of passion and relying only on cold rationality as a guide to behavior with emotions confusing the issue.

The Enlightenment philosopher David Hume almost alone believed that the human species should be called *Homo emovere* ("emotional man") rather than *Homo sapiens*. According to Hume, "we perceive a situation, experience emotions, pass judgment on the situation based on the emotion it evokes, and only then do we attempt to provide *post hoc* rational reasons for that judgment" (Walsh, 2014: 216). Emotional stimuli are highly relevant to human behavior because we often must quickly detect and react to events in our social relationships before we have time to reflect on them. We saw in Chapter 1 that Hume's position, that rationality is subordinate to emotion, is supported by neuroscience, and that emotion and cognition are integrated (like Plato's black and white horses) and operate simultaneously. We also saw, however, that when they conflict, emotion takes control of the bus.

Primary and Secondary Emotions

Emotions are divided into primary and secondary. Primary emotions are immediate visceral responses (anger, fear, disgust, etc.) to events or situations that narrow our focus. Secondary emotions are reactions to primary emotions, are more complex, and arise from higher cognitive processes. For instance, we may feel the secondary emotions of guilt or shame after directing anger toward someone. However, the extent to which we feel them is influenced by many factors, such as our temperaments and socialization experiences. The terms "primary" and "secondary" do not denote levels of importance; both are important to functional human relationships. Fear, anger, and disgust focus our attention on an immediate unpleasant situation and narrow our responses toward alleviating it. Anger at some injustice may prevent similar injustices in the future; fear and disgust motivate escape and avoidance, and joy is a feeling of experiencing an unexpectedly pleasant outcome. In evolutionary environments, this would have meant encountering situations that impacted fitness, such as finding new food and water resources and sexual opportunities, motivating our ancestors to seek similar rewarding situations.

Social emotions such as shame, embarrassment, and guilt are mixtures of primary emotions that broaden rather than narrow our focus, and are vital to social life. Whereas primary emotions are visceral and experienced consciously or subconsciously, social emotions are feelings that cognitively interpret them ("I was angry; now I feel guilty about it"). Social emotions evolved as essential parts of our social intelligence because they provide cues about the kinds of relationships (cooperative vs. uncooperative) we are likely to have with others. Social emotions such as empathy and guilt adjust our social behavior by arousing, focusing, and modifying brain activity in ways that habitually lead most people to choose prosocial responses in social situations. They are moral emotions that "function as an emotional moral barometer by providing immediate and salient feedback on our social and moral acceptability. That is, when we sin, transgress, or err, aversive feelings of shame, guilt, or embarrassment are likely to ensue" (Tangney, Stuewig, & Mashek 2007: 347). The alarm bells sounded by the social emotions prompt most people to attend to long-term consequences rather than surrender to the temptations of the moment.

Because others typically react negatively toward those who violate prosocial norms, it is adaptive to have evolved social emotions to monitor and restrain antisocial impulses by evoking self-reflection and evaluation of behavior. If we do something harmful to others, it is socially functional for us to be motivated to take remedial action. Guilt involves anxiety, remorse, and concern about how one's actions have negatively impacted others. Guilt is psychologically punitive and motivates both avoidance and approach behavior because it motivates us to avoid transgression in the future. It also motivates approach behavior by moving us toward apologies, promises, and restitution. Guilt is positively related to empathy since we are unlikely to feel bad about offending others if we don't "feel their pain" (Silfver & Helkama, 2007). Social emotions are integral to understanding criminal behavior because they are the components of conscience. The bite of conscience keeps us on the straight and narrow, and the relative lack of bite grants permission to criminals to prey on others.

The Autonomic Nervous System and Conscience

Conscience is an inner self-regulatory mechanism that informs us that it is wrong to harm others and right to behave well toward them. It is a sort of mental self-knowledge or self-assessment of the kind of person we are. The voice is strong in some people and weak to nonexistent in others. It is an emotional voice from the limbic system informed by cognitive content engaged when what we are doing or thinking about doing does not conform to learned moral standards of right and wrong. Charles Darwin asserted that conscience is based on "the social instincts [social emotions]—the prime principle of man's moral constitution—with the aid of active intellectual powers and the effects of habit, naturally lead to the golden rule" (1981: 106). Thus, for Darwin, conscience is a combination of cognitive faculties providing information about what is morally right or wrong and the affective faculties that we "feel." Conscience may only concern the subjective dimension of morality since it can lead one to opposite conclusions. However, we are only concerned with conscience as it affects behaving or contemplating behaving in ways that harm others.

Robert Levenson remarks: "When it comes to emotion, all roads lead to the autonomic nervous system (ANS). Whether it is the generation, expression, experience, or recognition of emotion, the role of the ANS is critical" (2014: 100). Each emotional episode we experience involves ANS activity, and the strength of an emotion depends on both innate temperament and classical conditioning factors. The ANS coordinates a complex network of nerves, organs, and sensors distributed throughout the body. It is a control system that functions unconsciously to automatically maintain homeostasis in the viscera, such as the heart, lungs, kidneys, and other internal organs. However, we are only concerned with its role in determining the strength of the conscience.

The ANS has two branches: the sympathetic system ("fight or flight") and the parasympathetic system ("rest and digest"). When we perceive threats, networks associated with the amygdala signal the sympathetic branch to release epinephrine and norepinephrine to dilate the pupils and lungs and increase heart rate. The changes mobilize the body for action (to fight, flee, or freeze). When the threat is over, the parasympathetic system restores the body to normal functioning. Our discussion of human nature revealed that we are not born with an innate desire to behave as others would like us to. Nothing matters to infants except their immediate desires, and toddlers throw temper tantrums, strike out, and take whatever they want when the urge strikes them. Parents must tame the raw energy of the Freudian id and teach their children to behave in socially acceptable ways. They do this by providing consequences for their actions in the socialization process. The extent to which this is successful depends on parents' ability and willingness to monitor their children's behavior, the warmth of the attachment relationship, and how effectively children have been reinforced for good behavior and punished for bad behavior.

However, the best childhood predictor of how well it learns moral lessons is the physiology it brings to the socialization process (Choy, Farrington, & Raine, 2015). The child's ratio of rewards to punishments engages operant conditioning, but classical conditioning is most salient in the early stages of conscience development (Choy, Farrington, & Raine, 2015). Classical conditioning is passive and visceral in contrast to operant conditioning, which forms mental associations between behavior and its consequences. Classical conditioning forms subconscious associations between behavior and visceral responses. The cornerstone of conscience is the unpleasant guilt or shame felt after transgressing because it dissuades us from such acts in the future. However, these feelings are not equally unpleasant for everyone. How well moral lessons are learned depends not only on parental efforts but also on the level of ANS arousal—how quickly and how strongly it reacts to clues of imminent disciplinary responses to transgression. Choy, Farrington, and Raine (2015, p. 190) explain the route from low ANS arousal to conscience:

> Lower levels of arousal cause poorer conditioning to environmental stimuli. It is assumed that the strength of the conscience depends on passive avoidance conditioning by parents. Impaired conditioning may result in the absence of or decrease in anticipatory anxiety regarding the consequences of a criminal or antisocial act, which causes a weak conscience.

ANS arousal thresholds are often measured by heart rate. A low resting heart rate (< 60 beats per minute) has been called the "best-replicated biological correlate of antisocial behavior in child and adolescent populations" (Ortiz & Raine, 2004, p. 159). Choy, Farrington, and Raine (2015: 194) report that "lower heart rate was strongly and consistently associated with active disregard reflected by negative and aggressive responses to others' distress and higher heart rate was associated with greater empathy and likelihood of intervening to help." People with a high resting heart rate (RHR) within the normal healthy range are more affected by stress, and thus it is not surprising that they are more empathetic than people with low resting heart rates (Lischke et al., 2018). A low resting heart rate is one of the most consistent biological correlates of antisocial behavior, with meta-analyses highlighting that the relationship exists among both children and adolescents (Ortiz & Raine, 2004; Portnoy & Farrington, 2015). Increasing evidence from longitudinal studies also suggests that lower RHR is associated with crime in adulthood after adjusting for a wide range of physical, socioeconomic, and psychiatric confounders (de Looff et al., 2022; Gao, Huang, & Li, 2017).

ANS arousal measures are normally distributed, with most individuals clustered around the mean. Individuals situated toward the *hyper*arousable tail of the distribution are easily aroused by punishment cues (fear) and will thus avoid behaving in ways that signal those cues. They learn their prosocial lessons well because arousal produces punishing visceral feelings indicative of anxiety, fear, guilt, and shame (rapid heart rate, flushing, "butterflies" in the stomach). If hyperarousable children contemplate behaving in ways contrary to parental expectations, memories of the consequences they experienced when they behaved badly in the past flood the amygdala to engage the ANS, producing anxiety or fear. When they subconsciously decide not to act on their impulse, the parasympathetic system engages to restore the ANS to homeostasis, which amounts to physiological reinforcement (reward) for conforming behavior. Barkow (1989: 121) describes the emotional component of the conscience as an involuntary "limbic system override" that adjusts our behavior in conforming ways.

Thus, the degree to which the sympathetic ANS is activated in the face of threat and/or the speed at which the parasympathetic returns the body to homeostasis is the primary determinant of conscience development (Gao et al., 2010). The development of conscience involves more than cognitive mechanisms since a developed conscience typically moves us to do the "right" thing before we have had an opportunity to cognitively assess our options (Barkow's "limbic system override"). People with strong moral consciences habitually ignore criminal opportunities; they do not consciously calculate cost/benefit ratios before doing so. Rational contemplation provides the content of our conscience; that is, the lessons we learn relate to what things we should feel guilty, ashamed, and embarrassed about, and what things we should feel good about, but the conscience's strength, power, and resilience are provided by emotion.

Conscience is thus the cooperative output of limbic emotional and prefrontal rational cognitive mechanisms that enable us to internalize the moral norms of our society. Simply being cognitively aware of what is right or wrong is not enough; that knowledge must be paired with emotional salience for it to be effective. Even the worst criminals of sound mind know the rational words of the social contract, but their poor emotional voices render them unsuited for the social choir. Individuals with a strong conscience will feel guilt, shame, and anxiety when they violate social norms, but those with a weak conscience will not experience these emotions. As Kochanska and Aksan (2004: 304) put it, "An impaired conscience is the core aspect of conduct disorders, antisocial development, and psychopathy. Conversely, the capacity for remorse and empathy, an appreciation of right and wrong, and engaging in behavior compatible with rules all mark successful adaptation."

Several studies have shown that males living in criminogenic environments who remain free of their influence show hyperactive ANS arousal under conditions of threat (Lacourse et al., 2006). Youths with highly reactive ANSs reared in criminogenic environments are less likely to commit antisocial acts than youths with hyporeactive ANS arousal levels reared in non-criminogenic environments (Brennan et al., 1997). A longitudinal study of a birth cohort found that measures of poor ANS conditioning (measured electrodermally) at age 3 successfully predicted criminal offending (official records) at age 23, independent of controls for several social adversities (Gao et al., 2010). Moffitt and Walsh (2003) attribute hyperactive ANSs to those rare individuals who abstained from antisocial behavior altogether during adolescence. Individuals with hypoactive ANSs, on the other hand, are not viscerally reinforced for conforming behavior because they are not aroused to fear in the first place and thus do not receive reinforcement for conforming behavior by way of a return to ANS homeostasis.

It is not news that criminals have poorly developed consciences. Most do not feel guilt or shame when inflicting harm on others. They are cognitively aware that their activities violate standards of moral decency but don't care or can neutralize any feelings that may prevent their antisocial activities. Many follow their nefarious lifestyle without experiencing pangs of conscience because they have faulty pathways connecting their brain's rational and emotional networks. For neuroscientists, this is the defining characteristic of chronic criminals and psychopaths (Patrick, 2022). Psychopaths know what is right and wrong as well as the rest of us, but poorly integrated rational and emotional systems do not activate the appropriate emotions, which leads them to discount that knowledge and to behave according to the call of immediate self-gratification.

Using diffusion tensor imaging (DTI), Craig et al. (2009) analyzed the structural integrity of neuropathways integrating the rational and emotional systems. They used a sample of violent criminal inmates and control inmates matched for IQ. Hare's Psychopathy Checklist Revised (PCL-R) was used, with scores ranging between 25 and 34. They examined the uncinate fasciculus (UF), a white matter tract connecting the anterior temporal lobes (where the amygdala is located) with the frontal lobes. Significant correlations were obtained between PCL-R factor 2 scores and tract volume in the left and right UF ($r = -0.88$). Psychopaths (PCL-R score 30 or higher) had significantly reduced fractional anisotropy (FA) in the right UC. FA is a measure ranging from zero (isotropy) to 1 (anisotropy), providing information about water diffusion along myelinated axons. Isotropy is random movement in all directions, and anisotropy is directional and non-random. Higher FA values thus signal greater integrity of the connections between brain areas. Significantly reduced mean FA values were found in the right UF between psychopaths and controls ($p = 0.003$). Craig et al. conclude: "Taken together, our findings suggest that abnormal connectivity in the amygdala-OFC limbic network may contribute to the neurobiological mechanisms underpinning the impulsive, antisocial behaviour and emotional detachment associated with psychopathy" (2009: 950) Another study of prison inmates with PLC-R scores ranging from 5 to 36 found PCL-R scores to be significantly inversely related in a graded fashion to right UC FA scores and that psychopaths had significantly lower UF FA than inmates with lower psychopathy scores (Wolf et al., 2015).

Decety et al. (2013) examined incarcerated males classified as high on psychopathy (PCL-R $\geq$ 30; $n = 37$), intermediate (between 21 and 29; $n = 44$), and low ($\leq$ 20; $n = 40$). Inmates were scanned using fMRI while viewing images of bodily injuries and asked to imagine either themselves or others suffering those injuries. Imagining themselves injured, those scoring high showed a normal response in the anterior insula ($r = .372$) and the right amygdala, indicating awareness of their imagined suffering. However, when asked to imagine others similarly suffering, they showed blunted activation in the emotional and rational brain areas (anterior insula, amygdala, and frontal cortex), indicating a lack of empathetic care for others. Furthermore, PCL-R scores correlated with response in the ventral striatum—part of the brain's reward system ($r = .212$) among inmates with high PCL-R scores when imagining others' suffering. Psychopaths are thus not only deficient in empathy but also feel callous pleasure when imagining the pain of others.

Empathy and Callous-Unemotionality

Empathy is the cognitive and emotional ability to understand and identify with the feelings and distress of others and has been described as the social emotion par excellence (Pfattheicher, Sassenrath, & Keller, 2019). As a form of compassionate relatedness, empathy is a potent inhibitor of victimizing behavior and an important facilitator of social cooperation. Empathy is an ancient capacity that predates the arrival of *Homo sapiens* by millions of years and evolved rapidly in mammals in the context of parental care (de Waal, 2008). Shirtcliff et al. (2009: 140) note: "The ontogenetic roots of empathy likely arose within the mammalian brain to support social bonds between a mother and child." The affiliative circuitry of empathy is stronger in females than males (Swain et al., 2007). The prolonged and intensive infant care required by our species is doubtless why females are universally found to be more empathetic than males (Silke et al., 2018), and high female empathy goes a long way in explaining why they are less antisocial than males. Because most people feel distressed when they witness the distress of others, the empathy neurocircuitry produces an affective resonance between self and others and urges us to take steps to alleviate that distress. When we do, we thereby alleviate our own distress. Empathy channels altruistic behavior in social species because it is a response mode by which conspecifics can rapidly assess a situation without relying on time-consuming conscious reflection to determine the appropriate response.

Empathy has a significant genetic component. Affective empathy has stronger genetic effects than cognitive empathy because the latter involves learning. Melchers et al. (2016) found heritability estimates for affective empathy between 0.52 and 0.57 among MZ, DZ, and sibling pairs of adults but an average estimate of only 0.27 for cognitive empathy. A meta-analysis of the genetics of empathy (Abramson et al., 2020) found that genetics accounted for an average of 48.3% of the variance in emotional empathy and 26.9% in cognitive empathy. All the remaining variance in emotional empathy was accounted for by non-shared environment and measurement error, whereas shared environment accounted for 9.2% of the variance in cognitive empathy. The heritability differences between the two components of empathy may be explained by the fact that emotional empathy is more tied to innate temperament and physiology, such as emotional reactivity and regulation, and cognitive empathy has a much larger learned component (Abramson et al., 2020). Parent–child relationship quality—determined by warmth, attachment security, and consistent discipline practices—is robustly linked to the development of a child's cognitive empathy and fine-tuning of its emotional empathy (Waller & Hyde, 2018).

Callous unemotionality (CU) is in many ways the opposite of empathy. It is composed of such attitudes as apathy, coldness, and indifference to others, and in children, it is a key precursor of adult psychopathy (Hyde & Dotterer, 2022). CU traits are consistently linked to reduced amygdala fear responses to socio-affective cues, such as viewing the fearful expressions of others (Cardinale et al., 2021; Dugré et al., 2020). A meta-analysis revealed statistically significant moderate-to-large negative associations between measures of CU traits and empathy ($r = -0.57$), guilt ($r = -0.40$), and prosociality ($r = -0.66$) (Waller et al., 2020). CU youths are deficient in social emotions, but not in primary emotions, as Waller et al. (2020: 9) note,

> whereas youth high on CU traits are "unemotional" in response to others' distress (i.e., low empathic arousal or concern), they exhibit strong and wide-ranging emotions in other contexts, including showing anger when their goals are frustrated or joy after breaking the rules and getting away with it.

Bezdjian et al. (2011) found heritability estimates for CU traits to be 0.64 for males and 0.49 for females in a sample of 605 twin pairs. Nonshared environmental effects of 0.36 for boys and 0.44 for girls were observed, implying zero shared environment effects for boys but 7% for girls. "One of the nurture risk factors that has been most studied specifically with regard to CU traits is parenting. A growing body of literature links harsh parenting and parenting that is low in warmth and involvement to CU traits" (Hyde & Dotterer, 2022: 549). However, they also note that the association between parenting and CU traits could exist because parents and children share common genes (passive rGE), and harsh parenting may reflect parents' CU traits. Alternatively, they suggest that children's CU traits elicit negative reactions from their parents (evocative rGE). It has been shown that harsh parenting is moderated by parental risk for CU, especially among children with elevated genetic risk for CU themselves (Trentacosta et al., 2019).

Low Fear

Low fear is the second leg of Walsh and Vaske's (2015) minimal two individual-level causes of crime and its prevention. Low ANS arousal is a marker of fearlessness and predisposes individuals to engage in crime. Cardinale, Ryan, and Marsh (2020: 41) remark:

> Lack of negative arousal during transgressions that result in punishment in children with fearless temperaments is believed to prevent the development of guilt and empathy in response to such transgressions and ultimately lead to the development of CU traits and antisocial behavior.

Brain imaging studies find deficient fear conditioning to be associated with altered regional brain function in the amygdala and anterior cingulate cortex in adult antisocial individuals (Cohn et al., 2013). Youths with CU are often found to have bold and fearless temperaments and low fear may be expected to lead to high levels of approach behavior, reward dominance, and low sensitivity to punishment (Berluti, Ploe, & Marsh, 2023; Trentacosta et al., 2019).

Anne Campbell's (1999) *staying alive* hypothesis provides a fear-based evolutionary explanation for sex differences in criminality. It involves sex-differentiated biology relevant to parental investment and has been characterized as: "Perhaps the best attempt to account for gender differences in criminality" (Roach & Pease, 2013: 66). For instance, Ellis, Beaver, and Wright (2009) surveyed over 500 studies from around the world and found that males are invariably more involved in all crimes and other forms of antisocial behavior than females. Campbell's (1999) hypothesis proposes that ancestral human females had less to gain from taking risks and more to lose. Each child represents an enormous investment in time and energy for females that they will not relinquish without the most compelling reasons. Infants' dependence on their mothers means a mother's presence is more critical to their survival than a father's. The practice of keeping nursing children close in ancestral environments posed an elevated risk to mother and child if the mother placed herself in risky situations.

The evolved mechanism to avoid doing so is the propensity for females to perceive more situations as fearful and avoid them than males. This accounts for the tendency of females to avoid potentially violent situations and to employ indirect and low-risk strategies in dispute resolution. Experimental risk studies show that females experience fear more readily and strongly than males whether assessed in early childhood, the school years, or among adults across cultures. A meta-analysis of 150 such studies found that sex differences were greater when the risk involved means carrying out a behavioral response rather than simply responding to hypothetical scenarios that only involved cognitive appraisals of possible risk (Byrnes, Miller, & Schafer, 1999).

The female HPA axis is activated faster than males when stressed. Estrogen increases the stress responses of the HPA axis, while testosterone dampens it (Heck & Handa, 2019). Lee et al. (2009) found that males had less activity in the insula and orbitofrontal cortex (OFC) than females when making risky decisions. The insula brings signals from the amygdala and HPA axis into cognitive awareness in the OFC to guide decision-making. The OFC is responsible for anticipating and assessing rewards and punishments, regulating emotions, and anticipating and evaluating rewards and punishments. They also showed that punishment had less impact on how male brains processed future risky decisions than female brains. Raine et al. (2011) found the OFC to be about 12% smaller in males than females and that sex differences in the OFC volume explained 65.9% of the variance in sex differences in self-reported antisocial behavior. This suggests that female brains function better at regulating negative emotional signals or that male brains may be less sensitive to threatening stimuli and less easily integrate emotional information and signals from the amygdala into their decision-making processes.

Meyer-Bahlburg et al. (2006) found that males with the low-activity allele of the MAOA gene had less connectivity between the OFC and amygdala, compared to females with the low-activity allele and males with the high-activity allele. Lower connectivity between the OFC and amygdala may prevent the OFC from receiving signals sent from the amygdala, and emotional signals of fear may not reach the OFC, thus inhibiting males from engaging in antisocial behavior. Campbell (2006) notes that studies have shown that females report higher levels of fear of physical threats and that females' fear of retaliation and feelings of guilt may prevent them from engaging in aggressive behavior.

Fear is a vital, evolved instinctive response to danger; if we didn't experience it, we wouldn't be able to take steps to protect ourselves from threats. As Lykken (1995: 144) explains this vital function: "Like the ability to experience pain, the fear mechanism is especially useful early in life before the individual's judgment and reason are sufficiently dependable guides to behavior." Fear is useful to guide children's behavior in the desired direction before their cognitive understanding of what kinds of behavior are expected of them. On the other hand, low fear makes it difficult to appreciate dangers. It gives rise to the tendency to take risks and favor an approach over avoidance behavior in potentially rewarding situations. Bush, Lengua, & Colder (2010: 358) found that in socially disorganized neighborhoods, the impact of parental socialization depends on children's fear levels. They remark:

> [P]oorly socially organized neighborhoods predicted worse prosocial adjustment only for low-fear children just as poor relationships with mothers were related to poor conscience development only for low-fear children. Fearful children are more likely to be socially competent than their low-fear peers. It may be that the superior conscience development associated with higher fear is protective against the detrimental effects of poor neighborhood social organization on social competence.

Of course, when we speak of fear, we mean a normally distributed range of levels. Excessive fearfulness can have many negative consequences. It can lead people to never step out of their comfort zone to take mildly risky chances to better their lives and can lead to anxiety disorders if fear overwhelms them. As with many other things, fear engages Aristotle's Golden Mean. For Aristotle, an appropriate balanced fear level lies between extremes of too much fear (cowardice) and too little (recklessness).

Section 3

Issues of Crime Causation

10 Social Learning Versus Social and Self-Control Theories

Broad Assumptions of the Theories

There are two major interconnected fault lines in criminology. We have discussed the rift based on sociopolitical ideology (hard left versus moderate liberalism or conservatism); the second plays out among traditional criminologists and is based on assumptions about human nature. These are social learning and control theories. The connection between these two fault lines is that criminologists who favor control theories tend to identify as conservatives and moderates, and criminologists who favor the social learning tradition identify themselves as liberals and radicals (Cooper, Walsh, & Ellis, 2010). According to Pratt, Gau, and Franklin (2010), scholars from the social control and social learning traditions vehemently disagree on many issues relating to crime and criminals. Both traditions emphasize learning but disagree about what is to be learned. Social learning theories maintain that people must learn to be antisocial, and control theories argue that people must learn to be prosocial.

Unlike in the hard sciences, where theories are abandoned if they fail to provide supporting data, few social science theories are abandoned but tend to get added to, repackaged, and renamed, such as Sutherland's differential association theory, morphing into Akers' social learning theory. Ward, McConaghy, and Bennett (2018) point out that disciplines progress via theoretical competition or integration. The problem with competition among theories in criminology is that "A modicum of truth can usually be found in each theory" (Akers & Sellers, 2013: 275), thus accounting for why they are not abandoned. Concerning the integration of social learning and control theories, Ward, McConaghy, and Bennett (2018: 511) remark: "Complicating integration efforts are the conflicting assumptions about human nature, which have been viewed as practicably irreconcilable." Social learning theory assumes the human mind is a blank slate at birth, and control theories assume the classical notion that humans have an innate nature that is inherently self-serving. As noted in Chapter 3, the latter view was held by all three founding fathers of sociology: Durkheim, Marx, and Weber.

DOI: 10.4324/9781003662495-13

Differential Association Theory

Sutherland's differential association theory (DAT) is the longest-lived learning theory. Sutherland's ambition was to develop a theory that could explain both individual criminality and aggregate crime rates by identifying conditions that must be present for crime to occur and are absent when crime is absent (Sutherland & Cressey, 1974). He stressed that the social context in which people are embedded determines how they will behave and attempted to provide mechanisms by which social context influences crime. DAT focuses on how people become delinquent via social definitions of reality and attitude formation. Definitions refer to the meaning experiences have for us and how our attitudes, values, and habitual ways of viewing the world are derived from them and are weakly or strongly embraced according to the frequency, duration, priority, and intensity of exposure to them.

DAT is a theory of peer influence, and the type of peer groups individuals have access to is contingent on the neighborhoods in which they reside. Delinquent peer groups convey their attitudes, values, motivations, and criminal techniques to group members. DAT argues that criminal conduct is learned by modeling oneself after and identifying with individuals we admire, respect, and value. It contains nine propositions, with the key being number 6, which reads: "A person becomes delinquent because of an excess of definitions favorable to violations of law over definitions unfavorable to violations of law." This proposition smacks of tautology because "an excess of definitions favorable to violations of law" and "delinquent" are the same; if we know one, we automatically know the other in DAT's framework. However, this can be rectified by biopsychosocial insights that specify how and why some in the same environment learn more definitions favorable to law violation than others via G*x*E and rGE processes. Walsh and Jorgensen (2020: 126) explain DAT by noting that humans, like chameleons, take on the hues and colors of their environments, blending in and conforming with natural ease:

> Most Americans probably like baseball, hot dogs, apple pie, and Chevrolets, as a Chevrolet commercial used to remind us. But do we prefer these things over, say, soccer, bratwurst, strudel, and Volkswagens because the former are demonstrably superior to the latter or simply because we are Americans and not Germans? We view the world differentially according to the attitudes, beliefs, and expectations of the groups around which our lives revolve; it could hardly be otherwise, particularly during our formative years. Sutherland's basic premise is that delinquent behavior is learned just as readily as we learn to play the games we enjoy, the food we eat, and the cars we drive, which are integral parts of our cultural lives.

Sutherland rejected individual differences in his later work but recognized them in an earlier work by noting that they affect relationship patterns:

"Individual differences among people in respect to personal characteristics or social situations cause crime only as they affect differential association or frequency and consistency of contacts with criminal patterns" (1939, p. 8). That is, differential association *intervenes* between individual traits at one end and criminal behavior at the other. Put otherwise, people self-select into delinquent and criminal groups, as numerous studies have recognized (Benedict, 2019; Schindler et al., 2021). Reviews of relationship patterns find that delinquent behavior *precedes* gang membership and that association with other like-minded individuals (rGE) simply speeds up and enhances delinquent behavior among those predisposed to it rather than being a stimulator of uncharacteristic behavior among the innocent. Flocking together in delinquent groups doubtless facilitates and accentuates delinquent activities but does not cause them. Ruth Kornhauser noted that Sutherland had an overly benign view of delinquents as "slum boys who become delinquent as nice friendly lads, available for indoctrination into the delinquent subcultures" (1978: 201).

Gottfredson (2006: 92) summarized several studies addressing this issue and noted: "The evidence is consistent with the proposition that much of the variance in peer effects on delinquency is attributable to the selection effect of like individuals associating together." TenEyck and Barnes (2015) found that once self-selection into different peer groups was accounted for, there was no significant direct influence of peer groups on delinquency. Nevertheless, it is undeniable that children associate with and become friends with children in neighborhoods that their parents provide for them. In socially disorganized neighborhoods, it is not unreasonable to assume that delinquent peers may cause delinquency among youths who are otherwise insulated from it, as well as accelerate it among youths who are attracted to it. The self-selection notion is valid for children in better neighborhoods with equal access to both prosocial and antisocial peers to select from, but not for those who grow up in the urban slums, where prosocial peers are rare. Even in those neighborhoods, Mark Warr (2002) distinguishes between private acceptance and compliance and notes that DAT has only private acceptance in mind and ignores the idea of mere compliance. Anderson's (1999) study of Black urban areas notes that "decent" families publicly comply with antisocial values ("code-switch") without privately accepting them. However, the neighborhood ambiance is set by "street" families who do.

Akers' Social Learning Theory

All meaningful behavioral learning is social, and social learning theory (SLT) seeks to elucidate the mechanisms by which it is. SLT is an extension of DAT associated primarily with Ronald Akers, who, with Robert Burgess (Burgess & Akers, 1966), added the concepts of operant psychology. They noted that operant principles amplify or extinguish behavior and that SLT rests on four principles: differential reinforcement, differential association, imitation, and definitions (as defined in DAT). Differential reinforcement is "the balance of anticipated or actual rewards and punishments that follow or are consequences of behavior" (Akers, 2011: 66–67). For some people, the balance of anticipated or actual rewards and punishments processes moves them in prosocial directions; for others, it moves them in antisocial directions, but the balance may fluctuate over time.

The most salient principle of SLT is differential reinforcement, which is that future behavior is governed by its past consequences. When we behave, we generate consequences that we interpret as positive or negative. Behavior is either positively reinforced, in which case it is likely to be repeated, or positively punished and will likely not be repeated. The most effective reinforcements and punishments are social and are derived primarily from one's intimate social groups, as one receives various forms of praise or admonition from others whose opinions we respect and value. Positive reinforcement may be instrumental (the loot from a burglary) or emotional (enhanced status from antisocial peers or the pure joy of successfully pulling off the burglary). Negative reinforcement occurs when an aversive condition is avoided or removed, such as the removal of the reputation of a coward when peers learn of one's daring crime. Both positive and negative reinforcement strengthen and amplify criminal behavior. Punishment leads to the weakening or elimination of behavior and can also be positive or negative. Positive punishment is the application of something undesirable, such as a prison term. Negative punishment is the removal of a pleasant stimulus, such as the loss of "street cred" in the neighborhood. Thus, from SLT's perspective, acquiring Sutherland's "definitions favorable" to antisocial behavior depends on an individual's history of reinforcement and punishment.

Each peer group member participates in the reinforcement/punishment process via the reciprocal effects each member has on their peers since it is them that hand out the cheers and boos. Of course, what is reinforcing for some may be punishing for others. For teens who value the approval of their parents and teachers, an arrest is experienced as punishment. However, for teens who value the approval of antisocial peers, an arrest is a reinforcer since it marks them officially as "badass." The social context is an important component of SLT because most learning occurs in the presence of others who provide both the social context and the available social reinforcements or punishments.

Discrimination is another key component of SLT. Discriminative stimuli are signals from others indicating what behavior may be rewarded or punished in a particular social context. Reinforcing or punishing stimuli *follow* a person's behavior, but discriminative stimuli precede behavior. Discrimination involves distinguishing between stimuli that have been reinforced or punished in the past and similar stimuli you expect will result in the same response in the future. An unlocked car with the keys present, for example, is a discriminative stimulus that signals "immediate reward" for a criminal, but signals only a careless driver for the average person.

The Neglect of Individual Differences

SLT adds to DAT by specifying how definitions favorable to law violation are learned through operant conditioning, but neglects individual differences in the ease or difficulty with which persons learn what kind of behavior is acceptable. All social behavior, including crime, is socially learned, but as Fox (2017: 25) observes, "This begs the question: why are some individuals more likely to associate or model antisocial peers, or feel reinforcement and rewards for their antisocial behavior?" Some people find hell-raising exciting and reinforcing and are more susceptible to short-term rewards. Others can appreciate the long-term rewards of behaving well because they can self-regulate. While the former are much more likely to be found in disadvantaged neighborhoods, it is not all about the environment. Many people in poor neighborhoods reject criminal activity, and some in more affluent neighborhoods embrace it.

But why are some people inclined to learn one thing, while others are inclined to learn other things, and what makes them succeed or fail in their learning endeavors? Cao (2004: 97) opines that SLT assumes "a passive and unintentional actor who lacks individuality and [is] better at explaining the transmission of criminal behavior than its origins." And, because of their "limited conception of human nature, learning theories generally also ignore the differential receptivity of individuals to criminal messages." Kornhauser likewise criticized learning theories as resting on the untenable assumptions that "man has no nature, socialization is perfectly successful, and cultural variability is unlimited" (1978: 34). If there is no human nature and "socialization is perfectly successful," the subculture in which delinquent values and norms are transmitted is deviant, not the individuals who conform to them. But humans do have a nature, and some individuals have genetic variations in that nature (differences in self-control, IQ, fearlessness, empathy, and so forth) that render them more ready to engage in antisocial behavior than others because of their personalities and will find such behavior is reinforced in delinquent areas. As Gwynn Nettler (1984: 295) put it, "Constitutions affect the impact of environment. What we learn and how well we learn it depends on constitution. The fire that melts the butter hardens the egg."

Akers denies that SLT ignores individual differences when he writes:

> An individual in a low crime group or category who is nevertheless more exposed to criminal associations, models, definitions, and reinforcement than someone in a high crime group or category will have a higher probability of committing criminal or deviant acts.
>
> (1999: 482)

However, this is an argument about different environments a person is exposed to, not about individuals. It assumes automaton-like individuals who enter environments at one end and emerge at the other end as criminal or non-criminal based on exposure to different "associations, models, definitions, and reinforcement" only, and it ignores the characteristics they bring with them to the environment.

Social Control/Bonding Theory

A peaceful and predictable social existence requires mechanisms designed to minimize nonconformity and deviance, which collectively are called social control. Social control may be direct, formal, and coercive, as exemplified by symbols of the state and the criminal justice system. Social control may be indirect and informal, which is preferable to the former because it leads to prosocial behavior regardless of the presence or absence of external coercion such as the possibility of arrest and imprisonment. Obeying society's rules of proper conduct because we believe the rules are right, not because we fear formal sanctions, means we have our own internalized police officer and judge in the form of a functioning conscience.

Travis Hirschi's (1969) social bond theory maintains that society's institutions are "good" and humans, in the absence of proper training, are "bad." Nettler (1984, p. 313) put the control argument colorfully: "If we grow up 'naturally,' without cultivation, like weeds, we grow up like weeds—rank." Development psychologists are virtually unanimous in support of this. They note that young children exhibit impulsive and aggressive behavior, which diminishes in time with proper socialization (Eme, 2015). Nettler's "weediness" is the natural outcome for children who are not properly socialized. A longitudinal study of children from 2 to 12 years of age found that the frequency of hitting, biting, and kicking peaked at 27 months and declined by about 66% by age 12 (Tremblay & LeMarquand, 2001). Tremblay (2008: 2619) sums up the literature on this issue: "By monitoring the development of physical aggression from infancy onwards, recent longitudinal studies show that human infants spontaneously use physical aggression and that humans learn not to physically aggress rather than learn to aggress." Toddlers are too young to have learned antisocial definitions and are not associating with deviant peers, so their aggressive and impulsive behavior must be innate. From this perspective, criminals are simply toddlers who have failed to learn to control their natural impulses.

Social bonding/control theory concentrates on the role of social relationships that bind people to the social order. This is the classical view of human nature, which maintains that antisocial behavior will emerge automatically if controls are lacking; it needs no motivating factors because humans are assumed to be naturally self-centered. The classical assumption of self-interested people seeking pleasure and trying to avoid pain is foundational to the theory. It attempts to account for why some people pursue their self-interest in legitimate ways and others do not. Prosocial socialization practices produce individuals capable of reining in their natural impulses, and poor socialization practices do not. Hirschi formulated his theory with some foundational facts about the "typical" criminal. The typical criminal is a young male who grew up in a fatherless home in an urban slum, is poorly educated, and is unemployed. From this, he deduced that those most likely to commit crimes lack the four elements of the social bond that form the foundation of prosocial behavior: attachment, commitment, involvement, and belief.

Attachment is the emotional component of conformity and refers to the emotional bonds between the individual and key social institutions, particularly the family. Attachment to prosocial others, particularly to parents, provides the foundation for all other social bonds because it leads us to feel valued, respected, and admired and to value the favorable judgments of those who made us feel that way. Much of our behavior is an attempt to gain favorable judgments from people and groups we care about. A lack of attachment to parents and respect for their rules spills over into a lack of attachment and respect for other social groups. Much of the controlling power of others outside the family lies in the threat of reporting misbehavior to parents. If the child has little respect for parents, the control exercised by others has little effect because parental control has minimal effect. As Hirschi (1969: 127) explains, "If a person feels no emotional attachment to a person or institution, the rules tend to be denied legitimacy." Of course, people can be emotionally attached to deviant parents and peers, and thus their deviant behavior can be viewed as conforming to deviant expectations. This is the sort of criticism social learning theories might level. However, Hirschi explicitly refers to attachment to prosocial others to explain prosocial behavior, not to all attachments that may lead to antisocial behaviors (Pratt, Gau, & Franklin, 2010). Additionally, attachment to antisocial others does not produce the other elements of the social bond: commitment, involvement, and a prosocial belief system.

Commitment is the rational component of conformity and refers to a lifestyle in which one has invested considerable time and energy pursuing a lawful career. People who invest heavily in a conventional career have a valuable stake in conformity and are unlikely to risk it by engaging in antisocial behavior. School dropouts and unemployed adults lack investment in conventional behavior and thus risk less by committing crimes. Acquiring a stake in conformity requires a disciplined application to tasks children do not necessarily relish but complete to gain approval from their parents and teachers. Attachment is thus the essential foundation for commitment to a prosocial lifestyle.

Involvement is a direct consequence of commitment and an overall conventional pattern of social existence. Involvement is a matter of time and energy constrictions by the demands of our lawful activities that reduce exposure to illegal opportunities. Conversely, idleness or non-involvement in conventional activities increases the possibility of exposure to antisocial activities. As Hirschi put it: "Idle hands are the devil's workshop" (1969: 187).

Belief is the moral component of social conformity and is the acceptance of conventional morality. People lacking social bonds tend not to accept moral norms and are concerned only with narrow self-interest. Unlike DAT and SLT, social control theory does not view a criminal belief system as motivating criminal behavior. Rather, criminals act according to their urges and then justify or rationalize their behavior with statements such as "Do unto others as they would do unto you—only do it first." Control theorists maintain that behavior gives birth to the belief rather than the belief giving birth to the behavior. It should be noted that crime is not motivated by the absence of these social bonds; their absence merely represents social deficiencies that result in a reduction of the perceived potential costs of committing a crime.

Self-Control Theory

With Michael Gottfredson, Hirschi added self-control to criminology's pantheon of theories. Self-control is defined as the "extent to which [different people] are vulnerable to the temptations of the moment" (Gottfredson & Hirschi, 1990: 87). The theory maintains that crime results from unrestrained natural human impulses to gain pleasure and avoid pain. These impulses often lead to crimes when the opportunity arises, which Gottfredson and Hirschi (1990) define as "acts of force or fraud undertaken in pursuit of self-interest" (p. 15). Most crimes and analogous behaviors (e.g., alcohol or drug abuse, DUI, casual sex) are spontaneous acts requiring little skill or motivation and earn the individual immediate short-term satisfaction. People with low self-control lack patience, persistence, and diligence and are oriented to the present rather than to the future, and crime affords them quick and easy ways to obtain money, sex, revenge, etc. Their low self-control leads them to take risks that they find exciting, and their extreme egoism allows them to take what they want without experiencing pangs of guilt for causing the suffering of others (Gottfredson & Hirschi, 1990: 89–90).

Self-control theory maintains that low self-control is established by incompetent parenting during early childhood and tends to persist throughout life. It also avers that children *do not* learn low self-control, but rather, they learn self-control; low self-control is the default outcome that occurs in the absence of proper socialization. Brannigan (1997: 425) notes that: "In the absence of interaction designed to promote empathy, identification, delayed gratification, a long-time horizon, and prosocial values, the infant appears to exhibit older evolutionary scripts of adaptation which favor immediate gratification and egoism." To produce self-control in offspring requires parental warmth, nurturance, vigilance, and a willingness to practice "tough love." Effective parenting requires consistent and fair discipline when a child misbehaves. Overly harsh, overly permissive, or erratic discipline is unlikely to produce self-control. Factors that may result in low self-control include parental criminality (criminals are not very successful socializing agents), family size (the bigger the family, the more difficult it is to monitor children's behavior), single-parent families (two parents are generally better than one), and working mothers (who negatively impact the development of self-control if no positive substitute monitors are provided and children are left to their own devices) (Gottfredson & Hirschi, 1990).

Gottfredson and Hirschi argue that children acquire or fail to acquire self-control during the first decade of life, after which the attained level of control remains stable across the life course. Subsequent experiences, situations, and circumstances have little independent effect on the probability of offending. Because low self-control is a stable component of a criminal personality, most criminals fail in things that require long-term commitment, such as school, employment, or marriage, because such commitments impede the immediate satisfaction of their desires. Self-control is imperative for prosocial behavior, but self-control is not a motivator of behavior; it is a brake, not an accelerator.

Low self-control alone is not sufficient to account for offending. Gottfredson and Hirschi consider self-control to be stable across the life course, so variation in self-control cannot explain criminal behavior. What explains the variation in criminal behavior among low self-control individuals is the variation in *opportunities* to commit it. A criminal opportunity is "a situation that presents itself to someone with low self-control by which he or she can immediately satisfy needs with minimal mental or physical effort" (Gottfredson & Hirschi, 1990: 12–13). Self-control theory is like routine activities theory: Crime results when people with low self-control (a motivated offender) meet a criminal opportunity (a suitable target lacking a capable guardian). The difference is that the low self-control theory emphasizes the motivated offender and ignores the target and guardian, whereas the routine activities theory does the opposite.

Gottfredson and Hirschi illustrate the intersection of low self-control and opportunity by describing typical criminal incidents not as the culmination of foresight and planning, but as situational opportunities observed by someone ready to take advantage of them. Both social control and self-control theories assume a natural inclination to pursue selfish interests with little effort and without regard for others, and both maintain that what distinguishes law-abiding people from criminals is the control that prevents the former from acting on their natural impulses. Hirschi (2004: 543) recognized this by noting that, like self-control, "differences in social control are stable, that social control and self-control are the same thing." He unites the two theories in two sentences: "Self-control is the set of inhibitions one carries with one wherever one goes. Their character may be initially described by going to the elements of the bond identified by social control theory: attachment, commitment, involvement, and belief" (2004: 543–544). Hirschi now says that self-control and the social control exercised by others in the family, school, and workplace mutually affect one another constantly across the life course and that self-control and social control theories are now integrated.

If we combine both theories as Hirschi did, more criminologists in the Cooper, Walsh, and Ellis (2010) survey checked it as the theory that best explains serious criminal behavior than any other. Matt DeLisi (2011: 103) calls self-control theory the "T-Rex of criminology," stating that "in terms of empirical tests of its theoretical ideas, citations, [and] influence on the field, self-control theory is 'peerless.'" A meta-analysis of 150 studies (n = 215,212) examining self-regulation in childhood and subsequent achievements and behaviors found that low self-control in childhood produces many adverse outcomes in later childhood, adolescence, and adulthood. In addition to things such as academic achievement and mental and physical health, low self-control was positively related to aggressive and criminal behavior and alcohol and drug abuse at a mean age of 36.5 (Robson, Allen, & Howard, 2020). The classic self-control experiment included in this meta-analysis is the "marshmallow test" in which 600 preschoolers were told they may eat a marshmallow placed before them immediately or wait 15 minutes and be rewarded with another. Follow-up studies of some of the children in their adolescence found robust correlations between delay time before succumbing to temptation and outcomes associated with SES such as SAT scores and thinking and planning for the future (Shoda, Mischel, & Peake, 1990).

Casey et al. (2011) brain-scanned 26 original participants in the marshmallow test in their mid-40s and found that self-control levels remained stable. High delayers more strongly activated regions in the prefrontal cortex than impulsive low delayers, and low delayers showed more activity in the ventral striatum, an area involved in desire and reward processing. Thus, the approach system is stronger in low delayers, and the avoidance system is stronger in high delayers. A study (Moffitt et al., 2011) correlated reward delay levels of 1,000 children between the ages of 3 and 11 with life outcomes at age 32, such as substance abuse, health status, criminal conviction, giving birth out-of-wedlock, financial problems, and adult SES. Controlling for childhood SES and IQ, all outcomes were more positive for those who demonstrated the ability to delay gratification as children than those who did not.

Child Effects and Genetics

Gottfredson and Hirschi's theory attributes variation in self-control solely to variation in parental behavior and ignores child effects. The child development literature is unequivocal in asserting that socialization is a two-way street in which parental behavior is shaped by the evocative behavior (evocative rGE) of their children, just as children's behavior is shaped by their parents (Kuo et al., 2021). Children bring self-control levels with them to the socialization process, rather than socialization alone producing variable levels. Lilly, Cullen, and Ball (2007: 110) point this out: "Research suggests that parents may affect levels of self-control less by their parenting styles and more by genetic transmission." This is supported by many studies that have found a strong genetic and neurobiological component to low self-control (Javakhishvili & Vazsonyi, 2022; Wright & Beaver, 2012). A meta-analysis of 31 twin studies found the heritability of self-control to be 0.60 (Willems et al., 2019).

The primary gene product underlying self-control has been consistently found to be poor serotonergic functioning (Boisvert et al., 2018).

This does not mean that parenting is irrelevant. Indeed, loving and conscientious parenting means more than anything else for the healthy development of prosocial children. However, a more sophisticated level of understanding of self-control is needed, which requires genetically informed samples and the assessment of the influence of children's evocative behavior on parenting behavior. For instance, Belsky and Beaver (2011) examined several alleles in the dopaminergic and serotonergic systems associated with antisocial behavior and low self-control. They found significant interactions between parenting quality and self-control among 1,588 youths (754 males and 832 females). Males raised in homes with strong parenting qualities showed moderate to excellent self-control depending on their genetic risk; that is, children with a genetic tendency for low self-control may not display it if effectively parented, and children with a genetic propensity for high self-control may not display it if they are inadequately socialized: nature and nurture are of equal importance. This effect was not seen for females, which they explain thus: "Perhaps females are simply more easily socialized, so parenting affects the self-regulation of all girls to the same extent irrespective of their genetic make-up" (Belsky & Beaver, 2011: 624). Studies of gender differences in self-control have shown, without exception, that females have higher levels of self-control than males, regardless of the methods used, or the culture, race/ethnicity, or age of subjects (Chapple & Johnson, 2007).

In sum, there is a "modicum of truth" in both learning and control theories; the primary difference is where they place the emphasis. Learning theory must address the question of why some individuals are more likely than others to respond to negative life experiences with antisocial behavior and why they are more likely to self-select into deviant peer groups. I see little movement within the theory in that direction among traditional criminologists, although biopsychosocial criminologists have done so. Control theories acknowledge that negative experiences weaken social bonds and lead to low self-control but have traditionally ignored genetic effects. Biopsychosocial criminologists have rectified this over the last two or three decades through many studies. In short, only by paying attention to all of Tinbergen's levels of analysis (particularly ontogeny and cause) can we move our discipline forward.

11 Radical/Critical Idealism Versus Orthodox Realism

The Radical/Critical Perspective and the Nature of Crime

I use the term "radical/critical" in this chapter as an umbrella term for theories with a strong leftist political orientation. They all share the assumptions that power relations among classes of people best characterize the nature of society and that crime has no ontological reality. These theories slot neatly into Platonic idealism and Sowell's unconstrained vision in their yearning for a perfect socialist society. Adherents of these diverse theories quarrel among themselves and coin new names for their theories, such as *radical*, *critical*, *cultural*, *anarchic*, *Marxist*, and *neo-Marxist*. They are united, however, in their disdain for capitalism and "bourgeois" morality: "Critical criminology can be described as focusing on the crime-producing forces of capitalism, with critical criminologists positing that a capitalist political economy promotes a devaluation of humankind, which encourages crime" (Dollar, 2014: 1162). What is most noticeable about this perspective is that it ignores all of Tinbergen's questions except causation, which it relegates to amorphous sociopolitical causes. As Madfis and Cohen (2016: 1) describe this perspective:

> Leftist political ideology and a concern with the larger structural forces at work in society often lead scholars to be attracted to critical criminology and its radical alternative perspectives on the definition, causation, and prevention of crime. ... Consequently, such radical scholars sought not the social amelioration and reform proposed by realists but advocated large-scale social restructuring, dramatic changes to legal codes or law enforcement, and/or paradigm shifts in correctional ideology.

The birth of modern radical/critical criminology with its notion that crime is a social construct can be traced to the politicized atmosphere of the late 1960s and early 1970s and the neo-Marxist criminology developed by Taylor, Walton, and Young (1973) in the UK. These theorists envisioned a utopian society where inequalities of wealth, power, property, and crime would be eliminated: "The elimination of crime is possible under certain social arrangements ... The task is to create a society in which the facts of

DOI: 10.4324/9781003662495-14

human diversity, whether personal, organic or social, are not subject to the power to criminalise" (Burke, 2009: 281–282). It seems that they are saying that because humans have a wide diversity of traits, whatever they do should be free from the fear of criminalization. Radical idealists downplay system reforms because such reforms stifle revolutionary progress. As Madfis and Cohen (2016: 6) observe:

> Idealists shun any solutions to crime that fall short of full-scale social revolution. Engels, for example, states that "in communist society, we eliminate the contradiction between the individual man and all others, we counterpoise social peace to social war, we put the ax to the root of crime."

The Ontological Status of Crime

Radical/critical criminologists vigorously deny the ontological reality of crime. Because radical/critical criminologists lean toward nominalism, they view crime (the concept, not a behavior so defined) as an abstraction lacking form and substance and thus cannot be real. Hence, Darnell Hawkins (1995: 41) maintains, "We cannot know what *real* crime is, or who *real* criminals are." And Hulsman (1986: 71) remarks: "Crime has no ontological reality. Crime is not the object but the product of criminal policy. Criminalization is one of the many ways to construct social reality." Although Hawkins and Hulsman do not deny that criminal acts have real consequences for their victims, they maintain that they are considered criminal only because some legislative body has defined them as such. Thus, crimes are defined into existence rather than discovered. Pronouncements such as these lead to endless language games and add nothing to our understanding of criminal behavior. No one doubts that the classification of crime is inherently social, as are the classifications of social class, intelligence levels, blood pressure levels, emotions, grade point averages, and many other such things. However, that does not render the phenomena they point to ontologically unreal.

We recognize that social facts are only facts by human agreement and that crimes can be defined in and out of existence, even acts considered crimes for centuries. Until the United States Supreme Court invalidated sodomy statutes in 2003, homosexual behavior was legally punishable, as was adultery, although it was rarely criminally punished. Burning the American flag was illegal until 1989, when the Supreme Court ruled anti-flag burning statutes unconstitutional. Up until the early 2020s, except for medical marijuana, the use and distribution of marijuana were criminalized, but now pot dispensaries dot the landscape. Much the same thing can be said about the formerly illegal status of gambling and the fact that gambling casinos are now everywhere.

Crimes can also be legislated into existence. In 1885, no state in the United States had an age of consent above 12 (Friedman, 2005), but having sex with someone that old today would get the perpetrator in serious trouble. Until the Harrison Narcotics Act of 1914, there were few legal restrictions in the United States on the sale, possession, or use of most drugs such as heroin and cocaine. Following the Harrison Act, many drugs became controlled substances, and drug sales and possession became a crime. Before the 1980s, the rape of one's spouse was not criminalized but now it is. Thus, what constitutes a crime can be defined in or out of existence by legislative or judicial action. Because human societies are diverse and dynamic, there will always be a moving target of behaviors with the potential for nomination as crimes and formerly illegal activities may be decriminalized. Categorization always requires a series of human judgments, but that fact does not render the categorizations arbitrary. Most of the so-called "victimless" crimes cause some harm (drug addiction, compulsive gambling, ruined marriages), although the act of prohibiting them by law often causes more harm than it prevents.

Criminologists distinguish between inherently evil (*mala in se*) and evil by convention (*mala prohibita*) when making harm judgments. Ellis and Walsh (2000: 7) refer to the former as "stationary core" offenses that are "universally condemned offenses" and the latter as "moving targets" because they move around from culture to culture and from one historical period to another. They point to the International Criminal Police Organization (Interpol) data to support the stationary core perspective. Interpol's data show that such acts as murder, assault, rape, and theft are considered serious crimes in every one of its 188 member nations. That some nations may turn a blind eye when certain perpetrators or victims are involved is more a commentary on their disdain for human rights than on the ontological status of the crimes.

Many people actively seek to be "victimized" by perpetrators of *mala prohibita* crimes—prostitutes, drug dealers, and bookies—but who wants to be murdered, raped, robbed, or have their house burgled? Being victimized by a *mala in se* crime evokes physiological reactions in victims such as anger, helplessness, depression, and a desire to see perpetrators punished. They evoke these responses in all cultures and would do so even if the acts were not punishable by law or custom. Inherently evil crimes engage these emotions not because some legislative body has defined them as wrong but because they hammer at our deepest concerns and harm us to the core. Emile Durkheim noted this:

> We must not say that an action shocks the common conscience because it is criminal, but rather that it is criminal because it shocks the common conscience. We do not reprove it because it is a crime, but it is a crime because we reprove it.
>
> (1933: 81).

Evolutionary scientists propose that these emotional responses occur because *mala in se* crimes were the most serious fitness-reducing threats faced by our distant ancestors. That is, they threatened their survival and reproductive success, the ultimate concerns of all sexually reproducing animals. The emotions they evoke motivate people to take steps to prevent the recurrence of such acts and to punish them if they do (Braman et al., 2010; Krebs, 2008; O'Manique, 2003).

However, criminologist Callie Burt (2023: 90) denies that even murder, the most serious of inherently evil acts, is a socially constructed crime because it is sometimes culturally accepted. She writes:

> Consider killing, which in its criminal form as murder is invariably deemed the most serious crime; one that is often pointed to as inherently criminal, immoral, unconventional, and universally condemned. Except it is not. Murder, like other crimes, is socially constructed. The intentional, even premeditated, killing of one person by another—generally the definition of criminal murder—can be expected (as in honor killings or duels), lauded (as in war or battles), excused or justified (as in self-defense), or even ignored (e.g. plantation owners killing "their" slaves in the "Old South").

This is cultural relativism. Of course, Burt does not deny that murder, or any other crime, is real: "Crime is real; we do not always agree on the definition; and it varies across space and time, but we have acts classified as crimes that are committed in the material world" (2023: 95). Honor killings typically involve the murder of daughters because they have "dishonored" the family by engaging in an unsanctioned romantic relationship with an "unapproved" person. Honor killings are distinguished legally from other types of murder in some Arab states, with perpetrators of the former benefiting from reduced penalties or even avoiding punishment altogether (Feldner, 2000). My claim, however, is that murder, regardless of whether it is punishable by law or custom, is an inherently evil universal crime against humanity. As for dueling in former times, at least the deceased duelist consented to the duel, and thus, the winner was rarely prosecuted; if he was, it was for dueling, not murder.

War is the ultimate evil, but sometimes necessary to defend the realm, and is a matter of "kill or be killed." This "premeditated" killing is not murder. Neither is the private killing of another in self-defense, since it is recognized that one has a natural right to protect one's life or the lives of others. Slavery ranks with war as the ultimate evil, but unlike war, it can never be justified. Fede (2017) tells us that after independence, the United States equated the murder of a slave with the murder of a free man, but there were only a few cases in which a slave owner was executed for killing a slave. The murder of a slave was thus recognized as such in theory but rarely punished in practice. As the international community has broadened the circle of humanity, it has come closer to recognizing the inherent evil of the intentional premeditated killing of another without excuse or justification. If a *mala in se* act is not defined as criminal in a particular culture, it says more about the moral anarchy of that culture than about the act.

The ontological status of crime is a primary issue for radical/critical criminologists who tend to dismiss the issue of crime causation. Empirical criminology seeks to discover the causes and correlates of crime, while critical criminology focuses on how and why some acts are defined as crimes and others are not. For instance, Carrier and Walby (2014: 4–5) criticize what they call the "psychopathologizing" of psychological/psychiatric approaches to crime causation and claim those approaches have died, "but critical criminological practices devoid of aetiological speculations flourished." They also maintain that the biosocial approach is an "effort to imprison criminology in an aetiological space where the ontological status of crime goes unquestioned."

We avoid the problem of defining crime by occupying Carrier and Walby's "aetiological space" and studying individuals who commit predatory, harmful acts, regardless of the legal status of the acts. When criminologists do this, they are concerned with criminality, a scientific term defined independently of legal definitions of crime. Crime is an intentional act of commission or omission contrary to the law; criminality is an individual property that signals the propensity or willingness to commit predatory, harmful acts against others for their own benefit (Gottfredson & Hirschi, 1990). Criminality is a continuous trait ranging from saint to sociopath, composed of a mixture of sub-traits such as low self-control, low empathy, callousness, impulsiveness, and negative emotionality that vary greatly among people. Defining criminality as a continuous trait acknowledges that no sharp line separates individuals on this trait; it is not a trait that one has or does not have, since we all fall somewhere along the continuum. People can harm others for personal instrumental gain or emotional gratification, regardless of whether the means they use have been defined as criminal.

Labeling Theory

Labeling theory is another critical theory that denies the inherent reality of criminal acts:

> Labelling theorists fundamentally argue that no behavior is inherently deviant or criminal, but only comes to be considered so when others confer this label upon the act. Thus, it is not the intrinsic nature of an act, but the nature of the societal reaction that determines whether a "crime"' has taken place.
>
> (Burke, 2018: 168)

The theory does not ask why crime rates vary or why individuals differ in their propensity to commit crimes. Rather, it asks why some behaviors are labeled criminal and not others and thus shifts the focus from the actor (the criminal) to the reactor (the criminal justice system). The theory distinguishes between primary and secondary deviance. Primary deviance is the initial act that comes to the authorities' attention and arises from various reasons, but they are of little interest to the theory.

The idea that primary deviance is of little consequence was derived from self-report studies of delinquency. Official statistics consistently show higher arrest rates for males, the poor, and African Americans, but self-report data tended to show no significant differences among these groups, thus, their overrepresentation in official statistics reflects police bias (Paternoster & Iovanni, 1989). Most tests of this theory occurred in the 1960s–1970s and were conducted with subjects in high schools or colleges. Such places are not criminological labs where we find people seriously involved in criminal activity; the real labs are prisons, jails, and probation and parole departments. Furthermore, such studies asked students to report whether they had committed such peccadillos as fighting, smoking, or disobeying parents. Who has not done such things? It is hardly surprising that the data lacked the variation required to distinguish individuals and groups on criminal behavior. Braithwaite (1981: 42) notes that one study required "boys to admit to either drinking or to drinking and heterosexual relationships in order to get into the most delinquent category." This makes almost all of us crooks.

Primary deviance is of interest to labeling theorists only insofar as it is detected and reacted to by those with the power to pin a stigmatizing label on the offender. The real criminogenic effect comes *after* a person is caught and labeled, and thus, the central concern of the theory is to explain the consequences of being labeled. According to the theory, secondary deviance results from the reactions of others to primary deviance. The stigma of a criminal label may alter a person's self-concept in conformity with the label ("I am called a criminal and will act more like one in the future"). The label may exclude them from conventional life domains and lead to losing ties to prosocial others. This may lead them to seek criminal opportunities to fulfill their financial needs, and other criminals to fulfill their friendship needs, further strengthening their growing conception of themselves as "really" criminals. The criminal label becomes a self-fulfilling prophesy because it is more powerful than other social labels.

No one doubts that a criminal label stigmatizes and results in future difficulties, but some wear the label proudly while others strive to neutralize it (Hadjimatheou, 2016). However, this says nothing about the acts that led to the labeling or about the characteristics of those who wear the label as a badge of pride versus those who wish to lose it. Neither should be surprised that persons labeled criminals are likely to commit further crimes—past is prologue—and that likelihood has more to do with their traits, characteristics, and environmental experiences than with the negative influences of the label. The theory's position that the causes of delinquent and criminal acts (primary deviance) are of little consequence and its overemphasis on the importance of official labeling draws much criticism. For instance, Akers notes:

> One sometimes gets the impression from reading this literature that people go about minding their own business, and then—wham—bad society comes along and slaps them with a stigmatized label. Forced into the deviant role, the individual has little choice but to be deviant.
> (Bernard, Snipes, & Gerould, 2010: 230)

The overemphasis on societal reaction at the expense of the individual's choice to commit crime leads to the tendency to view offenders as victims, and thus to infantilize them and has "the paradoxical consequence of inviting us to view the deviant as a passive nonentity who is responsible neither for his suffering nor its alleviation – who is more 'sinned' against than sinning" (Lumsden, 2013: 7).

Romanticizing Criminals

Marx and Engels were disdainful of criminals, describing them as: "The dangerous class, the social scum, that rotting mass thrown off by the lowest layers of the old society" (1948: 22). Marx and Engels considered criminals as people belonging to the *lumpenproletariat* (the "rag" proletariat), or what we might term the "underclass" today. These folks would play no decisive role in the expected socialist revolution. For Marx and Engels (1965: 367), crime was the product of unjust and alienating social conditions—"the struggle of the isolated individual against the prevailing conditions." This notion became known as the "primitive rebellion hypothesis," which essentially states that "Crime in capitalist societies is often a rational response to the circumstances in which people find themselves" (Bohm, 2001: 115).

Despite the Marxist lineage claimed by radical/critical criminologists, many of them excuse, justify, or even laud criminals. For instance, Chambliss (1976: 6) viewed criminal acts as "no more than the 'rightful' behavior of persons exploited by the extant economic relationships," and Taylor (1999: 151) defined the criminal as "an additional victim of the routine operations of a capitalist system—a victim, that is of 'processes of reproduction' of social and racial inequality." Greenberg (1981: 28) even elevated Marx's despised criminals to revolutionary leaders: "Criminals, rather than the working class, might be the vanguard of the revolution." Marxist criminologists view the class struggle as the *only* source of *all* crime, accuse other criminologists of being parties to class oppression, and view "real" crime as such things as racism, sexism, imperialism, and capitalism. In an interview with Elliott Currie, Anthony Platt said that criminology is

> used to repress and maintain the powerlessness of poor people, workers, people of color, and young people, *it is not too far-fetched to*

> *characterize many criminologists as domestic war criminals.* ... The new criminology must understand and reject the role we have played historically as architects of repression.
>
> (Currie, 1973: 28; emphasis added)

It is plain that radical criminologists are not shy about wearing their ideology proudly on their sleeves.

Much of the romanticizing of criminals and disdain for empirical criminology came from the old 1970s Berkley School of Criminology, but we see similar expressions in more modern times. For instance, Lynch (2000: 152) joins Platt in viewing criminology as the science of oppression and argues that criminology should be

> (a) interpreted as one of the many "sciences of oppression" that (b) emerged following the Enlightenment (c) whose purpose was to help legitimize and place into practice principles that justified the oppression of the dangerous classes, (d) which had emerged as the primary threat to the "rational" societies based upon capitalist social, economic and political relations.

Presdee (2004: 281) similarly opines from a primitive rebellion hypothesis standpoint that:

> Now we can begin to see that much crime, but not all; much disorder, but not all, is no more or less than the everyday life of the oppressed and the "excluded." From this perspective, crime should be viewed as everyday responses to lives lived out within deprived, brutalised and often lonely social locations. Moreover, the responses from within the structures of domination are often truly masochistic in that the reaction to such disorder is often further acts of cruelty by the dominant over the dominated.

Left Realism

During the 1980s, left-wing criminologists calling themselves left realists emerged as a reaction to both left idealism and right realism (which they see as any theory that includes criminogenic individual differences). Criminologists in this camp recognized the weak theorization in left idealism and its absence of realistic policy recommendations, and that these weaknesses led to the dominance of right realism in criminology. "Take crime seriously" is left realism's battle cry because it is oriented to the present while not abandoning left idealism's future dreams. Left realism remains radical in its politics but pragmatically realist in its policies, which makes its adherents hybrids of Sowell's constrained and unconstrained visions. According to Akers and Sellers (2008: 260), "Left realists are former radical or critical criminologists who have recognized the reality of crime [and] have softened their critique of capitalist society and the criminal justice system."

Left realists acknowledge predatory crime as ontologically real and a real concern for the working class, and they understand that they must translate their concern for the working class into practical, realistic social policies. This theoretical shift signaled a move away from the former singular emphasis on the capitalist economy to embrace the interrelatedness of the offender, the victim, the community, and the state in the causes of crime. It also signals a return to a more orthodox Marxist view of criminals (without the pejorative language) whose activities are against the interests of the working class. Although left realists are socialists who disdain capitalism, they are criticized by left idealists who view their advocacy of solutions to the crime problem within a capitalist context as a sellout (Bohm, 2001).

One of the original architects of left realism is Roger Matthew, who, according to Winlow and Hall (2016: 82), "could no longer tolerate the naïve idealism, crude structuralism and political inefficacy of the radical social constructionism that had colonised Leftist thought and politics."

Left realist criminology contains four major concepts: relative deprivation, marginalization, subculture, and the square of crime. Relative deprivation is a person's perception that they are poor relative to others in society. Such perceptions can lead to feelings of unfairness, frustration, envy, resentment, and anger ("strain") that can trigger criminal behavior in people burdened with personalities that do not allow them to deal with strain constructively (although neither left idealists nor right realists talk of individual differences in people's responses, apparently assuming that responses to perceived situations are uniform).

Marginalization is a spatial metaphor for people or groups excluded from fully participating in the "center" of society and relegated to its "margins." Marginalized people or groups have little social, economic, or political power, and like the experience of relative deprivation, marginalization can lead to resentment and crime. Subcultures form when a significant number of marginalized people congregate and forge a lifestyle different from mainstream society and often at odds with it. For instance, Elijah Anderson's ethnographic work in African American neighborhoods in Philadelphia found a hostile subculture that lauded such things as "rap music that encourages its young listeners to kill cops, to rape, and the like" (1999: 107). Subcultural theorists such as Albert Cohen maintain that most criminal behavior in marginalized communities is an expression of short-run hedonism; that is, the immediate gratification of desires without regard for any long-term consequences. Because people in such subcultures cannot live up to what Cohen calls "middle-class measuring rods," they experience status frustration and spawn an oppositional culture with behavioral norms contrary to those of the middle class. To gain status and respect, members of criminal subcultures establish "new norms, new criteria of status which define as meritorious the characteristics they *do* possess, the kinds of conduct of which they *are* capable" (Cohen, 1955: 66; emphasis original).

The Square of Crime and Crime Prevention

The final concept in left realism is the square of crime. The square of crime is the core of left realist criminology as "a framework for the analysis of crime and crime control in terms of the interaction between four 'participants' in the process: offenders, victims, criminal justice agencies and communities" (Lea, 2016: 58). These four interacting elements place the offender and victim at one side of the square as actors and the state (formal crime control) and communities (informal crime control) at the other as reactors. The offender commits the crime, the victim decides whether to report it, state agencies attempt to solve and punish it, and members of the public decide what they can do for themselves to prevent criminal victimization.

Left realists counsel that crime prevention efforts rest on improving police-community relations.

The efficacy of the police in their crime-fighting efforts lies primarily in this relationship with the communities they serve. If relationships are good, they will clear more crimes due to witness cooperation and other information relevant to solving the crimes they are investigating. If they do not enjoy good relationships, their efforts will be frustrated. We saw evidence of this in the 2022 FBI crime statistics. In 2022, police cleared only 36.7% of violent crimes and 12.1% of property crimes. Only 52.3% of the murders were cleared, which is the lowest clearance rate for homicide on record, and homicide has a higher clearance rate than all other crimes (Walsh & Jorgensen, 2025). In contrast, homicide clearance rates have remained steady in Western Europe for years, ranging from 98% in Finland to 80% in Sweden (Liem et al., 2019). The FBI reported a national homicide clearance rate of 93% in 1962 (Cook & Mancik, 2024); thus, the 52.3% clearance reported in 2022 is a 43.7% decline from 1962. This decline has occurred despite the technological advances available to the police such as computerized databases, DNA analysis, advances in forensic science, and video surveillance cameras almost everywhere. It appears that the police-community side of the square of crime has been severely compromised. Rather than rectifying this situation, some radical criminologists want to get rid of all forms of formal social control. For instance, Seigel (2017: 484) makes a case for police abolition, arguing that "abolition of the police must take place, of course in the context of an overall move towards the abolition of prisons, for otherwise police will simply be replaced by another mechanism of control." One wonders who Seigel would call if a group of thugs released from a now-abolished prison were hammering on his door.

As for lowering crime rates, left realists are united with left idealist colleagues in remaining committed to advocating for major structural, cultural, economic, and political changes while simultaneously advocating for short-term policies. There are two broad approaches to crime prevention advocated by left realists. The first is identifying those at risk of criminal offending and taking action to limit their offending. It is important to understand why people offend, but both left idealists and realists resist efforts that focus on individual personality and biological factors, preferring to look only at criminogenic structural factors. Left realists offer nothing new in the prevention and treatment areas and rely on traditional treatment programs such as the well-established risk-needs-responsivity (RNR) model for treatment and early intervention, such as the Nurse-Family Partnership (NFP) program. Both these programs have shown moderate success. Radical/critical criminologists also maintain that inequalities in wealth and income must be reduced, but they do not show how this can be done within a meritocratic economic system that enjoys wide public support.

Community-based approaches involve the local community in combating crime because everyone, not just the police, is needed in the fight against crime. Ninety percent of the crimes cleared by the police result from information the public provides (Cook & Mancik, 2024).

Crime flourishes in communities where many people have a "no one cares" attitude. Wilson and Kelling (1982: 8) suggest that when an act of vandalism or a crime is committed in such communities, community members act as if nothing serious has happened and this invites further antisocial acts:

> The key is to identify neighborhoods at the tipping point—where the public order is deteriorating but not unreclaimable, where the streets are used frequently but by apprehensive people, where a window is likely to be broken at any time, and must quickly be fixed if all are not to be shattered.

Left realists doubtless agree with Wilson and Kelling, but just as doubtless they would disagree with their "zero-tolerance" policing as the solution.

It is also important to understand what makes people vulnerable to victimization. According to the 2023 National Crime Victimization Survey (NCVS) (Thompson & Tapp, 2023), the individual most likely to be victimized is a young Black unmarried male living in an urban environment. Victimization, like criminal offending, drops precipitously from 25 years of age onward. It also drops with employment, increasing income, and marriage. These protective factors against victimization are the same protective factors against criminal behavior. Given this, the distinction between offender and victim is sometimes blurred because

> [p]redators prey on each other as well as upon innocent members of the public ... When youth gangs feud with each other by carrying out "drive-by" shootings, the young members who get gunned down are casualties of their own brand of retaliatory street justice.
>
> (Karmen, 2005: 14)

Prior victimization is the best predictor of future victimization (King & Bostaph, 2024; Tseloni & Pease, 2003), but this does not mean, of course, that most crime victims carry any measure of blame for their victimization.

According to routine activities theory, crime, and therefore victimization, involves the presence of motivated offenders, the availability of suitable targets, and the absence of capable guardians. Left realists would recommend that to minimize the probability of victimization, members of the public should evaluate their lifestyles (routine activities) because certain lifestyles disproportionately expose people to the risk of victimization. Some victim advocates reject crime-prevention tips that victimologists endorse as "ideologically tainted" (Karmen, 2005: 129), but crime-prevention strategies are ignored at our peril. Strategies include avoiding crime hot spots, not frequenting bars late at night, avoiding provocation, locking the car and house, and many other common-sense measures.

While the components of each side of the square of crime are relatively easy to operationalize and generate hypotheses about, the complexity of the square renders it difficult to operationalize in its totality. In an interview with Sozzo and Fonseca (2016: 103), Jock Young, one of its architects, says of the square of crime: "It is something which really appeals to me and interests me and I don't totally understand it, but it's got something about formal sociology in it." To the degree that it has "got something about formal sociology in it," any analysis is abstract since it does not refer directly to individual behavior or interpersonal interactions. Although many studies have tested each side of the square, we have yet to see a study that engages with all sides together. Given the abstract nature of the square of crime, the skepticism about empiricism, and the reliability of official crime data of both left idealists and left realists, we should not expect to.

12 What is Intelligence and How is it Related to Crime?

What is Intelligence?

When most of us hear the word "intelligence," we understand what it means, yet some scholars find it ill-defined and controversial. Stuart Ritchie (2015: 8) warns:

> Just mention IQ in polite company, and you'll be informed (sometimes rather sternly) that IQ tests don't measure anything real and reflect only how good you are at doing IQ tests ... and that those who are interested in intelligence testing must be elitists, or perhaps something more sinister.

For instance, Henry Schlinger (2003) writes of "the myth of intelligence," and accuses Charles Spearman, a pioneer of the scientific study of intelligence, of reifying it: "He took an abstract mathematical correlation and reified it as the general intelligence that someone possesses" (p. 17). He also writes: "We are fooled into believing that the term refers to a tangible entity because other words in our language, such as cat or table, have tangible referents" (p. 24), and that "some psychologists persist in believing in intelligence is that they have a significant personal and professional investment in it" (p. 29).

Schlinger appears to say that because intelligence is an abstraction, it does not exist; thus, we cannot possess it. For him, for something to be "really" real, it must occupy space, which is extreme nominalism. We previously noted that physicists can't define abstract energy other than its ability to perform work, but they can measure it in many ways as it moves physical objects around. We can think of intelligence similarly as operationalized "mental energy" that moves the concepts in our minds around to find adaptive solutions to life's problems. Like energy, we can quantify mental energy by IQ test scores and/or various physiological tests, such as brain glucose consumption, and those scores tell us how much mental work people are capable of.

The Latin root word of intelligence is *intelligo* ("to select among"). Intelligence thus implies the ability to select from among a variety of mental elements and to analyze, synthesize, and arrange them in such a way as to

DOI: 10.4324/9781003662495-15

provide satisfactory, and sometimes novel, solutions to problems. The speed and efficiency with which this is done differ among people; that is what we call intelligence. There is doubtless more to intelligence than IQ scores, although they are the only way we have of operationalizing the concept, and they have great predictive power.

Snyderman and Rothman (1988) surveyed 1,020 PhDs in developmental psychology and behavioral genetics. Responses were placed into three categories: (1) those for which there was virtual unanimity: "abstract thinking or reasoning," checked by 99.3%, "problem-solving ability" 97.7%, and "capacity to acquire knowledge," 96%; (2) those checked by the majority; "memory," 80.5%, "adaptation to one's environment," 77.2%, and "mental speed," 71.7%; (3) those rarely checked included "achievement motivation," 18.9% and "goal-directedness," 24%. These elements conform to David Wechsler's definition of intelligence:

> The aggregate or global capacity of the individual to act purposefully, to think rationally, and to deal effectively with his environment. It is aggregate or global because it is composed of elements or abilities (features) which, although not entirely independent, are qualitatively differentiable.
>
> (Matarazzo, 1976: 79)

The terms "aggregate" and "global" alert us that different mental tests measure different cognitive abilities, but there is also a common factor. Psychometricians call this factor *Spearman's g*, or simply *g ("g" for* "general" intelligence*)*, a statistical measure derived from factor analyses of tests represented by the first unrotated principal component. Spearman's *g* is the only factor common to all measures of intelligence. What this means is that in any tasks that tax the mind, however different they may be from one another, if a person is good at one mental task, they are is likely to be good at others, although not necessarily to the same degree (correlations between a specific test and the general factor across several mental tests are in the range of 0.50 to 0.90) (Deary, Spinath, & Bates, 2006). Thus, there is no measure of cognitive ability independent of *g*, and psychometricians agree that *g* conforms to what both they and laypersons mean by intelligence (Buschkuehl & Jaeggi, 2010).

General intelligence consists of two types: crystallized and fluid, characterized by somewhat different neurocognitive architectures (Simpson-Kent et al., 2020). Crystallized intelligence depends on acquired knowledge and refers to the ability to use learned skills and knowledge; fluid intelligence reflects the ability to analyze problems in novel ways and relies minimally on learning. Fluid intelligence is more strongly related to mathematical and complex logical skills than reading and foundation skills. It is "the ability to cope with new situations for which previously acquired knowledge is only minimally useful" (Buschkuehl & Jaeggi, 2010: 266). Fluid intelligence is an "on-the-spot" cognitive *process*, and crystallized intelligence is the stored *product* of learning. Most modern tests rely heavily on items that tap into fluid intelligence to minimize the effects of acquired knowledge due to different levels of educational attainment.

People with high fluid intelligence acquire knowledge more readily than those with lower levels, so fluid and crystallized intelligence are not entirely separate. Both kinds are used in many different circumstances. When taking a math exam, we rely on fluid intelligence to find a strategy for arriving at the correct answer. Crystallized intelligence is needed to recall the correct mathematical concepts (such as the foil method in algebra) before fluid intelligence is engaged to arrive at the correct answers. With practice, we engage mathematical concepts largely automatically and no longer require fluid intelligence because those concepts have become part of one's store of crystallized knowledge. Thus, fluid and crystallized intelligence function together as one.

The crystallized-fluid distinction tells us why intelligence is not learned. Intelligence is not how much you know, but your capacity to acquire it. If intelligence is acquired through education, it would increase dramatically across the life course as knowledge increases, but it does not. IQ scores are remarkably stable across the life course, with test-retest correlations as high as 0.94 over 10 years (Deary et al., 2000) and remain stable even as a person acquires vast storehouses of knowledge from childhood to old age. A 60-year-old professor may have acquired the knowledge to expound on subjects that would have mystified him or her at age 15, but their IQ would differ minimally at age 60 from what it was at 15, and fluid intelligence may have declined. It is agreed that fluid intelligence increases into early adulthood before steadily decreasing with age (Simpson-Kent et al., 2020).

IQ tests are composed of verbal IQ (VIQ) and Performance IQ (PIQ) subscales that are combined to give a measure of an individual's full-scale IQ (FSIQ). There are various IQ tests for people of all ages with different difficulty levels. The higher a test's *g*-load, and the more it is *g*-loaded, the more it depends on the common *g* factor rather than on a specific content domain, and the greater its complexity and the more *g*-loaded a test the higher its heritability (Lubinski, 2004). The Raven Standard Progressive Matrices test is the most widely used of all tests of intelligence because it relies minimally on cultural learning, is recognized as the best measure of general intelligence, and has the highest *g* loading of all IQ tests (Arce-Ferrer & Martinez Guzman, 2009). It has reported split-half, test-retest, and internal consistency reliabilities between 0.80 and 0.90 (Arce-Ferrer & Martinez Guzman, 2009). This level of reliability sits head and shoulders above the reliability of all other pencil and paper psychological measures. Their validity, especially criterion-related validity, the degree to which a scale measures what it is supposed to measure and predicts what it should, is superb (Nisbett et al., 2012).

Humans have many tools in their toolboxes to navigate their lives that are context-specific, but intelligence is a more general tool that is useful in almost all contexts. It is perhaps the "master" attribute that differentiates humans from other animals. Intelligence has always been of prime importance to our species, particularly in increasingly more complex societies where strong backs and broad shoulders are no longer sufficient to move up in the world unless one is a professional athlete. As Linda Gottfredson noted: "Intelligence has a profound effect on the structure of society, not necessarily because it is the most highly valued of individual differences—although conceivably it is—but rather because it may have the widest and most stable distribution among all the traits that are valuable in industrialized nations" (1986: 406).

Silver (2019: 1) notes that intelligence is one of the few variables "consistently shown to influence a swath of human outcomes." Thus, life is one continual intelligence test, with different levels predicting life outcomes such as poverty, lack of education, out-of-wedlock birth, and unemployment, all of which are associated with antisocial behavior. Herrnstein and Murray (1994) examined data from 12,686 White males and females in the National Longitudinal Study of Youth (NLSY). The study began in 1979 when study subjects were between 14 and 17 years old, and data were collected in 1989 when they were between 24 and 27. The sample was divided into the bottom 20% (IQ scores of 87 and below) and the top 20% (IQ of 113 and above). Among those who dropped out of high school, 66% of the low scorers and 2% of the high scorers did. Sixty-four percent of male low scorers versus 4% high scorers were unemployed the entire previous year, and 57% of lows versus 2% of highs were chronic welfare recipients. Among females, 52% of the lows had a child out of wedlock and 3% of the highs. In criminal terms, 62% of the low IQ category had been interviewed in jail or prison sometime during the study period versus 2% of the high category, a ratio of 31:1.

Neurobiology and Intelligence

IQ is among the most heritable human traits, with estimates ranging from 0.50 in childhood to 0.80 in old age (Neubauer & Fink, 2009). The once-controversial idea that genes are involved in intelligence has slowly disappeared as we have discovered more about its biological underpinnings (Nisbett et al., 2012). Neurobiological differences have much to do with how well people perform on IQ tests and provide tangible referents that Henry Schlinger felt were wanting. A simple way to physically define intelligence using EEG is to correlate IQ scores with nerve impulses that reflect individuals' speed and accuracy in information processing by reaction time (RT). The premise of RT studies is that higher-IQ people possess brains that can spot, differentiate, and respond to relevant stimuli faster than lower-IQ people. Correlations between reaction time and IQ range from -0.25 to -0.50 (higher IQ = shorter reaction time), with the largest correlations obtained with the most challenging RT tasks (Deary, 2003).

Higher correlations are found in more sophisticated measures of brain activity, such as cerebral glucose metabolism (CGM). CGM is measured by positron emission tomography (PET) scans, which reveal metabolic functioning as the brain takes up positron-emitting glucose. A computer reveals colorized maps of the brain identifying the parts activated (mainly areas crucial for integrating abstract relationships) while engaged in an intellectual task as the energy supplied by glucose is metabolized. Glucose metabolic rates at various brain slice levels are correlated with scores on highly g-loaded IQ tests. Depending on the brain slice level, correlations ranging between -0.44 and -0.84 are found, which means that high IQ subjects expend less brain energy when performing intellectual tasks and possess brains that are speedier, more accurate, and more "energy efficient" than low IQ subjects (Gray & Thompson, 2004).

Based on neuroimaging studies, Jung and Haier (2007) developed a theory of intelligence called the Parieto-Frontal Integration Theory (P-FIT). P-FIT stipulates a network of brain regions predominantly involved in complex reasoning and suggests that fluid intelligence is related to how efficiently information processing is shunted around the brain and how well the relevant brain areas communicate. As van den Heuvel et al. (2009: 7619) put it, "human intellectual performance is likely to be related to how efficiently our brain integrates information between multiple brain regions. Most pronounced effects between normalized path length and IQ were found in frontal and parietal regions. Our findings indicate a strong positive association between the global efficiency of functional brain networks and intellectual performance."

Most of these brain areas are clustered in the frontal and parietal lobes, connected by curving white-matter fibers called the arcuate fasciculus (Deary, Penke, & Johnson, 2010). Using fMRI with 115 children, Langeslag et al. (2013) found that higher nonverbal intelligence was associated with increased functional connectivity between the right parietal and right frontal regions. The function of these areas is to integrate sensory information, among several other things. This fits well with the body of research showing that the parietal-frontal network is strongly activated under situations where conflicting alternatives are possible and when response selection is required (Brass & von Cramon, 2004). Resolving conflicting possibilities by making the correct selection is what one engages in when taking an IQ test.

Dennis Garlick's (2002; 2003) neuroplasticity model posits that intelligence is "created" when neural connections are forged and strengthened by environmental input, and more or less of it will be created according to the differential capacity of one's neurons to adapt. Garlick argues that there is a critical period in which the developing brain fine-tunes its ability to adapt to novel phenomena. This adaptation refers to efficient signal transduction via molecules that promote brain development and plasticity. The primary molecules are brain-derived neurotrophic factor (BDNF), cyclic AMP response element binding protein (CREB), and extracellular signaling-related kinases. These three molecules work together to promote gene expression and brain plasticity (Ehrlich & Josselyn, 2016). A 10-year longitudinal MRI study of more than 300 children and adolescents found strong evidence for Garlick's model. Shaw et al. (2006) showed an identical pattern of brain maturation occurring in all subjects (the cortex gets thicker, peaks, and then gets thinner with pruning). He also found that the rate of these brain changes differed significantly according to IQ levels. The cortices of subjects with the highest IQs started thinnest, quickly got thicker, peaked relatively late, and thinned quickly. Average and below-average subjects experienced these same changes but at slower rates, suggesting that rapid brain changes in response to learning reflect a high degree of neural plasticity and that greater neuroplasticity suggests a more agile mind and higher IQ.

The Human Connectome Project (HCP) is a consortium of neuroscientists from multiple labs worldwide that investigates the neuroscience of behavior and cognitive function. It is designed to enable neuroscientists to navigate the geography of the brain by diagramming its structural and functional connectivity using every available brain imaging tool. The objective of functional network connectivity research is to characterize brain functions that can identify an individual from others with an astounding accuracy of up to 99.5% (Finn et al. 2015). Finn et al. (2015) looked at the connectome of 118 individuals finding that the integrity of the frontoparietal networks predicted fluid intelligence scores at r = 0.55 and concluded: "That the frontoparietal networks were most distinguishing of individuals—and the most predictive of behavior—is consistent with the role these networks play in cognition. Nodes in these networks tend to act as flexible hubs, switching connectivity patterns according to task demands" (p. 1669). Using data from 889 subjects, Cai et al. (2019) looked at connections in multiple brain areas. They found the frontoparietal to be significantly related to fluid intelligence (r = 0.548), cognitive flexibility (r = 0.50), inhibition/executive function (r = 0.493), and language comprehension (r = 0.535).

Intelligence and Crime

The notion that intelligence impacts criminal offending has a long history, dating back to Richard Dugdale's *The Jukes* and Henry Goddard's *The Kallikak Family*. These works were initially well received, but when eugenicists began using them as evidence for their position, critics threw the intelligence baby out with the eugenic bathwater (Selden, 2007). However, reviews of the IQ/crime relationship find it robust (e.g. Ellis & Walsh, 2003; Lynn, Fuerst, & Kirkegaard, 2018). Several Scandinavian cohort studies have provided the best evidence. Moffitt et al. (1981) studied 4,552 Danish army draftees on IQ and criminal records drawn from the Danish National Police Register, finding that men who committed two or more criminal offenses by age 20 had IQ scores averaging one full standard deviation below nonoffenders. Pudney and Galloway (2011) examined the relationship among five birth cohorts of Norwegian conscripts from 1977 to 2004 and found risk ratios between the highest and lowest IQ categories ranging from 4.65 for alcohol offenses to 7.74 and 9.33 for violent and serious theft offenses, respectively. They conclude: "The empirical IQ-crime gradient is very strong for all categories of crime and is only reduced to a modest degree when we make allowance for family circumstances and history" (p .37).

Frisell, Pawitan, and Långström (2012) examined the Swedish military's Conscript Register data from 1980 to 1993 and violent criminal convictions in Sweden's Crime Register among 700,514 men. They examined the relationship between IQ at age 18 obtained from both the Conscript Register and official criminal arrests and convictions. The most salient finding was:

> Men convicted of violent crime had more than a standard deviation lower cognitive ability than those without such convictions. ... this is clear evidence that violent individuals managed in courts, prison and probation, and forensic psychiatric services, on average have weaker cognitive resources.

Schwartz et al. (2015) examined a Finnish birth cohort of boys (n = 21,513) born in 1987 using official criminal convictions and IQ tests administered by the military upon conscription. They concluded:

> The clearest takeaway from this research is that low intelligence is a strong and consistent correlate of criminal offending. ... the risk of acquiring a felony conviction by age 21 is nearly four times (3.6) higher among those in the three lowest categories of total intelligence as compared to those scoring in the top three categories ... cognitive ability is an important correlate of individual differences in criminal offending, a finding that criminological theories ignore at their own peril.
>
> (p. 115)

Jacob, Haro, and Koyanagi (2019) studied a British national representative sample of 6,872 individuals. After controlling for age, sex, and race/ethnicity, the proportion of violent perpetrators increased monotonically from IQ scores of 70–79 to IQs of 120–129. There is no such thing as immaculate data in the human sciences, but verified convictions and IQ scores are as reliable and valid as it gets.

The IQ-offending relationship is stronger than often indicated because most studies tend to lump together boys who commit only minor delinquent acts during their teenage years with boys who will continue to seriously and frequently offend into adulthood. Casual and low-level offending (which is relatively common among adolescents) differ from non-offenders by only about one IQ point, while serious persistent offenders differ from non-offenders by about 17 points (Gatzke-Kopp et al., 2002; Moffitt, 1993). Pooling these two groups, since low and infrequently offending boys greatly outnumber the more serious and persistent offenders, hides the magnitude of IQ differences between minor and serious offenders if the latter have lower IQs than the former, which they doubtless do. Lower IQ individuals tend to have an earlier onset of offending and longer criminal careers than higher IQ individuals (McGloin & Pratt, 2003; Piquero & White, 2003).

Intellectual Imbalance and Crime

Just as pooling serious and frequent offenders with minor and infrequent offenders leads to underestimation of the IQ/antisocial behavior relationship, so does pooling the two subscales of the IQ test. David Wechsler's (1958: 176) statement, "The most outstanding feature of the sociopath's test profile is the systematic high score on the performance as opposed to the verbal part of the scale," sparked another way of examining the relationship between IQ and antisocial behavior. Most IQ studies look at full-scale IQ (FSIQ). While most people have VIQ and PIQ scores that closely match (balanced), criminal offender populations are almost always found to have significantly lower than average VIQ scores, but not significantly lower PIQ scores, than non-offenders. This PIQ>VIQ discrepancy is called *intellectual imbalance*.

As Miller (1987: 120) notes: "This PIQ>VIQ relationship [is] found across studies, despite variations in age, sex, race, setting, and form of the Wechsler scale administered, as well in differences in criteria for delinquency." Isen's (2010) meta-analysis of 131 PIQ > VIQ-antisocial behavior studies found, averaged across studies, that VIQ was 85.9 and the average PIQ score was 93. Thus, offenders score only 7 points below the general population average on PIQ but 14.1 points below average on VIQ. The PIQ > VIQ profile was found for both male and female offenders. A literature review found that overall, VIQ>PIQ boys are underrepresented in delinquent populations by a factor of about 2.6, and PIQ>VIQ boys are overrepresented by a factor of about 2.2 (Walsh, 2003). Thus, P>V boys are almost five times more likely to appear in delinquent samples than V>P boys.

Recall that Shaw et al.'s (2006) longitudinal study showed that high-IQ children had neural cortices that thinned more quickly than those of lower-IQ children. It is thus more likely that the lower VIQ of most offenders, rather than their superior PIQ relative to their VIQ that is salient to their offending. VIQ is more g-loaded than PIQ and is more important in navigating the nuances of social life (Pietschnig et al., 2022). However, it is not the case that a high PIQ makes a person prone to crime. Offenders have higher PIQ *relative* to their VIQ but are below the population average on both subscales. PIQ is highly important to quantitative disciplines such as physics and math. One study of the mathematically gifted showed they have an average PIQ score of 125 and a VIQ score of 138 (Kennedy, Willcutt, & Smith, 1963). Intellectually gifted people almost always show a VIQ>PIQ profile, but PIQs significantly above average (Lang et al., 2019).

Factors Mediating the IQ/Crime Relationship

One straightforward explanation for the IQ/crime relationship centers on the idea that people with low IQ may lack sufficient moral awareness of how to behave and are thus more likely to offend. A related argument is that individuals with lower IQs may be less able "to foresee the consequences of their offending and to appreciate the feelings of victims" (Farrington & Welsh, 2008: 41). It also may be that those with lower cognitive ability are less likely to develop self-control and thus be more likely to engage in criminal activity. However, some scholars argue that the IQ-crime relationship disappears once the effects of school performance, SES, poverty, and so forth, are considered.

The most usual explanation for the IQ/delinquency link is that it works via poor school performance, which leads to dropping out of school and associating with delinquent peers. Thus, poor school performance allegedly makes the IQ-crime relationship statistically disappear, implying that the effect of IQ is spurious. Measures of academic achievement such as GPA are probably better predictors of antisocial behavior than IQ given that academic achievement is a measure of IQ plus many other personal and situational characteristics such as conscientious study habits, ambition, and supportive parents: talent + effort + encouragement. However, IQ predicts these things. Children with low IQ, particularly low verbal IQ, lack the abilities for a rewarding and successful school experience. Unrewarding school experiences lead to frustration and failure and contribute to delinquency by creating non-attachment to school and negative attitudes toward authority figures. They also induce children to seek rewards among delinquent peers who provide a sense of belonging, a set of alternate values, and a source of self-esteem. Another explanation is that children with low verbal IQ fail to fully develop higher-order social skills such as empathy and moral reasoning. In a meta-analysis of 50 studies of moral reasoning and delinquency, Stams et al. (2006) found that low levels of moral reasoning were associated with higher levels of delinquency, especially for adolescents with low IQ. Stams et al. conclude: "The conclusion is that moral judgment is strongly associated with juvenile delinquency, even after controlling for socioeconomic status, culture, gender, age, and intelligence" (p. 708).

All variables that allegedly render IQ spurious are intervening variables between cause and effect, and IQ undergirds them all. Intelligence is an attribute that comes temporally before these variables that supposedly render it weak or spurious. For instance, the high correlation between IQ and school achievement has been found to range between 0.53 and 0.93 in studies (Sternberg, Grigorenko, & Bundy, 2001), and we have seen how well it predicts the correlated panoply of life outcomes that themselves predict crime. Adjusting relationships between IQ and criminal behavior for variables such as SAT scores and SES weeds out much of the influence of IQ we are trying to detect. Spuriousness only exists when a correlation is wrongly taken as a causal relationship when their association is due to a third, unaccounted-for variable. The IQ-crime relationship is not like that. IQ is a distal variable that has a causal relationship with intervening variables X, Y, and Z, which are the more proximately alleged causes of crime.

Another objection to the IQ/crime relationship, which may render it spurious, is that lower-IQ offenders are more likely to be caught and arrested. This must be true at least occasionally, but this would be true only for offenses for which police have discretion in their arrest decisions. For more serious crimes for which they do not have discretion, arrest is assured regardless of an offender's attitude. Herrnstein and Murray (1994) admit that the differential detection hypothesis has intuitive appeal, but they failed to find support for it. They state that given the millions of offenders who pass through the system and whose IQs are known, "there is barely enough crime left unaccounted for to permit such a population's [above-average IQ offenders] existence" (p. 243). This is not to say, of course, that above-average IQ offenders do not exist.

Moffitt and Silva (1988) designed an elegant test of the differential detection hypothesis based on a large birth cohort of New Zealand males. Subjects were asked to self-report delinquent activity, which was then compared with official police records, resulting in three distinct groups: (1) self-reported delinquents with a police record; (2) self-reported delinquents without a police record; and (3) nondelinquents as assessed both by self-reports and police records. Comparing IQ scores among the groups, they found that the FSIQ, VIQ, and PIQ means of both delinquent groups did not significantly differ from one another; i.e., undetected delinquents were no brighter than their less fortunate peers who were. Both groups had significantly lower full-scale and VIQ means than verified nondelinquents, but not lower PIQ means. The nature of the sample (a large birth cohort) and the ability to match self-reports with official records make these findings compelling.

On the other hand, Yun, and Lee (2013) found that low IQ offenders were more likely to get arrested, but only in "adequate neighborhoods" and not in "disadvantaged neighborhoods" One would intuitively expect the exact opposite, but this study was based on self-reports only, and thus the truth of respondents' answers could not be ascertained by consulting police records. Additionally, the sample was school-based and may have missed low-IQ youths who may have been absent, dropped out, or expelled. More replication studies are needed following the Moffitt/Silva verification model to gain confidence about the truth or falsity of the differential detection hypothesis.

Offending Among High-IQ People

A high IQ does not necessarily make one wise, nor does it necessarily make one moral. As Albert Einstein said: "We should take care not to make the intellect our god; it has, of course, powerful muscles, but no personality" (Lagerfeld, 2004: 34). IQ has been shown to predict success in almost every domain of life from good marriages to prestigious careers, so if a high IQ person chooses to follow an illegitimate path in life, it should predict success in a criminal career if paired with a crime-prone personality. For people who are callous, bold, and lack empathy, a high IQ would make them more successful in manipulating and victimizing others. High-IQ white-collar criminals cost the economy billions of dollars, leading to bankruptcy and sometimes suicide. Political tyrants are men of high intelligence coupled with a lack of morality. The mean IQ for all Nazi war criminals tested was 127. Albert Speer had an IQ of 128, Hermann Goering 138, and although we do not have Adolf Hitler's IQ, there is little doubt that he was an "evil genius" and a master of psychological manipulation (Zillmer, Archer, & Castino, 1989).

Serial killers are often described as having very high IQs because of (1) the high IQs of notorious killers such as Ted Kaczynski (IQ = 167), Ted Bundy (IQ = 124), and Ed Kemper (IQ = 135), and (2) they are hard to catch. However, the *Radford/FGCU Annual Report on Serial Killer Statistics*, a database of 5,334 serial killers as of 2020, finds that the average IQ of tested serial killers is 92.5 with a median of 85, which is more indicative of ordinary criminals than of the general population (Aamodt, Leary, & Southard, 2020). The IQ of the most prolific serial killer in American history, Samuel Little, who confessed to killing 93 (most of them verified) was 96, just under the population average (Hannan, 2020). The reason they are hard to catch is not because they are too smart to get caught but because they typically target strangers, making the solving of a case particularly challenging.

The evidence about offending among high-IQ people is sparse. If such people are criminals, it is more a function of personality deficits than their IQ. Johansson and Kerr (2005) examined a sample of 370 incarcerated Swedish men sentenced for attempted murder, murder, or manslaughter on psychopathy and intelligence. Psychopathic and non-psychopathic criminals did not differ significantly in intelligence, but they differed in how intelligence was related to the seriousness of misbehavior. Among non-psychopaths, those with higher intelligence had a later start in committing violent crimes. Among psychopaths, however, those with high intelligence had an early start in violent offending and more problematic behavior both inside and outside of prison walls. A British study conducted by Coid, Freestone, and Ullrich (2012) found that offenders they called "successful psychopaths" had high IQ scores and high social class but low involvement with the criminal justice system.

We are all capable of criminal behavior regardless of our IQ, but an average or above IQ is a protective factor. However, such an IQ is only a Kevlar vest that covers only vital areas, and not something that covers all risks. As in all areas of life, a high IQ can make people more successful in a life of crime if they possess a personality profile that may lead them to embark on such a lifestyle. If the potential rewards are sufficiently great and the risk of detection is sufficiently low, many may cross the criminality threshold regardless of IQ level. IQ is neither necessary nor sufficient to explain offending, but it is one of the most powerful predictors we have.

13 Issues Related to Socioeconomic Status, Poverty, and Crime

Socioeconomic Status

Socioeconomic status (SES) is a central concept in the social sciences, and poverty is a perennial concern of scholars in many disciplines. Understanding SES and poverty is important to many disciplines because these variables are strongly related to many things, such as mental and physical health and criminal status. People in poverty are on the bottom rung of the SES ladder. It is generally the case that people with higher SES have more material and nonmaterial resources, including income, education, prestigious occupations, and neighborhood quality. These dimensions are correlated with one another, but far from perfect. For instance, a PhD college professor has more education than a star athlete but makes much less money.

It is hard to find a social science study that does not include SES as an independent variable, but SES is also a dependent variable with causes of its own. For many, the only cause of a person's SES is parental SES, and parental SES is caused only by structural factors. Social structure is a nexus of connections among individuals that undeniably causally affect their actions but do not determine them in any absolute way (Sampson & Bean, 2006). The structural model "asserts that institutions treat different groups of people unequally, making success less attainable for some groups than for others" (Lopez, Gurin, & Nagda, 1998: 305). Lopez, Gurin, and Nagda call any individual trait explanations of SES "system-justifying," implying they neither support our meritocratic system nor the notion that people can achieve higher SES by talent and effort.

Merton's (1938) anomie/strain theory emphasized structure and culture to explain the relationship between SES and crime/delinquency. He stressed that the social structure systemically denies opportunities to some people to realize the overweening American cultural goal of monetary success. He asserted that people sort themselves into his "modes of adaptation" based on class-linked perceptions about how middle-class financial goals are achieved legitimately. This appears to say that SES causes SES, which gives the impression that Merton saw it as static and self-perpetuating. Of course, SES was

DOI: 10.4324/9781003662495-16

relatively static for some groups, such as Blacks and women, when he wrote his article in the 1930s, and many still believe that it remains so. Merton dismisses the idea that SES is caused by individual characteristics. For him, it is deeply tied to power dynamics, access to resources, and available opportunities based on family SES, implying that SES is largely ascribed. However, the alleged strong effect of parental SES on offspring SES is held by few outside sociology. For instance, Kingston (2006: 121) writes: "The net impact of measured family background on economic success is easy to summarize: very little. The conclusion holds across different data sets with different model specifications and measurements and applies to both occupational success and earnings."

IQ and SES

If SES is achieved, how does it happen? Some say it is not a question that should be asked lest it result in invidious comparisons, especially if genetics is linked to IQ. Lee Ellis (1996: 28) noted the tendency toward self-censorship on the question of SES causation: "Someday historians of social science will be astounded to find the word intelligence is usually not even mentioned in late-twentieth-century textbooks on social stratification." The relationship between intelligence (IQ) and moving up the SES ladder has long been controversial. The publication of *The Bell Curve* by Herrnstein and Murray (1994) brought the issue of IQ and SES to the fore. No one claims that IQ is the only cause of SES, although it is an important cause. It is without question that being born into an upper- or middle-class family confers many advantages and that being born into a lower-class family brings many disadvantages. Family SES thus has effects, but they are both genetic and environmental (Deming, 2017). Genes become important in determining SES in proportion to the equalization of environments because it is a mathematical truism that the more equal the access to opportunities the society provides, the greater the genetic effects (Adkins & Guo, 2008; Nolan, Richiardi, & Valenzuela, 2019).

When sociologists consider the correlation between IQ and SES, the inclination is to view a child's IQ as a direct effect of the SES of his or her parents; a reified measure of class advantage or disadvantage. If this is the case, an adult's SES is not meritoriously achieved but is a social ascription—SES of origin → SES of destination. Noting that the IQs of parents and offspring are correlated, Spirtes, Glymour and Scheines (2001: 150) conclude that SES causes IQ: "It seems very unlikely that the child's intelligence causes the family socioeconomic status, and the only sensible interpretation is that SES causes IQ, or they have a common unmeasured cause." The first clause amounts to a vacuous truism, the second is minimally true, and as for the third, genes are the "common unmeasured cause" they find elusive, and they are continually measured.

Plomin and Von Stumm (2018, p. 3) note:

> Across studies, parents' education correlates 0.30 with children's intelligence, implying that it accounts for 9% of the variance in children's intelligence. This association is, however, confounded by genetics because children inherit the DNA differences that predict their intelligence from their parents.

The correlation between parental SES and children's IQ is not an appropriate test of the status attainment issue; it is the correlation between children's IQ and their SES in adulthood. As Jensen points out: "If SES were the cause of IQ, the correlations between adults' IQ and their attained SES would not be markedly higher than the correlation between children's IQ and their parents' SES" (1998: 491). Across many studies, the correlations between adult IQ and a person's attained SES are in the 0.50 to 0.70 range (Jensen, 1998). Thus, the variance explained by the offspring's IQ in their adult-attained SES is at least four times greater than that explained by parental SES. In Strenze's (2007: 411) meta-analysis of 86 SES studies, he noted:

> Looking at the "best studies," we can observe the corrected sample size weighted correlations of .56, .45, and .23 between intelligence and education, occupation, and income, respectively. These correlations can be treated as the most appropriate estimates of the relationship between intelligence and socioeconomic success.

The corresponding correlations with parental SES were .41, .30, and .15, so parental SES also significantly affects offspring attained SES, even if less than offspring IQ.

Murray (2002: 340) examined data from the National Longitudinal Survey of Youth asking: "How much difference would it make to income inequality if, magically, every child in the country could be given the same advantages as the more fortunate of our children?" To address this question, he created two samples of sibling pairs: a "utopian" sample of 733 pairs who were born in wedlock, had not experienced parental divorce by age 8, and whose families had a median income of $64,586 ($125,300 in 2025 dollars), and a control sample of 1,075 sibling pairs with family histories failing one or more of the criteria for inclusion in the utopian sample. Murray compared paired sibling life outcomes—median family income, marital status, and out-of-wedlock childbearing—between the samples when subjects were 30 to 38. He also compared outcomes within each sample by IQ levels broken down into five categories ranging from 120+ to ≤ 80. The first division compared between-sample differences, and the second compared within-sample differences.

The utopian sample enjoyed a family SES advantage over the control sample; they made more money, were more likely to be married, and were less likely to have children out of wedlock. However, within-sample differences based on IQ levels were much greater than between samples. The median family income in the 120+ IQ category was $70,700 in the utopian and $65,100 in the control sample, a $5,600 advantage. However, *within* the samples, the 120+ IQ siblings enjoyed a median income of $47,100 more than their ≤ 80 IQ siblings in the utopian sample and $46,700 more in the control sample. Two percent of the women in the utopian sample with an IQ of 120+ had a child out of wedlock, versus 10% of women in the control sample. In the ≤ 80 IQ group, 44% in the utopian sample and 69% in the control group had a child out of wedlock. These data convincingly show that IQ is more important than the SES of the family of origin in determining a variety of life outcomes.

A longitudinal study of 4,298 British males found that meritocratic factors (intelligence, aspirations, motivation, and possession of educational qualifications) assessed when they were 11 and 16 years old accounted for 48% of the variance in occupational status at age 33. All measured background variables (parental SES, type of housing, type of school, and parents' aspirations) accounted for 8% of the variance. Based on this six-fold difference in the proportion of variance explained, the authors concluded that "occupational selection in Britain appears to take place largely on meritocratic principles" (Bond & Saunders, 1999: 217). Another British longitudinal study (Nettle, 2003) followed a cohort of all children born in one week in 1958 to the age of 42. All children had their mental abilities tested at the age of seven. The primary finding of this study was that childhood intellectual ability is associated with class mobility in adulthood uniformly across all social classes of origin. Nettle found an IQ difference of 24.1 points between those who attained professional status and those in the unskilled class, regardless of the class of origin. Nettle concluded that "intelligence is the strongest single factor causing class mobility in contemporary societies that has been identified" (2003: 560).

Environmental Effects on IQ

Nothing points more clearly to the environmental effects on intelligence than the Flynn Effect. Many of these effects are related to SES. Flynn noted increases in average national IQ levels of 21 points from 1932 to 2000, and because gene pools change over that period, the effect has to be environmental. The bulk of the IQ increase has been in similarities ("How is a dog like a rabbit?"), which has increased by 24 points, whereas the vocabulary, arithmetic, and information components have increased by only three (Flynn, 2007). Dickens and Flynn (2001) note that the high heritability of IQ in tandem with large IQ gains attributed to the environment, is a paradox. Flynn (2007: 90) maintains that the direct genetic effect on IQ is only about 36%, with 64% resulting from G*x*E effects. The G*x*E interplay results in what Dickens and Flynn call a multiplier effect because "genes can get matched with environments of corresponding quality only through genetically influenced traits" (2001: 349). A match between parents and offspring results in what may be a small genetic advantage at birth (passive rGE) being multiplied into a large phenotypic advantage in adulthood by accumulating evocative and active rGE effects. Genes and environments are reciprocally causative, inflating genetic and environmental advantages such that higher IQ leads to better environments, which, in turn, result in higher IQ. In earlier times, children born into advantaged and disadvantaged environments lived in different worlds, so the multiplier effect suppressed the power of environmental effects: "The match between genes and environment means that environmental factors, however potent, to a large extent just reinforce the advantage or disadvantage that genes confer. So the match masks the potency of environmental factors" (Dickens & Flynn, 2001: 351).

During the period the Flynn Effect has worked, the masking has slipped because of the better environments (better health care, nutrition, education, and so forth) to which successive generations have been exposed, and now: "The potency of environmental factors stands out in bold relief" (Dickens & Flynn, 2001: 351). The modern advances noted earlier have had a major impact on cognitive abilities. Eppig, Fincher, and Thornhill (2010) attribute a substantial part of the Flynn effect to the huge decrease in infectious diseases in Western nations during the relevant period. They found correlations between average IQ in countries worldwide and parasite stress ranging from -0.76 to -0.82. They note the mechanism behind the relationship: "From an energetics standpoint, a developing human will have difficulty building a brain and fighting off infectious diseases at the same time, as both are very metabolically costly tasks" (p. 3801).

Another paradox is that while the population's mean IQ has increased, scores on the Scholastic Aptitude Test (SAT) have declined. How can IQ increase at the same time that SAT scores, which largely rely on IQ, have decreased? Pietschnig and Voracek (2015: 290) explain:

> In this regard, changes in educational systems might have allowed individuals from all educational backgrounds (i.e., lower-performing individuals) to seek entry into higher education, thus explaining a rise of IQ scores in the presence of a decline of scores on the Scholastic Aptitude Test.

The decline in SAT scores is thus attributable to the same source as the rise in IQ; greater equality has led to more children with lower IQs taking the SAT and lowering mean SAT scores.

The Flynn effect has ended in developed nations as we have wrung all the IQ-enhancing juice from the environment we can, and we are even witnessing a decline in mean IQ in those nations since the high point in 1998 (Flynn, 2013). Rietveld et al. (2016) found that among the 70 IQ experts surveyed, most expected continued IQ gains in developing countries but a decline in Western countries. The most likely reasons they gave for this "anti-Flynn effect" were dysgenic fertility (low-IQ individuals having more children), immigration from low-IQ countries, and declining education standards. A study over three decades of Norwegian birth cohorts found evidence for this. Bratsberg and Rogeberg (2018, p. 6674) note: "A negative intelligence–fertility gradient is hypothesized to have been disguised by a positive environmental Flynn effect, revealing itself in data only once the ceiling of the Flynn effect was reached."

We should briefly note environmental factors that lead to lower cognitive functioning. Child maltreatment results in cognitive impairment, which is hypothesized to result from disruptions to normal brain development. As numerous studies have documented, maltreated children have lower IQs than children in similar environments (Tingberg & Nilsson, 2020). Crozier and Barth's (2005) based on the National Study of Child and Adolescent Wellbeing showed that 32.6% of maltreated children scored at or lower than one standard deviation below the mean on IQ. According to national norms, only 15.8% of children would be expected to score this low.

The most preventable cause of low IQ is maternal alcohol ingestion during pregnancy. During embryogenesis, immature neurons migrate from their birthplace to their assigned location guided by molecular messengers. The brain is most vulnerable to insults during this migratory phase because molecular guides are susceptible to attacks by teratogens, which may direct neurons to the wrong area or to self-destruct (Prayer et al., 2006). Mothers who drink while pregnant introduce their fetuses to neurotoxins that produce several neuro disorders, the most serious of which is fetal alcohol syndrome (FAS). FAS affects the behavior of children via its effects on the frontal lobes, various subcortical regions, the serotonergic system, and the myelination process (Little et al., 2021).

Lead, found mostly today in paint dust in older homes in low SES neighborhoods, also decreases IQ. The IQ decrement per unit increase in micrograms per deciliter of blood (μg/dl) of lead is an average of 0.50 points (Koller et al., 2004). Toxic levels of lead (>40 μg/dl) distort enzymes, interfere with the development of the endogenous opiate system, disrupt the dopamine system, and reduce serotonin and other brain chemicals (Wright et al., 2008). An fMRI study found that grey matter was inversely correlated with mean childhood lead concentrations in mostly Black young adults (Cecil et al., 2008). Their mean childhood blood lead concentration was 13.3 μg/dl, far above the 2006 average of 1.5 μg/dl in the general population (Bellinger, 2008). The grey matter lost was concentrated in the frontal lobes and the anterior cingulate cortex, both vital behavior-moderating areas responsible for cognitive and executive functioning.

Temperament and SES

Intelligence and temperament are "the two great pillars of differential psychology" (Chamorro-Premuzic & Furman, 2005: 352). Temperament must thus also be considered important for SES attainment. A 30-year longitudinal study of children from *middle-class* families with or without a history of temper tantrums in childhood discovered a variety of negative outcomes that can arise from a single temperamental dimension (Caspi, Bem, & Elder, 1989). The majority of bad-tempered boys ended up in lower-status occupations than their fathers, had erratic work histories, experienced more unemployment, and were more than twice as likely to be divorced by age 40 than males with more tranquil temperaments. Women with ill-tempered dispositions as children tended to marry men from classes lower than their own, were more than twice as likely as their more pleasant sisters to be divorced, and had significantly more marital conflict. This study illustrates that people with a tendency to be disagreeable and to respond more often with negative rather than positive emotionality, take their temperamental style with them wherever they go, from home to school, to work, to marriages, and that its cumulative effect can land one at the low end of the SES hierarchy via erratic work histories and marital disruptions. Thus, a middle-class upbringing does not guarantee achieving middle-class status in adulthood. Individuals with bad temperaments lack the personal resources to move up the status hierarchy, or to prevent themselves from sliding down it.

Because SES reflects patterns of cognition and behavior, certain traits such as conscientiousness, agreeableness, and self-control contribute considerably to SES. Conscientiousness consists of sub-traits such as being well-organized, disciplined, scrupulous, orderly, responsible, and reliable at one end of the continuum, and disorganized, careless, unreliable, irresponsible, and unscrupulous at the other. Agreeableness is the tendency to be friendly, considerate, courteous, helpful, and cooperative with others. Agreeable people tend to trust others, compromise with them, empathize with and aid them. This list of sub-traits suggests a high degree of concern for prosocial conformity and social desirability. Disagreeable persons display the opposite characteristics. Conscientiousness and agreeableness are positively correlated but far from perfect: someone can be conscientious at work but thoroughly disagreeable as a person, and can be agreeable but lackadaisical at work. Conscientiousness and agreeableness undergird the social skills that Deming (2017) shows are becoming more important in today's labor market.

In three intergenerational studies following subjects from early childhood to retirement, Judge et al. (1999) found that conscientiousness measured in childhood predicted adult occupational status ($r = 0.49$) and income ($r = 0.41$) in adulthood, which are only slightly less than the correlations between general mental ability (GMA) and the same variables ($r = .51$ and $.53$, respectively). Schmidt and Hunter's analysis of GMA and personality variables in attaining occupational success concluded that "the burden of prediction [of attained

SES] is borne almost entirely by GMA and conscientiousness" (2004: 170). Another longitudinal study of 7,081 individuals from infancy to 37 from the National Longitudinal Survey of Youth 1979—Child and Young Adult (NLSY79-CYA), with outcome measurements taken at 27.7 years, looked at temperament traits such as activity, fearfulness, positive affect, and found several interesting results (Wright & Jackson, 2022). This study found that temperament predicted SES level, incarceration, divorce, family relationships, and occupational success at significant levels, in addition to various health-related variables.

Poverty and SES

Poverty and SES are related, but they are not synonymous. Poverty is a state of deprivation based on income, usually at or below 50% of the median household income. SES is based on the level of education and occupational prestige, in addition to income. A grad student or adjunct professor may have an income below the poverty line but a high level of education. We have looked at putative causes of SES variability, but what causes poverty? It is estimated that 58% of Americans have tasted poverty for at least one year, but only about 12–15% of the population are mired in poverty long-term (Hacker, 2006). A US Department of the Treasury (2007) study showed that 57.6% of taxpayers in the lowest income quintile in 1996 had moved to higher quintiles (5.3% to the highest quintile; from the bottom fifth to the highest fifth) by 2005. The study showed that more than half of the 2005 top quintile in 2005 were not there in 1996, which indicates considerable income mobility in both directions. Poverty is thus a short-term blip for most people. However, for those in deep poverty, it may be permanent and even intergenerational. According to the US Census Bureau (2021), single-parent mothers are most likely to be in this sad condition. Thirty-five percent of single-parent households were in poverty versus 9.5% of two-parent households.

Brady (2023) examined several models that attempt to explain poverty. Structural models emphasize demographic and labor market contexts, such as deindustrialization, which has resulted in the loss of millions of well-paying jobs for the working class. The second model is cultural, which he describes as "the argument that a problematic or pathological culture causes counter-productive behavior and risks that cause poverty. Furthermore, poverty feeds back into and reinforces that problematic culture, often intergenerationally" (p. 9). The political model emphasizes power, policies, and institutions that indirectly cause poverty by moderating the relationship between cultural risks and poverty. The behavioral model (which he calls "fixing the poor") is tightly related to the cultural model. All models doubtless tell part of the SES story. However, as the Department of Treasury data showed, there is much mobility up and down the SES ladder. This mobility must be caused by individual actions aided by heritable differences in the traits previously discussed.

People vary in how they respond to environmental conditions according to the characteristics they bring with them via G*x*E and rGE processes.

Poverty and Crime

The link between poverty and crime is a common feature in criminology, but it has been undertheorized. A question rarely asked is "Does poverty cause crime, or does crime cause poverty"? Sampson (2000: 711) notes that:

> [E]veryone believes that "poverty causes crime" it seems; in fact, I have heard many a senior sociologist express frustration as to why criminologists would waste time with theories outside the poverty paradigm. The reason we do ... is that the facts demand it.

Sawhill (2003: 82) also avers that academic thought "has coalesced around the view that bad behaviors are a consequence, rather than a cause, of poverty. The result was that scholars continued to define the underclass simply in economic terms." Schmalleger (2004: 223) likewise notes that the underlying assumption of all structural theories is that the "root causes" of crime are poverty and social injustices. But he also notes: "Some now argue the inverse of the 'root causes' argument, saying that poverty and what appear to be social injustices are produced by crime, rather than the other way around." This is an important point, but neither may directly cause the other because some third set of variables may cause both crime and poverty, or the effect may be bidirectional, suggesting that poverty causes crime, but crime also causes concentrated disadvantage, as studies by Hipp (2010) and Vélez (2018) show.

Merton's anomie/strain theory avers that crime is a way for people denied access to legitimate opportunities by social structure to obtain what their culture has taught them to want. More recent theorists using the anomie paradigm emphasize personal disabilities that may prevent some individuals from taking advantage of the available opportunities (Agnew, 1992; 2005; Walsh, 2000). Vold, Bernard, and Snipes (1998: 177) remark, "It is not merely a matter of talented individuals confronted with inferior schools and discriminatory hiring practices. Rather, a good deal of research indicates that many delinquents and criminals are untalented individuals who cannot compete effectively in complex industrial societies." Whether people are denied access to legitimate means of achieving middle-class success by "the system" or by personal deficiencies, the result is the same—frustration, alienation, envy, rage, and resentment—all of which generate pressure among some individuals to realize their financial aspirations and status in criminal ways. The causal direction of the poverty/crime relationship is thus immaterial in this view because something else (either a discriminatory social system or personal deficiencies inimical to occupational success) has led to both poverty and crime.

Sawhill notes that "in order to achieve a middle-class life, an individual must do a few specific things: graduate from high school, defer having a baby until marriage, and obtain steady employment" (2003: 81). These are things people choose to do or not to do. Wright (2009: 73–89) also writes about choices:

> It should be expected that individuals with similar traits and abilities, who have made many of the same choices over their life course, should tend to cluster together within economic and social spheres. In other words, a degree of homogeneity should exist within neighborhoods, within networks in those neighborhoods, and within families in those neighborhoods.

This is similar to Kornhauser's (1978: 104) question, "How do we know that area differences in delinquency rates result from the aggregated characteristics of communities rather than the characteristics of individuals selectively aggregated into communities?"

Sampson and Bean (2006: 29) also maintain that structure (neighborhood conditions) versus culture (norms and values) arguments produce a false dichotomy because each is created by and creates the other: "The relational approach understands culture not as a simplistic adaptation to structure in a one-way causal flow, but an intrasubjective organizing mechanism that shapes unfolding social processes and that is constituent of social structure." Moffitt and Beckley (2015: 122) likewise argue that areas of concentrated disadvantage are created and sustained by people: "People who have behaved antisocially 'end up in' criminogenic environments selectively. ... Thus, selection effects account for much of the observed correlations between crime and many of its putative environmental risk factors." However, there are limits to how much accountability we can rightfully demand from people because, as our discussion of free will pointed out, the choices we make depend on many things that may be beyond our control, to which we may add such things as illness, economic recessions, and just plain bad luck.

It is undeniable that childhood poverty is associated with a myriad of negative outcomes that are associated with crime. We surveyed some of these, such as maltreatment and exposure to teratogens, in Chapter 8. Sarsour et al. (2011) showed that family SES and single-parent families predicted children's inhibitory control and cognitive flexibility. Low-SES children living with a single parent performed lower on executive function tests than children with similarly low SES in two-parent homes. Other research suggests that chronic physiological stress among children living in poverty is responsible for their reduced executive function and self-regulation (Duncan, Magnuson, & Votruba-Drzal, 2017). Our hearts must go out to these children who bear no responsibility for the conditions in which they are born. Various government programs have been implemented to address the problem, beginning with Lyndon Johnson's "War on Poverty" in 1964.

The War on Poverty and Other Anti-Poverty Programs

The War on Poverty was not a crime prevention policy per se, although most criminologists assumed that reducing poverty would significantly reduce crime because poverty was considered its "root cause." Anti-poverty programs derived from Johnson's policy currently involve 126 different federal and state programs that have consumed $23 *trillion* from 1964 to 2018 (Tanner, 2019). Despite the multitude of programs and rivers of dollars, the problem of poverty remains intractable, and the anti-poverty programs have had no effect in terms of reducing crime. Indeed, crime became more prevalent after the War on Poverty began. Bitler and Karoly (2015: 640) criticize the program because it increased what it was supposed to alleviate:

> The House Budget Committee's appraisal of the War on Poverty, which emphasized the existence of a multiplicity of programs that create a "poverty trap," leading to hundreds of billions of dollars in spending with unclear benefit given that the official poverty rate has remained little changed.

Many scholars view the war on poverty as partly the cause of the rise in unwed motherhood and believe that welfare benefits partly account for unwed motherhood. Walter Williams (2011: 8) remarks, "Using National 1979 Longitudinal Survey of Youth data, Anne Hill and June O'Neill found that a 50 percent increase in the monthly value of welfare benefits led to a 43 percent increase in out-of-wedlock births." In response to this and other evidence, Congress passed the Personal Responsibility and Work Opportunity Reconciliation Act (PRWORA) in 1996. When President Bill Clinton signed the act, he stated that it "gives us a chance we haven't had before to break the cycle of dependency that has existed for millions and millions of our fellow citizens, exiling them from the world of work. It gives structure, meaning and dignity to most of our lives."

PRWORA reduced nonmarital births minimally, but it produced a heightened sense of personal responsibility and self-worth among those who left welfare and went to work, and it reduced child poverty. Blank and Schoeni (2003) report that poverty among Black children reached a historical low of 30% in 2001, with the greatest income increases in evidence in single-parent families, and that the states producing the greatest increase in the income of single-parent families were states that adopted the strongest carrot-and-stick incentives. Lichter, Graefe, and Brown (2003, p. 60) note the positive effects of PRWORA:

> If measured by employment take-up rates among single mothers and by reductions in welfare case-loads, the success of "work first" welfare programs is unprecedented. Caseloads have been cut by more than 50% after peaking in 1994, while poverty rates among female-headed families with children were the lowest on record in 2000.

O'Neill and Hill report that "By the end of the second year after leaving welfare their [single mother's] incomes were 50 to 70% above poverty" (2003: 2).

Of course, PRWORA had its critics who mostly decried its emphasis on individual failure and irresponsibility. It has also been accused of racism because it disproportionately targeted Black women as more likely to give birth non-maritally, sexism because it violated women's rights to reproductive choices and privacy, and "enforced" heterosexual marriage, and blanket discrimination in "involuntary servitude" (e.g., Bailey, 1995; Brush, 2003; Thomas, 2000). It encouraged, not enforced, marriage (heterosexual because, after all, it focused on reproduction), and it is hard to see how working for one's daily bread can be called involuntary servitude. Liebertz and Bunch (2018: 481) describe some of the major impacts of the PRWORA ignored by its critics:

> The critics' worst fears failed to materialize in the earliest years of TANF's implementation, and many analysts declared PRWORA to be a great success. The number of welfare recipients had been decreasing prior to the legislation and continued at an even greater rate afterward. From 1993 to 1997, the national welfare rolls declined by 31%. By 1999, the number had jumped to 50%. The new welfare system did not appear to cause a spike in poverty either, as the Urban Institute and others had cautioned. Although nearly a third of female-headed households with children were impoverished in 2000, that percentage was one of the lowest levels in recent history.

14 Religion: Barrier or Bridge to Antisocial Behavior?

Religion: The Moral Institution

Sociologists view religion as society's moral institution that binds people with a core of common beliefs and a source of unity, stability, and informal social control (Walsh, 2023). It is, therefore, intuitively reasonable to believe that because religion is the institution that carries society's moral torch, it is a powerful barrier against all forms of antisocial behavior, particularly crime and delinquency. However, we rarely see discussions of the role of religion in criminology textbooks, perhaps because the benefits or drawbacks of religion are most strongly argued by theists and atheists rather than criminologists. The retreat of religion in our increasingly secularized society has given rise to people who maintain that religion is a source of intolerance and violence and, therefore, more of a bridge to crime and delinquency than a barrier.

Of course, religion can be both a bridge and a barrier at different times, places, and circumstances, depending on which religion we are discussing and what crimes are involved. Examining the issue at various levels of analysis (demographic areas versus individuals), how religion was measured (attendance at places of worship, religiosity scores, or the percentage of religious adherents in counties or states), the specific religion or type of crime examined, where to sample was obtained (secularized California versus high-religious states such as Utah) or in terms of intrinsic versus extrinsic religious motivation of individuals. Using different measures may produce results showing that religion has a positive influence on preventing crime and delinquency or that it points to the opposite conclusion.

There is little doubt where the sentiments of the American founding fathers lay. In George Washington's farewell address on leaving his second presidential term, he remarked:

> Of all the dispositions and habits which lead to political prosperity, religion and morality are indispensable supports. In vain would that man claim the tribute of patriotism, who should labor to subvert these great pillars of human happiness, these firmest props of the duties of men and citizens. ... Whatever may be conceded to the influence of refined

DOI: 10.4324/9781003662495-17

> education on minds of peculiar structure, reason and experience both forbid us to expect that national morality can prevail in exclusion of religious principle.
>
> (Virginia Museum of Culture & History Website)

Free societies assume the voluntary compliance of their citizens to moral rules, which is best accomplished when religion is free and independent of the state. As Martin Luther King, Jr. noted, religion "is not the master or the servant of the state, but rather the conscience of the state" (1986: 501). The Jeffersonian maxim states, "government is best which governs least, because its people discipline themselves" (Peterson, 1960: 79). Democratic societies provide wide space for personal freedom, but also require equally high standards of self-governance, and disciplining ourselves requires a sound basis of an objective morality seen as absolute. If we fail in moral self-governance, the state will intervene, as Benjamin Franklin noted: "Only a virtuous people are capable of freedom. As nations become more corrupt and vicious, they have more need of masters" (Boyack, 2012: 235). Moving forward almost a century, Robert Winthrop, a 19th-century Speaker of the House of Representatives, similarly remarked:

> All societies of men must be governed in some way or other. The less they may have of stringent State Government, the more they must have of individual self-government. The less they rely on public law or physical force, the more they must rely on private moral restraint. Men, in a word, must necessarily be controlled, either by a power within them, or by a power without them; either by the Word of God, or by the strong arm of man; either by the Bible, or by the bayonet.
>
> (1952: 172)

Preserving a free society by moral restraints on the behavior of rulers and the ruled is religion's most valuable secular function. Glen (2012: 38) quotes Alexis de Tocqueville as noting: "Despotism may govern without faith, but liberty cannot. Religion is much more necessary in the republic they advocate than in the monarchy which they attack; and in democratic republics most of all." Similarly, historian Will Durant opined:

> Conduct, deprived of its religious supports, deteriorates into epicurean chaos; and life itself, shorn of consoling faith, becomes a burden alike to conscious poverty and to weary wealth. In the end a society and its religion tend to fall together, like body and soul, in a harmonious death.
>
> (1935: 71)

In another work with Ariel Durant, it was observed that: "There is no significant example in history ... of a society successfully maintaining moral life without the aid of religion (Durant & Durant, 1968: 51).

Religion as a Bridge to Antisocial Behavior

The notion that religion provides the basis of morality and prosocial behavior has been under attack by the New Atheism movement. The movement came into prominence following the tragic events of 9/11, with New Atheism's leaders citing these events as emboldening them to attack all religions. New Atheism is a kind of fundamentalist atheism led by the gifted and articulate "Four Horsemen" of atheism: biologist Richard Dawkins, philosopher Daniel Dennett, neuroscientist Sam Harris, and journalist Christopher Hitchens. In the hands of these clever wordsmiths, "old atheism" (simply the non-belief in God or gods) has been repackaged as a doctrinal commitment and delivered aggressively and dogmatically, tactics that make people sit up and take notice. Between them, these four authors have sold millions of books; Dawkins's *The God Delusion* alone remained almost a year on the *New York Times* best-seller list.

War is the ultimate form of antisocial behavior. The events of 9/11 precipitated a war in Afghanistan, which the American-led coalition viewed as one of retaliation with the primary objective being the capture of Osama Bin Laden, but which the Afghans viewed as a jihad or holy war (Guest, 2010). If we take the Afghan view, it provides ammunition for the position that throughout history, war has been largely precipitated by religion. For instance, Sam Harris boldly states that religion has been "the most prolific source of violence in our history" (2005: 27). Dawkins also claims that: "Religious wars really are fought in the name of religion, and they have been horribly frequent in history" (2006: 316). Harris and Dawkins are good scientists, but their grasp of history is suspect, as Robin Schumacher's examination of Philip and Axelrod's three-volume *Encyclopedia of Wars* demonstrates. Schumacher notes that the *Encyclopedia* lists 1,763 wars waged throughout recorded human history and that "[o]f those wars, the authors categorize 123, as being religious in nature, which is an astonishingly low. However, when one subtracts out those waged in the name of Islam (66), the percentage is cut by more than half to 3.23%" (2012: np). However, if Harris and Dawkins believe that religion is the driving force behind war, it is understandable that they should attribute lesser evils, such as crime and delinquency, to religion.

As for crime, delinquency, and other forms of antisocial behavior, Richard Dawkins wrote in *The God Delusion*): "My uninformed opinion is that religious believers loot and destroy more than unbelievers" (2006: 261), and "Such research evidence as there is certainly doesn't support the common view that religiosity is positively correlated with morality" (p. 229). In his *God is Not Great*, Christopher Hitchens goes a step further than Dawkins to claim that evidence not only fails to support the claim that religiosity is positively correlated with morality, but that religion encourages antisocial behavior. Citing claims that Christianity promotes prosocial behavior, he writes: "In fact, if a proper statistical inquiry could ever be made, I am sure the evidence would be the other way [i.e., non-believers commit fewer anti-social acts than Christians]" (2008: 4). Hitchins also wrote:

> It is impossible to claim that religion makes people behave in a more kindly or civilised manner. ... The worse the offender the more devout he turns out to be. The chance that a person committing crimes was 'faith-based' was almost 100%.
>
> (2008, p. 66).

There are certainly occasions when religion is manipulated by its leaders to serve antisocial ends, such as encouraging terrorism. "In such cases, a 'warped' anti-mainstream religious message is communicated externally (by proponents of terroristic action) to individuals to encourage them to violence in the name of either religious obligation or potential transcendental rewards (i.e., heaven, '72 virgins' etc.)" (Topalli, Brezina, & Bernhardt, 2013: 53–54). Topalli, Brezina, and Bernhardt conducted interviews with 48 active non-incarcerated African American criminals, 44 of whom self-identified as Christians. They do not claim that there is a causative association between religion and crime, but rather that their study highlights the co-existence of conventional religious beliefs and criminal offending because criminals can justify or neutralize their offending by appealing to them, as the following excerpts from their interviews reveal:

Subject:	I believe in God and the Bible and stuff. I believe in Christmas, and uh, you know the commitments and what not.
Interviewer:	You mean the Commandments?
Subject:	Yeah that. I believe in that.
Interviewer:	Can you name any of them?
Subject:	Ahhh ... well, I don't know ... like don't steal, and uh, don't cheat and shit like that.

> Uhmm ... I can't remember the rest. I didn't really go to church enough to know like all the details, just the important shit, like Jesus forgives you for all your bad shit if you donate some money to the church, or pray and say you're sorry.
>
> (Topalli, Brezina, & Bernhardt, 2013: 59)

Another offender stated that his crimes are excusable because, as he perceives it, he has no choice in the matter and thus he will be forgiven:

> Well, you do get punished for doing wrong, but not if you don't have no choice. It's like this here. See, if I go and rob a motherfucker then I'm still going to Heaven because ... uhm ... it's like, Jesus knows I ain't have no choice, you know?
>
> (Topalli, Brezina, & Bernhardt, 2013: 60)

These offenders use their limited knowledge of Christianity to rationalize their criminality. Some claimed that God permitted or even wanted them to continue in their criminal ways! However, a vague and distorted understanding of Christian principles hardly qualifies as Topalli, Brezina, and Bernhardt's "adherence to religious doctrine" or justifies calling such people religious just because they call themselves Christians and report that they believe in certain Christian doctrines while being woefully ignorant about their content. It seems incongruous to take these data as any more than poorly articulated justifications ("techniques of neutralization") for their antisocial behavior.

Certain ecological and cross-cultural studies provide data that lend support to the notion that more religion equals more crime. For instance, Ellison, Burr, and McCall (2003) argue that a major factor accounting for disproportionate rates of violence in the Southern United States is its density of conservative evangelical Protestants in the South and that these people have a higher tolerance for violence when threats are perceived to one's honor, family, or property, or in defense of women. They examined the link between homicide rates and the density of evangelical Protestants in a sample of almost 250 metropolitan statistical areas and found that homicide rates were higher in areas with larger proportions of conservative evangelical Protestants. Lee (2006) counterpunches with a study that showed violent crime rates across the United States are, on average, consistently lower where there are more churches per capita. Then there is Phil Zuckerman's point that:

> If religion, prayer, or God-belief hindered criminal behavior, and secularity or atheism fostered lawlessness, we would expect to find the most religious nations having the lowest murder rates and the least religious nations having the highest. But we find just the opposite. Murder rates are actually lower in more secular nations and higher in more religious nations where belief in God is deep and widespread.
>
> (2009: 955)

Zuckerman is correct. According to the United Nations Office on Drugs and Crime (as cited in Walsh & Jorgenson, 2025), murder rates are many times higher in most Central and South American countries than in the more secularized countries of Europe and North America. The US murder rate was 6.8 per 100,000 in 2020, while for El Salvador, it was almost 10 times higher at 67.1. Other high-rate homicide countries include Honduras (41.0), Jamaica (56.4), and Venezuela (49.9). However, to claim that these data are indicative of a "more religion equals more crime" notion begs the question of the ecological fallacy. Piantadosi, Byar, and Green (1988: 893) note: "Serious errors can result when an investigator makes the seemingly natural assumption that the inferences from an ecological analysis must pertain either to the individuals within the groups or to individuals across groups."

Ecological studies are valuable in their own right when confined to the appropriate level of analysis. However, when analysis goes beyond it to imply that what is true of the amalgamated population is also true of subgroups and individuals within the whole, we confront the error of aggregation bias (the ecological fallacy). Countries and their subdivisions are divided in many ways other than religion. High homicide nations tend to be politically failed third-world countries with high poverty rates, corrupt governments, the absence of effective police power and a trusted system of justice, and high levels of narcotics-driven organized crime. These are conditions that virtually invite high crime rates, but it cannot be said that religious groups and individuals within them are responsible for it. The same can be said of studies of the density of conservative evangelical Protestants in a population or the number of churches per capita in a population. Neither can be cited as supporting either the notion that religion equals more crime or less crime, except in ecological terms, which says nothing about the enabling or constraining effect of religion on individuals living there.

W. S. Robinson, who coined the term "ecological fallacy," asks, "whether ecological correlations can validly be used as substitutes for individual correlations." He replied, "They cannot" (1950/2009: 341). Among the examples Robinson provided were the English literacy rates and the percentage of foreign-born individuals age 10 or older in all 48 states of the USA (in 1930). The ecological correlation was 0.53, which might lead some to conclude that the foreign-born are more illiterate than the native-born. However, when computed at the individual level, the correlation was in the opposite direction (-0.11), indicating that the foreign-born are more likely to be literate in English than the native-born. The opposite directions of the correlations show how wrong it is to use aggregated population data to make inferences about specific groups or individuals within the population.

Religion as a Barrier to Antisocial Behavior

We have seen that New Atheists such as Dawkins and Hitchens are prominent adherents of the notion that religion is positively associated with crime and delinquency. However, both Dawkins and Hitchens failed to do their homework, although Dawkins at least acknowledged that his opinion was uninformed. There are hundreds of what Hitchins calls "proper statistical inquiries" in the criminological literature relating to religion and antisocial behavior, which invariably show that the religiously committed are more prosocial than secularists.

In an examination of 113 studies linking attendance at religious services to criminal offending, the authors concluded, "attending religious services is the best documented correlate of [the prevention of] crime" (Ellis & Walsh, 2000: 205). In another review of 270 studies, the authors concluded:

> Finally, our updated systematic review suggests the beneficial relationship between religion and crime is not simply a function of religion's constraining function or what it discourages—opposing drug

> use, violence, or delinquent behavior—but also through what it encourages—promoting prosocial behaviors.
>
> (Johnson & Jang 2010: 129)

A study of over 17,000 adults from 13 industrial nations found that religious people are more law-abiding than non-religious people, and that: "The relationship was more pronounced in the case of 'overt' aspects of religiosity (especially church attendance and membership) than in the case of any specific religious beliefs" (Ellis & Peterson, 1996: 761). A representative sample of almost 184,000 young men and women concluded:

> Results indicate that the protective relationship between religiosity and criminal behaviors such as drug selling and theft is consistent across gender as well as across the developmental periods of adolescence and young adulthood. This study provides support for the validity of the invariance hypothesis as the protective effect of religiosity on criminal behavior was consistently observed across important sociodemographic differences.
>
> (Salas-Wright, Vaughn, & Maynard, 2014: 673)

Kelly et al.'s (2015) meta-analysis of 62 studies containing a total of 193,656 adolescents found that higher religiosity and church attendance resulted in less delinquency, regardless of how delinquency was measured. They remark:

> Mounting evidence points to the nonspurious effects of religiosity on crime and drug use, which are partly attributable to religiosity's prosocial outcomes. In other words, religiously involved adolescents are less likely to commit delinquency or use illicit drugs partly because they are more attached to their parents, more committed to educational goals, more conventional in moral beliefs, and less likely to have delinquent or drug-using friends than their nonreligious peers.
>
> (p. 507)

The attachment to parents, commitment to education, conventional moral beliefs, and involvement in a prosocial lifestyle are elements of the social bond and reflect better self-control. This was demonstrated in a study by Johnson et al. (2000). They analyzed data from a representative sample of interviews with 2,358 African American youths living in high-poverty neighborhoods where crime is rampant in Boston, Chicago, and Philadelphia and hypothesized:

> Church-attending youths are expected to show stronger attachment to parents, greater commitment to school, and/or more involvement in conventional activities because of their beliefs; in turn, these attachments

> reduce their chances of making delinquent friends and engaging in deviant activities, as compared with youths who do not attend church. It is also likely that church-attending youths live with parents who teach these values and behaviors.
>
> (p. 380)

They found that church attendance has a significant preventative impact on delinquency among disadvantaged youths after controlling for several background variables. For instance, the probability of drug usage declined by 46% from low or non-church attendance to high levels of church attendance; for drug dealing, the decline was 57%, and for non-drug crimes, the decline was 39%. Thus, even in the worst of criminogenic environments, serious religious commitment exerts a constraining effect on antisocial behavior. Similarly, almost 40 years ago, using three large national databases, Freeman (1986) found that church attendance is associated with substantial positive differences in the behavior of young Black males from poverty-stricken inner-city neighborhoods, which greatly increased their chances of escaping many of the problems that exist in America's inner cities.

Most people have an intuitive sense that belief in God is central to morality and that antisocial acts are more likely to arise from non-belief (Kelly, Kramer, & Shariff, 2024). French philosopher and skeptic Voltaire had this intuition: "I want my attorney, my tailor, my servants, even my wife to believe in God ... because then I shall be robbed and cuckolded less often" (Wilson, 1993: 219). Voltaire buttressed this with his famous pronouncement: "*Si Dieu n'existait pas, il faudrait l'inventer* [If God did not exist, it would be necessary to invent Him]" (Roca, 1978: 29). It is not only the religious who believe morality depends on belief in God. Arch-atheist philosopher Friedrich Nietzsche noted: "Christian morality is a command: its origin is transcendental ... it possesses truth only if God is truth—it stands or falls with the belief in God" (Nietzsche & Hollingdale, 1990: 80–81). Joel Marks (2012: 2) is another philosopher who believes it: "The long and the short of it is that I became convinced that atheism implies amorality; and since I am an atheist, I must therefore embrace amorality." He notes that people he calls "soft atheists" believe that a person can be an atheist and still believe in morality but dismisses them: "So was I [a softie], until I experienced my shocking epiphany that the religious fundamentalists are correct: without God, there is no morality." Marks also says he "has long been laboring with an unexamined assumption that there is such a thing as right and wrong. I now believe there isn't" (2016: 2). That is *really* a position that commends itself to those prone to harm others.

Will Gervais tested the intuition that belief in God is central to morality in five experiments with 1,152 participants who were asked to judge several immoral acts as more representative of Christianity or atheism. Participants, even atheist participants, judged each immoral act as more representative of atheists than of Christians. Gervais concluded: "These findings demonstrate a prevalent intuition that belief in God serves a necessary function in inhibiting immoral conduct" (2014: 7). Similar experimental data from Wright and Nichols (2014: 93) found: "Participants' (both Christian and atheist) moral appraisals of atheists were more negative than those of Christians who performed the same moral and immoral actions." They also reported immoral behavior "as more (internally and externally) consistent for atheists, and moral behavior more consistent for Christians." In a study of over 33,000 respondents from every inhabited continent, Lilienfeld et al. (2014) found a statistically significant tendency for professed atheists and agnostics to report higher levels of traits suggestive of a psychopathic personality, especially low self-control and a lack of empathy, than professed religious believers. This does not mean that atheists are psychopaths; it only means that atheists score higher on certain personality traits associated with psychopathy than theists.

Likewise, no one claims that atheism is inherently amoral or immoral. Many atheists are great people who live more moral lives than many theists, who subscribe to the universality of human rights, care about justice, value the good, and denounce evil. However, as Marks and Nietzsche point out, they cannot provide an ultimate justification necessary for a universal objective morality by which good and evil are delineated and understood. The Ten Commandments have provided all Western legal systems with religious guidance about right and wrong. Without such a basis, we do not have an objective basis for moral judgments and are left with a moral relativism that asserts what is deemed "good" and "bad"depends on culture or on whom we ask. If morality is not objective, we cannot, in good conscience, condemn evil practices if good and evil are only arbitrary and subjective, or, as Joel Marks claimed above, "there is such a thing as right and wrong" (2016: 2).

Religion and Self-Control

Self-governance presupposes high levels of adherence to moral standards of right and wrong. Moral prescriptions are "ought" propositions that inform people that they ought to do this or ought not to do that because it is right or wrong and for no other reason. Religion helps to clarify and reinforce society's moral prescriptions and proscriptions. The cultural basis of these rules in all Western nations and the bedrock of all modern Western systems of law is the Ten Commandments ("Thou shalt not kill," "Thou shalt not steal," and so forth) and other religious injunctions such as the Christian admonition to "Love thy neighbor as thyself" or the Jewish "What is hateful to you, do not do to your fellow man." These moral codes imply that people professing their belief in them will be more likely to behave accordingly.

Religion has a role in building and strengthening regulatory self-government, better known as self-control, in the face of temptation. Low self-control is considered the major correlate of antisocial behavior in criminology and is the default option in the absence of moral socialization. An important aspect of self-control is the ability of those who possess it to reconcile discrepancies between their behavior and beliefs, attitudes, and values. This self-regulatory strength is strengthened over time through repeated use. Religious congregations provide incentives for self-regulation and self-sanctions (self-monitoring guilt or shame) for failure to align one's behavior with moral standards. Living up to the standards of the Judeo-Christian tradition, accommodating the needs of others, volunteering one's time, and giving blood and money all strengthen the empathetic impulse that prevents one from harming others. McCullough and Willoughby (2009) concluded their review of the literature on religion and self-control by stating: "There is strong evidence for our proposition that religion is positively related to self-control as well as to traits such as Agreeableness and Conscientiousness that are considered to be the basic personality substrates of self-control" (p. 86).

This assumes that religion increases self-control, but it could be the case that people with high levels of self-control are more likely to be religious and that statistically controlling for self-control renders the negative religion-antisocial behavior relationship spurious. Kerley et al. (2011) found this to be so. When self-control was introduced into their model, the religion-antisocial behavior relationship was no longer statistically significant. Of course, one cannot determine temporal causal primacy using cross-sectional data, and which variable is rendered spurious depends on which one is considered in a model to be the primary causative variable and which is secondary. If they had entered religion as the control variable, it would have rendered self-control spurious.

Welch et al. (2006: 1615) found that both variables operate independently and that the association between religiosity and antisocial behavior was not "spuriously attributable to prior levels of self-control." Laird, Marks, and Marrero (2011) also found that while both religiosity and self-control were associated with less antisocial behavior, self-control did not render religiosity spurious. It was also found that the more meaningful their religious beliefs and the more they attended church services, the more likely they were to have good self-control. Similarly, Antonaccio and Tittle (2008) found that self-control and morality (religiosity was the major component in this measure) were significantly related to reducing criminal and deviant propensities. As they note, "morality is also shown to be a strong independent predictor with strength that seems to exceed substantially that of self-control. In addition, taking morality into account significantly reduces the coefficients for self-control, sometimes eliminating them entirely" (p. 479). More recently, Marcus and McCullough's (2021: 167) review of research from "lab and life" stated that:

> Religion is associated with a wide range of socially desirable behaviors and outcomes (particularly among adolescents), including lower rates of crime and delinquency, better school performance, and abstinence from risky sexual practices and substance use. ... we focus on evidence rituals (most notably, prayer), along with exposure to religious

> environments and institutions in the real world (e.g. religious schooling) influence self-control on the scale of weeks, months, and years—a conclusion that is also supported by rigorous longitudinal research.

Religion has thus been shown by a large number of cross-sectional, longitudinal, and experimental studies to be positively related to several prosocial life outcomes, especially to crime prevention.

Section 4

Issues in Criminal Justice

15 Abolish the Police: Why or Why Not?

Do the Police Prevent Crime?

The debate over whether policing in the United States should be reformed, transformed, or abolished is old. It lay moribund for a long time but was revitalized after the killing of George Floyd at the hands of the police in Minneapolis in 2020. African American activist Mariame Kaba, who self-describes as an anti-criminalization organizer and is perhaps the most radical proponent of police abolition, views the debate in entirely racial terms. She writes:

> I've been advocating the abolition of the police for years. Regardless of your view on police power — whether you want to get rid of the police or simply to make them less violent — here's an immediate demand we can all make: Cut the number of police in half and cut their budget in half. Fewer police officers equals fewer opportunities for them to brutalize and kill people.
>
> (Kaba, 2020: 1)

Kaba means literal abolition, as the title of her article shows: *Yes, we mean literally abolish the police*. She said in an interview with the *New Yorker*: "I am looking to abolish what I consider to be death-making institutions, which are policing, imprisonment, sentencing, and surveillance. ... Our current criminal justice system is rooted in the assumption that millions of people require policing, surveillance, containment, prison." Kaba wants to promote systemic thinking (crime is the fault of society) and to get rid of what she calls "our society's obsession with 'personal responsibility'" (Taylor, 2021: np). For Kaba, personal responsibility is bad, and believing you are a victim of society is healthy, but there is nothing healthy about disowning one's agency. This thinking feeds into the cult of victimhood and infantilizes Blacks as incapable of taking charge of their own lives. George W. Bush (2000) called this "soft bigotry of low expectations." Her position is another iteration of racial identity politics in which Blacks are homogenized and must

DOI: 10.4324/9781003662495-19

think alike. Recall Joe Biden's 2020 election claim: "You ain't black if you vote for Trump!" Biden's claim made African Americans mere appendages of the Democratic Party.

The Black Lives Matter (BLM) movement also racializes the police abolition debate, as the Black Lives Matter Global Network clearly shows: "Black Lives Matter is an ideological and political intervention in a world where *Black lives are systematically and intentionally targeted for demise*" (2016, np; my emphasis). Its 32-page agenda appeals for the abolition of capitalism and the traditional family, an unconditional basic income for all Blacks, a trillion-dollar job program, and reparations for slavery (Szetela, 2020: np). BLM's anti-police rhetoric was revealed in the comments of Melina Abdullah on the trial of Jussie Smollett, the Black man who falsely accused Trump supporters of beating him up. Abdullah called it a "white supremacist charade" and stated: "Black Lives Matter will continue to work towards the abolition of police and every unjust system" (Garger, 2021, np). BLM's demand for defunding the police gains little support from either Black (29%) or White (26%) communities. Most support for it is found among White liberals (49%) (Edwards-Levy & Robillard, 2020).

According to Cobbina-Dungy et al. (2022: 148), "the slogan defund the police was coined by protesters opposed to state sanctioned violence and the lack of accountability for those who use deadly force against Black civilians." However, no officer wants to kill anyone. Doing so is a traumatic experience that may haunt the officer for many years. Neither the public nor the media appreciate the profound difficulty police officers face in shoot/don't shoot situations, which are generally fraught with danger. They must make split-second decisions based on incomplete information and fundamentally unpredictable circumstances as to whether their lives or the lives of others are in danger. The BLM's narrative of homicidal White cops hunting down innocent Blacks is false, pernicious, and dangerous to both police officers and civilians, especially Black civilians (Chalfin et al., 2020; Mourtgos et al., 2022).

The incendiary nature of BLM rhetoric led Barbara Reynolds, a prominent Black civil rights activist, to condemn the movement. Drawing contrasts with the civil rights protesters in the 1960s, she notes,

> [A]t protests today, it is difficult to distinguish legitimate activists from the mob actors who burn and loot. The demonstrations are peppered with hate speech, profanity, and guys with sagging pants that show their underwear. Even if the Black Lives Matter activists are not the ones participating in the boorish language and dress, neither are they condemning it.
>
> Clayton, 2018: 457

Other scholars have a more nuanced view of abolition, such as reallocating funds from policing to social work and/or public health agencies. There is an almost Platonic idealism in such views. For instance, Bell (2021: 61) remarks,

> [T]he abolitionist goal of not giving power to state systems in order to build self-sustaining, self-determining communities commits abolitionists to not calling the police under any circumstances, to not seeking retribution when violence occurs within the movement community, when we ourselves or our loved ones are harmed.

So, we should not call the police when someone harms us or seek redress in the courts when harmed, or when our property is stolen. In this view, policing is a useless institution that does nothing to protect us or prevent crime. However, Fryer (2023: 556) notes that most abolitionists don't view things this way "because police actually do perform valuable societal functions." Braga, Papachristos, and Hureau (2012: 2) note their useful function in a meta-analysis of 65 studies of hot spot policing:

> The extant evaluation research suggests that hot spots policing is an effective crime prevention strategy. The research also suggests that focusing police efforts on high-activity crime places does not inevitably lead to crime displacement; rather, crime control benefits may diffuse into the areas immediately surrounding the targeted locations.

But there are others, such as Siegel et al. (2021: 262) who deny this:

> Reducing the size of police forces and the scope of their duties, as protesters have recently called for in the wake of George Floyd's killing by Minneapolis police officers, could reduce the number of police-civilian encounters and thereby reduce police killings. There is evidence that reductions in proactive policing may be associated with decreases in violent crime.

They cite evidence from Sullivan & O'Keeffe (2017), who noted that citizen crime complaints dropped by 3% to 6% during a seven-week NYPD work-to-rule strike. Reduced policing would necessarily mean fewer complaints and less violent crime in police data because no one will be around to arrest perpetrators or record them, but to say that fewer police officers result in fewer *actual* violent crimes is counterintuitive. Siegel et al. (2021: 247) also noted: "Several studies have documented that many cities have in fact over-deployed the police in direct proportion to the level of minority representation at the neighborhood level." The police deploy in crime hot spots, but the adverb "over" implies that they *excessively* deploy in those neighborhoods. However, this is not the view of those living in those neighborhoods. A national poll found that 81% of Black respondents want the police to spend either more or the same amount of time as before in their neighborhoods

(Saad, 2020). Several recent studies have found significant relationships between reduced police force size and higher crime rates (reviewed in Piza & Connealy, 2022).

The Effects of De-Policing

It is often noted that the value of something is best noticed by its absence, and we have seen many examples of the effects of police absence. David Bernstein remarks:

> In reaction to looting, rioting, and other forms of illegal behavior that threatened the well-being of the public, many police departments received implicit or explicit orders from their political supervisors to "stand down." The most famous example is the mayor of Seattle allowing—even encouraging—an anarchist zone to take root in Seattle, but there are many others.
>
> (2021: 180)

The reference is to Seattle's Capitol Hill Occupied Protest (CHOP) zone, a six-block radius occupied by armed BLM and Antifa followers in June 2020. The city's mayor, Jenny Durkan, surrendered the area to them, along with a police precinct, for a cop-free "safe zone" and forecasted "a summer of love." Not only did she allow it, but she also provided barriers and portable toilets to sustain it. However, the CHOP zone became a real-life version of the dystopian movie *The Purge*, in which America declares an annual national holiday in which all crimes become legal for 12 hours. Mayor Durkan said that since the East Police Precinct had been abandoned, shootings (including two fatal shootings), rapes, assaults, burglaries, and vandalism had been reported in the area: "The cumulative impacts of the gatherings and protests and the night-time atmosphere and violence has led to increasingly difficult circumstances for our businesses and residents. The impacts have increased and the safety has decreased" (BBC News, 2021, np). Not exactly the naïve "summer of love" she expected.

Similar events marred many US cities in 2020, and Bernstein notes that one of the dangers of the absence of police protection is vigilantism: "If law enforcement is unwilling or unable to preserve basic law and order, citizens will inevitably try to address the breach themselves" (2021: 180). He quotes two Black Atlantans interviewed by the press: "The police just don't seem to care anymore" about surging crime; "all this craziness is causing people to arm themselves." Another agreed: "If the police back off, there's really only two things left to do: defend yourself or be a victim" (p. 199). Even as parts of Chicago plunged into mayhem in 2020, Mayor Lori Lightfoot feared vigilantism and told citizens, "Do not pick up arms and try to be police. If there's a problem, call 911" (Spielman, 2020). This is the same mayor who pledged to reduce the police budget by $80 million when she took office in 2019. But as Chicago's homicide rate jumped 40% from 2019 to 2020, she asked the federal government for additional law enforcement resources to crack down on rampant crime (Miller & Golding, 2021).

Chicago also experienced huge increases in crime following the protests over the 2014 shooting death of Michael Brown by a White Ferguson, Missouri, police officer. Brown severely beat the officer while he was seated in his squad car. Cassell and Fowles (2018) found that fatal shootings increased by 66%, and non-fatal shootings increased by 44% in Chicago. They report that the most likely cause of the large increase in the 2016 Chicago homicide rate was the 80% reduction in police frisk stops. This led to more illegal guns on the streets and thus, more gun crimes. Chicago was not the only city that suffered. With anti-police rhetoric reaching feverish levels and stop-and-frisks banned, many US cities saw large increases in gun violence. Homicides in Minneapolis were up by a shocking 114% in 2020 from 2019 (Bernstein, 2021). The number of shooting victims in New York City more than doubled from 923 in 2019 to 1,868 in 2020, and homicides rose almost 45% from 2019, mostly attributable to less aggressive proactive policing in the wake of the protests/riots following the George Floyd killing (Chapman, 2021). The de-policing we witnessed in many cities in 2020/21 produced killing zones where the victims were overwhelmingly young Black males.

Chalfin et al. (2020: 1) notes:

> While there is now a strong consensus in the academic literature that the number of police officers combined with their presence and visibility reduces crime, the extent to which the benefits of additional law enforcement accrue equally to Black and white Americans remains a surprisingly open question.

Rosenfeld and Wallman (2019: 51) state: "Ample research findings have demonstrated the effectiveness of proactive policing practices, such as targeted patrol, in reducing crime rates." Bradford (2011) reviewed several studies on the effect of proactive policing and the number of police officers on the streets on crime. The overall conclusion was that more policing reduced crime, but more consistently on property crime than on violent crime. Bradford noted that this makes sense since property crime is usually committed by people who weigh the relative risks and rewards involved, and the presence of the police increases the risk. On the other hand, violent crime is usually committed in the heat of the moment in bars or the home, in which case, the deterrent effect of police officers on the street is not a particularly salient factor.

Is There a War on the Police?

Many people refer to the anti-police rhetoric as a war on the police. The term "war" may be hyperbolic, but as Morin et al. (2017a) note, 92% of police officers and 79% of the public agree that anti-police bias provided much of the impetus for the protests and riots. Ninety-one percent of Black police officers say that anti-police feelings are a reason for the protests, as do 56% of the Black public. Silver et al. (2022: 345) note that one national poll of likely voters found that 58% agreed that there is "a war on police in America today." Another poll found that 63% of Americans agreed with the statement "there is currently a war on police." As a result of this anti-police sentiment, the Pew Research Center's nationwide sample of 8,000 officers found that 72% of officers say they are less willing to question suspicious activity, and 76% are less willing to use appropriate force when necessary (Morin et al., 2017b). This inevitably entails fewer criminals being taken off the streets and more people, especially Black people, being victimized.

Police officers responded to the lack of support from their political supervisors by exhibiting low morale, backing off from enforcing the law, and retiring early or resigning in record numbers. Mourtgos et al. (2022: 22) note that there was a 279% increase in police resignations following the 2020 riots, and:

> On a large scale, turnover can lead to a police agency's inability to respond to calls for service, increased crime, and erosion of public trust. Indeed, some studies indicate that more police officers are associated with less crime. Recent research suggests a correlation between police force size and community violence, such that each additional 10 officers abates approximately one homicide.

They also note:

> Although the total reduction in homicide is roughly equal across Black and white victims, the decline in homicide is twice as large for Black victims in per capita terms. Thus, a rapid departure of police officers from a jurisdiction may have a disproportionately negative impact on communities of color.
>
> (Mourtgos et al., 2022: 22).

Police officers can't do their jobs when they know that city hall won't back them because of the fear of unrest. Thus, the tendency of the police in such jurisdictions is to back off, which further erodes public perceptions of the police. The 2021 UCR crime report shows that the number of arrests nationwide plummeted 24% in 2020 from 2019. It is thus no mystery why crime rose precipitously in 2020, including almost 5,000 more murders in 2020 than in 2019. Officers in my hometown have related that if they stop a Black person who claims "You only stopped me because I'm Black!" they are likely to say to themselves FIDO—"Fuck it; drive off." This kind of attitude was evidenced long before 2020. A police lieutenant applying for a professorship in my department told of a fatal shooting he attended shortly after the 1991 Rodney King riots in Los Angeles. When he arrived at the scene, the officer who had shot the armed suspect was sitting on the curb, saying over and over: "Thank God he was White, thank God he was White." Had the suspect been Black, a moment's hesitation may have cost the officer his life.

Indeed, anti-police bias has resulted in the death of many officers. Lott and Moody (2021: 2) note:

> The resulting anti-police sentiment has led to several "ambush killings" of police officers in Dallas, New York, and Baton Rouge. From January 1 to September 17, 2016, felonious police killings were up 61 percent compared to the same period in 2015.

This is what makes BLM's rhetoric dangerous. It feeds racial hatred by stoking historical grievances, demanding reparations for those who did not suffer the indignity of slavery, paid for by those who had no part in it. It is enlarging the racial cracks in our society that we may never be able to caulk over. It is a rhetoric that treats people as members of a group—Democrats or Republicans, liberals or conservatives, Blacks or Whites—rather than as individuals.

Rosenfeld and Lopez (2020) estimated that de-policing caused the death of more than 700 people and led to the shooting of more than 2,800 others, although they said other things, such as the COVID-19 pandemic and increased gun sales, played their parts. In an updated report, they remark, "the connection, if any, between the social unrest and heightened violence remains uncertain" (Rosenfeld & Lopez, 2021: 17). Uncertain or not, the fact remains that the 2021 UCR reported that there were 21,570 homicides in the US in 2020, which is a 30% increase over 2019, and the largest single-year increase ever recorded in the UCR. Furthermore, the police cleared only 54% of the homicides in the United States in 2020, the lowest clearance rate ever recorded (FBI, 2021). The police used to clear 90% of homicides in the 1960s, when most people respected them and cooperated with them (Keel, Jarvis, & Muirhead, 2009).

Police Shootings of Blacks and Crime Statistics

BLM's claim that black lives don't matter refers to police shootings of Blacks, which it attributes to police racism and the belief that "police have one trigger finger for whites and another for blacks" (Takagi, 1974: 30). The police indeed use lethal force against Blacks more often than their proportion of the population would lead us to expect. As the *Washington Post* points out:

> Although half of the people shot and killed by police are white, black Americans are shot at a disproportionate rate. They account for less than 13 percent of the U.S. population but are killed by police at more than twice the rate of White Americans.
>
> (2021: np)

However, in most instances, these people were either shot while committing a crime or resisting arrest when officers feared for their lives or the lives of others.

Police Shootings and Race-Differentiated Crime Levels

Using population proportion to assess the claim that "police have one trigger finger for whites and another for blacks" is unrealistic since it seems to imply that justice demands that people of each race be shot according to their population proportions. Police shootings are a function of how often police officers encounter armed, perceived to be armed, or aggressively resisting, suspects. Worrall et al. (2018: 13) found that an aggressively resisting suspect "was 29 times more likely to be shot than a nonaggressive suspect." If Blacks and Whites are involved in criminal activity proportionate to their population, and Blacks are still killed at twice the White rate, then we could validly claim that police trigger fingers are race-conscious, but this is not the case. Blacks have proportionately greater involvement in crime-related situations that lead them to potentially fatal police exposure. Thus, the correct criterion used to calculate racial disparity in fatal police shootings is their proportion to their frequency of police exposure in criminal situations, not their population proportions. As Cesario, Johnson, and Terrill (2019: 587) put it:

> If different groups are more or less likely to occupy those situations in which police might use deadly force, then a more appropriate benchmark as a means of testing for bias in officer decision making is the number of citizens within each race who occupy those situations during which police are likely to use deadly force.

They further add: "A more effective means of reducing racial bias [racial disproportion] in shootings would be to eliminate racial differences in crime rates" (p. 592). Worrall et al. (2018) make similar claims.

Ross, Winterhalder, and McElreath (2021) agree and, "find reliable evidence that lethal force by police occurs in direct proportion to race-specific rates of violent crime (p. 330), and "we acknowledge that they do hold for the case of armed criminals killed by police, but they do not hold for racial disparities in the killing of unarmed citizens by police" (p. 328). But "unarmed" does not equate with "not dangerous." Unarmed suspects are sometimes shot trying to grab an officer's gun or by an accidental discharge triggered by their attacks on an officer. Sometimes, it is the case that unarmed bystanders are accidentally struck by shots intended for armed targets, such as when a person shot is a passenger, where some other person in the car had shot at the police (VerBruggen, 2022). However, when the public hears that an unarmed person is shot by the police, and does not have all the details, the impression imparted is that an officer callously shot an innocent person for no reason. Such a perception may lead some to join the chorus shouting for the defunding or abolition of the police. The nuances of an officer/offender encounter are lost in news reports that do not go beyond noting if the suspect was unarmed. If an unarmed offender aggressively resists an officer, overpowers him or her, or reaches for the officer's gun, the unarmed offender becomes an armed offender, and the officer may be dead.

Ross, Winterhalder, and McElreath (2021) acknowledge that it is undeniable that, compared to other racial/ethnic groups in the United States, Black crime rates are disproportionately high. African Americans constitute 13.4% of the US population, so arrest rates should fluctuate randomly around that percentage if race were irrelevant to predicting the probability of criminal behavior. However, according to the 2021 Uniform Crime Report (FBI, 2021), the percentages of Blacks arrested for each Part I index crime in 2020 were: murder (51.0%), rape (25.4%), Robbery (49.3%), aggravated assault (33.1%), burglary (27.6%), larceny/theft (28,7%), motor vehicle theft (26.4%), and arson (22.9%). African Americans are thus overrepresented by large margins based on their proportion of the population in each of the eight most serious crimes. Blacks are also overrepresented as serial killers and perpetrators of mass killings. The 2020 *Radford/FGCU Report on Serial Killer Statistics* (Aamodt, Leary, & Southard, 2020: 34) notes that between 1900 and 2019, 40% of known serial killers were Black, and from 2010 to 2019, Blacks were 57.2% of known serial killers. Lankford (2016) notes that 42.9% of the 308 mass shootings that took place in the United States between 2006 and 2014 were committed by Blacks. Based on population proportion, Blacks thus had over four times the expected number of serial killers and over three times the expected number of mass shooters.

However, arrest rates inevitably raise the specter of racial profiling. The alternative hypothesis is the differential offending hypothesis; that is, Blacks are arrested more than other racial/ethnic groups because they offend more often. Blacks are arrested proportionately more than Whites, but so are Whites relative to Asians, males relative to females, and the young relative to the old. Scholars acknowledge that Whites proportionately commit more crimes than Asians, males more than females, and the young more than the old. They would also agree that the arrest rates of these groups reflect their crime rates, but when Black/White comparisons are made, this logic is often tossed aside in favor of police discrimination. One could plausibly blame racist police if the UCR is the only source of statistics, but the appearance of the National Incident-Based Reporting System (NIBRS) has changed the narrative. NIBRS provides detailed information on individual crimes, including the race/ethnicity of both offenders and victims and many other relevant properties, such as whether a victim-identified offender was arrested.

Using NIBRS data, D'Alessio and Stolzenberg (2003) looked at 335,619 violent crimes (rape, robbery, aggravated and simple assault). They found that Blacks were arrested in greater numbers than their proportion of the population would lead us to expect, but less often than the proportion of *offenses* they commit would lead us to expect. Whites committed 2,620 robberies, 30.8% of whom were arrested; Blacks committed 5,278 robberies, of whom 21.4% were. Arrest rates for aggravated assault were 53.1% versus 42.5%, and for simple assault, 46.8% versus 36.8%. No significant difference was found for rape. They concluded that the high Black arrest rate is attributable to their disproportionately higher involvement in crime.

Fogliato et al. (2021) found similar results from NIBRS data from 2007 to 2016 (103,309 rapes, 101,133 robberies, 596,324 aggravated assaults, and 2,669,399 simple assaults). Black suspects were significantly less likely (42%) to be arrested than White suspects (56%) for all crimes. Blacks were overrepresented in all crimes, from a low of 31% for rape to a high of 76% for robbery. The arrest gap is largest for robbery (36% vs 19%) and aggravated assault (62% vs 44%), followed by simple assault (57% vs 43%), and smallest for rape (27% versus 25%). Also using NIBRS data, Pope and Snyder (2003) analyzed 102,905 incidents of violent crime committed by juveniles. White youths were less involved in delinquency but were more likely to be arrested (40.5%) than Black youths (34.5%). These figures tell us much about the circumstances surrounding police shootings. The overwhelming majority of people shot by the police were engaging in behavior that brought the police to the scene. The NIBRS statistics unequivocally inform us that the police are called to deal with such behavior disproportionately more for Black perpetrators.

Circumstances in Which Officers Are Justified in Using Lethal Force

This leads us to look at police shootings and the behavior of those shot. Roland Fryer examined 4,500 police shootings in Austin, Dallas, Houston, Denver, Seattle, nine large Florida counties, Jacksonville, and Los Angeles County, controlling for the vitally important crime-related situation in officer-involved shootings and concluded:

> Given the stream of video "evidence", which many take to be indicative of structural racism in police departments across America, the ensuing and understandable outrage in black communities across America, and the results from our previous analysis of non-lethal uses of force, the results displayed in Table 4 are startling. Blacks are 23.5 percent *less likely* to be shot by police, relative to whites, in an interaction. Hispanics are 8.5 percent less likely to be shot.
>
> (2019: 1241; my emphasis)

Fryer is not asking, "Are the police more likely to shoot Blacks than Whites?" He is asking if an officer is more likely to shoot if the subject is

Black than if he is White, *given* a confrontation in which the officer would be justified in using lethal force. Because Blacks are less likely to be killed in a crime-related situation in which police guns are drawn, police seem more hesitant to fire on Black than White suspects. Cesario, Johnson, and Terrill (2019) found this when they looked at 1,561 fatal police shootings in 2015 and 2016 controlling for racial differences in criminal activity: "Although Blacks have greater odds of being fatally shot given population proportions, Whites overall were more likely to be fatally shot given each group's involvement in those situations where the police may be more likely to use deadly force" (p. 588).

The hesitation to fire on Black subjects is probably related to the fears officers have if they shoot a Black suspect, relative to the fear they have if they shoot a White suspect. This has potentially lethal consequences for officers. James, James, and Vila (2016: 457) reach a similar conclusion to Fryer concerning police hesitancy to use lethal force against Blacks:

> We found that ... officers were slower to shoot armed Black suspects than armed White suspects, and they were less likely to shoot unarmed Black suspects than unarmed White suspects. These findings challenge the assumption that implicit racial bias affects police behavior in deadly encounters with Black suspects.

Roussell et al. (2019) attacked James, James, and Vila's (2016) article because they claim reverse racism is "impossible." They aver that they have a faulty understanding of race and racism: "We argue the crucial flaw of the article is a substantive lack of knowledge of race/racism by James et al., leading them to make the unsubstantiated claim of 'reverse racism'" (p. 1). They claim that "To study 'race and policing' is, by definition, to study 'racism and policing'" (p. 6). They take it as axiomatic that policing is synonymous with racism and that reverse racism is impossible; that is, the police are inherently racist, and only Whites can be racist. However, a Rasmussen national telephone survey (2013) found that more Black respondents (31%) considered "most Blacks" to be racist than "most Whites" (24%). As for cops being "by definition" racists, only 22% of Blacks and 9% of Whites reported they believe this.

When a situation is such that officers hesitate to shoot when confronted by an armed Black suspect, they may end up dead themselves. Hesitancy may be part of the reason that police officers are more likely to be proportionately fatally shot by a Black perpetrator than a White one. As the *Chicago Tribune* reports: "There were 511 officers killed in felonious incidents and 540 offenders from 2004 to 2013, according to FBI reports. Among the total offenders, 52 percent were white, and 43 percent were black" (Lee, 2015, np). So, while in proportion to population, Blacks are shot and killed by police at twice the rate of Whites, Blacks shoot and kill police officers at more than *three* times the rate of Whites by population proportion.

Shootings by Black Police Officers

Nix and colleagues (2017) write of "implicit bias" when accounting for police shootings of Blacks, but what if the officer shooting is Black and the suspect killed is White, is that also implicit bias? Most police killings of suspects of any race are committed by White officers, which is to be expected given that White officers comprise about 75% of officers nationally (Menifield, Shin, & Strother, 2019). However, Black officers are more likely to shoot both Black and White suspects than White officers:

> Black officers had more than three times greater odds of shooting than White officers. This finding runs counter to concerns that white officers are overrepresented among officers using lethal force and is consistent with several previous studies of officer race and police use-of-force.
>
> (Ridgeway, 2016: 5)

Phillips & Kim (2021: 765) found that Black officers shot in 19.86% of encounters with dangerous suspects versus 9.92% of White officers similarly confronted. They further noted:

> The findings of this study indicate that police officers, White officers in particular, do not disproportionally target Black or Hispanic citizens. The results demonstrate consistency with other research, indicating that *situational factors* are the force related to the officer's decision to shoot at a citizen.
>
> (pp. 771–772; my emphasis)

Fryer also found that "The only statistically significant differences by race demonstrate that black officers are more likely to shoot unarmed whites, relative to white officers" (Fryer, 2019: 1257). Lott and Moody's (2021: 14) analysis of 2,699 police shootings between 2013 and 2015 found: "In all four models, black officers are significantly more likely than white officers to shoot a black suspect." They further noted a crucial difference in the media's reporting behavior: "But it could also mean that the media finds it less newsworthy to report cases where a black officer rather than a white officer shoots a suspect." (See Lankford, 2016; Lott and Moody, 2021; and Walsh, 2005, for the national media's reluctance to report on shooting incidents other than those involving a Black suspect.

Menifield, Shin, and Strother (2019: 62) note that "while African Americans are disproportionately killed by police, they are killed at much higher rates by nonwhite officers than by white officers." They conclude their study by noting:

> Consistent with prior research, our study finds no support for the popular narrative of the "racist white cop" as being the key driver of

> the killing of black suspects. The present research provides real-world corroboration of recent laboratory experimental research finding no evidence of race-based targeting of suspects for killing. Indeed, we find that nonwhite officers kill both black and Latino suspects at significantly higher rates than white officers.
>
> (p. 65)

The Donner et al. (2017) examination of the Philadelphia Police Department from the 1990s reported that Black officers were more likely to have been involved in a shooting than White officers. Data from the US Department of Justice (Fachner & Carter, 2015) of the Philadelphia Police Department also found that Black and Hispanic officers were more likely than White officers to shoot unarmed (again, "unarmed" does not mean "not dangerous") Black or White suspects. White suspects were unarmed in 8 of 32 officer-involved shootings (25%), and Black suspects were unarmed in 45 of 285 (15.8%) shootings. Note that Black suspects were almost nine times (285/32 = 8.9) more likely to be in potentially deadly confrontations than White suspects and 10 times more likely to be armed (240/24). This is the best explanation for why Blacks are proportionately more likely to be shot than Whites.

16 Issues in Criminal Punishment

Consequentialism and Punishment Justification

The first sentence of 19th-century American novelist Nathaniel Hawthorne's (2003: 1) book *The Scarlet Letter* reminds its readers of two disquieting truths about the human condition:

> The founders of a new colony, whatever Utopia of human virtue and happiness they might originally project, have invariably recognized it among their earliest practical necessities to allot a portion of the virgin soil as a cemetery, and another portion as the site of a prison.

In these words of wisdom and woe, Hawthorne points out two things we cannot avoid—human mortality and the human penchant for iniquity—and that we must make arrangements for both. We set the dead apart, and as James Q. Wilson remarked, we must also set the wicked apart: "Wicked people exist. Nothing avails except to set them apart from innocent people" (1975: 391). Setting wicked people apart is utilitarian in the Benthamite sense—the greatest good for the greatest number.

Because punishment for criminal behavior involves the state doing deliberate harm to individuals in the name of the people, in modern liberal societies, it is considered a practice in need of moral justification. Arguments for and against punishment engage the concepts of free will and determinism. The usual justifications for criminal justice punishment—deterrence, incapacitation, rehabilitation, and retribution—ebb and flow in primacy according to the ideology of the times. Moral philosophers refer to the first four punishment justifications as *consequentialist*; they are justified by the consequences presumed to flow from them, a means to a positive end. Retribution is the only non-consequentialist position because it justifies punishment based on its intrinsic moral worth ("just deserts') regardless of any benefits that may flow from its application. All punishment justifications assume that criminals should and could have behaved differently. However, some scholars dismiss this as naïvely resting on the assumption of free will and are against the notion of punishment as commonly understood.

DOI: 10.4324/9781003662495-20

Deterrence has long been considered the primary function of punishment. Specific deterrence is the effect of punishment on the behavior of the person being punished, with the hope that he or she will be dissuaded from future criminal acts. However, it is a forlorn hope. A study of 404,638 prisoners released in 2005 from 30 state prisons found that 68% were arrested within three years after release and 77% within five years. These offenders were responsible for around 1,173,000 new arrests between 2005 and 2010, these were just the ones who were caught (Dunrose, Cooper, & Snyder, 2014). However, this reflects the *specific* effect of deterrence (or lack thereof) on offenders; *general* deterrence is the effect of punishment on the general population aware that crime entails punishment. As Radzinowicz and King put it:

> People are not sent to prison primarily for their own good, or even in the hope that they will be cured of crime. Confinement is used as a measure of retribution, a symbol of condemnation, a vindication of the law. It is used as a warning and deterrent to others. It is used, above all, to protect other people from the offender's depredations.
>
> (1979: 296)

The justification for incapacitation is summarized by James Q. Wilson above. Incapacitation works while criminals are incarcerated. Currie (1999) notes that in 1995, there were 135,000 inmates whose most serious crime was robbery, and that each robber, on average, committed five robberies per year. Had these robbers not been incapacitated, they would have committed 135,000 × 5, or 675,000 additional robberies. The value of incapacitating serious criminal offenders was supported by a large Italian study that followed the offending patterns of released inmates. Due to budgetary and overcrowding concerns, the government released one-third of Italy's prison inmates with three years or less to serve in 2006. Buonanno and Raphael's (2013) analysis of released convicts found that the released offenders committed an average of 16 robberies or thefts per year after release. The estimated financial costs of these crimes were between 466 million and 2.2 billion euros (about $606 million and $2.9 billion). In an American study, Matt DeLisi (2005) studied the post-release offenses among 39 murderers and found that between 1996 and 2000, they had 122 arrests for serious violent crimes (including seven additional murders), 218 arrests for serious property crimes, and 863 other arrests.

Rehabilitation is a consequentialist justification that is forward-looking by its focus on the future behavior of criminals rather than looking backward at what they have done. Rehabilitation was birthed in the twentieth century by the medical model, which viewed criminal behavior as a moral sickness requiring treatment. More modern rehabilitative models view criminal behavior as emanating from faulty thinking rather than moral sickness and in need of programming rather than treatment. The rehabilitative goal is to change offenders' attitudes so that they come to accept that their behavior was wrong and to use the time they are under correctional supervision to prepare them to reenter society as well-equipped as possible. Judging by the Dunrose, Cooper, and Snyder (2014) recidivism study, rehabilitation is minimally effective. However, we must keep trying because whatever helps the offender down the straight and narrow path benefits the community. As former United States Supreme Court Chief Justice Warren Burger put it: "To put people behind walls and bars and do little or nothing to change them is to win a battle but lose a war. It is wrong. It is expensive. It is stupid" (Stohr & Walsh, 2012: 246). Most of us would agree, but if we justify punishment from a consequentialist position, we are using the person being punished as an instrument for the greater social good, which is immoral according to non-consequentialists.

Non-Consequentialism and Retribution

Retribution—punishment for its own sake—is a non-consequentialist or deontological justification. Probably more criminologists oppose retribution than all other justifications combined, seeing it as little more than state-sanctioned revenge (Rosebury, 2009). This position carries the unspoken assumption that the strong emotions behind the retributive urge are immoral and antisocial. Non-consequentialism is a deontological position that maintains that if any practice or behavior is to be judged moral, it must be judged by what motivated it, not by the consequences that flow from it. If punishment is justified only by its intrinsic merits, it must be retributionist.

Immanuel Kant is the best-known apologist of retributive justice. Kant believed that humans are different from other animals because they are commanded by reason. It is from reason that we derive all duties and obligations, and reason leads us to the concept of the categorical imperative. Kant wanted to find "the ground of a possible categorical imperative," which should be an "end in itself, and absolute value." He finds his ground in man, who "exists as an end in himself, not merely as a means for arbitrary use for this or that will" (1964: 95). A categorical imperative is a principle stating that a moral act is objectively necessary (should or ought to be done) regardless of any further end; it says "Do this," not "Do this *if*." Any action consistent with such an imperative is moral, regardless of its consequences. For Kant, categorical imperatives are universal laws that guide us toward duty: "Act as if the maxim of your action were to become through your will a universal law of nature" (1964: 89). Kant thus arrived at his definition of the categorical imperative: "Act in such a way that you always treat humanity, whether in your own person or in the person of any other, never simply as a means, but always at the same time as an end" (1964: 96).

Kant notes that, like everyone else, criminals are commanded by reason and must thus live by universal moral standards. When criminals victimize others, they both violate the autonomy of others and endorse criminality as a universal law. When the state punishes criminals, it is thus treating them according to their maxims; that is, the state allows criminals to decide how they will be treated, which respects their autonomy. Retribution is a just deserts model that demands punishments match the degree of harm criminals have inflicted. Retribution is the most honestly stated justification for punishment because it taps into our primitive punitive urges, posits no secondary purpose for it, and is typically viewed as a right-wing position. However, Karl Marx endorsed it, and you don't get more left wing than that. In an editorial in *The New York Daily Tribune* in 1853, Marx noted, "There is only one theory of punishment which recognizes human dignity in the abstract, and that is the theory of Kant" (Murphy, 1979: 93–94).

Rejecting Punishment

Several scholars have voiced their desire to abolish criminal punishment and prisons. Ironically, they rest their cases in Kant's deontology. However, they differ from Kant in viewing humans not as autonomous beings with free will, but rather as beings whose actions are entirely determined by their genes and environments. Michael Zimmerman (2011) considers retribution immoral and that people should be punished only for what they are responsible for and can control. He contends that it is "possible to have an excuse for doing something morally wrong ... [and] if you have such an excuse, then you are not to blame—you are not culpable" (p. 72). Of course, all criminals find some excuse for their behavior. Like Kant, Zimmerman wants people to be their own lawmakers by deciding what is and is not morally wrong, but he draws different conclusions. While Kant says that a man's decision to commit a crime "draws punishment upon himself," Zimmerman says that if criminals do not believe what they have done is morally wrong, they do not deserve punishment. Zimmerman rejects the view of humans as free-willed agents in his assumption that many of our actions are beyond our control. But does he believe that if a would-be robber sees a police officer nearby, he will still have an irresistible compulsion to complete the robbery? However, Zimmerman only calls retribution immoral; he recognizes that the state must respond to criminal harm and has no quarrel with incapacitation and rehabilitation, but isn't incapacitation and mandatory programming punishment?

Rafi Reznik is another who wants to abolish punishment because he believes no one deserves it. He writes:

> Retributivism's answer to the question *why do we punish*? is: because *a blameworthy offender deserves it*. In contrast, alternative, non-punishment methods guided by utilitarian considerations reach a different conclusion than both retributivist and traditional utilitarian accounts of punishment: that *no one deserves it*.
>
> (2019: 155–156; emphasis original)

He wants to strip blameworthiness of its legitimacy because "human agency amounts to little more than dollhood" (p. 159). Reznik further says that we cannot find a political authority with moral legitimacy to punish because: "Abolitionists find the United States unworthy of their trust" (p. 167). He further wants to abandon the "concept of crime, as wrongdoing to which the community should respond with condemnation, substituting it with a private conflict between members of the community that is a mere civil matter" (p. 154).

However, it is difficult to see how people could stop emotionally condemning evil acts to themselves or others because, as Canton (2015: 62) remarks, "retributive emotions reflect a decent compassion for a victim's (or survivor's) distress and a virtuous expression of solidarity with members of our community." Applying an experimental approach, Pfattheicher, Sassenrath, and Keller (2019) showed that compassion for victims intensified moral outrage in proportion to the harm caused by the criminal act, as did the increase in third-party punishment they were willing to assign. If we did not have these emotional responses to the plight of others and were callously indifferent to their suffering, we would all be psychopaths. A study from five continents found that in all populations, people are willing to altruistically punish those who have harmed unknown others (Henrich et al., 2006). Punishment is altruistic in the sense that criminal acts are potentially damaging to the social welfare of everyone, and although someone may not have been victimized themself, upon becoming aware of someone who had been, the caring person recruits inherent tendencies of sympathy for the victim and desire to punish the offender. John Mackie maintained that morality is "an outgrowth from retributive emotions" (1978: 463).

Reznik is joined in his sentiment of turning crimes into civil matters by Bagaric, Hunter, and Svilar (2021: 367) who write: "A popular proposed alternative to the institution of punishment is to treat what are presently categorized as criminal acts in the same manner as civil wrongs, where the emphasis is on reconciliation and reparation." For them, crimes should be redefined as torts and disputes that require negotiation, mediation, and arbitration rather than as events requiring guilt and punishment. They do not answer how a burglary victim would be able to sue the perpetrator who claims poverty for financial loss, and how one compensates victims for the emotional violation that accompanies such victimization. They note that prison abolitionists share sentiments with others who call for defunding the police and abolishing ICE, the Border Patrol, and probation/parole departments. They further note that "Children's separation from their incarcerated parents can have an extremely detrimental impact on them. It is estimated that 2.7 million American children have a parent who is in prison" (p. 361). Bagaric, Hunter, and Svilar (2021) are not so naïve as to think that abolitionist notions will result in the immediate bulldozing of prisons; they opt for gradual implementation and want to reserve prisons for the most serious violent offenders.

Dobchuk-Land and Walby even argue for the elimination of criminality, writing: "Criminalization is a kind of toxic exhaust that over time disintegrates over whole neighborhoods of people. Public police are the dispensers of this effect." They go on to argue that prisons create harm, and "Prisons do this by displacing members of communities, thus taking away their capacity to contribute to the local economy and to family and neighborhood associations" (2021: 18–19). Thus, the criminal justice system, not criminals, causes criminalization, and if unhindered, criminals would contribute to the local economy (redistributing wealth by robbery?) and neighborhood associations (local gangs?). However, as Jaffee et al. (2003: 120) note:

> When highly antisocial fathers reside with the family, children experience a double whammy of risk for antisocial behavior. They are at genetic risk because antisocial behavior is highly heritable. In addition, the same parents who transmit genes also provide the child's rearing environment.

Greg Caruso (2021) is another skeptic of individual responsibility, but he is not as radical as the prison abolitionists. He wants to apply a public health quarantine model to criminal justice and outlines his reasoning as follows:

> (1) free will skepticism maintains that criminals are not morally responsible for their actions in the basic desert sense; (2) plainly, many carriers of dangerous diseases are not responsible in this or in any other sense for having contracted these diseases; (3) yet, we generally agree that it is sometimes permissible to quarantine them, and the justification for doing so is the right to self-protection and the prevention of harm to others; (4) for similar reasons, even if a dangerous criminal is not morally responsible for his crimes in the basic desert sense (perhaps because no one is ever in this way morally responsible) it could be as legitimate to preventatively detain him as to quarantine the non-responsible carrier of a serious communicable disease.
>
> (2021:123)

Caruso's notion is that although criminals are no more responsible for their actions than people who have contracted a dangerous disease, we can justifiably incapacitate them in the name of social defense just as it is justified in quarantining carriers of infectious diseases as necessary to protect public health. I think we can all agree on this. He also avers that just as the public health system takes active steps to prevent outbreaks of infectious diseases, society should seek to prevent crime from occurring. Of course, we would all like to see this and have been trying to realize it for a very long time, with trillions of dollars and with minimal success. The "disease" of Criminality cannot be put in a test tube to devise pharmacological agents that would be successful preventative vaccines or viable treatments for those already in its grip, so we are left with quarantining them. But isn't quarantining a euphemism for prison incapacitation?

Punishment as an Evolutionary Adaptation

It is rare for social scientists outside the biopsychosocial perspective to think of the ultimate sources of phenomena (such as punishment) in terms of the evolutionary history of the species. The driving force behind evolution is the tendency of beneficial traits to increase in frequency in a population via natural selection. When a trait arises that results in fitness, it will likely become common in the mating population. The urge to punish those who victimize us or others is considered one such adaptive trait (Levy, 2022; Nakao & Machery, 2012).

Punishment is both a loss-cutting and a cost-imposing strategy in that it is designed to avoid future exploitation and impair a violator's capacity to impose further harm. That these strategies do not always have these consequences is not crucial to the evolution of punishment. As with most other behavioral adaptations, punishment involves emotions. We feel contentment and joy when we acquire resources and moral outrage when others take them from us (Wu, Luan, & Raihani, 2022). However, we have seen that natural selection does not pass judgment on emotions or the behaviors they motivate if they do not enhance evolutionary fitness. It is the fitness *consequences* of the behavior motivated by the emotion upon which natural selection operates. Moral outrage against crime is useless if it does not generate behavior designed to prevent its reoccurrence. Negative feelings accompanying victimization of self or others are assuaged to some degree by punishing violators because it signals a measure of the restoration of justice. The positive feelings accompanying the punishment of those who have wronged us or others provide powerful reinforcement, as suggested by the popular saying, "Vengeance is sweet." Several brain imaging studies have shown increased blood flow to the brain's reward centers when subjects witness the punishment of those who have wronged them or others in lab game-theoretical experiments (Bellucci et al., 2020; de Quervain et al., 2004; Klein, 2012).

The human urge to punish is also found among many social animal species due to its ability to increase social cooperation in the face of exploiters (game theorists call them "cheats"). Some evolutionary biologists argue that punishment evolved as a precondition for stable cooperation among conspecifics rather than an evolved response to cheating (Levy, 2022). Because reproductive success is the raison d'être of all sexually reproducing organisms, the emotions accompanying the loss of resources that facilitate this goal became the basis for detecting cheats and the desire to retaliate against those who may have expropriated their resources. The cooperative goals of social species such as our own suggest that altruism and punishment coevolved in the sense that: "Third-party punishment of norm violations ('I punish you because you harmed him') seems especially crucial for the evolutionary stability of cooperation and is the cornerstone of modern models of criminal justice" (Buckholz & Marois, 2012: 655).

A population of cooperators provides a target-rich niche for cheaters to gain resources at zero cost. Cheats will prosper in a population of unconditional cooperators (naïve altruists), what game theorists call "suckers." A sucker strategy is not an evolutionarily stable strategy (ESS) because cheats would soon drive them to extinction. It is consistently shown in computer simulation games that in a mixed population of naïve cooperators ("suckers"), cheats, and conditional cooperators, cheats always do better than naïve cooperators (Klein, 2012; Nowak, 2006). Few humans are suckers, rather, they are conditional cooperators (reciprocal altruists), or what game theorists call "grudgers." Because they abide by the norms of mutual trust and cooperation and expect the same from others, grudgers are liable to be cheated, but unlike suckers, once cheated grudgers will react differently to cheaters in the future by "bearing a grudge," not offering cooperation, or retaliating (Wiebe, 2011). The cheater strategy is more an ESS than the sucker strategy, as evidenced by the huge excess of criminals relative to the saints who forgive "not seven times, but 70 times 7" as the Bible counsels. It remains stable because it exists alongside a few suckers and a large series of different grudgers, cheats can victimize and could only be driven to near extinction in the unlikely case that the population was composed mostly of cheaters, in which case natural selection for grudgers would ensue since such a society could not long endure. The grudger strategy is the dominant strategy in all human societies.

Detecting Cheats in Cooperative Groups

To be successful in cooperative social groups, humans evolved mechanisms for detecting cheats and dissuading them from further cheating (Nowak, 2006). The continued presence of chronic cheaters among us indicates that we are not all that good at detecting them. Evolutionary biologists posit that a co-evolutionary "arms race" similar to the co-evolution of predator and prey has molded the sensibilities of cooperators and cheats alike. Cooperators have undergone evolutionary tuning of their senses for detecting cheats, and cheats have evolved mechanisms that serve to hide their true intentions, such as the dulling of the neurohormonal mechanisms that regulate social emotions (Gorelik, Shackelford, & Salmon, 2011; Patrick, 2022). Natural selection is morally neutral; it pounces on anything, repugnant or not, that leads to greater fitness in both saints and sinners in a species.

Reciprocal altruism generates positive emotions that reinforce further altruism, which sustains the *modus vivendi* of any social species, but because this is so, punitive emotions arise when cheats renege. As de Waal (1996: 160) points out, "A taste of revenge is the other side of the coin of reciprocity." Victims feel angry and hurt when treated unjustly, and confused and frustrated at losing the expectation of predictability ("I scratched your back, but you didn't scratch mine"!). The sum of these evolved emotions amounts to "moral outrage." Without moral outrage, there would be no motivation to react against those who violate the norms of reciprocity; cheats would have thrived without the threat of punishment in our ancestral environments, and we would have evolved as a quite different species of animal (Nowak, 2006).

However, the desire to "get even" is a primitive one, which, if left untamed, can tear a social group apart by generating a cycle of tit-for-tat blood feuds, which have been the norm throughout human history (Boehm, 2011). Even if there are well-founded evolutionary reasons for retributionist feelings aimed at wrongdoers, we must reflect on the moral propriety of always acting on them. For instance, Chagnon (1988) estimates that approximately 30% of adult male deaths among the Yanomamo Indians are related to revenge feuds, which generate and expand the very injustice that "righteous" revenge was supposed to assuage. The urge for vengeance, while an *adaptation*, is not *adaptive* in large social groups. As Jacoby (1983: 13) puts it:

> The struggle to contain revenge has been conducted at the highest level of moral and civic awareness at each stage in the development of civilization. The self-conscious nature of the effort is expectable in view of the persistent state of tension between uncontrolled vengeance as destroyer and controlled vengeance as an unavoidable component of justice.

Cultural norms may engage or neutralize the emotions that temper punishment with mercy or allow vengeful passions to run wild. Cesare Beccaria's lasting influence on our discipline rests on his recognition that brutal acts of retribution common in his time resulted in general distrust and social alienation. For Beccaria, punishment's purpose is deterrence, not vengeance, and is accomplished by punishments that exceed in relatively small measure the benefits of a specific crime. Beccaria's reform ideas tapped into and broadened other evolved emotions, such as sympathy and empathy, among the intellectual elite of Enlightenment Europe. We tend to feel empathetic towards those we view as being "like us," and empathy often leads to sympathy, which may translate into the vicarious experience of the pains of others into active concern for their welfare. With cognition and emotion gelling into the Enlightenment ideal of the basic unity of humanity, justice became more refined and more equitably dispensed.

Emile Durkheim (1964) saw crime and punishment as central to social life. Just as evolutionary psychologists view cheating as vital to the evolution of cooperation, Durkheim viewed deviance as necessary for social solidarity. Durkheim's view is analogous to the coevolution of altruism and punishment in that the former needs the latter. Punishing criminals maintains solidarity, in part, because punishment rituals reaffirm the justness of the social norms, particularly norms concerning reciprocal altruism. Durkheim recognized that the urge to punish is inherent in human nature and serves an expiatory role, but he also believed that it should be tempered with sympathy. Throughout social evolution, he observed that humankind had largely moved from retributive to restitutive justice. For Durkheim, retributive justice is driven by the natural passion for punitive revenge that "ceases only when exhausted"... only after it has destroyed" (1964: 86). Restitutive justice, on the other hand, is driven by simple deterrence, and is more humanistic and tolerant, although it is still "at least in part, a work of vengeance"... since it is still "an expiation" (1964: 88–89). Both forms of justice satisfy the human urge for social regularity by punishing miscreants, but repressive justice oversteps its adaptive usefulness and becomes socially destructive. Restitutive justice offers a balance between helping to calm moral outrage on the one hand and exciting the emotions of empathy and sympathy on the other.

Forgiveness Strategies

Although a simple strategy of tit-for-tat reciprocity is highly effective in generating cooperative behavior in small groups, and tit-for-tat is modified by punishment for defectors in larger groups, natural selection operates simultaneously on too many alternate strategies to opt for fixity. If two strict tit-for-tat strategists play one another and one cheats, it tends to launch a long series of mutual punitive responses, resulting in a loss to both. Work in game theory indicates that a measure of forgiveness works better to maintain social cooperation rather than always paying back defectors in kind (Rand, Ohtsuki, & Nowak, 2009). If we play strict tit-for-tat (always punishing non-cooperation) in our relationships, we risk losing valuable relationships if the cheating incident was uncharacteristic of the person or accidental. As Machalek and Cohen (1991: 221) put it, "Forgiving strategies can transform a pattern of mutual cheating by not remaining permanently punitive but instead by cooperating, even when the other strategy cheats." Several game theory studies have found that strict tit-for-tat can amount to punishment that is too costly for the punisher, that all parties tend to suffer to some extent, and that the generous (forgiving) tit-for-tat strategy invariably prevails (Rand, Ohtsuki, & Nowak, 2009).

The generous tit-for-tat strategy forgives a one-shot betrayal by responding with cooperation rather than retaliation in the next round of the game, and in most instances, it returns the players to a cooperative strategy. Of course, we are dealing with game theory here with idealized lab conditions and the assumption of rational actors; the real world is expected to be far more complicated. However, the predictions based on game theoretical models have been remarkably consistent with real-world findings on numerous occasions (Levitt & List, 2007). Cosmides and Tooby (1992) provide the example of the Ache of Paraguay (and other hunter/gatherer tribes) who respond differently to hunters who cheat than to gatherers who cheat. Meat is a scarce resource shared equally by all when available, and obtaining it is often a matter of luck and hunting skills. Plant food is a low-variance item, the availability of which depends only on the effort spent on gathering it. Arguments erupt when plant gatherers are perceived as not pulling their weight, and punishing lazy gatherers has no adverse effect on plant food availability. Given the highly variable nature of meat acquisition, tribal members are more forgiving of hunters they perceive as cheating. It is recognized that charges of cheating may result from false perceptions since hunting is often a matter of sheer luck as much as effort. If, as a result of a false charge, the hunter is ostracized, the tribe will lose a valuable cooperator in the difficult business of hunting meat, and the meat supply will become less stable and predictable.

Continuing to invite cooperation in the face of defection is not a sucker strategy because it does not tolerate continued cheating. It is like sentencing an offender to probation rather than prison, leaving the door open to future mutually advantageous cooperation between the offender and the community. The "forgiving tit-for-tat" strategy is captured most familiarly in Braithwaite's (1989) concept of reintegrative shaming. Braithwaite maintains that we should retaliate against tit-for-tat defectors, but retaliation should be conciliatory rather than punitive. Punishment should be reintegrative and motivate offenders to evaluate themselves and their behavior, not disintegrative. The offender and the community benefit from methods used to express our disapproval of offenders who conform to the reintegrative ideal. If we always respond to defecting with strong punitive reactions, the community loses a potentially valuable cooperator, and the offender becomes, to his or her great disadvantage, alienated from it.

Reconciliatory behavior is not "natural" (i.e., forged by natural selection) in the same sense that moral outrage and the desire to punish are. It is more a rational evaluation of the costs and benefits rather than an emotional one. However, in restorative justice programs, victims who confront their victimizers in controlled settings and offer forgiveness to them report feeling positive (a sense that justice has been done) about the experience (Latimer, Dowden, & Muise, 2005). Forgiveness is contingent on the wrong not being too egregious, payment of restitution, written and verbal apologies, and the assurance of some consequences for the offender. Thus, even forgiveness has elements of punishment. Restorative justice principles tap into the offender's capacity for empathy with the victim. Forgiveness tit-for-tat in game theory provides a degree of justification for restorative justice, the only corrections model aimed at reintegrating offenders into the community with the community's help. It is a consequentialist position at odds with Kantian deontology, but it is more practical, and contrary to Kant, I believe it is more moral than punishment for its own sake. Even if it means treating criminals as a means to an end, it is an end beneficial to both offenders and the community.

17 Issues in Criminal Sentencing

Race and Criminal Sentencing

Sentencing is the post-conviction stage of the criminal justice process aimed at implementing one or more punishment philosophies discussed in the previous chapter. There are many issues related to criminal sentencing, but perhaps no issue is as controversial as the relationship between race and sentencing. The racial discrimination issue gets batted back and forth in the literature like a ping-pong ball with claims of racial bias and counterclaims that no such bias exists. Without a doubt, historically, Blacks and other minorities have received harsher criminal justice treatment in the United States than Whites, and it is still a fact that African American offenders receive harsher sentences on average than White or Asian American offenders.

Is this differential treatment indicative of racism? It would be if all ethnic/racial groups committed roughly the same level of crime, but not if Blacks commit more serious crimes and have lengthier criminal histories than other groups. As has been shown, they do, even though the NIBRS data previously discussed show they are less likely to be arrested for their crimes. However, the question is whether this racial disproportionality in offending is sufficient to account for racial disparity in sentencing. Kansal (2005: 17) doesn't think so: "Racial bias continues to pervade the US criminal justice sentencing system [although] the effects of this bias are somewhat hidden... or may even have less to do with the race of the defendant than with the race of the victim." A study of over 322,000 cases by the United States Sentencing Commission (2018) found that after controlling for a variety of relevant factors, Black males received longer sentences than similarly situated White males.

Franklin and Henry (2020: 9) state that: "Kleck (1981) argued that acknowledging past discrimination could motivate 'criminal-justice decision-makers to consciously or unconsciously compensate with more lenient treatment of black defendants' or adjust for 'greater prior criminal records which black defendants bring into court.'" To what extent has this been implemented? Sampson and Lauritsen's 66-page review of hundreds of sentencing studies noted such a trend. They found that: "in the aggregate, blacks

DOI: 10.4324/9781003662495-21

tend to be convicted less than whites ...With or without control of type of crime, then, there is no consistent evidence that minorities are disadvantaged at the stage of criminal conviction" (1997: 345–346). They did find that the studies show greater sentencing severity for Blacks, but "the racial disparities in sentencing (e.g., prison) arose from the greater proportional involvement of minorities in criminal behavior, which was in turn reflected in longer or more serious prior records" (1997: 347). Siegel (2006: 578) also noted: "Although critics of American race relations may think otherwise, research on sentencing has failed to show a definitive pattern of racial discrimination." In addition, he noted that the more stringent studies are in controlling for legally relevant variables (crime seriousness and criminal record), the less likely they are to find racial discrimination.

Sentencing research is complicated and typically reports average effects, but many nuances are lost in averaging. For instance, victim characteristics play a role; if the victim is a child, is elderly, has a disability, or is female, the sentence is typically harsher for offenders of any race (Hatch & Walsh, 2016). Ideology also plays a role, with more conservative "law and order" jurisdictions sentencing more harshly across the board (Ulmer, 2012). Wu and Walsh (2007) found that conservative probation officers recommended harsher sentences (regardless of race) than liberal officers and that judges followed the recommendations of both sets of officers closely. Muhlhausen (2004) found that Black judges in Pennsylvania gave longer prison sentences than White judges, regardless of the offender's race. A study of the sentencing practices of 18 Ohio judges who sentenced 5,467 offenders in 2005 found that nine did not consider any extralegal factors at sentencing; of the nine that did, five sentenced Blacks more leniently, and four sentenced Blacks more harshly (Wooldredge, 2010). The harsh and lenient judges cancel each other out if one looks only at the averaged data from all judges and ignores the sentencing practices of individual judges.

A study of more than 46,000 federal defendants found no evidence of racial bias after controlling for crime seriousness and prior record (Wang & Mears, 2010), although Jordan and Freiburger (2015) maintained that studies continue to show that Blacks are sentenced more severely than Whites. All these contradictory studies starkly reveal that sentencing research is fraught with difficulties. For instance, Franklin and Henry (2020) examined the federal sentencing of 122,270 offenders using United States Sentencing Commission data from 2010 to 2012. They found that: "African Americans received notably *longer* sentences [7.4% longer than Whites] at the low end of the criminal history scale and notably *shorter* sentences [7.4% shorter] at the high end of the scale" (2020: 25). They also note:

> We found no evidence across the eight racial and ethnic comparisons that comporting with prevalent criminal stereotypes further exacerbates

> race- or ethnic-based sentence disparities. Put differently, when Black, Latino, and Native American offenders exhibit extensive criminal histories—congruent with race/crime stereotypes—this does not aggravate sentence disadvantages for these offenders.
>
> (Franklin & Henry, 2020: 24)

Then, there is the issue of how thoroughly researchers can account for all aspects of crime seriousness and prior record data that court officials have. Researchers typically have access only to unnuanced data, such as the crime for which offenders were sentenced and the number of their criminal convictions; this hides a wealth of data surrounding the circumstances of each crime. The circumstances of each robbery conviction, for instance, may differ enormously, such as whether a gun was involved and whether the victim was physically harmed, and prior convictions may have been all for violent offenses in one case and all property offenses in another. Judges have full access to these additional factors from trials or probation officers' presentence reports, but researchers typically do not, making it difficult to argue for or against racial bias. So, is there racial discrimination involved in sentencing? The short answer is that it depends on the quality of the data, where you look, how hard you look, and even what you expect to find based on your ideological assumptions.

Is Criminal History a Proxy for Race?

Prior record is second only to crime seriousness as a predictor of sentence severity, but several researchers disdain the role of criminal record in sentencing as racist. For instance, Omori and Petersen (2020) note that Blacks are sentenced more harshly than Whites, and this is:

> [I]n large part, a result of the use of criminal history and increased criminal records. ... Our findings indicate that inequality is, in part, institutionalized through legal case factors, suggesting these factors are not "race neutral" but instead racialized and contribute to inequalities in court outcomes.
>
> (p. 684)

Harcourt (2015) takes a similar view. Although he believes the objective of actuarial prediction scales is noble (to reduce mass incarceration and reduce crime), he resists them as proxies for race and as "troubling" when used in sentencing decisions. He says:

> I argue here that we should resist the political temptation to embrace the progressive argument for risk-prediction instruments [which include an offender's criminal history] because their use will unquestionably

> aggravate the already intolerable racial imbalance in our prison populations. The fact is, risk today has collapsed into prior criminal history, and prior criminal history has become a proxy for race.
>
> (Harcourt, 2015: 237)

Monahan and Skeem's (2016: 499) take on this proxy argument is:

> [T]he label "proxy" conveys little more than an observation that these predictors of recidivism overlap. Criminal history and race are correlated, but it is not clear that criminal history is intended to proxy for race (i.e., to camouflage discrimination) ... Criminal history is not a proxy for race; instead, it overlaps race and possibly mediates race's relation to recidivism.

A proxy is an authority given to someone or something to represent somebody else, and the original person or concept is held to be synonymous by the stand-in, such as someone given power of attorney to sign their name in place of yours. In such an instance, your and your proxy's signatures have a "correlation" of 1.0, meaning they have the same force in law. Are those claiming that criminal history and race are synonymous in that they are similarly correlated? Criminal history and race are correlated, albeit far from perfect, and thus are far from a proxy as the term is normally used. To the extent that Blacks exceed Whites in their offending rates, the use of criminal history in sentencing will naturally produce disparate sentencing, disfavoring Blacks.

The positions taken by those such as Harcourt and Omori and Petersen claim that because criminal history is a proxy for race, race-neutral sentencing should not include offenders' criminal histories. If criminal history and correlated factors are not considered, we are back to the classical position of Cesare Beccaria that punishment must be based exclusively on the crime. This would lead to gross injustices, such as a poor mother with no criminal record convicted of grand theft receiving the same sentence as a career criminal convicted of the same crime with the same monetary value. A major concern of the American criminal justice system has long been moving away from such thinking and toward individualized sentencing consistent with justice. Justice entails treating people fairly according to what they deserve—"just deserts." Aristotle defines justice for our purposes: "Justice consists of treating equals equally and unequals unequally according to relevant differences" (Stohr & Walsh, 2025: 133). The "relevant differences" in sentencing are the legally relevant variables of crime seriousness and prior record. Thus, those who have committed the same crime *and* have similar criminal histories are "equals" and should be sentenced equally. People who have committed different crimes and/or have different criminal histories are "unequals" and should thus be sentenced unequally—either more leniently or more harshly according to the relevant differences.

Criminal Sentencing and Gender

Sentencing disparities also exist between the sexes, but the issue evokes much less moral outrage because the disparity favors women. As long as studies of criminal justice processing cases have been conducted, women have been treated more leniently than men similarly situated. For instance, Sonja Starr (2012: 17) looked at all federal criminal cases between 2001 and 2009 and concluded, "Conditional on arrest offense, criminal history, and other pre-charge observables, men receive 63% longer sentences on average than women. Women are also significantly likelier to avoid charges and convictions, and twice as likely to avoid incarceration if convicted." Scholars have explained this disparity by referring to the "chivalry hypothesis." The hypothesis maintains that men tend to have a "chivalrous" and paternalistic view of women as requiring protection and that this view extends into the male-dominated criminal justice system.

Beaver and Wright (2019) examined sentencing patterns among male and female offenders in a national sample and found that after holding crime seriousness, prior record, and a variety of demographic variables constant, women received more lenient sentences than men. Contrasting sentencing disparity patterns between the races and between the sexes, they remark that

> where several studies find that legally relevant variables account for all, or almost all, of racial disparities in processing, just the opposite is true of the literature on sex disparities in processing. Given our findings, and those reported by others, it would appear that the criminal justice system is sexist in its application of justice.
>
> (p. 869)

However, they contended that such sexism is rationally based because it reflects

> fundamental differences between men and women in their use of physical aggression. If true, women are more likely to be channeled out of the criminal justice system for reasons not entirely associated with their participation in a criminal event. In general, women are less physically dangerous than men and pose less a social threat than men even if they engage in the same criminal event with a male.
>
> (Beaver & Wright, 2019: 869)

Depending on one's politics, this statement may be acceptable since, for instance, the male homicide rate is about eight times greater than the female rate (Walsh & Jorgensen, 2025). However, sparks would fly if one were to claim that sentencing White males more leniently than Black males is rational because they "pose less a social threat" since the Black male homicide rate is about 5.6 times greater than the White male rate, which includes White-Hispanics thereby inflating the White-Anglo rate (Steffensmeier et al., 2010).

Sentencing disparity between men and women exists even for sex offenses, which are seen as a significant departure from gender norms for females and should thus negate the chivalry hypothesis, even more so than homicide (women commit about 6% of all reported sex crimes as opposed to about 11% of all homicides). Analyzing sex offender data from the US Department of Justice's National Corrections Reporting Program from 1994 to 2004, Embry and Lyons, Jr (2012) looked at the sentences that male and female sex offenders received for specific sex offenses and found that, even after the implementation of sentencing guidelines that are supposed to ensure equality in sentencing, on average, male sentences were between 6% and 31% longer than females similarly situated under the guidelines. They conclude that:

> Even after the implementation of sentencing guidelines to ensure equality in sentencing regardless of demographic characteristics, men continue to receive disproportionately higher sentences for a variety of offenses, including sex offenses. This leads to the supposition that women, regardless of the departure from social and gender norms committed in concurrence with the offense for which they are being sentenced, continue to be viewed as individuals who should be protected by the justice system. Obviously, as a social institution, the criminal justice system is reluctant to break those social norms and gender roles in response to atypical gendered behavior.
>
> (Embry and Lyons, 2012: 158)

Fazel, Sjöstedt, Grann, and Långström (2010) point to a reason beyond chivalry that female sex offenders might be treated more leniently than males. They compared 93 Swedish female sex offenders with 8,500 male sex offenders, and all females convicted of non-sexual violent offenses (n = 13,452) between the years 1988 and 2000. They also used a random sample of women from the general population (n = 20,597) for comparative purposes. They found that over the 13 years, 36.6% of female sex offenders had been admitted to psychiatric hospitals, and 7.5% had been discharged with a diagnosis of a psychotic disorder. Compared to women in the general population, female sex offenders showed a significantly increased risk of psychiatric hospitalization (age-adjusted odds ratio [AOR] = 15.4), being diagnosed with a psychotic disorder (AOR = 16.2), and substance abuse AOR = 22.6).

Serial killing is an even greater departure from gender norms than sexual offending. According to an FBI symposium on serial murder (2008), there are several myths floating around about serial killers, the biggest one being that they are all White males. The reality is that White males are underrepresented among serial killers in proportion to their numbers in the population (FBI, 2008; Aamodt, Leary, & Southard, 2020). It is also a myth that women never commit serial murders, although they are vastly underrepresented in proportion to their numbers in the population. Women have comprised 8.6% of known serial killers over all decades and 6.2% since 1900 (Aamodt, Leary, & Southard, 2020).

But what explains this severe departure from gender norm expectations? One study comparing 55 male serial killers with 55 female serial killers on their motivation and methods tested a "hunter-gatherer" model. The assumption was that differences between male and female serial killers may be byproducts of evolutionary tendencies. The researchers hypothesized that:

> MSKs [male serial killers] more frequently act as "hunters," stalking and killing targeted strangers in dispersed areas, while FSKs [female serial killers] more frequently are "gatherers," killing those who are around them and familiar to them and gaining profit from their crimes.
> (Harrison, Hughes, & Gott, 2019: 295)

Their model was supported in that it was found that 75% of MSKs versus 7.3% of FSKs killed for sexual gratification, while 16.7% of MSKs killed for financial gain versus 51.9% of FSKs. Kelleher and Kelleher's (1998) study of an international sample of 100 female serial killers found similar results.

A Google Scholar search revealed only one study that mentioned gender differences in the sentencing of female serial killers: that of Gurian (2017). From her total sample of 738 offenders, there were 340 cases of solo male killers, 71 cases of solo female serial killers, 97 of partnered offenders, 48 mixed sex cases of 93 male and 71 female offenders, 45 male/male cases of 125 total male offenders, and 4 female/female cases, for a total of 327 partnered offenders. Although Gurian's data came from several countries, she only mentioned sentencing in the United States, where female serial killers have historically been 62% less likely to be sentenced to death than male serial killers. The chivalry hypothesis cannot by itself explain such a large gap. I submit that the key explanation is the blood lust, torture, and sexual violence that often characterize male "hunter" serial killers as opposed to the typical female "gatherer" method of poisoning for profit.

Sentencing Guidelines

Sentencing guidelines provide structured sentencing and define a recommended sentence for convicted criminals based on their criminal histories and the seriousness of the criminal charge(s). More comprehensive guidelines include other items such as if the offender was on bail or probation/parole when the crime was committed, prior probation/parole revocations, and whether efforts have been made to compensate victims of property offenses. They were originally aimed at curtailing judicial discretionary power because unbridled discretion can lead to wide sentencing disparities based only on a judge's subjective evaluations and whims regarding the issue of justice. At one end of the sentencing curve, we might get "hanging" judges, and at the other, "bleeding heart" judges; thus a defendant's fate may have depended largely on the temperament of the judge by whom they had the good luck or misfortune to be sentenced. By pushing extremist judges to the center of the curve (especially if the guidelines are presumptive rather than merely advisory), guidelines provide a rational basis for sentencing, increase judicial accountability, and reduce sentencing disparity. As Frase (2019: 82) remarks, "The preguidelines regime of unstructured, highly discretionary sentencing is unacceptable. Guidelines offer the only proven sentencing reform model."

Sentencing guidelines are rules for numerically computing sentences that offenders should justly receive based on their crimes and criminal records. They may be binding or non-binding. If the crime is not so egregious as to require a prison sentence, a major concern is a defendant's risk of recidivating. Many modern risk-assessment tools are often integrated into sentencing guidelines and use machine learning algorithms, which generate risk models based on vast quantities of data and are adjusted as new data is obtained and computerized. Actuarial instruments vary widely in the number and type of risk factors they include, but to the chagrin of those who view criminal history as a proxy for race, it is second only to crime seriousness in weighing the scales. Indeed, the guidelines used by the federal government and some states are limited to crime seriousness and criminal history.

Making predictions about future behavior is a difficult endeavor, but as William Shakespeare wrote: "Whereof what's past is prologue." This common-sense observation tells us that criminal history best predicts an offender's future offending behavior and is the best justification we have for including it. Predictions about behavior may be based on expert diagnoses and evaluations made by professionals such as psychologists or psychiatrists, although such judgments are inferior to actuarial predictions. Like any data fed to a computer program, these methods are prone to error because they must rely on the quality of the data. However, as Gottfredson and Moriarty (2006: 180) note, actuarial methods are an improvement over clinical judgments because "in virtually all decision-making situations ... actuarially developed predictions outperform human judgments."

For instance, Hanson and Morton-Bourgon (2009) looked at the accuracy of recidivism risk assessments for offenders in 118 prediction studies comparing predictions made by statistical actuarial methods versus unstructured clinical judgment and structured professional judgment. The effect sizes (d) for sex offense recidivism for the unstructured clinical judgment, structured clinical judgment, and statistical actuarial methods were 0.42, 0.46, and 0.67, respectively. For the prediction of violent offense recidivism, they were 0.22, 0.31, and 0.51, respectively, and in predicting recidivism of any kind, the respective effect sizes were 0.11, 0.26, and 0.52. Thus, although actuarial methods improve clinical assessment methods, they still produce many false positives and false negatives, and their effect sizes are only moderate since a strong effect size is considered 0.80 or higher.

Although actuarial instruments perform better than clinician-based assessments, tools are only as good as those using them, and those charged with their use are not immune to scoring them according to their ideological biases. For instance, Wu and Walsh (2007) found that liberal and conservative probation officers scored subjective items (but not objective items) on sentencing guidelines significantly differently. Likewise, Miller and Maloney (2013) found that workers trained in the risk assessment LS/CMI instrument found that decisions were not always based on it. They noted that

> about half of the tool-using subgroup were "substantive" compliers who completed tools carefully and honestly and tended to use them for decision making. The remaining tool users were "formal" in their compliance: filling out the tools, but often making decisions that did not correspond with tool results, and in some cases even manipulating the information included in them.
>
> (Miller and Maloney, 2013: 716)

Although sentencing guidelines have proved useful in reducing sentencing disparity and curtailing judicial discretion, their future format and function are not ensured. Given the usefulness of guidelines in structuring sentencing, it is surprising that so few states use them, and among the states that do, they vary greatly in quality. In 2008, the National Center for State Courts (NCSC) evaluated the guidelines in all 21 states that use them (as of 2024, only 16 states retain them) and assigned them points according to several criteria. The most important were whether the guidelines were voluntary or mandatory, whether compelling and substantial reasons were required for departures from guideline-derived sentences, and whether written reasons must be provided for any such departures.

Wang et al, (2013) looked at three years of data including 27, 019 felony defendants sentenced in 60 large urban counties in 23 states. They examined sentencing practices in states (1) without sentencing guidelines, (2) with voluntary guidelines, and (3) with presumptive guidelines. They found that the probability of a jail sentence was greater in guideline states than in nonguideline states. Guidelines thus increased sentence severity for offenders with presumably less serious crimes and/or criminal histories. However, the opposite pattern was obtained for prison sentences: 40.97% of offenders were imprisoned in nonguideline states, 36.86% in voluntary guideline states, and 27.26% in presumptive guideline states. There was no evidence of racial disparities in any of the three state sentencing systems in sentence length.

Sentencing guidelines were mandatory in the federal system for many years after their creation, but they are currently only advisory. By *mandatory*, we mean that the sentences indicated by the guidelines had to be imposed unless there were compelling reasons for not doing so. Advisory guidelines are used to guide judges' decisions by providing a uniform set of standards for them to consult if they wish. This has opened the door again to unwarranted sentencing discrepancies that guidelines were meant to rein in. The change in federal guideline practices began with the US Supreme Court's ruling in *United States v. Booker* (2005), where the issue was the separation of responsibilities of the trial judge and the trial jury. The role of judges is to be finders of law; the role of juries is to be finders of facts. The circumstances of the case are that Freddie Booker was arrested in possession of 92.5 grams of crack cocaine. He also admitted to the police that he had sold an additional 566 grams. A jury found Booker guilty of possession with intent to sell at least 50 grams, for which the possible penalty ranged from 10 years to life. At sentencing, the judge used the information about the additional 566 grams and that Booker had obstructed justice to sentence him to 30 years. However, his sentence would have been 21 years and 10 months if it were based only on the facts presented to the jury. Booker appealed, arguing that his Sixth Amendment rights were violated because "finding facts" is the jury's role, not the judge's. Criminal history is the only fact not presented to juries that judges can use for increasing sentencing; anything must be submitted to a jury and proven beyond a reasonable doubt. The Supreme Court agreed that Booker's sentence violated the Sixth Amendment and sent the case back to the lower court with instructions either to sentence Booker within the sentencing range supported by the jury's findings or to hold a sentencing hearing before a jury.

The Supreme Court also held that the guidelines were to be advisory only and, therefore, no longer binding on judges. The Court did require judges to "consult" them, but there is no way of ensuring that judges comply. US Attorney General John Ashcroft called the decision "a retreat from justice" and Congressman Tom Feeney decried that "the extraordinary power to sentence" was now afforded to federal judges who are accountable to no one and that the decision "flies in the face of the clear will of Congress" (Bissonnette, 2006, p. 1499). Ironically, Booker was resentenced by the same judge to the same 30-year sentence. Because the sentencing guidelines had become merely advisory, the judge did not need to justify his sentence because it was within the range of the statutorily defined penalty.

Presentence Investigation Reports

Presentence investigation reports (PSIs), typically written by probation officers, assist judges in determining an appropriate sentence. Some states mandate a PSI for all felony cases, some only in certain felony cases, and others only at the request of the sentencing judge. There are few documents as important to the defendant as the PSI. It is used for other purposes besides sentencing, such as treatment planning, classification to supervision levels in probation and parole departments and prisons, and parole decisions. PSIs inform the judge of various aspects of the offense for which the defendant is being sentenced (since most cases are plea-bargained, judges have little knowledge of this) as well as information about the defendant's background (educational, family, and employment history), gang ties, substance abuse, character, and criminal history. Based on this information, officers make recommendations to the court regarding the sentence the offender should receive. Because probation officers have considerable discretionary power in how their reports are crafted to be favorable or unfavorable to offenders, many scholars view them as the agents who determine the sentences offenders receive (Champion, 2005). Other researchers suggest that the high rate of judicial agreement with officer recommendations reflects an anticipatory effect, whereby officers become adept at "second-guessing" a judge's likely sentence for a given case and recommend accordingly (Durnescu, 2008).

Although PSIs have generally been considered a positive aid to individualized justice, they are not without their problems. For instance, they are not mandatory in many states and are only written when judges require them. In Monaghan and Konefal's (2023) analysis of 717,163 cases from Pennsylvania from 2006 to 2016, only 25% had a PSI. Moreover, cases with a PSI received, on average, longer sentences than those that did not. Blacks received one extra month, and Whites received an extra 1.3 months. This may be because a PSI might contain information that judges otherwise would not have. Much of this information might be negative, such as a poor work history, a poor family environment, the defendant's attitude, and a victim impact statement. Of course, the whole point of individualized justice is to make sentencing decisions based on as much information as possible, both positive and negative.

Because a defendant's future depends to some extent on the reports, the information should be reliable and objective. All pertinent information must be verified by cross-checking with reliable sources. The officer must be careful in the terms they use to describe the offender (i.e., "morally bankrupt"), which may reveal more about the officer's attitudes and values than the defendant's character. Because of this, arguments about whether defendants and their attorneys should have access to their PSIs have arisen. Proponents of disclosure argue that defendants should be allowed to challenge any erroneous information harmful to the defendant. Opponents fear that if victims and other informants from whom the investigating officer has sought information know that the offender will see their comments, they will refuse to offer their information; thus, the judge would not have complete information on which to base the sentencing decision. However, 16 states currently require full disclosure; some require disclosure but redact information that may lead to retaliation, such as the officer's recommendation and negative comments from informants. Despite objections and concerns about confidentiality, the trend is to allow defendants access to their PSIs. For instance, in the federal system, Section 3552 of the US Code states:

> The court shall assure that a report filed pursuant to this section is disclosed to the defendant, the counsel for the defendant, and the attorney for the Government at least ten days prior to the date set for sentencing,

> unless this minimum period is waived by the defendant. The court shall provide a copy of the presentence report to the attorney for the Government to use in collecting an assessment, criminal fine, forfeiture or restitution imposed.

In the federal judicial system and some state systems, probation officers no longer write PSIs. Rather, they merely complete sentencing guidelines and other risk-assessment tools and calculate the presumptive sentence (Abadinsky, 2009). This, and the decreasing use of sentencing guidelines, may be signaling a move away from individualized justice (the idea that punishment should be tailored to the individual and be consistent with rehabilitation) and back to the classical position that the punishment should fit the crime (with only criminal history now added) and serve as a retributive or deterrent effect.

18 The Death Penalty Issue

The Death Penalty and Public Opinion

The most controversial issue in American criminal justice is the death penalty. Throughout human history, capital punishment has been considered a legitimate and appropriate form of punishment, even for offenses considered minor misdemeanors today. As standards of decency and justice have evolved, 138 of the world's 193 countries (71.5%) have abolished capital punishment. According to the British Broadcasting Corporation (BBC, 2024), of the 55 countries that retain it, 23 have not used it for 10 years, and nine have used it only for the most serious crimes, such as multiple murders or war crimes. Of the developed democratic nations, only the United States and Japan have executed a significant number of people this century. South Korea and Taiwan formally retain the death penalty, but there has been a long moratorium on it in those countries. At the beginning of 2025, 23 states, the US government, and the military retain the death penalty, 23 states have abolished it, and four have a pause on executions (Death Penalty Information Center, 2025).

According to a Gallup Poll (Jones, 2024), 53% of the American public favors the death penalty, 43% oppose it, and 4% have no opinion. In 1966, more people opposed the death penalty (47%) than supported it (42%). Support for the death penalty was greatest during the 1980s and 1990s, with 1994 having the highest level of support (80%) in the Gallup Poll's history. Public opinion waxes and wanes with the crime rate—as crime goes up, support for the death penalty increases. According to UCR data, the violent crime rate in 1994 was 713.6 per 100,000 population, which is 3.25 times higher than the 1966 violent crime rate of 220 per 100,000 (FBI, 2013). Walsh and Hatch (2018) note that polls in Britain and Canada show public support for returning the abolished death penalty hovers in the 60-to-65% range.

This begs the question of why public opinion on the death penalty issue is an important consideration in the US but not in other Western democracies. Garland (2012: 4) answers by appealing to the tension between liberalism and democracy in centralized unitary countries versus federated countries such as

DOI: 10.4324/9781003662495-22

the US where local state democracy enjoys a measure of independence from centralized government: "America's distinctive emphasis on the value of local popular democracy [public opinion]—together with the Supreme Court's interpretation of the meaning of liberty—explains why the United States still has capital punishment." A study by Sarat et al. (2019) supports Garland by showing that public opinion in state referenda is almost always decisive in deciding whether their state capital punishment codes would be retained or abolished.

Interpreting Death Penalty Studies

The death penalty issue is so fraught with emotion, and strongly held pro or con opinions, that studies assessing it should be viewed with great caution, unless we are to assume that researchers are immune to such charges. (Full disclosure: I am against the death penalty on moral [most Christian and Jewish denominations are against it], financial [it is inordinately expensive to pursue], and possible innocence grounds). Charles Manski (2011) writes that reluctance to consider views contrary to our own often results in claims of "incredible certitude" for scholarly work congenial to our views and asserts that almost all arguments about social policies with moral content such as the death penalty involve "dueling certitudes" that conflate science and advocacy and engage wishful extrapolation. Gross and Simmons (2007) show that social scientists have a strong leftward lean, with 58% self-identified as either liberal or radical, 36.9% as moderate, and only 4.9% as conservative, so we should expect "certitude" to be in evidence in death penalty research to be anti-death penalty and claims of racial bias.

Statisticians Gerritzen and Kirchgässner (2013) demonstrate advocacy research. Using data from 102 US death penalty studies from 1975 to 2011, they show how opposite findings can be derived from the same data set with only slight changes in assumptions. They further concluded that pro- or anti-death penalty ideological bias may account for most contradictory findings: "Our results also reinforce the considerations...that selective perceptions might be the cause for divergent findings. If rather different results can be obtained under reasonable assumptions, researchers will consider those outcomes as being reliable which correspond to their pre-conceptions" (p. 24). Scheidegger (2012: 161) also notes that, "many academics who do research on the death penalty reliably produce results that favor one side, raising a suspicion of partisan bias." For instance, Paternoster and Brame (2003) looked at 1,130 death-eligible homicide cases in Maryland and found no race-of-defendant bias but significant race-of-victim effects. That is, Black defendants with White victim cases were *more* likely to receive a death sentence. On the other hand, Berk, Li, and Hickman (2005: 381) looked at the same data and found the opposite: "When race surfaces, cases with a Black defendant and White victim or 'other' racial combinations are *less* likely to have death sentences imposed."

Race and the Death Penalty

The history of capital punishment in the United States is inextricably tied to questions of race. The history of race relations in the United States has been disturbing, to say the least. Blacks have historically been executed in numbers highly disproportionate to their crimes, even for crimes for which Whites may have received only a prison sentence (or none at all). Some scholars suggest that history is just that—history—and that the situation has changed dramatically in modern times. For instance, Elliot Cramer's (2006) testimony before the House Select Committee of North Carolina on the death penalty indicated that from 1910 to 1961, 133 Blacks and 36 Whites were executed in North Carolina. However, he also noted that from 1984 to 2008, the situation changed with 13 Blacks and 28 Whites being executed in the state. Only a fraction of homicides is death-eligible, and an even smaller proportion (about 2% to 6%) receive a death sentence (Berk, Li, & Hickman, 2005). To be eligible for the death penalty, a murder must satisfy several elements, including such things as premeditation, being particularly brutal, involving multiple victims, being committed during the commission of some other felony such as robbery or rape, or involving the killing of a law enforcement officer during the commission of his or her duties, or having a prior homicide conviction.

Kleck (1981) found that from 1930 onwards in the Northern states, Whites were more likely to receive the death penalty, and that the discrimination against Blacks in death penalty cases in earlier years in the South disappeared in later years. Greenfeld and Hinners (1984) looked at 1,405 people sentenced to death and found that 15.8 per thousand White murderers were sentenced to death versus 11.6 per 1,000 Black murderers. Gross and Mauro (1989) looked at death sentences in over 14,000 cases and found that Whites received a death sentence in 26.5% cases involving felony circumstances and 1.4% involving non-felony circumstances, compared to 17.2% of Blacks convicted in felony and 0.4% in non-felony circumstances. A US Justice Department (2001: 2) study of federal death-eligible cases found similar results:

> United States Attorneys recommended the death penalty in smaller proportions of cases involving Black or Hispanic defendants than in those involving White defendants; the Attorney General's capital case review committee likewise recommended the death penalty in smaller proportions of involving Black or Hispanic defendants. ... In the cases considered by the Attorney General, the Attorney General decided to seek the death penalty for 38% of the White defendants, 25% of the Black defendants, and 20% of the Hispanic defendants.

Blume, Eisenberg, and Wells (2004) looked at the racial disproportion issue using data from 5,953 death sentences in the 31 states that sentenced 10 or more individuals to death from 1977 through 1999. They compared the proportion of convicted Black murderers in each state with their proportion on death row. In California, Nevada, and Utah, Blacks were overrepresented relative to the proportion of Blacks convicted of murder. In Nevada, the percentage of Blacks convicted of murder during that period was 30.2%, and the percentage of Blacks on death row was 33.1%. In Utah, the respective percentages were 8.6% and 10.5%; in California, they were 33.8% and 35.3%, respectively. In all other 28 death penalty states, Blacks were greatly underrepresented. The states where they were most underrepresented are those where we least expect to find them: in the South. In Tennessee, Blacks committed 60.4% of murders, but their percentage on death row was 33.3%. In Mississippi, the respective percentages were 77.9% of murders and 59.0% on death row, and in Missouri, they were 62.6% and 41.1%, respectively.

When Blacks were disproportionately executed for capital crimes, it could easily be explained by racism. However, it is the Southern states where Blacks are most underrepresented on death row relative to the number of murders they commit. One explanation is that the Southern states have relatively large Black populations, and Blacks are less likely to favor the death penalty than Whites (Blume, Eisenberg, & Wells, 2004). With more Blacks on Southern juries, perhaps prosecutors are less likely to seek the death penalty, and Black jurors may not convict if the death penalty is on the table, especially if the defendant is Black. Or perhaps prosecutors, judges, and juries are more careful in handling Black cases in an attempt to convince themselves they are impartial and are keen to avoid the racist label.

Despite such evidence, some still charge the death penalty with anti-Black bias. For instance, Ford (2014: np) states: "The national death-row population is roughly 42 percent black, while the US population overall is only 13.6 percent black, according to the latest census. We've long known that the death penalty disproportionately kills people of color." Acker, Bohm, and Lanier (2014: 531) likewise claim,

> even if it were clear that blacks and non-black defendants were treated fairly and consistently in America's death-sentencing system, there are also concerns about the substantial over-representation of blacks on death row in America (13 percent of the nation's civilian population versus 42 percent of the death row population).

These statistics are accurate, but the interpretation is flawed. Neil Gilbert (1997: 102) calls such statements examples of "advocacy research" that purposely paints a grim picture to reinforce public perceptions that the death penalty is biased against people of color. As much as I applaud consciousness-raising and advocacy for victims in various bad situations that can be alleviated, it harms the status of social science. Gilbert (1997) cites many examples of this in his article.

Scholars know that claims of disproportionality cannot be evaluated by comparing percentages of total racial populations with those executed or on death row, but public consumers of the information do not. The percentages of each race who are eligible to be executed or on death row are sub-populations, and to assess a bias claim logically, we must compare the proportion of death penalty-eligible murderers of each race with its proportion executed or on death row, not with the total population of each race. As Robinson (2008: 191) notes: "Although they are overrepresented among death row populations and executions relative to their share of the U.S. population, blacks are underrepresented based on their arrests and convictions for murder."

The Death Penalty and Victim Race

With the evidence now showing that Blacks are less likely to receive a death sentence than Whites, the race issue has become victim-centered rather than defendant-centered. The literature consistently shows that before controlling for aggravating and mitigating factors, killers of Whites (regardless of the perpetrator's race) are more likely to receive the death penalty than killers of Blacks. The apparent reluctance of prosecutors to seek the death penalty when the victim is Black is often viewed as devaluing Black victims compared with White victims. The race issue in death penalty discourse is thus still alive, but it has done a U-turn. McAdams (1998) contends that now that a larger proportion of convicted Whites are sentenced to death and executed than convicted Blacks, capital punishment opponents have turned from an offender-centered argument to a victim-centered argument, as more Whites than Blacks are executed. He notes:

> Had they maintained a philosophical consistency, the opponents might have lauded the current situation on the ground that a sort of affirmative action was being employed. That is, against a historic background of harsh treatment of black people in most aspects of public policy, black offenders are getting favorable treatment from the criminal justice system.
>
> (McAdams, 1998: 160)

The victim-centered argument began with the work of Baldus, Pulaski, and Woodworth (1983), who examined over 2,000 murder cases in Georgia during the 1970s. This study was widely cited in *McCleskey v. Kemp* (1987) before the United States Supreme Court. McCleskey was a Black man convicted of murdering a White police officer in Georgia and sentenced to death, whose attorneys claimed that the death penalty was racially biased in favor of White victims. The raw numbers in the Baldus study showed that 4% of the Black defendants received the death penalty and 7% of the White defendants. However, the issue in the case was the race of the victim, not the race of the defendant. Denying McCleskey's claim and writing the majority opinion, Justice Powell wrote, "defendants charged with killing white victims were

4.3 times as likely to receive a death sentence as defendants charged with killing blacks" (Weatherspoon, 1998: 193–194).

Powell's statement has become a meme in anti-death penalty discourse. For instance, Bedau (1997: 254) writes, "defendants charged with killing white victims are 4.3 times as likely to receive a death sentence as defendants charged with killing blacks." Likewise, Baumgartner, Grigg, and Masto (2015: 2) write: "They [Baldus et al.] found that those accused of killing white victims were four times as likely to be sentenced to death than those of killing black victims."

However, the "4.3" is misinterpreted as a 430% greater likelihood, but it was an odds ratio, which is a much different animal. Mathematician Arnold Barnett (1994) used the *McCleskey* quote in his guide to the *Six Deadly Sins of Statistical Misrepresentation* to illustrate the misuse of statistics and "to discourage fellow citizens from taking a strong position or course of action based solely on a press report" (p. 38). The problem is confusing probabilities with odds ratios. An odds ratio is the ratio of the probability of something happening compared with the probability of it not happening; i.e., the ratio between the odds represented by their respective probabilities, and a 4.3 odds ratio can mean as little as a 3% difference (Walsh & Hatch, 2018). The Baldus et al. (1983) study is not to blame; the blame lies with Powell's misinterpretation in the *McCleskey* case and others who misinterpret it, either out of unwitting innumeracy or purposely as an advocacy quote.

The Baldus et al. study looked at aggravating and mitigating circumstances and found that with zero or one aggravating factor, there was no racial discrimination, regardless of the racial makeup of the victim/offender dyad. At the other end of the scale, for offenders with multiple aggravating factors (multiple victims, a prior homicide conviction, child victims, torture, kidnapping for ransom, etc.), the risk of a death sentence was high regardless of the racial makeup of the victim/offender dyad. However, it was in the middle range of aggravating circumstances where racial disparities appear, and where the 4.3 odds ratio originated.

Katz (2005) looked at the same Georgia data that Baldus et al. did. In the 1,082-homicide defendant sample, 141 cases involved a White victim and a Black perpetrator. In 67.1% of the White victim-Black perpetrator (W/B) cases, the victim was killed during a robbery, compared to 7.4% in Black victim cases, and in 70.6% of the W/B cases, the victim was a stranger, compared with 9.6% of black victim cases. Katz (2005) noted that "White victim homicides show a greater percentage of mutilations, execution-style murders, tortures, and beaten victims, features which generally aggravate homicide and increase the likelihood of a death sentence" (p. 405). Katz (2005) cites several other studies finding similar results in 10 different states; that is, once the full array of aggravating and mitigating factors is considered, there is little or no discrimination evident in W/B cases that is not accounted for by aggravating circumstances and other legally relevant variables. As Cassell (2008: 23–24) notes: "Black-defendant-kills-white-victim cases more often involve the murder of a law enforcement officer, kidnapping and rape, mutilation, execution-style killing, and torture—all quintessential aggravating factors—than do other combinations."

To assess the victim race issue in federal death penalty cases, the National Institute of Justice commissioned studies by three independent teams. In the report of the findings, Klein, Berk, and Hickman (2006) showed that, without controlling for case characteristics, the death penalty is more likely when victims are White. However, racial disparities disappeared in all three studies when statistical adjustments were made for the nature of the crimes. After controlling for all aggravating and mitigating factors that influence sentencing, there was no evidence of a race effect regardless of whether they were examining just the race of the victim, the race of the offender, or the interaction between the victim's and defendant's race.

Looking at all first-degree murder convictions in Tennessee from 1976 to 2007, Sharma et al. (2013) found that prosecutors sought the death penalty for 76% of White defendants and 62.6% of Black defendants. Of those for whom the death penalty was sought, 37.3% of Whites received it versus 23.6% of Blacks. In terms of the victim race issue, prosecutors sought the death penalty in 64% of the cases where the victim was White and in 33% of the cases where the victim was Black. Controlling for a variety of aggravating and mitigating factors and evidentiary variables, they found that the killing of a law enforcement officer or child, a history of prior violent offenses, particularly a prior murder, and all evidentiary (scientific, co-perpetrator testimony, forensics, and eyewitness testimony) variables were by the strongest predictors of receiving a death sentence for defendants of any race. Their most salient finding was that the victim's race did not play any significant independent part, but the victim's sex (being female) did. The racial make-up of the offender/victim dyad had no significant independent effect, but the race of the defendant did, with Whites being significantly more likely to receive the death penalty than Blacks over the 30 years. Studies typically find insufficient numbers of White defendant/Black victim cases to include them (Ulmer, Kramer, & Zajac, 2020).

Jennings et al. (2014) looked at every death-eligible case (N = 1,356) in North Carolina from 1977 to 2009. After surveying several other studies with contradictory findings (but mostly supporting the white victim effect), they used propensity score matching (PSM) between those who received a death sentence and those who received a life-without-the-possibility-of-parole (LWOP) sentence. PSM is a statistical approximation of a quasi-experimental design by removing systematic differences between cases before comparing the outcome of interest—death versus LWOP. They estimated the White victim effect using logit regression models controlling for 50 legal and non-legal factors and found that regardless of the offender's race, there was a significant race-of-victim effect with an odds ratio of 1.39. When they looked at Black offender/White victim dyads, the odds ratio was 2.834. However, after applying PSM to the data, both effects were close to zero; that is, neither the race of the victim nor the racial makeup of offender/victim dyads had any independent effect on whether or not a defendant received the death penalty. The authors conclude that the "White victim effect' on capital punishment decision-making is better considered a 'case effect' rather than a 'race effect'" (p. 384). In other words, each case is unique and contains many case characteristics (aggravators and mitigators) and evidentiary qualities that must be considered. Given the ability to case-match, this quasi-experimental approach is the best that we have to tease out any discriminatory effects that may be present in sentencing.

Bjerregaard et al.'s (2017) study of 1,163 capital cases in North Carolina found that Blacks who killed Whites in "high severity" circumstances (multiple aggravating "heinous, atrocious, and cruel" factors) had an increased probability of a death sentence. Blacks who killed Whites at lower levels of severity had a decreased likelihood of receiving the death penalty. Under low-severity circumstances, a Black defendant who killed a White victim had almost half the odds of receiving a death sentence than a Black defendant who killed a Black victim or a White defendant who killed a victim of either race. The average number of aggravating factors in B/W cases (23.4% of the cases) was 2.20; the average in W/B cases (3.6% of the cases) was 1.47 factors (significant at $p < .01$). The average number of aggravating factors in B/B cases (30.9% of cases) was 1.96; for W/W (42.1% of cases) it was 1.84. Thus, B/W cases are more likely to have multiple aggravating factors than cases with any other defendant/victim dyad. This study adds to others showing that sentencing outcomes are conditioned by legally relevant factors.

Ulmer, Kramer, and Zajac (2020) examined death penalty decisions for 880 death-eligible murder convictions in 18 Pennsylvania counties that accounted for 87% of the state's first-degree murder convictions from 2000 to 2010. They focused on the defendant/victim race dyad and prosecutors' decisions to seek the death penalty and to retract a death penalty filing using propensity score weighting. Most cases were B/B (53.1%); 10.7% were B/W, and 3.8% were W/B. They did not find that Black defendants or Blacks who killed Whites were more likely to have the death penalty sought or imposed when all legal factors were considered. However, they did find that those who kill White victims, regardless of the defendant's race, were more likely to receive the death penalty. They describe the most surprising of their findings:

> Another notable effect was found in cases with black defendants and white victims, which saw an 8% smaller probability of death penalty filing than other types of cases, an effect that borders on statistical significance. Thus, there may be a modest tendency for prosecutors to seek the death penalty less often when the defendant is black and the victim is white.
>
> (Ulmer, Kramer, & Zajac 2020: 970)

Women and the Death Penalty

Although women have historically committed about 10% of the murders in the United States, they have constituted only about 3.6% of the total of 16,047 confirmed executions in the United States (including the colonies) between 1608 and 2022" (Death Penalty Information Center [DPIC], 2025). The first woman to be executed in the United States was Mary Surratt, a conspirator in the assassination of President Abraham Lincoln, and hanged in 1865 (Hatch & Walsh, 2016). According to the DPIC (2024), there were 52 women on death row as of March 11, 2024. This constitutes 2.12% of the total death row population, and 18 (13 White, 4 Black, 1 native American) have been executed since the reinstatement of the death penalty in 1976. Women have thus constituted 1.12% of the 1,610 people executed in the US from 1976 to the beginning of 2025. The last woman to be executed in the US was Amber McLaughlin, a 49-year-old transgender woman convicted and sentenced in Missouri for abducting, raping, and stabbing to death a former girlfriend in 2003. She was executed in January 2023.

Is this pro-female bias in the application of the death penalty, given that they commit an average of 10% of the murders each year? Many of these homicides are committed against spouses and boyfriends in self-defence situations, and rarely do we find women committing the heinous kinds of murders that draw down the death penalty on male murderers (Hatch & Walsh, 2016). However, Bohm (2003: 211) estimates that 4% to 6% of women murderers would receive death sentences "if women and men were treated equally [and if] no factor other than the offense was considered." Perhaps the chivalry hypothesis discussed in the previous chapter plays its part. For instance, in 1941, male inmates of San Quentin State Prison signed a petition to the governor of California to prevent the execution of Juanita Spinelli, who killed a young member of her gang she suspected would inform on her. The inmates wrote that to execute her would be "a blot on the reputation of the state and repulsive to the people of California because of her sex and her status as a mother" (Reza, 2005: 183). No one would think of appealing a male execution based on his sex or status as a father.

The pending 1998 execution of Karla Faye Tucker—a rock groupie, prostitute, and drug abuser convicted of the murders of a man and a woman—produced many protests, including from Colonel Oliver North, who exclaimed: "I don't think chivalry can ever be misplaced," and TV host Geraldo Rivera said, "Please don't let this happen. This is—it's very unseemly. Texas manhood, macho swagger.... What, are ya' going to kill a lady? Oh jeez. Why?" (Robinson, 2008: 205). Chivalry probably played a part in the case of Susan Smith, who, in 1994, strapped her two sons, ages 3 years and 14 months, into their car seats and rolled the car into a lake, drowning them. Smith wanted to reunite with her lover, who did not want her with her children. Smith was sentenced to life rather than death because, according to Reza

(2005: 188), she was viewed by the jury as a jilted victim "and loving mother with severe emotional issues."

Chivalry does not always prevail because 18 women have been executed since 1976. What was "special" about these 18 women? The counterpart to the chivalry hypothesis is the "evil woman" hypothesis, which maintains that women who defy traditional gender roles by not enacting a traditional feminine identity invite the wrath of the male-dominated criminal justice system (Reza, 2005). Both Tucker and Smith were good-looking young women who seemed to conform to the stereotype of femininity. Women who fit the evil woman hypothesis tend to be unattractive and "unladylike" and very much out of their prescribed gender roles by acting "manly" and being "man-hating." Ethel Spinelli deviated from gender role expectations in many ways. She was a career criminal, an ex-wrestler, and quite ugly. The warden of San Quentin called her the "coldest, hardest character, male or female" and added that she was "a hag, evil as a witch, horrible to look at" (Shatz & Shatz, 2011: 112). Four women executed since 1976—Wanda Jean Allen, Aileen Wuornos, and Lisa Coleman—may be considered to fit this description and were lesbians, and Amber McLaughlin was transgender.

If female murderers are treated more leniently based on nothing but their sex, it is a clear case of extra-legal bias. Streib (2003: 322) opines that if women want to be treated as men's equals, they should be treated as such, even in death penalty decisions: "Otherwise, women are lumped with juveniles and the mentally retarded as not fully responsible human beings." Reza (2005: 211) also opines:

> When women commit similar [death-eligible] crimes, we should not withhold capital punishment simply because the murderer is a mother, sister, or wife. ... The American judicial system must equalize the capital punishment system so that all, regardless of gender, are punished in a manner society and the legal system has deemed appropriate to impose on those who callously take the lives of others.

For people who support the death penalty, the answer to the sentencing equity issue is to execute more women convicted of first-degree murder until they attain parity with men convicted of similar crimes or to reduce the number of men executed. For those who oppose it, the only answer is to execute no one.

Life Without the Possibility of Parole (LWOP)

As the use of the death penalty has diminished in the US, it is not surprising that LWOP sentences have proliferated for our most serious offenders. It is also not surprising that questions have arisen regarding their fairness. For instance, Ogletree and Sarat (2012: 7) argue that LWOP is "America's new death penalty" and "riddled with racial disparity." Mauer and Nellis (2018:

103), however, although they want to abolish LWOP, declare that there is little "direct evidence" for "the impact of race on sentences of life imprisonment." Compared with the blizzard of death penalty studies, studies on LWOP are very sparse.

Johnson, Spohn, and Kimchi (2021) examined a sub-sample of 4,852 offenders eligible for LWOP under sentencing guidelines from a total of 366,612 non-immigration offenders sentenced in 90 federal district courts. Of those eligible for LWOP, only 23.3% received that sentence. A larger percentage of Black and Hispanic offenders were eligible for LWOP, and it was hypothesized that they would be more likely to receive it than White offenders after controlling for guideline scores. However, they found that, as in death penalty cases, case effects were the most important and stated:

> Contrary to social-psychological theories grounded in racial stereotypes and heuristics, we did not find evidence that federal judges are more likely to impose life sentences on eligible Black and Hispanic offenders. When we limit the sample to life-eligible offenders, both the descriptive statistics (table 1) and multivariate analysis (table 4) suggest that judges base these decisions primarily on legal factors; the likelihood of a LWOP sentence is substantially higher for eligible offenders convicted of violent crimes or racketeering/extortion and for those sentenced under mandatory minimums.
>
> (Johnson, Spohn, & Kimchi, 2021: 728)

At the state level, Garrett et al. (2021) examined the characteristics of the 1,627 LWOP sentences imposed in North Carolina from 1995 to 2017. They found that as the number of homicides with Black victims increases in a county, "LWOP sentencing is far less likely to occur if the defendant is Black (Model BB) but not so if the defendant is White. ... no significant correlation is found between White-victim homicide rate and LWOP sentencing for Black defendants" (p. 311). It thus appears that White rather than Black defendants were disadvantaged in this study and that there was no White-victim effect for Black defendants.

Although the studies in this chapter show that if there is any racial disadvantage in sentencing, it tends to disadvantage White defendants. Why this exists in a White-dominated system is hard to explain except perhaps in terms of the possible reasons given earlier (judges and prosecutors being more careful in Black defendant cases, etc.). However, Spohn (2017) asserts that although the widespread racism in the criminal justice system during the early part of the 20th century has largely been eliminated, she claims that racial disparities in sentencing remain. She bases her claim on the proportion of the general population imprisoned, not the proportion of crimes committed by each race: "In 2015, blacks comprised about 13% of the US population, but 39% of all state and federal prison inmates. ... By contrast, non-Hispanic whites made up 63% of the total population but only

37% of the prison population" (p. 171). As we saw earlier, however, Blacks are overrepresented in committing crimes and less likely to be arrested for them. This sub-population eligible for criminal sentencing is the correct comparison, not the entire Black population. She notes how Blacks are economically disadvantaged, and this is unfortunate and to be denounced, but this is not a concern of the criminal justice system, nor is it a mitigating factor for criminal behavior.

Bibliography

Aamodt, M., Leary, T., & Southard, L. (2020). *Radford/FGCU Annual Report on Serial Killer Statistics: 2020*. Radford, VA: Radford University.

Abadinsky, H. (2009). *Probation and parole: Theory and practice*. Saddle River, NJ: Prentice-Hall.

Abramson, L., Uzefovsky, F., Toccaceli, V., & Knafo-Noam, A. (2020). The genetic and environmental origins of emotional and cognitive empathy: review and meta-analyses of twin studies. *Neuroscience & Biobehavioral Reviews*, *114*: 113–133.

Acker, J., Bohm, R., & Lanier, C. (2014). *America's experiment with capital punishment: Reflections on the past, present, and the future of the ultimate sanction*. (3rd edn). Durham, NC: Carolina Academic Press.

Adkins, D., & Guo, G. (2008). Societal development and the shifting influence of the genome on status attainment. *Research in Social Stratification and Mobility*, *26*: 235–255.

Adolphs, R. (2009). The social brain: Neural basis of social knowledge. *Annual Review of Psychology*, *60*: 693–716.

Agnew, R. (1992). Foundation for a general strain theory of crime and delinquency. *Criminology*, *30*: 47–88.

Agnew, R. (2005). *Why do criminals offend? A general theory of crime and delinquency*. Los Angeles: Roxbury.

Agnew, R. (2013). Integrating assumptions about crime, people, and society: Response to the reviews of toward a unified criminology. *Journal of Theoretical & Philosophical Criminology*, *5*: 74.

Akers, R. (1999). Social learning and social structure: Reply to Sampson, *Morash, and Krohn. Theoretical Criminology*, *3*: 477–493.

Akers, R. (2011). *Social learning and social structure: A general theory of crime and deviance*. Transaction Publishers.

Akers, R., & Sellers, C. (2008). *Criminological theories: Introduction, evaluation, and application*. New York: Oxford University Press.

Akers, R., & Sellers, C. (2013). *Criminological theories: Introduction, evaluation, and application (6th edn)*. New York: Oxford University Press.

Alsharif, A., Salleh, N., & Baharun, R. (2021). The neural correlates of emotion in decision-making. *International Journal of Academic Research in Business and Social Sciences*, *11*: 64–77.

Anderson, E. (1999). *Code of the street: Decency, violence, and the moral life of the inner city*. New York: W.W. Norton.

Anderson, G. (2019). *Biological influences on criminal behavior*. Boca Raton, FL: CRC Press.

Andersen, T. (2015). Race, ethnicity, and structural variations in youth risk of arrest: Evidence from a national longitudinal sample. *Criminal Justice and Behavior*, 42: 900–916.

Ångström, A., Andersson, A., Garcia-Argibay, M., Chang, Z., Lichtenstein, P., D'Onofrio, B., Tuvblad, C., Ghirardi, L. and Larsson, H. (2024). Criminal convictions in males and females diagnosed with attention deficit hyperactivity disorder: A Swedish national registry study. *JCPP Advances*, *4*: p.e12217.

Apps, M., Rushworth, M., & Chang, S. (2016). The anterior cingulate gyrus and social cognition: tracking the motivation of others. *Neuron*, *90*: 692–707.

Antonaccio, O., & Tittle, C. (2008). Morality, self-control, and crime. *Criminology*, *46*: 479–510.

Arce-Ferrer, A., & Martinez Guzman, E. (2009). Studying the equivalence of computer-delivered and paper-based administrations of the raven standard progressive matrices test. *Educational and Psychological Measurement*, *69*: 855–867.

Ash, J., & Gallup, G. (2007). Paleoclimatic variation and brain expansion during human evolution. *Human Nature*, *18*: 109–124.

Avinun, R., & Knafo, A. (2014). Parenting as a reaction evoked by children's genotype: A meta-analysis of children-as-twins studies. *Personality and Social Psychology Review*, *18*: 87–102.

Baedke, J., Böhm, A., Reiners-Selbach, S., & Straetmanns, V. (2024). A synthesis without Darwin: Unification attempts in early theoretical biology. In R. Delisle, M. Esposito, & D. Ceccarelli (eds.) *Unity and disunity in evolutionary biology: Deconstructing Darwinism*, pp. 333–356. Cham: Switzerland. Springer International Publishing.

Bagaric, M., Hunter, D., & Svilar, J. (2021). Prison abolition. *The Journal of Criminal Law and Criminology*, *111*: 351–406.

Bailey, C. (1995). Workfare and involuntary servitude–What you wanted to know but were afraid to ask. *Boston College Third World Law Journal*, *15*: 285–321.

Bailey, D., & Geary, D. (2009). Hominid brain evolution: Testing climactic, ecological, and social competition models. *Human Nature*, *20*: 67–79.

Baker, L., Bezdjian, S., & Raine, A. (2006). Behavioral genetics: The science of antisocial behavior. *Law and contemporary problems*, *69*: 7–46.

Baldus, D., Pulaski, C., & Woodworth, G. (1983). Comparative review of death sentences: An empirical study of the Georgia experience. *The Journal of Criminal Law and Criminology*, *74*: 661–753.

Barnett, A. (1994). How numbers can trick you. *MIT Technology Review*, Oct.: 38–42.

Barkow, J. (1989). *Darwin, sex and status: Biological approaches to mind and culture*. Toronto: University of Toronto Press.

Barkow, J. (1992). Beneath new culture is old psychology: Gossip and social stratification. In J. Barkow, L. Cosmides, & J. Tooby (eds.), *The adapted mind: Evolutionary psychology and the generation of culture*, pp. 627–638. New York: Oxford University Press.

Barnes, J., & Boutwell, B. (2015). Biosocial criminology: The emergence of a new and diverse perspective. *Criminal Justice Studies*, *28*: 1–5.

Barrós-Loscertales, A., Ventura-Campos, N., Sanjuán-Tomás, A., Belloch, V., Parcet, M., & Ávila, C. (2010). Behavioral activation system modulation on brain activation during appetitive and aversive stimulus processing. *Social Cognitive and Affective Neuroscience*, *5*: 18–28.

Batrinos, M. (2012). Testosterone and aggressive behavior in man. *International Journal of Endocrinology and Metabolism*, *10*: 563–568.

Bateson, P., & Laland, K. (2013). Tinbergen's four questions: An appreciation and an update. *Trends in Ecology & Evolution*, *28*(12): 712–718.

Baumgartner, F., A. Grigg & A. Mastro (2015). #Black lives don't matter: Race-of-victim effects in US executions, 1976–2013. *Politics, Groups, and Identitities*. DOI: 10.1080/21565503.2015.1024262.

BBC News (2021) Seattle to end police-free protest zone after shootings. BBC News, June 23. https://www.bbc.com/news/world-us-canada-53146258

BBC (2024). How many countries still have the death penalty, and how many people are executed? BBC News Website. https://www.bbc.com/news/world-45835584

Bearman, P. (2008). Exploring genetics and social structure. *American Journal of Sociology*, *114*(S1), v–x.

Beaver, K., & Wright, J. (2019). Self-reported male-female differences in criminal involvement do not account for criminal justice processing differences. *American Journal of Criminal Justice*, *44*: 859–871.

Bedau, H. (1997). *The death penalty in America: Current controversies*. New York: Oxford University Press.

Bell, E., Kandler, C., & Riemann, R. (2018) Genetic and environmental influences on sociopolitical attitudes: Addressing some gaps in the new paradigm. *Politics and the Life Sciences*, *37*: 236–249.

Bell, M. (2021). Abolition: A new paradigm for reform. *Law & Social Inquiry*, *46*: 32–68.

Bellinger, D. (2008). Neurological and behavioral consequences of childhood lead exposure. *PLoS Medicine*, *5*: 690–692.

Bellucci, G., Camilleri, J., Iyengar, V., Eickhoff, S., & Krueger, F. (2020). The emerging neuroscience of social punishment: Meta-Analytic evidence. *Neuroscience and Biobehavioral Reviews*, *113*: 426–439.

Belsky, J. (1999). Conditional and alternative reproductive strategies: Individual differences in susceptibility to rearing experiences. In J. Rodgers & D. Rowe (eds.), *Genetic influences on fertility and sexuality*, pp. 62–63. Boston, MA: Klumer.

Belsky, J. (2024). The nature of nurture: Darwinian and Mendelian perspectives. *Development and Psychopathology*, 1–10.

Belsky, J., & Beaver, K. (2011). Cumulative-genetic plasticity, parenting and adolescent self-regulation. *Journal of Child Psychology and Psychiatry*, *52*: 619–626.

Belsky, J., Zhang, X., & Sayler, K. (2022). Differential susceptibility 2.0: Are the same children affected by different experiences and exposures? *Development and Psychopathology*, *34*: 1025–1033.

Benedict, R. (2019). *Patterns of culture*. New York: Routledge.

Bentham, J. (1948). *A fragment on government and an introduction to the principles of morals and legislation*. W. Harrison (ed.), Oxford: Basil Blackwell.

Bernard, T., Snipes, J., & Gerould, A. (2010). *Integrated theories. Theoretical criminology* (6th edn). New York: Oxford University Press.

Berk, R., Li, A., & Hickman, L. (2005). Statistical difficulties in determining the role of race in capital cases: a re-analysis of data from the state of Maryland. *Journal of Quantitative Criminology*, *21*: 365–390.

Berluti, K., Ploe, M., & Marsh, A. (2023). Emotion processing in youths with conduct problems: An fMRI meta-analysis. *Translational Psychiatry*, *13*(1), 105.

Bernstein, D. (2021). The right to armed self-defense in light of law enforcement abdication. *The Georgetown Journal of Law & Public Policy*, *19*: 177–209.

Bezdjian, S., Raine, A., Baker, L., & Lynam, D. (2011). Psychopathic personality in children: Genetic and environmental contributions. *Psychological Medicine*, *41*: 589–600.

Binotti, B., Jahn, R., & Pérez-Lara, Á. (2021). An overview of the synaptic vesicle lipid composition. *Archives of Biochemistry and Biophysics*, *709*: 108966.

Bissonnette, G. (2006). Consulting the federal sentencing guidelines after Booker. *UCLA Law Review*, *53*: 1497–1514.

Bitler, M., & Karoly, L. (2015). Intended and unintended effects of the war on poverty: What research tells us and implications for policy. *Journal of Policy Analysis and Management*, *34*: 639–696.

Bjerregaard, B., Smith, M., Cochran, J., & Fogel, S. (2017). A further examination of the liberation hypothesis in capital murder trials. *Crime & Delinquency*, *63*: 1017–1038.

Blank, R., & Schoeni, R. (2003). Changes in the distribution of children's family income over the 1990's. *American Economic Review*, *93*: 304–308.

Black Lives Matter Global Network (2016). Herstory. https://blacklivesmatter.com/about/herstory/

Bliss C. (2018). *Social by nature: The promise and peril of sociogenomics*. Stanford, CA: Stanford University Press.

Blume, J., Eisenberg, T., & Wells, M. (2004). Explaining death row's population and racial composition. *Journal of Empirical Legal Studies*, *1*: 165–207.

Boehm, C. (2011). Retaliatory violence in human prehistory. *British Journal of Criminology*, *51*: 518–534.

Bohm, R. (2001). *A primer on crime and delinquency* (2nd edn). Belmont, CA: Wadsworth.

Bohm, R. (2003). American death penalty opinion: Past, present, and future. In J. Acker, R., Bohm, & C. S. Lanier (eds.), *America's experiment with capital punishment: Reflections on the past, present, and future of the ultimate penal sanction*, pp. 27–54. Durham, NC: Carolina Academic Press.

Boisvert, D., Wells, J., Armstrong, T., & Lewis, R. (2018). Serotonin and self-control: A genetically moderated stress sensitization effect. *Journal of Criminal Justice*, *56*: 98–106.

Bond, R., & Saunders, P. (1999). Routes of success: Influences on the occupational attainment of young British males. *British Journal of Sociology*, *50*: 217–240.

Bonham, V., Warhauer-Baker, E., & Collins, F. (2005). Race and ethnicity in the genome era.*American Psychologist*, *60*: 9–15.

Bonnycastle, K., Davenport, E., & Cousin, M. (2021). Presynaptic dysfunction in neurodevelopmental disorders: Insights from the synaptic vesicle life cycle. *Journal of Neurochemistry*, *157*: 179–207.

Booth, A., Granger, D., Mazur, A., & Kivlighan, K. (2006). Testosterone and social behavior. *Social Forces*, *85*: 167–191.

Botescu, G. (2022). Comprehensive criminology — A reflective and Christian approach to the rationalist paradigm of free will. *Jurnalul Libertății de Conștiință*, *10*: 593–607.

Bouchard Jr, T., & McGue, M. (2003). Genetic and environmental influences on human psychological differences. *Journal of Neurobiology*, *54*: 4–45.

Box, S. (1987). *Recession, crime and punishment*. Bloomsbury Publishing.

Boyack, C. (2012). *Latter-day responsibility: Choosing liberty through personal accountability*. Springer Fork, UT: Cedar Fork.

Boyce, W., & Ellis, B. (2005). Biological sensitivity to context: I. An evolutionary–developmental theory of the origins and functions of stress reactivity. *Development and Psychopathology*, *17*: 271–301.

Boyce, W., & Kobor, M. (2015). Development and the epigenome: the "synapse" of gene–environment interplay. *Developmental Science*, *18*: 1–23.

Boyd, K. (2012). Levi's challenge and Peirce's theory/practice distinction. *Transactions of the Charles S. Peirce Society: A Quarterly Journal in American Philosophy*, *48*: 51–70.

Bradford, B. (2011). Police numbers and crime rates–a rapid evidence review. *HM Inspectorate of Constabulary*, 1–10.

Brady, D. (2023). Poverty, not the poor. *Science Advances*, *9*, eadg1469: 1–17.

Braga, A., Papachristos, A., & Hureau, D. (2012). Hot spots policing effects on crime. *Campbell Systematic Reviews*, *8*: 1–96.

Braithwaite, J. (1981). The myth of social class and criminality reconsidered. *American Sociological Review*, *46*: 36–57.

Braithwaite, J. (1989). *Crime, shame, and reintegration.* Cambridge, UK: Cambridge University Press.

Braman, D., Kahan, D., Hoffman, D., Robinson, P., Jones, O., Kurzban, R., & Darley, J. (2010). Some realism about punishment naturalism (with responses). *The University of Chicago Law Review*, *77*: 1531–1660.

Brannigan, A. (1997). Self-control, social control, and evolutionary psychology: Toward an integrated perspective on crime. *Canadian Journal of Criminology*, *39*: 403–431.

Brass, M., & Cramon, D. (2004). Decomposing components of task preparation with functional magnetic resonance imaging. *Journal of Cognitive Neuroscience*, *16*: 609–620.

Bratsberg, B., & Rogeberg, O. (2018). Flynn effect and its reversal are both environmentally caused. *Proceedings of the National Academy of Sciences*, *115*: 6674–6678.

Brembs, B. (2011). Towards a scientific concept of free will as a biological trait: Spontaneous actions and decision-making in invertebrates. *Proceedings of the Royal Society: Biological Sciences. 278*: 930–939.

Brennan, P., Raine, A., Schulsinger, F., Kirkegaard-Sorenen, L., Knop, J., Hutchings, B., Rosenberg, R., & Mednick, S. (1997). Psychophysiological protective factors for male subjects at high risk for criminal behavior. *American Journal of Psychiatry*, *154*: 853–855.

Brown, D. (1990). *Human universals.* New York: McGraw-Hill.

Brown, G., Dickins, T., Sear, R., & Laland, K. (2011). Evolutionary accounts of human behavioural diversity. *Philosophical Transactions of the Royal Society B: Biological Sciences*, *366*: 313–324.

Brunero, J. (2002). Evolution, altruism and internal reward explanations. *Philosophical Forum*, *33*: 413–424.

Brush, L. (2003). Impacts of welfare reform. *Race, Gender & Class*, *10*: 173–192.

Buckholtz, J., & R. Marois (2012). The roots of modern Justice: Cognitive and neural foundations of social norms and their enforcement. *Nature Neuroscience*, *13*: 655–661.

Buonanno, P., & Raphael, S. (2013). Incarceration and incapacitation: Evidence from the 2006 Italian collective pardon. *American Economic Review*, *103*: 2437–2465.

Burgess, R., & Akers, R. (1966). A differential association-reinforcement theory of criminal behavior. *Social Problems 14*: 128–147.

Burke, R. (2009). *An introduction to criminological theory.* Uffculme Cullompton, UK: Willan Publishing.

Burke, R. (2018). *An introduction to criminological theory.* New York: Routledge.

Burt, C. (2020). Self-control and crime: beyond Gottfredson & Hirschi's theory. *Annual Review of Criminology*, *3*: 43–73.

Burt, C. (2023). Irreducibly social: Why biocriminology's ontoepistemology is incompatible with the social reality of crime. *Theoretical Criminology*, *27*: 85–104.

Burt, C., & Simons, R. (2014). Pulling back the curtain on heritability studies: Biosocial criminology in the postgenomic era. *Criminology*, *52*: 223–262.

Burt, C., & Simons, R. (2015). Heritability studies in the postgenomic era: The fatal flaw is conceptual. *Criminology*, *53*: 103–112.

Burt. S. (2009). Rethinking environmental contributions to child and adolescent psychopathology: A meta-analysis of shared environmental influences. *Psychological Bulletin*, *135*: 608–637.

Buschkuebl, M., & Jaeggi, S. (2010). Improving intelligence: A literature review. *Swiss Medical Weekly*, *140*: 266–272.

Bush, G. (2000). George W. Bush's speech to the NAACP. *Washington Post.* https://www.washingtonpost.com/wp-srv/onpolitics/elections/bushtext071000.htm

Bush, N., Lengua, L., & Colder, C. (2010). Temperament as a moderator of the relation between neighborhood and children's adjustment. *Journal of Applied Developmental Psychology, 31*: 351–361.
Buss, D. (2001). Human nature and culture. *Journal of Personality, 68*: 955–978.
Byrd, A., & Manuck, S. (2014). MAOA, childhood maltreatment, and antisocial behavior: Meta-analysis of a gene-environment interaction. *Biological Psychiatry, 75*: 9–17.
Byrnes, J., Miller, D., & Schafer, W. (1999). Gender differences in risk taking: A meta-analysis. *Psychological Bulletin, 125*: 367–383.
Cai, B., Zhang, G., Zhang, A., Xiao, L., Hu, W., Stephen, J., Wilson, T., Calhoun, V., & Wang, Y. (2021). *Human Brain Mapping, 42*: 2691–2705.
Camilleri. K. (2005). Heisenberg and the transformation of Kantian philosophy. *International Studies in the Philosophy of Science, 19*: 271–287.
Campbell, A. (1999). Staying alive: Evolution, culture, and women's intrasexual aggression. *Behavioral and Brian Sciences, 22*: 203–214.
Campbell, A. (2006). Sex differences in direct aggression: What are the psychological mediators? *Aggression and Violent Behavior, 11*: 237–264.
Campbell, A., Muncer, S., & Bibel, D. (2001). Women and crime: An evolutionary approach. *Aggression and Violent Behavior*, 6: 481–497
Canton, R. (2015). Crime, punishment and the moral emotions: Righteous minds and their attitudes towards punishment. *Punishment & Society, 17*: 54–72.
Cao, L. (2004). *Major criminological theories: Concepts and measurements*. Belmont, CA: Wadsworth.
Cardinale, E., Ryan, R., & Marsh, A. (2021). Maladaptive fearlessness: An examination of the association between subjective fear experience and antisocial behaviors linked with callous unemotional traits. *Journal of Personality Disorders, 35* (Supplement A): 39–56.
Carrier, N., & Walby, K. (2014). Ptolemizing Lombroso: The pseudo-revolution of biosocial criminology. *Journal of Theoretical and Philosophical Criminology, 6*: 1–45.
Caruso, G. (2021). Précis of rejecting retributivism: Free will, punishment, and criminal justice. *Journal of Legal Philosophy, 46*: 120–125.
Casey, B., Somerville, L., Gotlib, I., Ayduk, O., Franklin, N., Askren, M., Jonides, J., Berman, M., Wilson, N., Teslovich, T., & Glover, G. (2011). Behavioral and neural correlates of delay of gratification 40 years later. *Proceedings of the National Academy of Sciences, 108*: 14998–15003.
Caspi, A., Bem, D., & Elder, G. (1989). Continuities and consequences of interaction styles across the lifecourse. *Journal of Personality, 57*: 375–406.
Caspi, A., Langley, K., Milne, B., Moffitt, T., O'Donovan, M., Owen, M., & Thapar, A. (2008). A replicated molecular genetic basis for subtyping antisocial behavior in children with attention-deficit/hyperactivity disorder. *Archives of General Psychiatry, 65*: 203–210.
Caspi, A., McClay, Ju., Moffitt, T., Mill, J., Martin, J., Craig, I., Taylor, A., & Poulton, R. (2002). Role of genotype in the cycle of violence in maltreated children. *Science, 297*: 851–854.
Caspi, A., Moffitt, T., Silva, P., Stouthamer-Loeber, M., Krueger, R. Schmutte, P. (1994). Are some people crime-prone? Replications of the personality-crime relationship across countries, genders, races, and methods. *Criminology, 32*: 163–194.
Caspi, A., Williams, B., Kim-Cohen, J., Craig, I., Milne, B., Poulton, R., Schalkwyk, L., Taylor, A., Werts, H., & Moffitt, T. (2007). Moderation of breastfeeding effects on the IQ by genetic variation in fatty acid metabolism. *Proceedings of the National Academy of Sciences, 104*: 18860–18865.
Cassé, M. (2003). *Stellar alchemy: The celestial origin of atoms*. Cambridge, UK: Cambridge University Press.

Cassell, P. (2008). In defense of the death penalty. *Journal of the Institute for the Advancement of Criminal Justice*, *15*: 14–28.
Cassell, P., & Fowles, R. (2018). What caused the 2016 Chicago homicide spike: An empirical examination of the ACLU effect and the role of stop and frisks in preventing gun violence. *University of Illinois law Review*, *1581*: 1–92.
Cecil, K., Brubaker, C., Adler, C., Dietrich, K., Altaye, M., Egelhoff, J., ... Lanphear, B. (2008). Decreased brain volume in adults with childhood lead exposure. *PLoS Medicine*, *5*: 742–750.
Cesario, J., Johnson, D., & Terrill, W. (2019). Is there evidence of racial disparity in police use of deadly force? Analyses of officer-involved fatal shootings in 2015–2016. *Social Psychological and Personality Science*, *10*: 586–595.
Centers for Disease Control and Prevention (2022). Percent of babies born to unmarried mothers by state. https://www.cdc.gov/nchs/pressroom/sosmap/unmarried/unmarried.htm
Chagnon, N. (1988). Life histories, blood revenge, and warfare in a tribal population. *Science*, *239*: 985–992.
Chalfin, A., Hansen, B., Weisburst, E., & Williams, M. Jr. (2020). Police force size and civilian race. Working Paper 28202. National Bureau of Economic Research.
Chambliss, W. (1976). *Criminal law in action*. Santa Barbara, CA: Hamilton.
Chamorro-Premuzic, T., & Furman, A. (2005). *Intellectual competence. The Psychologist*, *18*: 352–354.
Chapman, B. (2021). New York City homicides and shootings rose dramatically in 2020. *Wall Street Journal*, January 7.
Champion, D. (2005). *Probation, parole, and community corrections*. Saddle River, NJ: Prentice-Hall.
Chapple, C., & Johnson, K. (2007). Gender differences in impulsivity. *Youth Violence and Juvenile Justice*, *5*: 221–234.
Chen, F. (2020). Behavioral Inhibition System function as the mediator in the pathway from electrodermal fear conditioning to antisocial behavior: Integrating the Reinforcement Sensitivity Theory. *Personality and Individual Differences*, *166*: 110179.
Cheung, R., Boise, C., Cummings, E., & Davies, P. (2018). Mothers' and fathers' roles in child adjustment: Parenting practices and mothers' emotion socialization as predictors. *Journal of Child and Family Studies*, *27*: 4033–4043.
Chiao, J., & Blizinsky, K. (2010). Culture-gene coevolution of individualism-collectivism and the serotonin transporter gene. *Proceedings of the Royal Society of London B; Biological Sciences*, *277*: 529–537.
Choy, O., Farrington, D., & Raine, A. (2015). The need to incorporate autonomic arousal in developmental and life-course research and theories. *Journal of Developmental and Life-Course Criminology*, *1*: 189–207.
Cicchetti, D., Hetzel, S., Rogosch, F., Handley, E., & Toth, S. (2016). An investigation of child maltreatment and epigenetic mechanisms of mental and physical health risk. *Development and Psychopathology*, November 28: 1305–1317.
Clark, T. (2007). *Encountering naturalism: A worldview and its uses*. Somerville, MA: The Center for Naturalism.
Clarke, R., & Cornish, D. (2001). Rational choice. In R. Paternoster & R. Backman (eds.), *Explaining criminals and crime*, pp. 23–42. Los Angeles, CA: Roxbury.
Clarkson, J., Chambers, J., Hirt, E., Otto, A., Kardes, F., & Leone, C. (2015). The self-control consequences of political ideology. *Proceedings of the National Academy of Sciences of the United States of America*, *112*: 8250–8253.
Clayton, D. (2018). Black lives matter and the civil rights movement: A comparative analysis of two social movements in the United States. *Journal of Black Studies*, *49*: 448–480.
Cobbina-Dungy, J., Chaudhuri, S., LaCourse, A., & DeJong, C. (2022). "Defund the police:" Perceptions among protesters in the 2020 March on Washington. *Criminology & public policy*, *21*(1): 147–174.

Coccaro, E., McCloskey, M., Fitzgerald, D., & Phan, K. (2007). Amygdala and orbitofrontal reactivity to social threat in individuals with impulsive aggression. *Biological Psychiatry*, *15*: 168–178.

Coffey, P. (2008) *Cathedrals of science: The personalities and rivalries that made modern chemistry*. Oxford: Oxford University Press.

Cohen, A. (1955). *Delinquent boys*. New York: Free Press.

Cohn, M., Popma, A., Van Den Brink, W., Pape, L., Kindt, M., Van Domburgh, L., Doreleijers, T., & Veltman, D. (2013). Fear conditioning, persistence of disruptive behavior and psychopathic traits: an fMRI study. *Translational Psychiatry*, *3*: 319–e319.

Coid, J., Freestone, M., & Ullrich, S. (2012). Subtypes of psychopathy in the British household population: Findings from the national household survey of psychiatric morbidity. *Social Psychiatry and Psychiatric Epidemiology*, *47*: 879–891

Collier-Spruel, L., Hawkins, A., Jayawickreme, E., Fleeson, W., & Furr, R. M. (2019). Relativism or tolerance? Defining, assessing, connecting, and distinguishing two moral personality features with prominent roles in modern societies. *Journal of Personality*, *87*: 1170–1188.

Cook, P., & Mancik, A. (2024). The sixty-year trajectory of homicide clearance rates: Toward a better understanding of the great decline. *Annual Review of Criminology*, *7*: 59–83.

Cooke, E., Connolly, E., Boisvert, D., Armstrong, T., Lewis, R., Kavish, N., Wells, J., & Harper, J. (2020). Examining how testosterone and cortisol influence the relationship between strain, negative emotions, and antisocial behavior: a gendered analysis. *Crime & Delinquency*, *66*: 1470–1501.

Cooper, J., Walsh, A., & Ellis, L. (2010). Is criminology ripe for a paradigm shift? Evidence from a survey of American criminologists. *Journal of Criminal Justice Education*, *21*: 332–347.

Cornea, A. (2012). Relativity and relativism: On a failed analogy. *Cultura*, *9*: 29–42.

Corning, P. (2002). The re-emergence of "emergence:" A venerable concept in search of a theory. *Complexity*, *7*: 18–30.

Corr, P. (2008). Reinforcement sensitivity theory (RST): Introduction. In P. Corr (ed.), *The Reinforcement Sensitivity Theory and personality*, pp. 1–28. Cambridge, UK: Cambridge University Press.

Corr, P. (2013). Approach and avoidance behaviour: Multiple systems and their interactions. *Emotion Review*, *5*: 285–290.

Cosby, B., & Poussaint, A. (2007). *Come on, people: On the path from victims to victors*. Nashville, TN: Thomas Nelson.

Cosmides, L., & Tooby, J. (1992). Cognitive adaptations for social change. In J. Barkow, L. Cosmides, & J. Tooby (eds.), *The adapted mind: Evolutionary psychology and the generation of culture*, pp. 163–228. New York: Oxford University Press.

Costa, P., Terracciano, A., & McCrae, R. (2001). Gender differences in personality traits across cultures: Robust and surprising findings. *Journal of Personality and Social Psychology*, *81*: 322–331.

Craig, M., Catani, M., Deeley, Q., Latham, R., Daly, E., Kanaan, R., Picchioni, M., McGuire, P., Fahy, T., & Murphy, D. (2009). Altered connections on the road to psychopathy. *Molecular Psychiatry*, *14*: 946–53.

Craig, S., Goulter, N., & Moretti, M. (2021). A systematic review of primary and secondary callous-unemotional traits and psychopathy variants in youth. *Clinical Child and Family Psychology Review*, *24*: 65–91.

Cramer, E. (2006). Statement to the North Carolina House Selection Committee on Capital Punishment. http://ourpaws.info/cramer/death/talk.txt

Crick, F. (1994) *The astonishing hypothesis: The scientific search for the soul*. New York: Charles Scribner's Sons.

Crocker, J., Canevello, A., & Brown, A. (2017). Social motivation: Costs and benefits of selfishness and otherishness. *Annual Review of Psychology*, *68*: 299–325.
Crozier, J. & Barth, R. (2005). Cognitive and academic functioning in maltreated children. *Children & Schools*, *27*: 197–206.
Csikszentmihalyi, M. & Wong, M. (2014). The situational and personal correlates of happiness: A cross-national comparison. In *Flow and the foundations of positive psychology*, pp. 193–212. Springer, Dordrecht.
Cullen, F. (2005). Challenging individualistic theories of crime. In S. Gua-Ghezzi & J. Trevino (eds.), *Understanding crime: A multidisciplinary approach*, pp. 55–60. Cincinnati, OH: Anderson.
Cullen, F. (2011). Beyond adolescence-limited criminology: Choosing our future—the American Society of Criminology 2010 Sutherland address. *Criminology*, *49*: 287–330.
Currie, E. (1973) Dialogue with Anthony M. Platt: An interview conducted and prepared for issues in criminology, *Issues in Criminology*, *8*: 19–34.
Currie, E. (1999). Confronting crime: Looking toward the twenty-first century. *Justice Quarterly*, *6*: 5–25.
Cziko. G. (1996). Three lessons of biology for psychology: The adapted mind, within organism selection, and perceptual control. *Presented at the Annual Meeting of the Human Behavior and Evolution Society*, Northwestern University, Evanston, Illinois, June, 1996.
D'Alessio, S. & Stolzenberg, L. (2003). Race and the probability of arrest. *Social Forces*, *81*: 1381–1397.
Darwin, C. (1981) *The descent of man, and selection in relation to sex*. Princeton, N.J.: Princeton University Press.
Dawes, C. & Weinschenk, A. (2020). On the genetic basis of political orientation. *Current Opinion in Behavioral Sciences*, *34*, 173–178.
Dawkins, R. (2006). *The God delusion*. New York: Houghton Mifflin.
Day, J. & Carelli, R. (2007). The nucleus accumbens and Pavlovian reward learning. *The Neuroscientist*, *13*: 148–159.
Deary, I. (2003). Reaction time and psychometric intelligence: Jensen's contributions. In Nyborg, H. (ed.), *The scientific study of general intelligence: Tribute to Arthur Jensen*, pp. 53–75. Elsevier.
Deary, I., Penke, L., & Johnson, W. (2010). The neuroscience of human intelligence differences. *Nature Reviews Neuroscience*, *11*: 201–211.
Deary, I., Spinath, F., & Bates, T. (2006). Genetics of intelligence. *European Journal of Human Genetics*, *14*: 690–700.
Deary, I., Whalley, L., Lemmon, H., Crawford, J., & Starr, J. (2000). The stability of individual differences in mental ability from childhood to old age: Follow-up of the 1932 Scottish Mental Survey. *Intelligence*, *28*: 49–55.
Death Penalty Information Center (2025). State by State. https://deathpenaltyinfo.org/state-and-federal-info/state-by-state
Decety, J., Chen, C., Harenski, C., & Kiehl, K. (2013). An fMRI study of affective perspective taking in individuals with psychopathy: imagining another in pain does not evoke empathy. *Frontiers in Human Neuroscience*, *7*: 489.
Deckers, L. (2018). *Motivation: Biological, psychological, and environmental*. New York: Routledge.
Degler, C. (1991). *In search of human nature: The decline and revival of Darwinism in American social thought*. New York: Oxford University Press.
De Haan, W. & Vos, J. (2003). A crying shame: The over-rationalized conception of man in the rational choice perspective. *Theoretical Criminology*, *7*: 29–54.
DeLisi, M. (2005). *Career criminals in society*. Thousand Oak, CA: Sage.
DeLisi, M. (2011). Self-control theory: The Tyrannosaurus rex of criminology is poised to devour criminal justice. *Journal of Criminal Justice*, *39*: 103–105.

DeLisi, M., Beaver, K., Vaughn, M., & Wright, J. (2009). All in the family: Gene× environment interaction between DRD2 and criminal father is associated with five antisocial phenotypes. *Criminal Justice and Behavior*, *36*: 1187–1197.

de Looff, P., Cornet, L., de Kogel, C., Fernández-Castilla, B., Embregts, P., Didden, R., & Nijman, H. L. (2022). Heart rate and skin conductance associations with physical aggression, psychopathy, antisocial personality disorder and conduct disorder: An updated meta-analysis. *Neuroscience and Biobehavioral Reviews*, *132*: 553–582.

Deming, D. (2017). The growing importance of social skills in the labor market. *Quarterly Journal of Economics*, *132*: 1593–640.

Dennett, D. (1995). *Darwin's dangerous idea: Evolution and the meanings of life*. New York: Simon & Schuster.

Depue, R. & Collins, P. (1999). Neurobiology of the structure of personality: Dopamine, facilitation of incentive motivation, and extraversion. *Behavioral and Brain Sciences*, *22*: 491–569.

De Quervain, D., Fischbacher, U., Valerie, T., Schellhammer, M., Schnyder, U., Buch, A., & Fehr, E. (2004). The neural basis of altruistic punishment. *Science*, *305*: 1254–1259.

DeWall, C., Finkel, E., & Denson, T. (2011). Self-control inhibits aggression. *Social and Personality Psychology Compass*, *5*: 458–472.

de Waal, F. (1996). *Good natured: The origins of right and wrong in humans and other animals*. Cambridge, MA: Harvard University Press.

de Waal, F. (2008). Putting the altruism back into altruism: The evolution of empathy. *Annual Review of Psychology*, *59*: 279–300.

DeWeerdt, S. (2019). How to map the brain. *Nature*. DOI: 10.1038/d41586-019-02208-0.

Dickens, W. & Flynn, J. (2001). Heritability estimates versus large environmental effects: The IQ paradox resolved. *Psychological Review*, *108*: 346–369.

Ding, Y., Chi, H., Grady, D., Morishima, A., Kidd, J., Kidd, K., Flodman, P., Spence, M., Schuck, S., Swanson, J., & Zhang, Y. (2002). Evidence of positive selection acting at the human dopamine receptor D4 gene locus. *Proceedings of the National Academy of Sciences*, *99*: 309–314.

Dinh, T., Haselton, M., & Gangestad, S. (2022). "Fast" women? The effects of childhood environments on women's developmental timing, mating strategies, and reproductive outcomes. *Evolution and Human Behavior*, *43*: 133–146.

Dobchuk-Land, B. & Walby, K. (2021). Police abolition as community struggle against state violence. *Social Justice*, *48*: 1–30.

Dobzhansky, T. (1973). Nothing in biology makes sense except in light of evolution. *The American Biology Teacher*, *35*: 125–129.

Dolan, M., Anderson, I., & Deakin, J. (2001). Relationship between 5–HT function and impulsivity and aggression in male offenders with personality disorders. *British Journal of Psychiatry*, *178*: 352–359.

Dollar, C. (2014). Conceptual remixing in criminology: Tracing Durkheim and Marx's influence on etiological theories of crime. *Sociology Compass*, *8*(10): 1157–1166.

Donner, C., Maskaly, J., Piquero, A., & Jennings, W. (2017). Quick on the draw: Assessing the relationship between low self-control and officer-involved police shootings. *Police Quarterly*, *20*: 213–234.

Dugré J., Radua J, Carignan-Allard M, Dumais A, Rubia K, Potvin S. (2020). Neurofunctional abnormalities in antisocial spectrum: A meta-analysis of fMRI studies on five distinct neurocognitive research domains. *Neuroscience Biobehavioral Review*, *119*: 168–83.

Duncan, G., Magnuson, K., & Votruba-Drzal, E. (2017). Moving beyond correlations in assessing the consequences of poverty. *Annual Review of Psychology*, *68*: 1–22.

Dunrose, M., Cooper, A., & Snyder, H. (2014). *Recidivism of prisoners released in 30 states in 2003: Patterns from 2005 to 2010*. Washington, DC: Bureau of Justice Statistics.

Durant, W. (1935). *Our oriental heritage*. New York: Simon & Schuster.

Durant, W. & Durant, A. (1967). *Rousseau and revolution*. New York: Simon and Schuster.

Durant, W. & Durant, A. (1968) *The lessons of history*. New York: Simon and Schuster.

Durkheim, E. (1933). *The division of labor in society*. New York: Free Press.

Durkheim, E. (1964). *The division of labour in society*. New York: Free Press.

Durkheim, E. (2005). The dualism of human nature and its social conditions. *Durkheimian Studies*, *11*: 35–45.

Durnescu, I. (2008). An exploration of the purposes and outcomes of probation in European jurisdictions. *Probation Journal*, *55*: 273–281.

Edwards-Levy, A. & Robillard, K. (2020). Most Americans want police reform but don't back "defund the police." *Huffington Post*, June 15.

Ehrlich, D. & Josselyn, S. (2016). Plasticity-related genes in brain development and amygdala-dependent learning. *Genes, Brain and Behavior*, *15*: 125–143.

Einstein, A. & L. Infeld (1938). *The evolution of physics*. Cambridge, UK: Cambridge University Press.

Ekins, E. (2019). *Poll: What Americans think cause wealth and poverty*. Washington, DC: The Cato Institute.

Eliaeson, S. (2002). *Max Weber's methodologies: Interpretation and critique*. Malden, MA: Blackwell Press.

Ellis, B., Boyce, W., Belsky, J., Bakermans-Kranenburg, M., & Van Ijzendoorn, M. (2011). Differential susceptibility to the environment: An evolutionary–neurodevelopmental theory. *Development and Psychopathology*, *23*: 7–28.

Ellis, L. (1996). A discipline in peril: Sociology's future hinges on curing its biophobia. *The American Sociologist*, *27*: 21–41.

Ellis, L. (2005). A theory explaining biological correlates of criminality. *European Journal of Criminology*, 2: 287–315.

Ellis, L., Beaver, K. & Wright, J. (2009). *Handbook of crime correlates*. Oxford: Academic.

Ellis, L. & Hoffman, H. (1990). Views of contemporary criminologists on causes and theories of crime. In L. Ellis & H. Hoffman (eds.), *Crime in biosocial, moral, and social contexts*, pp. 50–58. New York, NY: Praeger.

Ellis, L. & Peterson, J. (1996). Crime and religion: An international comparison among thirteen industrialized nations. *Personality and Individual Differences*, *20*: 761–768.

Ellis, L. & Walsh, A. (2000). *Criminology: A global perspective*. Needham Heights, MA: Allyn & Bacon.

Ellis, L. & Walsh, A. (2003). Crime, delinquency, and intelligence: A review of the worldwide literature. In H. Nyborg (ed.), *The scientific study of general intelligence: Tribute to Arthur R. Jensen*, pp. 343–365. Oxford, UK: Elsevier.

Ellison, C., Burr, J., & McCall, P. (2003). The enduring puzzle of southern homicide. *Homicide Studies*, 7: 326–52.

Ellwood, D. & J. Crane (1990). Family changes among black Americans: What do we know? *Journal of Economic perspectives*. *4*: 65–84.

Embry, R. & Lyons Jr, P. (2012). Sex-based sentencing: Sentencing discrepancies between male and female sex offenders. *Feminist Criminology*, 7: 146–162.

Eppig, C., Fincher, C., & Thornhill, R. (2010). Parasite prevalence and the worldwide distribution of cognitive ability. *Proceedings of the Royal Society B: Biological Sciences*, *277*: 3801–3808.

Erath, S., El-Sheikh, M., & Cummings, E. (2009). Harsh parenting and child externalizing behavior: skin conductance level reactivity as a moderator. *Child Development*, *80*: 578–592.

Eme, R. (2015). Beauchaine ontogenic process model of externalizing psychopathology: A biosocial theory of crime and delinquency. *Journal of Criminal Justice*, *43*: 443–449.

Errol, Z., Madsen, J., & Moslehi, S. (2021). Social disorganization theory and crime in the advanced countries: Two centuries of evidence. *Journal of Economic Behavior & Organization*, *191*: 519–537.

Eskridge, C. (2005). The state of the field of criminology: Brief essay. *Journal of Contemporary Criminal Justice*, *21*: 296–308.

Etkin, A., Egner, T., & Kalisch, R. (2011). Emotional processing in anterior cingulate and medial prefrontal cortex. *Trends in Cognitive Sciences*, *15*: 85–93.

Fachner, G. & Carter, S. (2015). Collaborative reform initiative: An assessment of deadly force in the Philadelphia police department. *Submitted by the CNA Corporation to the USDOJ Office of Community Oriented Policing Services.*

Farnier, J., Shankland, R., Kotsou, I., Inigo, M., Rosset, E., & Leys, C. (2021). Empowering well-being: Validation of a locus of control scale specific to well-being. *Journal of Happiness Studies*, *22*: 3513–3542.

Farrington, D. & Welsh, B. (2008). *Saving children from a life of crime: Early risk factors and effective interventions.* New York, NY: Oxford University Press.

Fazel S, Sjöstedt G, Grann M, Långström N. (2010). Sexual offending in women and psychiatric disorder: a national case-control study. *Archive of Sexual Behavior*, *39*: 161–167.

Fede, A. (2017). *Homicide justified: The legality of killing slaves in the United States and the Atlantic world* (Vol. 2). University of Georgia Press.

Federal Bureau of Investigation (2008). *Serial murder: Multidisciplinary perspectives for Investigators.* https://www.fbi.gov/stats-services/publications/serial-murder

Federal Bureau of Investigation (2013). *Crime in the United States: 2012.* Washington, DC: U.S. Government Printing Office.

Federal Bureau of Investigation (2021). *Crime in the United States: 2020.* Washington, DC: US Government Printing Office.

Federico, C. & Schneider, M. (2007). Political expertise and the use of ideology: Moderating effects of evaluative motivation. *Public Opinion Quarterly*, *71*: 221–252.

Feldner, Y. (2000). "Honor" murders—Why the perps get off easy. *Middle East Quarterly*, 7.

Felthous, A. (2008). The will: From metaphysical freedom to normative functionalism. *Journal of the American Academy of Psychiatry and the Law Online*, *36*: 16–24.

Fields, R. (2014). Myelin—more than insulation. *Science*, *344*: 264–266.

Fincher, C., Thornhill, R., Murray, D., & Schaller, M. (2008). Pathogen prevalence predicts human cross-cultural variability in individualism/collectivism. *Proceedings of the Royal Society B*, *275*: 1279–1285.

Finn, E., Shen, X., Scheinost, D., Rosenberg, M., Huang, J., Chun, M., Papademetris, X., & Constable, R. (2015). Functional connectome fingerprinting: identifying individuals using patterns of brain connectivity. *Nature Neuroscience*, *18*: 1664–1671.

Firestone, L., Firestone, A., & Catlett, J. (2013). *The self under siege: A therapeutic model for differentiation.* New York: Routledge.

Fish, J. (2013). Homo duplex revisited: A defence of Émile Durkheim's theory of the moral self. *Journal of Classical Sociology*, *13*: 338–358.

Flynn, J. (2007). *What is intelligence? Beyond the Flynn effect.* Cambridge, UK: Cambridge University Press.

Flynn, J. (2013). The "Flynn effect" and Flynn's paradox. *Intelligence*, *41*: 851–857.

Fogliato, R., Xiang, A., Lipton, Z., Nagin, D., & Chouldechova, A. (2021). On the validity of arrest as a proxy for offense: Race and the likelihood of arrest for violent crimes. In *Proceedings of the 2021 AAAI/ACM Conference on AI, Ethics, and Society*, pp. 100–111.

Fontao, M. & Ross, T. (2021). External locus of control and cognitive ability independently distinguish men in prison from community living non-offending men. *Criminal Behaviour and Mental Health*, *31*: 297–309.

Ford, M. (2014). Racism in the execution chamber. *The Atlantic*, June 23. http://www.theatlantic.com/politics/archive/2014/06/race-and-the-death-penalty/373081/

Forero, D., Pereira-Morales, A., & González-Giraldo, Y. (2017). Molecular genetics and human behavior. *Module in Neuroscience and Biobehavioral Psychology*. https://doi.org/10.1016/B978-0-12-809324-5.06489-0.

Fox, B. (2017). It's nature and nurture: Integrating biology and genetics into the social learning theory of criminal behavior. *Journal of Criminal Justice*, *49*: 22–31.

Fox, E. & Beevers C. (2016) Differential sensitivity to the environment: contribution of cognitive biases and genes to psychological wellbeing. *Molecular Psychiatry*, *12*: 1657–1662.

Francis, J. (2013). Deconstructing crime and nature or, what does post humanism have to do with criminology? *Critical Criminology*, *21*: 509–524.

Franklin, T. & Henry, T. (2020). Racial disparities in federal sentencing outcomes: Clarifying the role of criminal history. *Crime & Delinquency*, 66: 3–32.

Frase, R. (2019). Forty years of American sentencing guidelines: What have we learned? *Crime and Justice*, *48*: 79–135.

Freeman, R. (1986). Who escapes? The relation of churchgoing and other background factors to the socioeconomic performance of black male youths from inner-city tracts. Working Paper Series No. 1656, National Bureau of Economic Research, Inc., Cambridge, MA.

Freud, S. (1961). *Civilization and its discontents*. New York: Norton.

Friedman, L. (2005). *A history of American law*. New York: Simon & Shuster.

Frisell, T., Pawitan, Y., & Långström, N. (2012). Is the association between general cognitive ability and violent crime caused by family-level confounders? *PloS one*, 7: e41783.

Fritz, M., Rösel, F., Dobler, H., Streb, J., & Dudeck, M. (2021). Childhood trauma, the combination of MAO-A and COMT genetic polymorphisms and the joy of being aggressive in forensic psychiatric patients. *Brain Sciences*, *11*: 1008.

Fryer, D. (2023). Idealizing abolition. *Criminal Law and Philosophy*, *17*: 553–572.

Fryer Jr, R. (2019). An empirical analysis of racial differences in police use of force. *Journal of Political Economy*, *127*: 1210–1261.

Funk, C., Smith, K., Alford, J., Hibbing, M., Eaton, N., Krueger, R., Eaves, L., & Hibbing, J. (2013). Genetic and environmental transmission of political orientations. *Political Psychology*, *34*: 805–819.

Galison, P. (2008). Ten problems in history and philosophy of science. *Isis*, *99*: 111–124.

Gao, Y., Huang, Y., & Li, X. (2017). Interaction between prenatal maternal stress and autonomic arousal in predicting conduct problems and psychopathic traits in children. *Journal of Psychopathology Behavioral Assessment*, *39*: 1–14.

Gao, Y., Raine, A., Venables, P., Dawson, M., & Mednick, S. (2010). Association of poor childhood fear conditioning and adult crime. *American Journal of Psychiatry*, *167*: 6–60.

Gannett, L. (2010). Questions asked and unasked: how by worrying less about the "really real" philosophers of science might better contribute to debates about genetics and race. *Synthese*, *177*: 363–385.

Garger, K. (2021). BLM backs Jussie Smollett: "We can never believe the police." *New York Post*. December 8. https://nypost.com/2021/12/08/blm-backs-jussie-smollett-we-can-never-believe-the-police/

Garland, D. (2012). You asked: Why does the United States have *capital punishment*? http://photos.state.gov/libraries/amgov/133183/english/P_You_Asked_WhyCapitalPunishment_English.pdf

Garlick, D. (2002). Understanding the nature of the general factor of intelligence: the role of individual differences in neural plasticity as an explanatory mechanism. *Psychological Review*, *109*: 116–136.
Garlick, D. (2003). Integrating brain science research with intelligence research. *Current Directions in Psychological Science*, *12*: 185–189.
Garrett, B. (2009). *Brain and behavior: Introduction to biological psychology*. Los Angeles, CA: Sage.
Garrett, B., Seale-Carlisle, T., Modjadidi, K., & Renberg, K. (2021). Life without parole sentencing in North Carolina. *North Carolina Law Review*, *99*: 279–332.
Gatzke-Kopp, L, Raine, A., Loeber, R., Stouthamer-Loeber, M., & Steinhauer, S. (2002). Serious delinquent behavior, sensation seeking, and electrodermal arousal. *Journal of Abnormal Child Psychology*, *30*: 477–486.
Geary, D. (2005). *The origin of mind: Evolution of brain, cognition, and general intelligence*. Washington, DC: American Psychological Association.
Gerritzen, B. & Kirchgässner, G. (2013). Facts or ideology: What determines the results of econometric estimates of the deterrence effect of death penalty? A meta-analysis. Discussion Paper no. 2013–03, School of Economics and Political Science, University of St. Gallen.
Gavrilets, S. (2012). On the evolutionary origins of the egalitarian syndrome. *Proceedings of the National Academy of Sciences*, *109*: 14069–14074.
Gervais, W. (2014). Everything is permitted? People intuitively judge immorality as representative of atheists. *PloS one*, *9*(4): e92302.
Gilbert, N. (1997). Advocacy research and social policy. *Crime and justice*, *22*: 101–148.
Glenn, G. (2012). Situating Tocqueville between modern political philosophy and pre-modern Catholic political philosophy about what constitutes society. *Catholic Social Science Review*, *17*: 33–45.
Goldberg, E. (2001). *The executive brain: Frontal lobes and the civilized mind*. New York: Oxford University Press.
Goldstein, D. & Kopin, I. (2007). Evolution of the concept of stress. *Stress*, *10*: 109–120.
González-Forero, M. (2024). Evolutionary–developmental (evo-devo) dynamics of hominin brain size. *Nature Human Behaviour*, *8*: 1321–1333.
Gorelik, G., Shackelford, T., & Salmon, C. (2011). Between conflict and cooperation: New horizons in the evolutionary science of the human family. In C. Salmon & T. Shackelford (eds.), *Oxford handbook of evolutionary family psychology*, pp. 386–398. New York: Oxford University Press.
Gottfredson, L. (1986). Societal consequences of the g factor in employment. *Journal of Vocational Behavior*, *29*: 379–410.
Gottfredson, M. (2006). The empirical status of control theory in criminology. In F. Cullen, J. Wright, & K. Blevins (eds.) *Taking stock*, pp. 77–100. New Brunswick, NJ: Transaction.
Gottfredson, M. & Hirschi, T. (1990). *A general theory of crime*. Stanford: Stanford University Press.
Gottfredson, M. & Hirschi, T. (1997). National crime control policies. In M. Fisch (ed.), *Criminology, 97/98*, pp. 27–33. Guilford, CT: Dushkin Publishing.
Gottfredson, S. & Moriarty, L. (2006). Statistical risk assessment: Old problems and new applications. *Crime & Delinquency*, *52*: 178–200.
Gray, J. & Thompson, P. (2004). Neurobiology of intelligence: Science and ethics. *Nature Reviews Neuroscience*, *5*: 471–482.
Greenberg, D. (1981). *Crime and capitalism: Readings in Marxist criminology*. Palo Alto, CA: Mayfield.
Greene, J. & Cohen, J. (2004). For the law, neuroscience changes nothing and everything. *Philosophical Transactions of the Royal Society of London. Series B: Biological Sciences*, *359*: 1775–1785.

Greenfeld, L. and Hinners, D. (1984). Capital punishment, 1984. Washington, DC: Bureau of Justice Statistics, National Prisoner Statistics.
Gregor, A. (2017). *Marxism, China & development: Reflections on theory and reality*. New York: Routledge.
Gross, N. & Simmons, S. (2007). The social and political views of American professors. *Working Paper presented at a Harvard University Symposium on Professors and Their Politics*.
Gross, S. & Mauro, R. (1989). *Death and discrimination: Racial disparities in capital sentencing*. Boston, MA: Northeastern University Press.
Grosvenor, P. (2002). Evolutionary psychology and the intellectual left. *Perspectives in Biology and Medicine*, *45*: 433–448.
Grotzinger, A., Mann, F., Patterson, M., Tackett, J., Tucker-Drob, E., & Harden, K. (2018). Hair and salivary testosterone, hair cortisol, and externalizing behaviors in adolescents. *Psychological Science*, *29*: 688–699.
Guest, K. (2010). Dynamic interplay between religion and armed conflict in Afghanistan. *International Review of the Red Cross*, *92*: 877–897.
Gunnar, M. & Quevedo, K. (2007). The neurobiology of stress and development. *Annual Review of Psychology*, *58*: 145–173.
Guo, G., Roettger, M., & Shih, J. (2007). Contributions of the DAT1 and DRD2 genes to serious and violent delinquency among adolescents and young adults. *Human genetics*, *121*: 125–136.
Gurian, E. (2017). Reframing serial murder within empirical research: Offending and adjudication patterns of male, female, and partnered serial killers. *International Journal of Offender Therapy and Comparative Criminology*, *61*: 544–560.
Hacker, J. (2006). *The great risk shift: The new insecurity and the decline of the American dream*. New York: Oxford University Press.
Hadjimatheou, K. (2016). Criminal labelling, publicity, and punishment. *Law and Philosophy*, *35*: 567–593.
Haidt, J. (2001). The emotional dog and its rational tail: A social intuitionalist approach to moral Judgment. *Psychological Review*, *108*: 814–834.
Haller, J. (2018). The role of the lateral hypothalamus in violent intraspecific aggression—The glucocorticoid deficit hypothesis. *Frontiers in Systems Neuroscience*, *12*: 26: 10.3389/fnsys.2018.00026.
Han, Y., Yuan, M., Guo, Y., Shen, X., Gao, Z., & Bi, X. (2022). The role of enriched environment in neural development and repair. *Frontiers in Cellular Neuroscience*, *16*: 890666.
Hankin, B., Nederhof, E., Oppenheimer, C., Jenness, J., Young, J., Abela, J., Smolen, A. Ormel, J., & Oldehinkel, A. (2011). Differential susceptibility in youth: evidence that 5-HTTLPR x positive parenting is associated with positive affect "for better and worse". *Translational Psychiatry*, *10*: e44.
Hannan, S. (2020). The crimes of America's most prolific serial killer. *The Cleveland Magazine*, January. https://clevelandmagazine.com/in-the-cle/the-read/articles/in-the-shadows
Hannikainen, I., Cabral, G., Machery, E., & Struchiner, N. (2017). A deterministic worldview promotes approval of state paternalism. *Journal of Experimental Social Psychology*, *70*: 251–259.
Hanson, R. & Morton-Bourgon, K. (2009). The accuracy of recidivism risk assessments for sexual offenders: A meta-analysis of 118 prediction studies. *Psychological Assessment*, *21*: 1–21.
Harcourt, B. E. (2015). Risk as a proxy for race: The dangers of risk assessment. *Federal Sentencing Reporter*, *27*: 237–243.
Harpending, H. & Cochran, G. (2002). In our genes. *Proceedings of the National Academy of Science*, *99*: 10–12.
Harris, J. (1998). *The nurture assumption: Why children turn out the way they do*. New York: Free Press.

Harris, S. (2005). *The end of faith: Religion, terror, and the future of reason*. New York: WW Norton & Company.

Harrison, M., Hughes, S., & Gott, A. (2019). Sex differences in serial killers. *Evolutionary Behavioral Sciences, 13*: 295–310.

Hatch, V. & Walsh, A. (2016). *Capital punishment: Theory and practice of the ultimate Punishment*. New York, NY: Oxford University Press.

Hawking, S. & Mlodinow, L. (2010). *The Grand Design*. New York: Bantam Books.

Hawkins, D. (1995). Ethnicity, race, and crime: A review of selected studies. In D. Hawkins (ed.), *Ethnicity, race, and crime: Perspectives across time and space*, pp. 11–45. Albany, NY: State University of New York Press.

Hawks, J., Wang, E., Cochran, G., Harpending, H., & Moyzis, R. (2007). Recent acceleration of human adaptive evolution. *Proceedings of the National Academy of Science, 104*: 20753–20758.

Hawthorne, N. (2003). *The scarlet letter*. Barnes & Noble Classics.

Hecht, E. (2008). Energy conservation simplified. *The Physics Teacher, 46*: 77–80.

Heck, A. & Handa, R. (2019). Sex differences in the hypothalamic–pituitary–adrenal axis' response to stress: An important role for gonadal hormones. *Neuropsychopharmacology, 44*: 45–58.

Heck, K., Braveman, P., Cubbin, C., Chávez, G., & Kiely, J. (2006). Socioeconomic status and breastfeeding initiation among California mothers. *Public Health Reports, 121*: 51–59.

Henrich, J., McElreath, R., Barr, A., Ensminger, J., Barrett, C., Bolyanatz, A., Cardenas, J. Gurven, M., Gwako, E., Henrich, N., Lesorogot, C., Marlowe, F., Tracy, D., & Ziker, J. (2006). Costly punishment across human societies, *Science, 312*: 1767–1770.

Herba, C., Roza, S., Govaert, P., Hofman, A., Jaddoe, V., Verhulst, F., & Tiemeier, H. (2013). Breastfeeding and early brain development: The Generation R study. *Maternal & Child Nutrition, 9*: 332–349.

Herman, A. (2014). *The cave and the light: Plato versus Aristotle, and the struggle for the soul of Western civilization*. New York: Random House.

Herrnstein, R. & Murray, C. (1994). *The bell curve: Intelligence and class structure in American life*. New York: Free Press.

Hewig, J., Hagemann, D. Seifert, J., Naumann, E., & Bartussek, D. (2006). The relation of cortical activity and BIS/BAS on the trait level. *Biological Psychology, 71*: 42–53.

Hipp, J. (2010). A dynamic view of neighborhoods: The reciprocal relationship between crime and neighborhood structural characteristics. *Social problems, 57*: 205–230.

Hirschi, T. (1969). *Causes of delinquency*. Berkeley, CA: University of California Press.

Hirschi, T. (2004). Self-control and crime. In R. Baumeister & K. Vohs (eds.), *Handbook of self-regulation: Research, theory, and applications*, pp. 537–552. New York: Guilford.

Hirvonen, M., Laakso, A., Någren, K., Rinne, J., Pohjalainen, T., & Hietala, J. (2004). C957T polymorphism of the dopamine D2 receptor (DRD2) gene affects striatal DRD2 availability in vivo. *Molecular Psychiatry, 9*: 1060–1061.

Hitchens, C. (2008). *God is not great: How religion poisons everything*. Toronto, ON: McClelland & Stewart.

Hoffman, M. & Goldsmith, T. (2003). The biological roots of punishment. *Ohio State Journal of Criminal Law, 1*: 627–641.

Holt, J. (2012). *Why does the world exist? An existential detective story*. New York: WW Norton.

Howard, D. (2005). Albert Einstein as a philosopher of science. *Physics Today*, Dec.: 34–40.

Hublin, J. & Coqueugniot, H. (2006). Absolute or proportional brain size: That is the question. A reply to comments. *Journal of Human Evolution*, *50*: 109–113.

Hughes, K., Moore, R., Morris, P., & Corr, P. (2012). Throwing light on the dark side of personality: Reinforcement sensitivity theory and primary/secondary psychopathy in a student population. *Personality and Individual Differences*, *52*: 532–536.

Hulsman, L. (1986). Critical criminology and the concept of crime. *Contemporary Crises*, *10*: 63–80.

Hyde, L. & Dotterer, H. (2022). The nature and nurture of callous-unemotional traits. *Current Directions in Psychological Science*, *31*(6): 546–555.

Iofrida, C., Palumbo, S., & Pellegrini, S. (2014). Molecular genetics and antisocial behavior: Where do we stand? *Experimental Biology and Medicine*, *239*: 1514–1523.

Isen, J. (2010). A meta-analytic assessment of Wechsler's P> V sign in antisocial populations. *Clinical Psychology Review*, *30*: 423–435.

Jacob, L., Haro, J., & Koyanagi, A. (2019). Association between intelligence quotient and violence perpetration in the English general population. *Psychological Medicine*, *49*: 1316–1323.

Jacoby, S. (1983). *Wild justice: The evolution of revenge*. New York: Harper & Row.

Jaffee, S., Moffitt, T., Caspi, A., & Taylor, A. (2003). Life with (or without) father: The benefits of living with two biological parents depend on the father's antisocial behavior. *Child Development*, *74*: 109–126.

James, L., James, S., & Vila, B. J. (2016). The reverse racism effect: Are cops more hesitant to shoot black than white suspects? *Criminology & Public Policy*, *15*: 457–479.

James, W. (1988). *Writings 1902–1910*. New York: The Library of America.

Javakhishvili, M. & Vazsonyi, A. (2022). Empathy, self-control, callous-unemotionality, and delinquency: Unique and shared developmental antecedents. *Child Psychiatry & Human Development*, *53*: 389–402.

Jennings, W., Richards, T., Smith, M., Bjerregaard, B., & Fogel, S. (2014). A critical examination of the "white victim effect" and death penalty decision-making from a propensity score matching approach: the North Carolina experience. *Journal of Criminal Justice*, *42*: 384–398.

Jensen, A. (1998). *The g factor*. Westport, CT: Praeger.

Jin, Y., Wang, J., Bachtiar, M., Chong, S., & Lee, C. (2018). Architecture of polymorphisms in the human genome reveals functionally important and positively selected variants in immune response and drug transporter genes. *Human Genomics*, *12*: 1–13.

Johansson, P. & Kerr, M. (2005). Psychopathy and intelligence: A second look. *Journal of Personality Disorders*, *19*: 357–369.

Johnson, B., Spohn, C., & Kimchi, A. (2021). Life lessons: Examining sources of racial and ethnic disparity in federal life without parole sentences. *Criminology*, *59*: 704–737.

Johnson, B. & Jang, S. (2010). Crime and religion: Assessing the role of the faith factor. *Contemporary issues in criminological theory and research: The role of social institutions*, 117–149.

Johnson, B., Larson, D., De Li, S., & Jang, S. (2000). Escaping from the crime of inner cities: Church attendance and religious salience among disadvantaged youth. *Justice Quarterly*, *17*: 377–391.

Jones, J. (2024). Drop in death penalty support led by younger generations. *Gallup Poll*. https://news.gallup.com/poll/653429/drop-death-penalty-support-led-younger-generations.aspx

Jordan, K., & Freiburger, T. (2015). The effect of race/ethnicity on sentencing: Examining sentence type, jail length, and prison length. *Journal of Ethnicity in Criminal Justice*, *13*: 179–196.

Jost, J. (2006). The end of the end of ideology. *American Psychologist*, *61*: 651–670.

Judge, T., Higgins, C., Thoresen, C., & Barrick, M. (1999). The big five personality traits, general mental ability, and career success across the life span. *Personnel Psychology, 52*: 621–652.

Julvez, J., Guxens, M., Carsin, A., Forns, J., Mendez, M., Turner, M., & Sunyer, J. (2014). A cohort study on full breastfeeding and child neuropsychological development: The role of maternal social, psychological, and nutritional factors. *Developmental Medicine & Child Neurology, 56*: 148–156.

Jung, R. & Haier, R. (2007). The Parieto-Frontal Integration Theory (P-FIT) of intelligence: Converging neuroimaging evidence. *Behavioral and brain sciences, 30*: 135–154.

Kaba, M. (2020). *Yes, we mean literally abolish the police. Abolition Library Commons*, 1–2.

Kanazawa, S. (2008). Temperature and evolutionary novelty as forces behind the evolution of general intelligence. *Intelligence, 36*: 99–108.

Kanazawa, S. (2012). The evolution of general intelligence. *Personality and Individual Differences, 53*: 90–93.

Kansal, T. (2005). Racial disparity in sentencing: A review of the literature. The Sentencing Project, Washington, D.C.

Kant, I. (1964). *Groundwork of the metaphysics of morals*. Trans. by H. J. Paton. New York: Harper & Row.

Karasewich, T. & Kuhlmeier, V. (2020). Trait social anxiety as a conditional adaptation: A developmental and evolutionary framework. *Developmental Review, 55*, 100886.

Karmen, A. (2005). *Crime victims: An introduction to victimology*. Belmont, CA: Wadsworth.

Katz, J. (1988). *Seductions of crime: Moral and sensual attractions in doing evil*. New York: Basic Books.

Katz, J. (2005). Warren McClesky v. Ralph Kemp: Is the death penalty in Georgia racially biased? In E. Mandery (ed.), *Capital punishment in America: A balanced examination*, pp. 400–408. Sudbury, MA: Jones & Bartlett.

Keel, T., Jarvis, J., & Muirhead, Y. (2009). An exploratory analysis of factors affecting homicide investigations: Examining the dynamics of murder clearance rates. *Homicide studies, 13*: 50–68.

Kelleher, M. & Kelleher, C. (1998). *Murder most rare: The female serial killer*. Westport, CT: Praeger.

Kelly, J., Kramer, S., & Shariff, A. (2024). Religiosity predicts prosociality, especially when measured by self-report: A meta-analysis of almost 60 years of research. *Psychological Bulletin, 150*: 284–318.

Kelly, P., Polanin, J., Jang, S., & Johnson, B. (2015). Religion, delinquency, and drug use: A meta-analysis. *Criminal Justice Review, 40*: 505–523.

Kennedy, W., Willcutt, H., & Smith, A. (1963). Wechsler profiles of mathematically gifted adolescents. *Psychological Reports, 12*: 259–262.

Kerley, K., Copes, H., Tewksbury, R., & Dabney, D. (2011). Examining the relationship between religiosity and self-control as predictors of prison deviance. *International Journal of Offender Therapy and Comparative Criminology, 55*: 1251–71

Kennair, L. (2002). Evolutionary psychology: An emerging integrative perspective within the science and practice of psychology. *The Human Nature Review, 2*: 17–61.

Khodadadi, E., Fahmideh, L., Khodadadi, E., Dao, S., Yousefi, M., Taghizadeh, S., Asgharzadeh, M., Yousefi, B., & Kafil, H (2021). Current advances in DNA methylation analysis methods. *BioMed Research International, 2021*(1), 8827516.

Kim, J., Kim, B., Kim, J. W., Hong, S., Shin, M., Yoo, H., & Cho, S. (2017). Breastfeeding is associated with enhanced learning abilities in school-aged children. *Child and Adolescent Psychiatry and Mental Health, 11*: 1–7.

Kim, T., Hur, J., Kwak, S., Jang, D., Lee, S., & Kwon, J. (2020). Intrinsic functional connectivity of blue and red brains: Neurobiological evidence of different stress resilience between political attitudes. *Scientific Reports*, *10*: 1–10.

Kim-Cohen, J., A. Caspi, A. Taylor, B. Williams, R. Newcombe, I. Craig, & T. Moffitt (2006). MAOA, maltreatment, and gene-environment interaction predicting children's mental health: New evidence and a meta-analysis. *Molecular Psychiatry*, *11*: 903–913.

King, L. & Bostaph, L. (2024). That is not behavior consistent with a rape victim: The effects of officer displays of doubt on sexual assault case processing and victim participation. *Journal of Interpersonal Violence*, *39*: 973–995.

King, Jr., M. (1986). A knock at midnight. In M. Washington (ed.), *A testament of hope: The essential writings of Martin Luther King, Jr.* San Francisco, CA: Harper and Row.

Kingston, P. (2006). How meritocratic is the United States? *Research in Social Stratification and Mobility*, *24*: 111–130.

Kitayama, S., King, A., Hsu, M., Liberzon, I., & Yoon, C. (2016). Dopamine-system genes and cultural acquisition: The norm sensitivity hypothesis. *Current Opinion in Psychology*, *8*: 167–174.

Klasios, J. (2019). Aggression among men: An integrated evolutionary explanation. *Aggression and Violent Behavior*, *47*: 29–45.

Kleck, G. (1981). Racial discrimination in criminal sentencing: A critical evaluation of the evidence with additional evidence on the death penalty. *American Sociological Review*, *46*: 783–805.

Klein, R. (2012). The neurobiology of altruistic punishment: A moral assessment of its social utility. In K. Plaisance & T. Reydon (eds.), *Philosophy of behavioral biology*, pp. 297–313. Boston, MA: Springer Science.

Klein, S., Berk, R., & Hickman, L. (2006). Race and the decision to seek the death penalty in federal cases. Santa Monica, CA: Rand Cooperation.

Knight, D. (1992). *Ideas in chemistry: A history of the science.* New Brunswick, NJ: Rutgers University Press.

Kochanska, G. & Aksan, N. (2004). Conscience in childhood: Past, present, and future. *Merrill-Palmer Quarterly*, *50*: 299–310.

Koller, K., Brown, T., Spurfeon, A., & Levy, L. (2004). Recent developments in low-level lead exposure and intellectual impairment in children. *Environmental Health Perspectives*, *112*: 987–994.

Kolb. B. & Gibb, R. (2011). Brain plasticity and behaviour in the developing brain. *Journal of The Canadian Academy of Child and Adolescent Psychiatry*, *20*: 265–276.

Kolk, S. & Rakic, P. (2022). Development of prefrontal cortex. *Neuropsychopharmacology*, *47*: 41–57.

Kolla, N. & Bortolato, M. (2020). The role of monoamine oxidase A in the neurobiology of aggressive, antisocial, and violent behavior: A tale of mice and men. *Progress in Neurobiology*, *194*, 101875.

Kornhauser, R. (1978). *Social sources of delinquency: An appraisal of analytical methods*. Chicago: University of Chicago Press.

Koukkou, M. & Lehmann, D. (2006). Experience dependent brain plasticity: A key concept for studying nonconscious decisions. *International Congress Series*, *1286*: 45–52.

Kramer, M., Aboud, F., Mironova, E., Vanilovich, I., Platt, R., Matush, L., Igumnov, S., Fombonne, E., Bogdanovich, N., Ducruet, T., & Collet, J. (2008). Breastfeeding and child cognitive development: New evidence from a large randomized trial. *Archives of General Psychiatry*, *65*: 578–584.

Krebs, D. (2008). The evolution of a sense of justice. In J. Duntley & T. Shackelford (eds.), *Evolutionary forensic psychology*, pp. 230–246. Oxford: Oxford University Press.

Kruk, E. (2012). Arguments for an equal parental responsibility presumption in contested child custody. *The American Journal of Family Therapy*, *40*: 33–55.

Krupić, D., Gračanin, A., & Corr, P. (2016). The evolution of the Behavioural Approach System (BAS): Cooperative and competitive resource acquisition strategies. *Personality And Individual Differences*, *94*: 223–227.

Kuo, S., Salvatore, J., Barr, P., Aliev, F., Anokhin, A., Bucholz, K., Chan, G., Edenberg, H., Hesselbrock, V., Kamarajan, C., & Kramer, J. (2021). Mapping pathways by which genetic risk influences adolescent externalizing behavior: the interplay between externalizing polygenic risk scores, parental knowledge, and peer substance use. *Behavior Genetics*, *51*: 543–558.

Lacourse, E., Nagin, D., Vitaro, F., Côté, S., Arseneault, L., & Tremblay, R. (2006). Prediction of early-onset deviant peer group affiliation: A 12–year longitudinal study. *Archives of General Psychiatry*, *63*: 562–568.

Lagerfeld, S. (2004). The revenge of the nerds. *The Wilson Quarterly (1976–)*, *28*: 28–34.

Laird, R., Marks, L., & Marrero, M. (2011). Religiosity, self-control, and antisocial behavior: Religiosity as a promotive and protective factor. *Journal of Applied Developmental Psychology*, *32*: 78–85.

Lang, M., Matta, M., Parolin, L., Morrone, C., & Pezzuti, L. (2019). Cognitive profile of intellectually gifted adults: Analyzing the Wechsler Adult Intelligence Scale. *Assessment*, *26*: 929–943.

Langeslag, S., Schmidt, M., Ghassabian, A., Jaddoe, V., Hofman, A., van der Lugt, A., Verhulst, F., Tiemeier, H., & White, T. (2013). Functional connectivity between parietal and frontal brain regions and intelligence in young children: The Generation R study. *Human Brain Mapping*, *34*: 3299–3307.

Lankford, A. (2016). Race and mass murder in the United States: A social and behavioral analysis. *Current Sociology*, *64*: 470–490.

Latimer, J., Dowden, G., & Muise, D. (2005). The effectiveness of restorative justice practices: A meta-analysis. *The Prison Journal*, *85*: 127–144.

Lawrence, R.M. & Lawrence, R.A. (2011). Breastfeeding: More than just good nutrition. *Pediatrics in Review*, *32*: 267–280.

Lea, J. (2016). Left realism: A radical criminology for the current crisis. *International Journal for Crime, Justice and Social Democracy*, *5*: 53–65.

Lee, M. (2006). The religious institutional base and violent crime in rural areas. *Journal for theScientific Study of Religion*, *45*: 309–324.

Lee, M. (2015). Fact checker: Are black or white offenders more likely to kill police? *Chicago Tribune*, January 10. https://www.chicagotribune.com/opinion/commentary/chi-fact-checker-police-killings-20150110–story.html

Lee, T., Chan, C., Leung, A., Fox, P., & Gao, J. (2009). Sex-related differences in neural activity during risk taking: An fMRI study. *Cerebral Cortex*, *19*: 1303–1312.

Lenski, G. (2005). *Ecological-evolutionary theory: Principles and applications*. New York: Routledge.

Levenson, R. (2014). The autonomic nervous system and emotion. *Emotion Review*, *6*: 100–112.

Levitt, S. & List, J. (2007). What do laboratory experiments measuring social preferences reveal about the real world? *The Journal of Economic Perspectives*, *21*: 153–174.

Levy, D. (2022). Optimizing the social utility of judicial punishment: An evolutionary biology and neuroscience perspective. *Frontiers in Human Neuroscience*, *16*, 967090.

Libet, B. (1985). Unconscious cerebral initiative and the role of conscious will in voluntary action. *Behavioral and Brain Sciences*, *8*: 529–539.

Libet, B. (1999). Do we have free will? *Journal of Consciousness Studies*, *6*: 47–57.

Libet, B., Wright Jr., E., & Gleason, C. (1983). Preparation-or intention-to-act, in relation to pre-event potentials recorded at the vertex. *Electroencephalography and Clinical Neurophysiology*, *56*: 367–372.

Lichter, D., Graefe, D., & Brown, J. (2003). Is marriage a panacea? Union formation among economically disadvantaged unwed mothers. *Social Problems*, *50*: 60–86.

Liebertz, S. & Bunch, J. (2018). Examining the externalities of welfare reform: TANF and crime. *Justice Quarterly*, *35*: 477–504.

Liem, M., Suonpää, K., Lehti, M., Kivivuori, J., Granath, S., Walser, S., & Killias, M. (2019). Homicide clearance in Western Europe. *European Journal of Criminology*, *16*: 81–101.

Lilienfeld, S., Latzman, R., Watts, A., Smith, S., & Dutton, K. (2014). Correlates of psychopathic personality traits in everyday life: Results from a large community survey. *Frontiers in Psychology*, *5*, 740.

Lilly, J., Cullen, F., & Ball, R. (2007). *Criminological theory: Context and consequences* (3rd edn). Thousand Oaks, CA: Sage.

Ling, S., Umbach, R., & Raine, A. (2019). Biological explanations of criminal behavior. *Psychology, Crime & Law*, *25*: 626–640.

Lischke, A., Pahnke, R., Mau-Moeller, A., Behrens, M., Grabe, H., Freyberger, H., Hamm, A., & Weippert, M. (2018). Inter-individual differences in heart rate variability are associated with inter-individual differences in empathy and alexithymia. *Frontiers in Psychology*, *9*: 134–142.

Little, B., Sud, N., Nobile, Z., & Bhattacharya, D. (2021). Teratogenic effects of maternal drug abuse on developing brain and underlying neurotransmitter mechanisms. *Neurotoxicology*, *86*: 172–179.

London, J. M., Troshynski, E. I., & Panos, G. (2021). Abolishing consensus criminology: Confronting the human nature assumption and ritual criminologists. *Justice Policy Journal*, *18*: 1–16.

Lopez, G., Gurin, P., & Nagda, B. (1998). Education and understanding structural causes for group inequalities. *Political Psychology*, *19*: 305–329.

Lopez-Vergara, H., Colder, C., Hawk Jr, L., Wieczorek, W., Eiden, R., Lengua, L., & Read, J. (2012). Reinforcement sensitivity theory and alcohol outcome: Expectancies in early adolescence. *The American Journal of Drug and Alcohol Abuse*, *38*: 130–134.

Lott, J. & Moody, C. (2021). Do white police officers unfairly target black suspects? *Economics, Law and Policy*, *4*: *SSRN 2870189*.

Loughran, T., Paternoster, R., Chalfin, A., & Wilson, T. (2016). Can rational choice be considered a general theory of crime? Evidence from individual-level panel data. *Criminology*, *54*: 86–112.

Lubinski, D. (2004). Introduction to the special section on cognitive abilities: 100 years after Spearman's (1904) "General intelligence," objectively determined and measured. *Journal of Personality and Social Psychology*, *86*: 96–111.

Lumsden, K. (2013). You are what you research: Researcher partisanship and the sociology of the "underdog". *Qualitative Research*, *13*: 3–18.

Lykken, D. (1995). *The antisocial personalities*. Hillsdale, NJ: Lawrence Erlbaum.

Lynch, M. (2000). The power of oppression: Understanding the history of criminology as a science of oppression. *Critical Criminology*, *9*: 144–152.

Lynn, R., Fuerst, J., & Kirkegaard, E. (2018). Regional differences in intelligence in 22 countries and their economic, social and demographic correlates: A review. *Intelligence*, *69*: 24–36.

Machado-Vieira, R., Manji, H., & Zarate Jr, C. (2009). The role of lithium in the treatment of bipolar disorder: Convergent evidence for neurotrophic effects as a unifying hypothesis. *Bipolar Disorders*, *11*: 92–109.

Machalek, R. & Cohen, L. (1991). The nature of crime: Is cheating necessary for cooperation? *Human Nature*, *2*: 215–233.

Machery, E. (2008). A plea for human nature. *Philosophical Psychology, 21*(3), 321–329.
Mackey, W. & Immerman, R. (2007). Fatherlessness by divorce contrasted to fatherlessness by non-marital births: A distinction with a difference for the community. *Journal of Divorce & Remarriage, 47*: 111–134.
Mackie, J. (1978). The law of the jungle: moral alternatives and principles of evolution. *Philosophy, 53*: 455–464.
Madfis, E. & Cohen, J. (2016). Critical criminologies of the present and future: Left realism, left idealism, and what's left in between. *Social Justice, 1*: 1–21.
Maestripieri, D. & Boutwell, B. (2022). Human nature and personality variation: Reconnecting evolutionary psychology with the science of individual differences. *Neuroscience and Biobehavioral Reviews, 143*: 104946–104946.
Mainali, P., Rai, T., & Rutkofsky, I. H. (2020). From child abuse to developing borderline personality disorder into adulthood: Exploring the neuromorphological and epigenetic pathway. *Cureus*, 12: e9474.
Manski, C. (2011). Policy analysis with incredible certitude. *Economic Journal, Royal Economic Society, 121*: 261–289.
Marcus, Z. & McCullough, M. (2021). Does religion make people more self-controlled? A review of research from the lab and life. *Current Opinion in Psychology, 40*:f 167–170.
Marks, J. (2012). *Ethics without morals: In defence of amorality*. New York: Routledge.
Marks, J. (2016). *Hard atheism and the ethics of desire: An alternative to morality*. Cham, Switzerland: Springer.
Martin, S. (2004). The links between alcohol, crime and the criminal justice system: Explanations, evidence and interventions. In E. McCance-Katz & H. Clark (eds.), *Psychosocial Treatments*, pp. 137–164. New York: Brunner-Routledge.
Marx, K. & Engels, F. (1948). *The communist manifesto*. New York: International Publishers.
Marx, K. & F. Engels (1965). *The German Ideology*. London: Lawrence and Wishart.
Massey, D. (2002). A brief history of human society: The origin and role of emotion in social life. *American Sociological Review, 67*: 1–29.
Matarazzo, J. (1976). *Wechsler's measurement and appraisal of adult intelligence*. Baltimore, MA: Williams and Wilkins.
Matthews, L. & Turkheimer, E. (2021). Across the great divide: Pluralism and the hunt for missing heritability. *Synthese, 198*: 2297–2311.
Mauer, M. & Nellis, A. (2018). *The meaning of life: The case for abolishing life sentences*. New York: The New Press.
Mazur, A. (2023). Testosterone and the "honor culture" of young Black men. *Qeios*, 1–15
McAdams, J. (1998). Racial disparity and the death penalty. *Law and Contemporary Problems, 61*: 153–170.
McBurnett, K., Lahey, B., Rathouz, P., & Loeber, R. (2000). Low salivary cortisol and persistent aggression in boys referred for disruptive behavior. *Archives of General Psychiatry, 57*: 38–43.
McCrae, T. & Terracciano, A. (2005). Universal features of personality traits from the observer's perspective: Data from 50 cultures. *Journal of Personality and Social Psychology, 88*: 547–561.
McCullough, M. & Willoughby, B. (2009). Religion, self-regulation, and self-control: Associations, explanations, and implications. *Psychological Bulletin, 135*: 1–25.
McDermott, R., J. Cowden, G. Frazzetto & D. Johnson (2009). Monoamine oxidase A gene (MAOA) predicts behavioral aggression following provocation. *Proceedings of the National Academy of Sciences, 106*: 7 2118–2123.
McGilchrist, I. (2009). *The master and his emissary: The divided brain and the making of the western world*. Connecticut, CT: Yale University Press.

McGloin, J. & Pratt, T. (2003). Cognitive ability and delinquent behavior among inner-city youth: A life-course analysis of main, mediating, and interaction effects. *International Journal of Offender Therapy and Comparative Criminology*, *47*: 253–271.
McLaughlin, K., Weissman, D., & Bitrán, D. (2019). Childhood adversity and neural development: A systematic review. *Annual Review of Developmental Psychology*, *1*: 277–312.
McLaughlin, V. & Mackey, W. (2008). Demographics of the upward-trending murder rate in Buffalo, New York: *A harbinger of societal stress. Journal of Social, Political, and Economic Studies*, *33*: 458–471.
Mead, M. (1935). *Sex and temperament in three primitive societies*. New York: Morrow.
Mealey, L. (1995). The sociobiology of sociopathy: An integrated evolutionary model. *Behavioral and Brain Sciences*, *18*: 523–59.
Meaney, M. (2010). Epigenetics and the biological definition of gene× environment interactions. *Child development*, *81*: 41–79.
Mehta, P. & Beer, J. (2009). Neural mechanisms of the testosterone-aggression relation: The role of the oribitofrontal cortex. *Journal of Cognitive Neuroscience*, *22*: 2357–2368.
Melchers, M., Montag, C., Reuter, M., Spinath, F., & Hahn, E. (2016). How heritable is empathy? Differential effects of measurement and subcomponents. *Motivation and Emotion*, *40*: 720–730.
Menifield, C., Shin, G., & Strother, L. (2019). Do white law enforcement officers target minority suspects? *Public Administration Review*, *79*: 56–68.
Merton, R. (1938). Social structure and anomie. *American Sociological Review*, *1938*: 672–682
Meyer-Bahlburg, H., Dolezal, C., Baker, S., Ehrhardt, A., & New, M. (2006). Gender development in women with congenital adrenal hyperplasia as a function of disorder severity. *Archives of Sexual Behavior*, *35*: 667–684.
Miczek, K., Fish, E., & De Bold, J. (2003). Neurosteroids, GABAA receptors, and escalated aggressive behavior. *Hormones and Behavior*, *44*: 242–257.
Miller, J. & Golding, B. (2021). Chicago mayor who pushed $80M defund of cops now pleads for feds to save city. *New York Post*, 12/21. https://nypost.com/2021/12/21/chicago-mayor-lori-lightfoot-wants-federal-help-to-stem-gun-violence/
Miller, J. & Maloney, C. (2013). Practitioner compliance with risk/needs assessment tools: A theoretical and empirical assessment. *Criminal Justice and Behavior*, *40*: 716–736.
Miller, L. (1987). Neuropsychology of the aggressive psychopath: An integrative review. *Aggressive Behavior*, *13*: 119–140.
Miller-Butterworth, C., Kaplan, J., Shaffer, J., Devlin, M., Manuck, S., & Ferrell, R. (2008). Sequence variation in the primate dopamine transporter gene and its relationship to social dominance. *Molecular Biology and Evolution*, *25*: 18–28.
Mills, M. & Tropf, F. (2020). Sociology, genetics, and the coming of age of sociogenomics. *Annual Review of Sociology*, *46*: 553–581.
Mitchell, K. (2007). The genetics of brain wiring: From molecule to mind. *PLoS Biology*, *4*: 690–692.
Moczek, A. (2012). The nature of nurture and the future of evodevo: Toward a theory of developmental evolution. *Integrative and Comparative Biology*, *52*: 108–119.
Moffitt, T. (1993). Adolescent-limited and life-course-persistent antisocial behavior: A developmental taxonomy. *Psychological Review*, *100*: 674–701.
Moffitt, T. & Beckley, A. (2015). Abandon twin research? Embrace epigenetic research? Premature advice for criminologists. *Criminology*, *53*: 121–126.
Moffitt, T. & Silva, P. (1988). IQ and delinquency: A direct test of the differential detection hypothesis. *Journal of Abnormal Psychology*, *97*: 330–333.

Moffitt, T. & Walsh, A. (2003) The adolescence-limited/Life-course persistent theory of antisocial behavior: What have we learned? In A. Walsh & L. Ellis (eds.), *Biosocial criminology: Challenging environmentalism's supremacy*, pp. 125–144, Hauppauge, NY: Nova Science.

Moffitt, T., Gabrielli, W., Mednick, S., & Schulsinger, F. (1981). Socioeconomic status, IQ, and delinquency. *Journal of Abnormal Psychology*, *90*: 152.

Moffitt, T., Arseneault, L., Belsky, D., Dickson, N., Hancox, R., Harrington, H., Houts, R., Poulton, R., Roberts, B., Ross, S., & Sears, M. (2011). A gradient of childhood self-control predicts health, wealth, and public safety. *Proceedings of the National Academy of Sciences*, *108*: 2693–2698.

Mogilski, J., Mitchell, V., Reeve, S., Donaldson, S., Nicolas, S., & Welling, L. (2020). Life history and multi-partner mating: A novel explanation for moral stigma against consensual non-monogamy. *Frontiers in Psychology*, 3033.

Monaghan, R. & Konefal, K. (2023). Presentence investigation reports and racial/ethnic disparities in sentencing. *Crime & Delinquency*, *69*: 2460–2483.

Monahan, J. & Skeem, J. (2016). Risk assessment in criminal sentencing. *Annual Review of Clinical Psychology*, *12*: 489–513.

Montagu, A. (1981). *Growing young*. New York: McGraw-Hill, p. 93.

Montagu, A. (1981). The adolescent's unreadiness for pregnancy and motherhood. *Pediatric Annals*, *10*: 52–56.

Morin, R., Parker, K., Stepler, R., & Mercer, A. (2017a). Police views, public views. Pew Research Center. https://www.pewresearch.org/social-trends/2017/01/11/police-views-public-views/

Morin, R., Parker, K., Stepler, R., & Mercer, A. (2017b). Behind the badge. Pew Research Center. https://www.pewresearch.org/social-trends/2017/01/11/behind-the-badge/

Mosing, M., Pedersen, N., Cesarini, D., Johannesson, M., & Magnusson, P. (2012). Genetic and environmental influences on the relationship between flow proneness, locus of control and behavioral inhibition. *Plos One*, 7–e47958.

Mourtgos, S., Adams, I., & Nix, J. (2022). Elevated police turnover following the summer of George Floyd protests: A synthetic control study. *Criminology & Public Policy*, *21*: 9–33.

Mrazek, A., Chiao, J., Blizinsky, K., Lun, J., & Gelfand, M. (2013). The role of culture–gene coevolution in morality judgment: Examining the interplay between tightness–looseness and allelic variation of the serotonin transporter gene. *Culture and Brain*, *1*: 100–117.

Muhlhausen, D. (2004). The determinants of sentencing in Pennsylvania: Do the characteristics of judges really matter? Center for Data Analysis Report #04–02. Washington, DC: The Heritage Foundation.

Müller, C. (2020). Mechanisms of a near-orthogonal ultra-fast evolution of human behaviour as a source of culture development. *Behavioural Brain Research*, *384*: 112521.

Murphy, J. (1979). Marxism and retribution. *Retribution, Justice, and Therapy: Essays in the Philosophy of Law*, 93–115.

Murray, C. (2002). IQ and income inequality in a sample of sibling pairs from advantaged family backgrounds. *American Economic Review*, *92*: 339–343.

Murray, D., Trudeau, R., & Schaller, M. (2011). On the origins of cultural differences in conformity: Four tests of the pathogen prevalence hypothesis. *Personality and Social Psychology Bulletin*, *37*: 318–329.

Myrdal, G. (1944). *An American dilemma: The Negro problem and modern democracy* (2 volumes). New York: Harper & Brothers.

Nakao, H. & Machery, E. (2012). The evolution of punishment. *Biology & Philosophy*, *27*: 833–850.

Narvaez, D. & Vaydich, J. (2008). Moral development and behaviour under the spotlight of the neurobiological sciences. *Journal of Moral Education*, *37*: 289–312.

Naumova, O., Lee, M., Koposov, R., Szyf, M., Dozier, M., & Grigorenko, E. (2012). Differential patterns of whole-genome DNA methylation in institutionalized children and children raised by their biological parents. *Development and Psychopathology*, *24*: 143–155.

Nettle, D. (2003). Intelligence and class mobility in the British population. *British Journal of Psychology*, *94*: 551–561.

Nettler, G. (1978). *Explaining crime*. New York: McGraw Hill.

Nettler, G. (1984). *Explaining crime* (3rd edn). New York: McGraw Hill.

Neubauer, A. & Fink, A. (2009). Intelligence and neural efficiency. *Neuroscience & Biobehavioral Reviews*, *33*: 1004–1023.

Newman, G. & Knobe, J. (2019). The essence of essentialism. *Mind & Language*, *34*: 585–605.

Nietzsche, F. & Hollingdale, R. (1990). Expeditions of an untimely man. In *Twilight of the Idols; and, The Anti-Christ*. Penguin Classics, London: Penguin Books.

Nisbett, R., Aronson, J., Blair, C., Dickens, W., Flynn, J., Halpern, D., & Turkheimer, E. (2012). Intelligence: New findings and theoretical developments. *American Psychologist*, *67*: 130–159.

Nix, J., Campbell, B., Byers, H., & Alpert, G. (2017). A bird's eye view of civilians killed by police in 2015: Further evidence of implicit bias. *Criminology & Public Policy*, *16*: 309–340.

Nolan, B., Richiardi, M., & Valenzuela, L. (2019). The drivers of income inequality in rich countries. *Journal of Economic Surveys*, *33*: 1285–1324.

Nowak, M. (2006). Five rules for the evolution of cooperation. *Science*, *314*: 1560–1563.

Nuño de la Rosa, L. & Müller, G. (2024). The legacy and evolvability of Pere Alberch's ideas. *Interface Focus*, *14*: 20240011.

Nurk, S., Koren, S., Rhie, A., Rautiainen, M., Bzikadze, A., Mikheenko, A., ... & Phillippy, A. (2022). The complete sequence of a human genome. *Science*, *376*: 44–53.

Nwankwo, B., Okechi, B., Okoh, A., Okolie, P., & Ogbonnaya, K. (2018). Locus of control and marital status as predictors of recidivism among prison inmates in Abakaliki. *IFE PsychologIA: An International Journal*, *26*: 120–133.

Oderberg, D. (2011). Essence and properties. *Erkenntnis*, *75*: 85–111.

O'Donnell, K. & Meaney, M. (2020). Epigenetics, development, and psychopathology. *Annual Review of Clinical Psychology*, *16*: 327–350.

Ogletree, C. & Sarat, A. (2012). *Life without parole: American's new death penalty?* New York: New York University Press.

O'Leary, M., Loney, B., & Eckel, L. (2007). Gender differences in the association between psychopathic personality traits and cortisol response to induced stress. *Psychoneuroendocrinology*, *32*: 183–191.

Olson, J., Vernon, P., & Harris, J. (2001). The heritability of attitudes: A study of twins. *Journal of Personality and Social Psychology*, *80*: 845–860.

O'Manique, J. (2003). *The origins of justice: The evolution of morality, human rights, and law*. Philadelphia, PA: University of Philadelphia Press.

Omori, M. & Petersen, N. (2020). Institutionalizing inequality in the courts: Decomposing racial and ethnic disparities in detention, conviction, and sentencing. *Criminology*, *58*: 678–713.

O'Neill, J. & Hill, A. (2003). Gaining ground, moving up: The change in the economic status of single mothers under welfare reform. Civic Report, Number 35. Center for Civic Innovation. New York, NY.

Ortiz, J. & Raine, A. (2004). Heart rate level and antisocial behavior in children and adolescents: A meta-analysis. *Journal of the American Academy of Child & Adolescent Psychiatry*, *43*: 154–162.

Papero, D., Frost, R., Havstad, L., & Noone, R. (2018). Natural systems thinking and the human family. *Systems*, *6*: 19–29.

Parente, R., Bergqvist, L., Soares, M., & Filho, O. (2011). The history of vaginal birth. *Archives of Gynecology and Obstetrics*, *284*: 1–11.

Park, S. (2014). Cultural relativism and the theory of relativity. *Filosopija Sociologija*, *25*: 44–51.

Paternoster, R. and Brame, R. (2003). An empirical analysis of Maryland's death sentencing system with respect to the influence of race and legal jurisdiction. Study commissioned by the Maryland Governor. http:urhome.umd.edu/newsdesk/pdf/finalrep.pdf

Paternoster, R. & Iovanni, L. (1989). The labeling perspective and delinquency: An elaboration of the theory and an assessment of the evidence. *Justice Quarterly*, *6*: 359–394.

Patrick, C. (2022). Psychopathy: Current knowledge and future directions. *Annual Review of Clinical Psychology*, *18*: 387–415.

Patterson, O. (1998). *The rituals of blood: Consequences of slavery in two American centuries*. Washington, DC: Civitas Counterpoint.

Peñaherrera-Aguirre, M., Dunkel, C., & Sarraf, M. (2021). Evidence for the Scarr–Rowe Effect on genetic expressivity in the Health and Retirement Study. *Twin Research and Human Genetics*, *24*: 110–115.

Penn, A. (2001). Early brain wiring: Activity-dependent processes. *Schizophrenia Bulletin*, *27*: 337–348.

Perry, B. (2002). Childhood experience and the expression of genetic potential: What childhood neglect tells us about nature and nurture. *Brain and Mind*, *3*: 79–100.

Perry, B. & Pollard, R. (1998). Homeostasis, stress, trauma, and adaptation: A neurodevelopmental view of childhood trauma. *Child and Adolescent Psychiatric Clinics of America*, *7*: 33–51.

Pessoa, L., Medina, L., Hof, P., & Desfilis, E. (2019). Neural architecture of the vertebrate brain: Implications for the interaction between emotion and cognition. *Neuroscience & Biobehavioral Reviews*, *107*: 296–312.

Peters, K., Cheer, J., & Tonini, R. (2021). Modulating the neuromodulators: dopamine, serotonin, and the endocannabinoid system. *Trends in Neurosciences*, *44*: 464–477.

Peters, T. (2014). *Playing God? Genetic determinism and human freedom*. New York: Routledge.

Peterson, C. (1997). *Psychology: A biopsychosocial approach*. New York: Longman.

Peterson, J., Smith, K., & Hibbing, J. (2020). Do people really become more conservative as they age? *The Journal of Politics*, *82*: 600–611.

Peterson, M. (1960). *The Jefferson image in the American mind*. Oxford: Oxford University Press.

Pfattheicher, S., Sassenrath, C., & Keller, J. (2019). Compassion magnifies third-party punishment. *Journal of Personality and Social Psychology*, *117*: 124–141.

Pham, H., DiLalla, L., Corley, R., Dorn, L., & Berenbaum, S. (2022). Family environmental antecedents of pubertal timing in girls and boys: A review and open questions. *Hormones and Behavior*, *138*: 105101.

Phelps, E., Lempert, K., & Sokol-Hessner, P. (2014). Emotion and decision making: Multiple modulatory neural circuits. *Annual Review of Neuroscience*, *37*(1): 263–287.

Phillips, S. & Kim, D. (2021). Exploring officer-involved shootings with interaction effects: A deeper understanding of how race/ethnicity interacts with other factors in the use of deadly force. *Criminal Justice and Behavior*, *48*: 755–775.

Piantadosi, S., Byar, D., & Green, S. (1988). The ecological fallacy. *American Journal of Epidemiology*, *127*: 893–904.

Pietschnig, J. & Voracek, M. (2015). One century of global IQ gains: A formal meta-analysis of the Flynn effect (1909–2013). *Perspectives on Psychological Science*, *10*: 282–306

Pietschnig, J., Gerdesmann, D., Zeiler, M., & Voracek, M. (2022). Of differing methods, disputed estimates and discordant interpretations: The meta-analytical multiverse of brain volume and IQ associations. *Royal Society Open Science*, *9*: 211621.

Pinker, S. (2002). *The blank slate: The modern denial of human nature*. New York: Viking.

Piquero, A. & White, N. (2003). On the relationship between cognitive abilities and life-course-persistent offending among a sample of African Americans: A longitudinal test of Moffitt's hypothesis. *Journal of Criminal Justice*, *31*: 399–409.

Piza, E. & Connealy, N. (2022). The effect of the Seattle Police-Free CHOP zone on crime: A microsynthetic control evaluation. *Criminology & Public Policy*, *21*: 35–58.

Plato (1960). *The Republic and Other Works*. Jowett, B. (Trans.). Garden City, NY: Dolphin.x

Ploeger, A. & Galis, F. (2021). Evo-Devo and cognitive science. In L. de la Rosa & G. Müller (eds.) *Evolutionary developmental biology: A reference guide*, pp. 1209–1220. Cham: Springer International Publishing.

Plomin, R. (2003). General cognitive ability. In R. Plomin, J. Defries, I. Craig, & P. McGuffin (eds.), *Behavioral genetics in the postgenomic Era*, pp. 183–201. Washington, DC: American Psychological Association.

Plomin, R. (2023). Celebrating a century of research on behavioral genetics. *Behavior Genetics*, *53*: 75–84.

Plomin, R. & Von Stumm, S. (2018). The new genetics of intelligence. *Nature Reviews Genetics*, *19*: 148. doi: 10.1038/nrg.2017.104.

Plomin, R. & von Stumm, S. (2021). Polygenic scores: prediction versus explanation. *Molecular Psychiatry*, *27*: 49–52.

Pockett, S. (2007). The concept of free will: Philosophy, neuroscience and the law. *Behavioral Sciences & the Law*, *25*: 281–293.

Polanía, R., Burdakov, D., & Hare, T. (2024). Rationality, preferences, and emotions with biological constraints: It all starts from our senses. *Trends in Cognitive Sciences*, *28*: 264–277.

Polderman, T., Benyamin, B., De Leeuw, C., Sullivan, P., Van Bochoven, A., Visscher, P., & Posthuma, D. (2015). Meta-analysis of the heritability of human traits based on fifty years of twin studies. *Nature Genetics*, *47*: 702–709.

Pope, C. & Snyder, H. (2003). Race as a factor in juvenile arrests. Juvenile justice bulletin. Washington, DC: Office of Juvenile Justice and Delinquency Prevention.

Popper, K. (1971). *The open society and its enemies: The spell of Plato*. Princeton, NJ: Princeton University Press.

Porteous, A. (1934). Platonist or Aristotelian? *The Classical Review*, *48*: 97–105.

Portnoy, J. & Farrington, D. (2015). Resting heart rate and antisocial behavior: An updated systematic review and meta-analysis. *Aggression and Violent Behavior*, *22*: 33–45.

Pourhamzeh, M., Moravej, F., Arabi, M., Shahriari, E., Mehrabi, S., Ward, R., Ahadi, R., & Joghataei, M. (2022). The roles of serotonin in neuropsychiatric disorders. *Cellular and Molecular Neurobiology*, *42*: 1671–1692.

Pratt, T., Gau, J., & Franklin, T. (2010). *Key ideas in criminology and criminal justice*. Thousand Oaks, CA: Sage.

Prayer, D., Kasprian, G., Krampl, E., Ulm, B., Witzani, L., Prayer, L., & Brugger, P. (2006). MRI of normal fetal brain development. *European Journal of Radiology*, *57*: 199–216.

Presdee, M. (2004). Cultural criminology: The long and winding road, *Theoretical Criminology*, *8*: 275–285.

Pudney, S. & Galloway, T. (2011). *Initiation into crime: An analysis of Norwegian register data on five birth cohorts* (No. 2011–11). Institute for Social and Economic Research.

Radzinowicz, L. & J. King (1979). *The growth of crime: The international experience*. Middlesex, England: Penguin Books.
Rafter. N. (2004) Earnest A. Hooton and the biological tradition in American criminology. *Criminology*, *42*: 735–772.
Raine, A. (2008). From genes to brain to antisocial behavior. *Current Directions in Psychological Science*, *17*: 323–328.
Raine, A., Yang, Y., Narr, K., & Toga, A. (2011). Sex differences in orbitofrontal gray as a partial explanation for sex differences in antisocial personality. *Molecular Psychiatry*, *16*: 227–236.
Rand, D., Ohtsuki, H., & Nowak, M. (2009). Direct reciprocity with costly punishment: Generous tit-for-that prevails. *Journal of Theoretical Biology*, *256*: 45–57.
Rasmussen Report (2013). *More Americans view blacks as racist than whites, Hispanics*. http://www.rasmussenreports.com/public_content/lifestyle/general_lifestyle/july_2013/more_americans_view_blacks_as_racist_than_whites_hispanics
Replogle, R. (1990). Justice as superstructure: How vulgar is vulgar materialism? *Polity*, *22*: 675–699.
Reza, E. (2005). Gender bias in North Carolina's death penalty. *Duke Journal of Law and Policy*, *12*: 170–214.
Reznik, R. (2019). Retributive abolitionism. *Berkley Journal of Criminal Law*, *24*: 124–193.
Richerson, P., Boyd, R., & Henrich, J. (2010). Gene-culture coevolution in the age of genomics. *Proceedings of the National Academy of Sciences*, *107* (supplement_2), 8985–8992.
Ridgeway, G. (2016). Officer risk factors associated with police shootings: A matched case–control study. *Statistics and Public Policy*, *3*: 1–6.
Ridley, M. (2003). *Nature via nurture: Genes, experience and what makes us human*. New York: Harper Collins.
Rieppel, O. (2010). New essentialism in biology. *Philosophy of Science*, *77*: 662–673.
Rietveld, C., Esko, T., Davies, G., Pers, T., Turley, P., Benyamin, B., Chabris, C., Emilsson, V., Rindermann, H., Becker, D., & Coyle, T. (2016). Survey of expert opinion on intelligence: Causes of international differences in cognitive ability tests. *Frontiers in Psychology*, *7*: 399.
Rigoni, D., Kühn, S., Gaudino, G., Sartori, G., & Brass, M. (2012). Reducing self-control by weakening belief in free will. *Consciousness and cognition*, *21*: 1482–1490.
Ritchie, S. (2015). *Intelligence: All that matters*. London: John Murray.
Roach, J. & Pease, K. (2013). *Evolution and crime*. New York: Routledge.
Robinson, M. (2008). *Death nation: The experts explain American capital punishment*. Upper Saddle River, NJ: Prentice Hall.
Robinson, W. (2009). Ecological correlations and the behavior of individuals. *International Journal of Epidemiology*, *38*: 337–341. Originally published in the *American Sociological Review* (1950).
Robson, D., Allen, M., & Howard, S. (2020). Self-regulation in childhood as a predictor of future outcomes: A meta-analytic review. *Psychological Bulletin*, *146*: 324–354.
Roca, S. (1978). Le deisme anglais et le problème de la religion de Voltaire. *Cuadernos de Investigación Filológica*, *4*: 29–38.
Rocque, M. & Posick, C. (2017). Paradigm shift or normal science? The future of (biosocial) criminology. *Theoretical Criminology*, *21*: 288–303.
Rogers, D., Deshpande, O., & Feldman, M. (2011). The spread of inequality. *PLoS One*, *6*:e24683.
Rogers, R. (2011). The roles of dopamine and serotonin in decision making: Evidence from pharmacological experiments inhumans. *Neuropsychopharmacology*, *36*: 114–132.
Rose, S. (1999). Precis of *Lifelines:* Biology, freedom, determinism. *Behavioral and Brain Sciences*, *22*: 871–921.

Rosebury, B. (2009). Private revenge and its relation to punishment. *Utilatus, 21*: 1–21.
Rosenfeld, R. & Lopez, E. (2020). Pandemic, social unrest, and crime in US Cities. *Washington, DC: Council on Criminal Justice.*
Rosenfeld, R. & Lopez, E. (2021). Pandemic, social unrest, and crime in US cities, 2020 year-end update. 2021. *Washington, DC: Council on Criminal Justice.*
Rosenfeld, R. & Wallman, J. (2019). Did de-policing cause the increase in homicide rates? *Criminology & Public Policy, 18*: 51–75.
Ross, C., Winterhalder, B., & McElreath, R. (2021). Racial disparities in police use of deadly force against unarmed individuals persist after appropriately benchmarking shooting data on violent crime rates. *Social Psychological and Personality Science, 12*: 323–332.
Rousseau, J. (1997). Discourse on the origin of inequality. In V. Gourevitch (ed.), *The discourses and other early political writings*. Cambridge, UK: Cambridge University Press.
Roussell, A., Henne, K., Glover, K. S., & Willits, D. (2019). Impossibility of a reverse racism effect: A rejoinder to James, James, and Vila. *Criminology & Public Policy, E5, 18*.
Rowe, D. (1996). An adaptive strategy of theory of crime and delinquency. In J. Hawking (ed.), *Delinquency and crime: Current theories*, pp. 268–314. Cambridge, UK: Cambridge University Press.
Rowe, D. (2002). *Biology and crime*. Los Angeles: Roxbury.
Rudland, J., Golding, C., & Wilkinson, T. (2020). The stress paradox: How stress can be good for learning. *Medical Education, 54*: 40–45.
Russell, B. (1988). The value of philosophy. In L. Pojman (ed.), *Philosophy: The quest for truth*, pp. 17–21. Belmont, CA: Wadsworth.
Saad, L. (2020). Black Americans want police to retain local presence. Gallup Poll, August 5. https://news.gallup.com/poll/316571/black-americans-police-retain-local-presence.aspx
Sagan, C. (1980). *Cosmos*. New York: Ballantine.
Salas-Wright, C., Vaughn, M., & Maynard, B. (2014). Religiosity and violence among adolescents in the United States: Findings from the National Survey on Drug Use and Health 2006–2010. *Journal of Interpersonal Violence, 29*: 1178–1200.
Salas-Wright, C., Vaughn, M., Hodge, D., & Perron, B. (2012). Religiosity profiles of American youth in relation to substance use, violence, and delinquency. *Journal of Youth and Adolescence, 41*: 1560–1575.
Sampson, R. (2000). Wither the sociological study of crime? *Annual Review of Sociology, 26*: 711–714.
Sampson, R. & Bean, L. (2006). Cultural mechanisms and killing fields: A revised theory of community-level racial inequality. In *The many colors of crime: Inequalities of race, ethnicity, and crime in America*, pp. 8–36. New York: New York University Press.
Sampson, R. & Lauritsen, J. (1997). Racial and ethnic disparities in crime and criminal justice in the United States. *Crime and Justice, 21*: 311–374.
Sarat, A., Malague, J., de los Santos, L., Pedersen, K., Qasim, N., Seymour, L., & Wishloff, S. (2019). When the death penalty goes public: Referendum, initiative, and the fate of capital punishment. *Law & Social Inquiry, 44*: 391–419.
Sarsour, K., Sheridan, M., Jutte, D., Nuru-Jeter, A., Hinshaw, S., & Boyce, W. (2011). Family socioeconomic status and child executive functions: The roles of language, home environment, and single parenthood. *Journal of the International Neuropsychological Society, 17*: 120–132.
Sawhill, I. (2003). The behavioral aspects of poverty. *Public Interest, 153*: 79–95.
Sayer, A. (1997). Essentialism, social constructionism, and beyond. *Sociological Review, 45*: 453–487.

Sayers, S. (2005). Why work? Marx and human nature. *Science & Society*, *69*: 606–616.
Schacht, R. & Kramer, K. (2019). Are we monogamous? A review of the evolution of pair-bonding in humans and its contemporary variation cross-culturally. *Frontiers in Ecology and Evolution*, 230.
Schafer, S. (1976). The problem of free will in criminology. *The Journal of Criminal Law and Criminology*, *67*: 481–485.
Scheidegger, K. (2012). Rebutting the myths about race and the death penalty. *Ohio State Journal of Criminal Law*, *10*: 147–165.
Schiffer, B., Pawliczek, C., Forsting, M., Gizewski, E., Leygraf, N., & Hodgins, S. (2014). Neural mechanisms underlying cognitive control of men with lifelong antisocial behavior. *Psychiatry Research: Neuroimaging*, *222*: 43–51.
Schindler, S., Querengässer, J., Bruchmann, M., Bögemann, N., Moeck, R., & Straube, T. (2021). Bayes Factors show evidence against systematic relationships between the anchoring effect and the Big Five personality traits. *Scientific Reports*, *11*: 7021.
Schlinger, H. (2003). The myth of intelligence. *Psychological Record*, *53*: 15–32.
Schmalleger, F. (2004). *Criminology Today* (3rd edn). Upper Saddle River, NJ: Prentice Hall.
Schmidt, F. & Hunter, K. (2004). General mental ability in the world of work: Occupational attainment and job performance. *Journal of Personality and Social Psychology*, *86*: 162–173.
Schmitt, D., Realo, A., Voracek, M., & Allik, J. (2008). Why can't a man be more like a woman? Sex differences in big five personality traits across 55 cultures. *Journal of Personality and Social Psychology*, *94*: 168–182.
Schury, K., & Kolassa, L. (2012). Biological memory of childhood maltreatment: Current knowledge and recommendations for future research. *Annals of the New York Academy of Sciences*, *1262*: 93–100.
Schuster, P. (2009). Free will, information, quantum mechanics, and biology: It pays to distinguish different forms of free choice and information. *Complexity*, *15*: 8–11.
Schutter, D. A. De Weijer, J. Meuwese, B. Morgan & J. Van Honk (2008). Interrelations between motivational stance, cortical excitability, and the frontal electroencephalogram asymmetry of emotion: A transcranial magnetic stimulation study. *Human Brain Mapping*, *29*: 574–580.
Schwartz, J., Savolainen, J., Aaltonen, M., Merikukka, M., Paananen, R., & Gissler, M. (2015). Intelligence and criminal behavior in a total birth cohort: An examination of functional form, dimensions of intelligence, and the nature of offending. *Intelligence*, *51*: 109–118.
Sedlak, A., Mettenburg, J., Basena, M., Peta, I., McPherson, K., Greene, A., & Li, S. (2010). Fourth national incidence study of child abuse and neglect (NIS-4). *Washington, DC: US Department of Health and Human Services*, *9*, 2010.
Selden, S. (2007). Biological determinism and the narrative of adjustment: The high school biology textbooks of Truman Jesse Moon, c. 1921–1963. *Curriculum Inquiry*, *37*: 159–196.
Selita, F. & Kovas, Y. (2019). Genes and Gini: What inequality means for heritability. *Journal of Biosocial Science*, *51*: 18–47.
Sharma, H., Scheb, J., Houston, D., & K. Wagers. (2013). Race and the death penalty: An empirical assessment of first degree murder convictions in Tennessee after *Gregg v. Georgia*. *Tennessee Journal of Race, Gender, & Social Justice*, *2*: 1–39.
Sharp, B. (2006). *Changing criminal thinking: A treatment program*. Alexandria, VA: American Correctional Association.
Shatz, S. & Statz, N. (2011). Chivalry is not dead: Murder, gender, and the death penalty. *Berkeley Journal of Gender, Law, & Justice*, *27*: 64–112.
Shaw, P., Lerch, J., Greenstein, D., Sharp, W., Clasen, L., Evans, A., Giedd, J., Castellanos, F., & Rapoport, J. (2006). Longitudinal mapping of cortical thickness and

clinical outcome in children and adolescents with attention-deficit/hyperactivity disorder. *Archives of General Psychiatry*, *63*: 540–549.
Shi, S., Cheng, T., Jan, L. & Jan, Y. (2004). The immunoglobin family member dendrite arborization and synapse maturation 1 (Dasm1) controls excitatory synapse maturation. *Proceedings of the National Academy of Sciences*, *101*: 13246–13351.
Shih, H., Kuo, M., Wu, C., Chao, Y., Huang, H., & Huang, C. (2022). The neurobiological basis of love: A meta-analysis of human functional neuroimaging studies of maternal and passionate love. *Brain Sciences*, *12*: 830.
Shimamura, A. (2000). The role of the prefrontal cortex in dynamic filtering. *Psychobiology*, *28*: 207–218.
Shirtcliff, E., Vitacco, M., Graf, A., Gostisha, A., Merz, J., & Zahn-Waxler, C. (2009). Neurobiology of empathy and callousness: Implications for the development of antisocial behavior. *Behavioral Sciences & the Law*, *27*: 137–171.
Shoda, Y., Mischel, W., & Peake, P. (1990). Predicting adolescent cognitive and self-regulatory competencies from preschool delay of gratification: Identifying diagnostic conditions. *Developmental Psychology*, *26*: 978–986.
Schumacher, R. (2012). The myth of religion as the #1 cause of war, CARM, April 22. https://carm.org/atheism/the-myth-that-religion-is-the-1–cause-of-war/
Siegel, L. (2006). *Criminology*. Belmont, CA: Thomson/Wadsworth.
Seigel, M. (2017). The dilemma of racial profiling: An abolitionist police history. *Contemporary Justice Review*, *20*: 474–490.
Siegel, M., Poulson, M., Sangar, R., & Jay, J. (2021). The Interaction of race and place: Predictors of fatal police shootings of black victims at the incident, census tract, city, and state levels, 2013–2018. *Race and Social Problems*, *13*: 245–265.
Silfver, M. & Helkama, K. (2007). Empathy, guilt, and gender: A comparison of two measures of guilt. *Scandinavian Journal of Psychology*, *48*: 239–246.
Silke, C., Brady, B., Boylan, C., & Dolan, P. (2018). Factors influencing the development of empathy and pro-social behaviour among adolescents: A systematic review. *Children and Youth Services Review*, *94*: 421–436.
Silver, E., Goff, K., & Iceland, J. (2022). Social order and social justice: Moral intuitions, systemic racism beliefs, and Americans' divergent attitudes toward Black Lives Matter and police. *Criminology*, *60*: 342–369.
Silver, I. (2019). Linear and non-linear: An exploration of the variation in the functional form of verbal IQ and antisocial behavior as adolescents age into adulthood. *Intelligence*, *76*: 101375.
Simpson-Kent, I., Fuhrmann, D., Bathelt, J., Achterberg, J., Borgeest, G., & Kievit, R. (2020). Neurocognitive reorganization between crystallized intelligence, fluid intelligence and white matter microstructure in two age-heterogeneous developmental cohorts. *Developmental Cognitive Neuroscience*, *41*: 100743.
Singh, J., Volavka, J., Czobor, P., & Van Dorn, R. (2012). A meta-analysis of the Val158Met COMT polymorphism and violent behavior in schizophrenia. *PLoS One* 7: e43423.
Smillie, L. (2008). What is reinforcement sensitivity? Neuroscience paradigms for approach-avoidance process theories of personality. *European Journal of Personality*, *22*: 359–384.
Smith, K., Oxley, D., Hibbing, M., Alford, J., & Hibbing, J. (2011). Linking genetics and Political attitudes: Reconceptualizing political ideology. *Political Psychology*, *32*: 369–397.
Snyderman, M. & Rothman, S. (1988). *The IQ controversy, the media and public policy*. New Brunswick, NJ: Transaction.
Solomon, R. (1977). The logic of emotion. *Nous*, *11*: 41–49.
Sowell, T. (1987). *A conflict of visions: Ideological origins of political struggles*. New York: Basic Books.

Sowell, E., P., & Toga, A. (2004). Mapping changes in the human cortex throughout the span of life. *Neuroscientist, 10*: 372–392.

Sozzo, M. & Fonseca, D. (2016). From critical criminology to the criminological imagination: An interview with Jock Young. *International Journal for Crime, Justice and Social Democracy, 5*: 95–110.

Spielman, F. (2020, June 1). Lightfoot: "We did not stand by to watch the South and West Sides burn." *Chicago Sun Times* https://chicago.suntimes.com/city-hall/2020/6/1/21276893/chicago-protests-looting-aldermen-national-guard-troops-protect-neighborhoods

Spiro, M. (1999). Anthropology and human nature. *Ethos, 27*: 7–14.

Spirtes, P., Glymour, C., & Scheines, R. (2001). *Causation, prediction, and search.* Cambridge, MA: MIT Press.

Spohn, C. (2017). Race and sentencing disparity. *Reforming criminal justice: A report of the Academy for Justice on bridging the gap between scholarship and reform, 4*: 169–186.

Stams, G., Brugman, D., Deković, M., Van Rosmalen, L., Van Der Laan, P., & Gibbs, J. (2006). The moral judgment of juvenile delinquents: A meta-analysis. *Journal of Abnormal Child Psychology, 34*: 692–708.

Starr, S. (2012). Estimating gender disparities in federal criminal cases. University of Michigan Law and Economics Research Paper, No. 12–018.

Steffensmeier, D., Ulmer, J., Feldmeyer, B., & Harris, C. (2010). Scope and conceptual issues in testing the race–crime invariance thesis: Black, White, and Hispanic comparisons. *Criminology, 48*: 1133–1169.

Stellar, J., Feinberg, M., & Keltner, D. (2014). When the selfish suffer: evidence for selective prosocial emotional and physiological responses to suffering egoists. *Evolution and Human Behavior, 35*: 140–147.

Stenger, V. (2009). *The new atheism: Taking a stand for science and reason.* Amherst, NY: Prometheus Books.

Sternberg, R., Grigorenko, E., & Bundy, D. (2001). The predictive value of IQ. *Merrill-Palmer Quarterly (1982–)*: 1–41.

Stohr, M. & Walsh, A. (2012). *Corrections: The essentials* (5th edn). Thousand Oaks, CA: Sage.

Streib, V. (1987). *Death penalty for juveniles.* Bloomington, IN: Indiana University Press.

Streib, V. (2003). Executing women, juveniles, and the mentally retarded: Second class citizens in capital punishment. *America's experiment with capital punishment*, 301–323.

Strenze, T. (2007). Intelligence and socioeconomic success: A meta-analytic review of longitudinal research. *Intelligence, 35*: 401–426.

Sullins, D. (2021). The case for mom and dad. *The Linacre Quarterly, 88*: 184–201.

Sullivan, C., & O'Keeffe, Z. (2017). Evidence that curtailing proactive policing can reduce major crime. *Nature Human Behaviour, 1*: 730–737.

Sutherland, E. (1939). *Principles of criminology.* Philadelphia, PA: J.B. Lippincott.

Sutherland, E. & Cressey, D. (1974). *Criminology* (9th edn). Philadelphia, PA: J.B. Lippincott.

Sutton, W. & Liin, E. (1976). *Where the money was: The memoirs of a bank robber.* New York: Viking.

Suwa, G., Asfaw, B., Kono, R., Kubo, D., Lovejoy, C., White, T. (2009). The *Ardipithecus ramidus skull* and its implications for hominid origins. *Science, 326*: 68e1–68e8.

Swain, J., Lorberbaum, J., Kose, S., & Strathearn, L. (2007). Brain basis of early parent–infant interactions: Psychology, physiology, and in vivo functional neuroimaging studies. *Journal of Child Psychology and Psychiatry, 48*: 262–287.

Sweetser, K. (2014). Partisan personality: The psychological differences between Democrats and Republicans, and independents somewhere in between. *American Behavioral Scientist*, *58*: 1183–1194.

Szetela, A. (2020). Black Lives Matter at five: Limits and possibilities. *Ethnic and Racial Studies*, *43*: 1358–1383.

Takagi, P. (1974). A garrison state in a "democratic" society. *Crime and Social Justice*, *1*: 27–33.

Tancredi, L. (2005). *Hardwired behavior: What neuroscience reveals about morality*. Cambridge, UK: Cambridge University Press.

Tangney, J., Stuewig, J., & Mashek, D. (2007). Moral emotions and moral behavior. *Annual Review of Psychology*, *58*: 345–372.

Tanner, M. (2019). *What's missing in the war on poverty?* San Francisco, CA: The Cato Institute.

Taylor, K.-Y. (2021). The emerging movement for police and prison abolition. *The New Yorker*, May 7. https://www.newyorker.com/news/our-columnists/the-emerging-movement-for-police-and-prison-abolition.

Taylor, E. (2022). Power emergentism and the collapse problem. *Philosophy of Science*, *89*: 302–318.

Taylor, I. (1999). Crime and social criticism. *Social Justice*, *26*: 150–168.

Taylor, I., Walton, P., & Young, J. (1973). *The new criminology: For a social theory of deviance*. London: Routledge and Kegan Paul.

TenEyck, M. & Barnes, J. (2015). Examining the impact of peer group selection on self-reported delinquency: A consideration of active gene–environment correlation. *Criminal justice and behavior*, *42*: 741–762.

Terbeck, S., Savulescu, J., Chesterman, L., & Cowen, P. (2016). Noradrenaline effects on social behaviour, intergroup relations, and moral decisions. *Neuroscience & Biobehavioral Reviews*, *66*: 54–60.

Terburg, D., Morgan, B., & van Honk, J. (2009). The testosterone–cortisol ratio: A hormonal marker for proneness to social aggression. *International Journal of Law and Psychiatry*, *32*: 216–223.

Thomas, S. (2000). Ending welfare as we know it, or farewell to the rights of women on welfare—a constitutional and human rights analysis of the Personal Responsibility Act. *University of Detroit Mercy Law Review*, *78*: 179–202.

Thompson, A. & Tapp, S. (2023). Criminal victimization, 2022. Washington, DC: U.S. Department of Justice.

Tielbeek, J., Barnes, J., Popma, A., Polderman, T., Lee, J., Perry, J., Posthuma, D., & Boutwell, B. (2018). Exploring the genetic correlations of antisocial behaviour and life history traits. *British Journal of Psychology*, *4*: 467–470.

Tingberg, B. & Nilsson, D. (2020). Child neglect-still a neglected problem in the global world: A review. *Journal of Advanced Pediatrics and Child Health*, *3*: 038–046.

Tinbergen, N. (1963) On aims and methods in ethology. *Zeitschrift für Tierpsychologie*, *20*: 410–433.

Topalli, V., Brezina, T., & Bernhardt, M. (2013). With God on my side: The paradoxical relationship between religious belief and criminality among hardcore street offenders. *Theoretical Criminology*, *17*: 49–69.

Tottenham, N. (2020). Early adversity and the neotenous human brain. *Biological Psychiatry*, *87*: 350–358.

Tremblay, R. (2008). Understanding development and prevention of chronic physical aggression: Towards experimental epigenetic studies. *Philosophical Transactions of the Royal Society B: Biological Sciences*, *363*: 2613–2622.

Tremblay, R. & LeMarquand, D. (2001). Individual risk and protective factors. In R. Loeber & D. Farrington (eds.), *Child delinquents: Development, interventions and service needs*, pp. 137–164. Thousand Oaks, CA: Sage.

Trentacosta, C., Waller, R., Neiderhiser, J., Shaw, D., Natsuaki, M., Ganiban, J., Reiss, D., Leve, L., & Hyde, L. (2019). Callous-unemotional behaviors and harsh parenting: Reciprocal associations across early childhood and moderation by inherited risk. *Journal of Abnormal Child Psychology*, *47*: 811–823.

Trigg, R. (1999). *Ideas of human nature: An historical introduction.* Malden, MA: Blackwell.

Tseloni, A. & Pease, K. (2003). Repeat personal victimization. "Boosts" or "Flags"? *British Journal of Criminology*, *43*: 196–212.

Turkheimer, E. (2000). Three laws of behavior genetics and what they mean. *Current Directions in Psychological Science*, *9*: 160–164.

Turkheimer, E., Haley, A., Waldron, M., D'Onofrio, B., & Gottesman, I. (2003). Socioeconomic status modifies heritability of IQ in young children. *Psychological Science*, *14*: 623–628.

Turkheimer, E. & Harden, P. (2014) Behavior genetic research methods: Testing quasi-causal hypotheses using multivariate twin data. In H. Reis & C. Judd (eds.) *Handbook of Research Methods in Social and Personality Psychology*, pp. 159–187. Cambridge, UK: Cambridge University Press.

Tuvblad, C. & Baker, L. (2011). Human aggression across the lifespan: genetic propensities and environmental moderators. *Advances in Genetics*, *75*: 171–214.

Twardosz, S. & Lutzker, J. (2010). Child maltreatment and the developing brain: A review of neuroscience perspectives. *Aggression and Violent Behavior*, *15*: 59–68.

Tyler, N., Heffernan, R., & Fortune, C. (2020). Reorienting locus of control in individuals who have offended through strengths-based interventions: Personal agency and the good lives model. *Frontiers in Psychology*, *11*: 553240.

Ulmer, J. (2012). Recent developments and new directions in sentencing research. *Justice Quarterly*, *29*: 1–40.

Ulmer, J., Kramer, J., & Zajac, G. (2020). The race of defendants and victims in Pennsylvania death penalty decisions: 2000–2010. *Justice Quarterly*, *37*: 955–983.

US Census Bureau (2021). *Current population survey, America's families and living arrangements.* https://www2.census.gov/programs-surveys/demo/tables/families/2021/cps-2021/

US Department of Health and Human Services (2009). Understanding the effects of maltreatment on brain development. https://www.childwelfare.gov/pubs/issue_briefs/braindevelopment/brain_development.pdf

US Department of Justice. (2001). The federal death penalty system: supplementary data, analysis and revised protocols for capital case review. http://www.justice.gov/archive/dag/pubdoc/deathpenaltystudy.htm

US Department of Treasury (2007). *Income mobility in the U.S. from 1996 to 2005.* http://www.treasury.gov/resource-center/tax-policy/Documents/incomemobilitystudy.pdf

United States v. Booker, 543 U.S. 220 (2005).

UvnäsMoberg, K., Ekström-Bergström, A., Buckley, S., Massarotti, C., Pajalic, Z., Luegmair, K., Kotlowska, A., Lengler, L., Olza, I., Grylka-Baeschlin, S., & Leahy-Warren, P. (2020). Maternal plasma levels of oxytocin during breastfeeding—A systematic review. *PloS one*, *15*: p.e0235806.

Valentova, J., Junior, F., Štěrbová, Z., Varella, M., & Fisher, M. (2020). The association between Dark Triad traits and sociosexuality with mating and parenting efforts: A cross-cultural study. *Personality and Individual Differences*, *154*: 109613.

Van As, A., Fieggen, G., & Tobias, P. (2007). Severe abuse of infants-an evolutionary price for human development?: opinion. *South African Journal of Child Health*, *1*: 54–57.

Van den Berghe, P. (1990). Why most sociologists don't (and won't) think evolutionarily. *Sociological Forum*, *5*: 173–185.

Van den Haag, F. (2003). Justice, deterrence, and the death penalty. In J. Aker, R. Bihm, & C. Lanier (eds.), *America's experiment with the death penalty*, pp. 233–249. Durham, NC: Carolina Academic Press.

Van Den Heuvel, M., Stam, C., Kahn, R., & Pol, H. (2009). Efficiency of functional brain networks and intellectual performance. *Journal of Neuroscience*, *29*: 7619–7624.

Van Goozen, S., Fairchild, G., Snoek, H., & Harold, G. (2007). The evidence for a neurobiological model of childhood antisocial behavior. *Psychological Bulletin*, *133*: 149–82.

Van Honk, J., Hermans, E., D'Alfonso, A., Schutter, D., Van Doornen, *L.* & De Haan, E. (2002). A left-prefrontal lateralized, sympathetic mechanism directs attention towards social threat in humans: Evidence from repetitive transcranial magnetic stimulation. *Neuroscience Letters*, *319*: 99–102.

Van Honk, J., Harmon-Jones, E., Morgan, B., & Schutter, D. (2010). Socially explosive minds: The triple imbalance hypothesis of reactive aggression. *Journal of Personality*, *78*: 67–94.

Van Voorhees, E., & Scarpa, A. (2004). The effects of child maltreatment on the hypothalamic- pituitary-adrenal axis. *Trauma, Violence, and Abuse*, *5*: 333–352.

Vélez, M. (2018). An elaboration and critique of "Reassessing 'Toward a theory of race, crime, and urban inequality.'" *Du Bois Review: Social Science Research on Race*, *15*: 35–46.

Velkley, R. (2002). *Being after Rousseau: Philosophy and culture in question*. Chicago: University of Chicago Press.

VerBruggen, R. (2022). Fatal police shootings and race: A review of the evidence and suggestions for future research. *Manhattan Institute Report*, 1–32.

Virginia Museum of Culture and History (ND). George Washington's Farewell address. https://virginiahistory.org/learn/george-washingtons-farewell-address

Vold, G., Bernard, T., & Snipes, J. (1998). *Theoretical criminology*. New York: Oxford University Press.

Wagstaff, G. (1998). Equity, justice, and altruism. *Current Psychology*, *17*: 111–134.

Wajzer, M. & Dragan, W. (2023). It is not only the f environment that matters: A short introduction to research on the heritability of political attitudes. *Political Studies Review*, *21*: 144–161.

Walker, J. & Cloete, T. (2023). Reductionism or holism? The two faces of biology. *HTS Teologiese Studies/Theological Studies*, *79* (Online) 2072–8050.

Wallace, W. (1990). Rationality, human nature, and society in Weber's theory. *Theory and Society*, *19*: 199–223.

Waller, R. & Hyde, L. (2018). Callous-unemotional behaviors in early childhood: The development of empathy and prosociality gone awry. *Current Oopinion in Psychology*, *20*: 11–16.

Waller, R., Wagner, N., Barstead, M., Subar, A., Petersen, J., Hyde, J., & Hyde, L. (2020). A meta-analysis of the associations between callous-unemotional traits and empathy, prosociality, and guilt. *Clinical Psychology Review*, *75*: 101809.

Wallenborn, J., Levine, G., dos Santos, A., Grisi, S., & Brentani, A. (2021). Breastfeeding, physical growth, and cognitive development. *Development*, *147*: e2020008029.

Walsh, A. (1981). *Human nature and love*. Washington, DC: University Press of America.

Walsh, A. (2000). Behavior genetics and anomie/strain theory. *Criminology*, *38*: 1075–1107.

Walsh, A. (2003). Intelligence and antisocial behavior. In A. Walsh & L. Ellis (eds.), *Biosocial criminology: Challenging environmentalism's supremacy*, pp. 105–124. Huntington, NY: Nova Science.

Walsh, A. (2005). African Americans and serial murder: The myth and the reality. *Homicide Studies*, *9*: 271–291.

Walsh, A. (2014). *Biosociology: Bridging the biology-sociology divide.* New Brunswick, NJ: Transaction Publishers.
Walsh, A. (2019). *Reinforcement sensitivity theory: A metatheory for biosocial criminology.* New York: Routledge.
Walsh, A. (2023). *The social institutions through the contrasting visions of Plato and Aristotle.* Bradford, UK: Ethics Press International.
Walsh, A & Bolen, J. (2012). *The neurobiology of criminal behavior: Gene-brain culture co-evolution.* Farnham, England: Ashgate.
Walsh, A. & Ellis, L. (2004). Ideology: Criminology's Achilles' Heel? *Quarterly Journal of Ideology, 27*: 1–25.
Walsh, A. & Hatch, V. (2018). Capital punishment, retribution, and emotion: An evolutionary perspective. *New Criminal Law Review, 21*: 267–290.
Walsh, A., Johnson, H., & Bolen, J. (2012). Drugs, crime, and the epigenetics of hedonic allostasis. *Journal of Contemporary Criminal Justice, 28*: 314–328.
Walsh, A. & Jorgensen, C. (2020). *Criminology: The essentials* (4th edn). Thousand Oaks, CA: Sage.
Walsh, A. & Jorgensen, C. (2025). *Criminology: The essentials* (5th edn). Thousand Oaks, CA: Sage.
Walsh, A., Jorgensen, C., & Wells, J. (2020). Evolution and punishment. *The SAGE Handbook of Evolutionary Psychology: Applications of Evolutionary Psychology*, p. 258.
Walsh, A. & Vaske, J. (2015). *Feminist criminology through a biosocial lens (*2nd edn) Durham, NC: Carolina Academic Press.
Walsh, A. & Wright, J. (2015). Biosocial criminology and its discontents: A critical realist philosophical analysis. *Criminal Justice Studies, 28*: 124–140.
Walsh, A. & Yun, I. (2016). evoked Culture and evoked nature: the promise of Gene-Culture Co-evolution theory for sociology. *Frontiers in Sociology, 1*: 1–11.
Walsh, A. & Yun, I. (2018). Examining the race, poverty, and crime nexus adding Asian Americans and biosocial processes. *Journal of Criminal Justice, 59*: 42–53.
Walsh, D. (2006). Evolutionary essentialism. *British Journal for the Philosophy of Science, 57*: 425–448.
Walters, G. (2015). The decision to commit crime: Rational or nonrational? *Criminology, Criminal Justice, Law & Society, 16*: 1–18.
Wang, X. & Mears, D. (2010). A multilevel test of minority threat effects on sentencing. *Journal of Quantitative Criminology, 26*: 191–215.
Wang, X., Mears, D., Spohn, C., & Dario, L. (2013). Assessing the differential effects of race and ethnicity on sentence outcomes under different sentencing systems. *Crime & Delinquency, 59*: 87–114.
Ward, J., McConaghy, M., & Bennett, J. (2018). Differential applicability of criminological theories to individuals? The case of social learning vis-à-vis social control. *Crime & Delinquency, 64*: 510–541.
Warr, M. (2002). *Companions in crime: The social aspects of criminal conduct.* New York: Cambridge University Press.
Washington Post (2021). 927 people have been shot and killed by police in the past year. Washington Post Data Base, September 22. https://www.washingtonpost.com/graphics/investigations/police-shootings-database/
Watts, S. & McNulty, T. (2016). Genes, parenting, self-control, and criminal behavior. *International Journal of Offender Therapy and Comparative Criminology, 60*: 469–491.
Weatherspoon, F. (1998). *African-American males and the law: Cases and materials.* Lanham, MD: University Press of America.
Weaver, I., Cervoni, N., Champagne, F., D'Alessio, A., Sharma, S., Seckl, J., Dymov, S., Szyf, M., & Meaney, M. (2004). Epigenetic programming by maternal behavior, *Nature Neuroscience, 7*: 847–854.

Wechsler, D. (1958). *The measurement and appraisal of adult intelligence*. Baltimore, MD: Williams & Wilkins.
Weinhold, B. (2006). Epigenetics: The science of change. *Environmental Health Perspectives, 114*: 161–167.
Weitoft, G., Hjern, A., Haglund, B., & Rosén, M. (2003). Mortality, severe morbidity, and injury in children living with single parents in Sweden: A population-based study. *The Lancet, 361*: 289–295.
Welch, M., Tittle, C., & Grasmick, H. (2006). Christian religiosity, self-control and social conformity. *Social Forces, 84*: 1605–1623.
Wiebe, R. (2011). The nature and utility of low self-control. In K. Beaver & A. Walsh (eds.), *The Ashgate research companion to biosocial theories of crime*, pp. 369–395. Farnham, England: Ashgate.
Wiebe, R. (2012). Integrating criminology through adaptive strategy and life history theory. *Journal of Contemporary Criminal Justice, 28*: 346–365.
Willems, Y., Boesen, N., Li, J., Finkenauer, C., & Bartels, M. (2019). The heritability of self-control: A meta-analysis. *Neuroscience & Biobehavioral Reviews, 100*: 324–334.
Williams, C. & Arrigo, B. (2006). Philosophy, crime, and theoretical criminology. In B. Arrigo & C. Williams (eds.) *Philosophy, crime, and criminology*, pp. 1–40. Urbana: University of Chicago Press.
Williams, E. & Robinson, M. (2004). Ideology and criminal justice: Suggestions for a pedagogical model. *Journal of Criminal Justice Education, 15*: 373–392.
Williams, N. (2011). Putnam's traditional neo-essentialism. *The Philosophical Quarterly, 61*: 151–170.
Williams, W. (2011). *Race & economics: How much can be blamed on discrimination?* Stanford, CA: Hoover Press.
Wilson, D. & Wilson, E. (2007). Rethinking the theoretical foundation of sociobiology. *The Quarterly Review of Biology, 84*: 327–348.
Wilson, E. (1990). Biology and the social sciences. *Zygon, 25*: 245–262.
Wilson, E. (1993). *The moral sense*. New York: The Free Press.
Wilson, E. (1998). *Consilience: The unity of knowledge*. New York: Knopf.
Wilson, E. (1978). *On human nature*. Cambridge, MA: Harvard University Press.
Wilson, J. (2000). *The marriage problem: How our culture has weakened families*. New York: HarperCollins.
Wilson, J. (1975). *Thinking about crime*. New York: Basic Books.
Wilson, J. & Kelling, G. (1982) Broken windows. *The Atlantic Online*, 8/3/09.
Wilson, M. & Daly, M. (1997). Life expectancy, economic inequality, homicide and reproductive timing in Chicago neighborhoods. *British Medical Journal, 314*: 1271–1274.
Winlow, S. & Hall, S. (2016). Realist criminology and its discontents. *International Journal for Crime, Justice and Social Democracy, 5*: 80–94.
Winthrop, R. (1952). *Addresses and speeches at various occasions*. Boston, MA: Little, Brown.
Wismer-Fries, A. Ziegler, T., Kurian, J., Jacoris, S., & Pollak, S. (2005). Early experience in humans is associated with changes in neuropeptides critical for regulating social behavior. *Proceedings of the National Academy of Sciences, 102*: 17237–17240.
Wolf, R., Pujara, M., Motzkin, J., Newman, J., Kiehl, K., Decety, J., Kosson, D., & Koenigs, M. (2015). Interpersonal traits of psychopathy linked to reduced integrity of the uncinate fasciculus. *Human Brain Mapping, 36*: 4202–4209.
Woodger, J. (1948). *Biological principles*. London: Routledge & Kegan Paul.
Wood, P., Gove, W., Wilson, J., & Cochran, J. (1997). Nonsocial reinforcement and habitual criminal conduct: An extension of learning theory. *Criminology, 35*: 335–366.

Wooldredge, J. (2010). Judges' unequal contributions to extralegal disparities in imprisonment. *Criminology, 48*: 539–67.
Worrall, J., Bishopp, S., Zinser, S., Wheeler, A., & Phillips, S. (2018). Exploring bias in police shooting decisions with real shoot/don't shoot cases. *Crime & Delinquency*, *64*: 1171–1192.
Wright, A. & Jackson, J. (2022). Childhood temperament and adulthood personality differentially predict life outcomes. *Scientific Reports*, *12*: 10286.
Wright, J. & Beaver, K. (2012). The behavioral genetics of predatory criminal behavior. In DeLisi & P. M. Conis (eds.), *Violent offenders: Theory, research, policy, and practice*, pp. 109–123. Burlington, MA: Jones and Bartlett.
Wright, J. & Boisvert, D. (2009). What biosocial criminology offers criminology. *Criminal Justice and Behavior*, *36*: 1228–1240.
Wright, J., Boisvert, D., Dietrich, K., & Ris, M. (2009). The ghost in the machine and criminal behavior: Criminology for the 21st century. In A. Walsh & K. Beaver. *Biosocial criminology: New directions in theory and research*, pp. 73–89. New York: Routledge.
Wright, J. & Cullen, F. (2012). The future of biosocial criminology: Beyond scholars' professional ideology. *Journal of Contemporary Criminal Justice*, *28*: 237–253.
Wright, J. & Nichols, R. (2014). The social cost of atheism: How perceived religiosity influences moral appraisal. *Journal of Cognition and Culture*, *14*: 93–115.
Wright, J., Dietrich, K., Ris, M., Hornung, R., Wessel, S., & Lanphear, B. (2008). Association of prenatal and childhood blood lead concentrations with criminal arrests in early childhood. *PLoS Medicine*, *5*: 732–740.
Wu, H.-H. & Walsh, A. (2007). Teaching statistical interaction in ANOVA and OLS regression in the context of ideology in criminal justice processing. *Free Inquiry in Creative Sociology*, *35*: 27–35.
Wu, J., Luan, S., & Raihani, N. (2022). Reward, punishment, and prosocial behavior: Recent developments and implications. *Current Opinion in Psychology*, *44*: 117–123.
Xue, S., Kidd, M., Le, A., Kirk, K., & Martin, N. (2020). The role of locus of control in adulthood outcomes: Evidence from Australian twins. *Journal of Economic Behavior & Organization*, *179*: 566–588.
Xygalatas, D., Maňo, P., Bahna, V., Klocová, E., Kundt, R., Lang, M., & Shaver, J. (2021). Social inequality and signaling in a costly ritual. *Evolution and Human Behavior*, *42*: 524–533.
Yacubian, J., Sommer, T., Schroeder, K., Glascher, J., Kalisch, R., Leuenberger, D., Braus, F., & Buchel, C. (2007). Gene-gene interaction associated with neural reward sensitivity, *Proceedings of the National Academy of Sciences*, *104*: 8125 –8130.
Yaldir, H. & Der, K. (2016). Hobbes and Rousseau on human nature. In H. Yaldir & R. Efee, E. (eds.), *Current topics in social sciences*, pp. 267–277. Sofia: St. Kliment Ohridski University Press.
Yao, S., Långström, N., Temrin, H., & Walum, H. (2014). Criminal offending as part of an alternative reproductive strategy: Investigating evolutionary hypotheses using Swedish total population data. *Evolution and Human Behavior*, *35*: 481–488.
Young, J. (2003) Merton with energy, Katz with structure: The sociology of vindictiveness and the criminology of transgression. *Theoretical Criminology* 7: 388–414.
Yun, I., Cheong, J., & Walsh, A. (2011). Genetic and environmental influences in delinquent peer affiliation: From the peer network approach. *Youth Violence and Juvenile Justice*, *9*: 241–258.
Yun, I. & Lee, J. (2013). IQ and delinquency: The differential detection hypothesis revisited. *Youth Violence and Juvenile Justice*, *11*: 196–211.
Yurdakök, K. (2014). Neonatal maltreatment and brain development. *Journal of Pediatric and Neonatal Individualized Medicine*, *3*: e030228–e030228.

Zack, N. (2002). *Philosophy of science and race*. New York: Routledge.
Zhang, J. (2013). Reference and perception: Towards a social relativism perspective. *Theory in Action*, 6: 148–173.
Zhuravel, V. & Kurumisawa, Y. (2020). Criminology in the system of scientific knowledge. *Yearbook of Ukrainian Law: Collection of Scientific Papers*. *12*: 372–383.
Zillmer, E., Archer, R., & Castino, R. (1989). Rorschach records of Nazi war criminals: A reanalysis using current scoring and interpretation practices. *Journal of Personality Assessment*, *53*: 85–99.
Zimmerman, M. (2011). *The immorality of punishment*. Buffalo, NY: Broadview Press.
Zuckerman, P. (2009). Atheism, secularity, and well-being: How the findings of social science counter negative stereotypes and assumptions. *Sociology Compass*, *3*: 949–971.

Index

academic achievement: and antisocial behavior 144; and IQ 144; measures of 144
ADHD *see* attention-deficit/hyperactivity disorder (ADHD)
African Americans: crime rates 181; *see also* Blacks
agency: and rational choice theory 46
aggression: reactive 81; and triple imbalance hypothesis (TIH) 81–2
Agnew, Robert 43
agreeableness: traits 153
Akers, Ronald 115, 117, 130
alcohol: and gamma and gamma-aminobutyric acid (GABA) 79
alcohol consumption: by mother, and low IQ 152
allele gene 53, 68, 69, 71, 73–4; and antisocial behavior 57, 123; low and high level 108; and monoamine oxidase A (MAOA) gene 70
allostasis 96
altruism: benefits 35; and empathy 106; punishment as 190, 194; reciprocal 31, 35, 194; and self-interest 34–5
American Revolution: French Revolution, comparison 18
amygdalae 75–6, 82
Anderson, Elijah 132; *Code of the Streets* 57
anomie/strain theory: Merton 46, 147–8, 155
ANS *see* autonomic nervous system (ANS)
anterior cingulate cortex (ACC): role 76
anti-poverty programs: criticisms of 157; failure 157–8
antisocial behavior: and academic achievement 144; and allele gene 57, 123; heritability of 191; and IQ 143; and maltreatment 95–6; and monoamine oxidase A (MAOA) gene 70; and non-belief 166–7; and religion 161–4; war as ultimate form of 161; *see also* crime
archetypal Forms: Plato 5
Aristotle: on justice 200; and Plato, modes of thought 16, 18
arrest rates: Blacks 181, 182; Whites 182
atomic theory 9
attachment: social bond theory 119
attention-deficit/hyperactivity disorder (ADHD) 69; and criminal behavior 78; drug treatment 78
autonomic nervous system (ANS): arousal levels 102–3, 104; and conscience 101–5; and free will 40; function 78, 95; Levenson on 101–2; parasympathetic system 102, 103; regulation 85; sympathetic system 102, 103

Barkow, Jerome 28; on social instincts 31
Barnett, Arnold: *Six Deadly Sins of Statistical Misrepresentation* 214
Beccaria, Cesare 43, 194
behavior: dual inheritance theory 27; explanatory framework 51; prediction, and sentencing guidelines 204; rational, definition 43; and self-interest 43–4; unpredictability, and free will 37–8; *see also* antisocial behavior; criminal behavior

behavioral activating system (BAS) 83, 85; location 84; *see also* behavioral inhibition system (BIS)
behavioral genetics 63–5; three laws 64
behavioral inhibition system (BIS) 84, 85; *see also* behavioral activating system (BAS)
belief: Nietzsche on 166; social bond theory 119–20; Voltaire on 166; *see also* non-belief
Bentham, Jeremy: on hedonism 82
Bernstein, David 176
Big Bang 27
biopsychosocial: beings 9–10; criminologists xi, 52, 82, 123; insights 114; perspective x, xiv, 51–2, 192; theorists 99
births: out-of-wedlock 157
Black judges: sentencing by 198
Black Lives Matter (BLM) movement: agenda 174; rhetoric 179
Blacks: arrest rates 181, 182; crime rates 181–2; death penalty, numbers 211–12; involvement in crime 180; police shootings of 179–80; sentencing 197–8; serial killers 181; *see also* Whites
Bohr, Niels 3, 42
Bongo-Bongo tribe: Buss on 29
Botescu, George 43
Box, Steven 43
brain *see* human brain
brain function: serotonin 70
brain-derived neurotrophic factor (BDNF) gene 98
breastfeeding: and emotional development 90; and human brain 89; and IQ 89–90
Brembs, Bjorn: on free will 39
Brodie, Benjamin 9
Brown, David: on human nature 28
Brown, Michael: killing by police 177
Burgess, Robert 115
Burt, Callie: on murder 127
Buss, David: on Bongo-Bongo tribe 29

callous unemotionality (CU): constituents 106; heritability 107; low fear 107; *see also* empathy
Campbell, Anne: staying alive hypothesis 107–8
capital punishment *see* death penalty
Caruso, Greg 43; on criminal justice 191
categorical imperative: definition 188; Kant on 188
causation: top-down 11
chariot allegory: Plato 83
cheater theory ("cad vs dad") 56–8; and criminal behavior 57–8; and mating effort 56
cheaters: detection of 193–5; and moral outrage 194; and retribution 194
Chicago: crime 176–7; homicides 177
child effects: and self-control theory 122
child maltreatment *see* maltreated children
church attendance: and crime prevention 165–6
class mobility: and intelligence 150
cognition: emotion, integration in brain 17
cognitive impairment: and maltreated children 152
Cohen, Albert 132
Coleridge, Samuel Taylor: on ideology 16
commitment: social bond theory 119
community-based approaches: crime prevention 134
compatibilism 41–3; and complementarity principle 42; and criminal justice systems 42–3; definition 41
complementarity principle: and compatibilism 42; and light 42
conditional adaptation theory 58–61; and criminal behavior 59
conscience: and autonomic nervous system (ANS) 101–5; constituents 104; Darwin on 101; definition 101; and guilt 102, 104
conscientiousness: measures 153; traits 153
consequentialism: punishment 186, 188
conservation of energy: law 6
constrained visionaries: vs unconstrained visionaries 18
control *see* locus of control
control theories 113
Cornea, Andrei 7
cortisol (CRT) 81; *see also* hypercortisolism
COVID-19 pandemic 179
Crick, Francis: on neuro-determinism 39
crime: Blacks involvement in 180; Chicago 176–7; concept, as abstraction 125; defined in/out of existence 125–6; definition 128; Durkheim on 126; and emotion 46–7; and intelligence 141–2; and IQ

142, 143–5, 146; as normal behavior 53–4; ontological status 125–8; and poverty 155–6; Whites involvement in 180; *see also* antisocial behavior
crime classification: Interpol 126
crime prevention: and church attendance 165–6; community-based approaches 134; and guilt 47; left realist criminology 133–4; and religion 164–7; zero-tolerance policing 134
crime rates: African Americans 181; Blacks 181–2; Whites 182
crime statistics 133
criminal: meaning of term 5
criminal behavior: and ADHD 78; and cheater theory ("cad vs dad") 57–8; and conditional adaptation theory 59; and dopamine polymorphisms 71–2; and mating effort 56–7; and norepinephrine (NE) 78; and rationality 44, 45; and self-control 121; and serotonin polymorphisms 69–70; as survival trait 54–5
criminal history: as proxy for race 200; and sentencing 199–200
criminal justice: Caruso on 191
criminal justice system: as cause of criminalization 191; and compatibilism 42–3; and the death penalty 209; involvement with, and IQ 146; need for 173; and race 219; and sentencing 197, 201; in square of crime 133
criminal opportunity: and low self-control 121
criminality: and hedonism 44, 46; meaning 5, 128; proposed elimination of 191; sex differences 107; and sexuality 54–6
criminalization: criminal justice system as cause of 191
criminals: and justification for incapacitation 187; Marxist view 130, 132; recidivism 187, 188; rehabilitation models 187; romanticizing 130–1
criminologists: fallibility of current beliefs 24; ideology, views on 23; locus of control, views on 21–4
criminology: competing theories 113; and evolutionary developmental biology (evo-devo) 52–4; ideological debates 14–15; left realism 131–2; and philosophy 3, 4; as science of oppression 131; *see also* radical/critical criminology
critical realism: and maps of reality 6
Cullen, Francis 51
cultural relativism 7, 127

Darwin, Charles 71; on conscience 101; on natural selection 53; *On the Origin of Species* 27
DAT *see* differential association theory (DAT)
Dawkins, Richard 161, 164; *The God Delusion* 161
death penalty: abolition and retention 209; alleged anti-Black bias 212; Blacks, numbers 211–12; and criminal justice system 209; interpretation of studies on 210; and public opinion 209–10; and race 211–13; in USA 209–10, 211; and victim race 213–16; Whites, numbers 211–12; and women 217–18; *see also* life without possibility of parole (LWOP)
Dennett, Daniel: on reductionism 10
determinism: consequences 38; and externalities 38; vs free will 37; and reductionism 8–9; *see also* neuro-determinism
differential association theory (DAT): environmental effects 114; individual differences 114–15; peer influence 114; *see also* social learning theory (SLT)
differential detection hypothesis 145
differential susceptibility hypothesis (DSH) 72–4
diffusion tensor imaging (DTI) 104
discrimination: social learning theory (SLT) 116
dizygotic (DZ) twins 64; *see also* monozygotic (MZ) twins
DNA structure 9
dopamine (DA) 68, 77, 84; polymorphisms, and criminal behavior 71–2
dual inheritance theory: human behavior 27
Dugdale, Richard: *The Jukes* 141
Durant, Will: on religion 160
Durkheim, Emile 9; on crime 126; on *homo duplex* concept 28–9; on punishment 194–5

ecological fallacy: example 164
egalitarianism 31–2
Einstein, Albert: on the intellect 145; on philosophy 3
emergentism 11
emotion: cognition, integration in brain 17; and crime 46–7; and rationality 16–17; and reason, complementarity 17
emotional development: and breastfeeding 90
emotions: Haidt on 17; Hume on 100; Kant on 99; Leibniz on 99; Massey on 17; moral 100–1; neuroscience evidence for 16–17; origins 17; primary 100; secondary 100; social 100–1
empathy: affective 106; and altruism 106; cognitive 106; definition 105; effects of 106; evolution of 105; in females 105–6; genetic component 106; and guilt 101, 107; *see also* callous unemotionality (CU)
Encyclopedia of Wars 161
energy: definition 6; Feynman on 6
The Enlightenment: and rationality 99–100
environmental effects: differential association theory (DAT) 114; and evolutionary developmental biology (evo-devo) 60; and heritability 65; on IQ 150–2; shared and non-shared components 65–6
epigenetics: definition 96; DNA methylation process 96–7; experiments 97; histone acetylation process 96, 97; and maltreated children 98; and nurturing 97; and orphanage-raised children 97–8; *see also* genes
epistemology: questions of 4
Eskridge, Chris 14
essentialism: base for categorization 13; biological 12, 27; debates about 12–13; definition 11–12; origin essentialism 12; *per accidens* property 12, 13; *per se* property 11–12, 13; and Platonic Forms 11; and race 11
evil: inherently evil/evil by convention, distinction 126
evo-devo *see* evolutionary developmental biology (evo-devo)
evolution: definition 53
evolutionary developmental biology (evo-devo): and criminology 52–4; and environmental effects 60; and the human brain 87–9
evolutionary psychology 53
evolutionary theory: explanatory role 53; Teilhard de Chardin on 60–1
externalities: and determinism 38

fatalism: and human agency 38
fathers: absence of 92; abusive 92
fear mechanism: and Aristotle's Golden Mean 109; function 108–9
Felthous, Alan 41
female pelvis size: and human brain size 88
females: avoidance of violence 108; brain, size, and pelvis size 88; empathy in 105–6; hypothalamic-pituitary-adrenal (HPA) axis 108; maltreated, hypercortisolism in 95; *see also* women
fetal alcohol syndrome (FAS): and IQ 152
Feynman, Richard: on energy 6
fight-flee-freeze system (FFFS) 84–5
Fish, Jonathan 28–9
Floyd, George: killing by police 173
Flynn Effect 150, 151–2
forgiveness: strategies 195–6; and tit-for-tat reciprocity 195–6
fractional anisotropy (FA) 105
Francis, Jenny: on human nature 25–6
free will: and autonomic nervous system (ANS) 40; and behavior unpredictability 37–8; Brembs on 39; constraints on 39; definition 38–9; vs determinism 37; and "free won't" 40–1; and freedom of action 42; and human agency 38; as illusion 40; Libet on 40–1; and locus of control 39; as quantitative 39; and rationality 43–6; Schopenhauer on 41; Shafer on 37; *see also* compatibilism
"free won't": and free will 40–1
freedom of action: and free will 42
French Revolution: American Revolution, comparison 18

gamma and gamma-aminobutyric acid (GABA) 78–9; and alcohol 79
Gannett, Lisa 28
Garlick, Dennis 140

gender: and sentencing 201–3
gene perpetuation: and high status 31
gene-environment correlation (rGE): active 67; evocative 66–7; and gene-environmental interaction (GxE) 66–8; MZ and DZ twins 67; passive 66
gene-environmental interaction (GxE): and gene-environment correlation (rGE) 66–8
general mental ability (GMA) 153–4
genes: and high status 32; influence of 63; Ridley on 63; and socioeconomic status (SES) 148–9; *see also* behavioral genetics; molecular genetics
genetic: determinism 62–3; polymorphisms 68
genetic component: empathy 106
genetics: and self-control 122–3
genome 53; rate of change 88; as reactive system 63; as recipe 96
Genome-Wide Polygenic scores (GPSs) 69
Goddard, Henry: *The Kallikak Family* 141
good and evil 31; driven by selfishness 33–6; subjectiveness of 167
guilt 101; and conscience 102, 104; and crime prevention 47; and empathy 101, 107; influences on 100; nature of 101; and self-control 120

Haidt, Jonathan: on emotions 17
Harris, Judith 54
Harrison Narcotics Act (1914) 126
Hawkins, Darnell 125
Hawthorne, Nathaniel: *The Scarlet Letter* 186
hedonism: Bentham on 82; and criminality 44, 46
Heisenberg, Werner 3; uncertainty principle 38
heritability: of antisocial behavior 191; callous unemotionality (CU) 107; definition 64; and environmental effects 65; gap, molecular genetics 69; IQ 150–1; measurement 64–5; sources 65
high status: evolutionary benefit of 31; and gene perpetuation 31; and genes 32
high-IQ people: Nazi war criminals 146; psychopaths 146; serial killers 146; successful criminals 145
hippocampus 76
Hirschi, Travis 118, 118–19
Hitchens, Christopher 164; *God is Not Great* 161–2
Hobbes, Thomas: on human nature 31; Rousseau, comparison 34
homicides: by women 217; Chicago 177; Minneapolis 177; New York City 177
homo duplex concept: complementarity 29; criticism of 29; Durkheim on 28–9
honor killings 7, 127
hormones 80–1
HPA *see* hypothalamic-pituitary-adrenal (HPA) axis
human agency: and fatalism 38; and free will 38
human brain: and breastfeeding 89; capacity increase 87–8; communication 77–8; encephalization quotient 88; evolution 80, 85–6; and evolutionary developmental biology (evo-devo) 87–9; neuroplasticity model 140–1; plasticity 94; size, and female pelvis size 88; structure 75–6
human brain development 80, 85–6; and childhood maltreatment 91–3; experience-dependent processes 93, 94; experience-expected processes 93–4
Human Connectome Project (HCP) 141
human nature: assumptions about 25; Brown on 28; constituents 26; and cultural determinism 30; definitions 26; denial of 26; Francis on 25–6; Hobbes on 31; Hume on 30; Lenski on 25; malleability 29–30; Mead on 29; and natural selection 27; perennial traits 30; Rousseau on 31; as social construction 25, 30; theory of, need for 35–6; universality of 27; *see also* self-interest
Hume, David: on the emotions 100; on human nature 30
hypercortisolism 95–6
hypothalamic-pituitary-adrenal (HPA) axis 81; arousal 95; female 108

ideology: Coleridge on 16; criminologists' views 23; debates, criminology 14–15; definition 15; formation 19; and sentencing 198; as subconscious roadmap 23; and temperament 16–17
immorality: and moral relativism 8
intellect: Einstein on 145

intelligence: and class mobility 150; and crime 141–2; crystallized 137, 138; definitions 136–7; etymology 136; fluid 137–8; general 137; influence 139; as master attribute 138–9; measure, Spearman's *g* 137; as mental energy 136; and neurobiology 139–41; Parieto-Frontal Integration Theory (P-FIT) 140; *see also* IQ
intermittent explosive disorder (IED) 82
Interpol: crime classification 126
involvement: social bond theory 119
IQ (Intelligence Quotient): and academic achievement 144; and antisocial behavior 143; and breastfeeding 89–90; and crime 142, 143–5; criticism of 136; environmental effects on 150–2; and fetal alcohol syndrome (FAS) 152; heritability 150–1; and involvement with criminal justice system 146; and lead poisoning 152; and maltreated children 152, 153; and maternal alcohol consumption 152; and moral awareness 143; Raven Standard Progressive Matrices test 138; and Scholastic Aptitude Test (SAT) 151; and socioeconomic status (SES) 148–50; stability of 138; tests 138; *see also* high-IQ people; intelligence

James, William: on temperament 16
justice: Aristotle on 200; as "just deserts" 200

Kaba, Mariame 173
Kant, Immanuel: on the categorical imperative 188; on the emotions 99; phenomenal/noumenal distinction 6; on retribution 188–9
Katz, Jack 46
King, Martin Luther, Jr: on religion 160
Kuo, Zing 9

labeling theory 128–30; primary deviance 129; secondary deviance 129
language: capacity for 93
lead poisoning: and IQ 152
left realist criminology 131–5; crime prevention 133–4; marginalization 132; relative deprivation 132; square of crime 133–5; subculture 132
left-right visions: conflict 17–18
Leibniz, Gottfried: on the emotions 99
Lenski, Gerhard: on human nature 25
Levenson, Robert: on the autonomic nervous system (ANS) 101–2
liberalism-conservatism: continuum 18–19; on sources of wealth and poverty 21–2
Libet, B.: on free will 40–1
life without possibility of parole (LWOP): and race 218–20
light: and complementarity principle 42
limbic system 17; functions 75–6
locus of control: continuum 19; criminologists' views 21–4; and environment 20; and free will 39; internal vs external 19; liberal/conservative divide 21; stability 20; variability 20
love: and brain activity 10–11
low fear: callous unemotionality (CU) 107

McCleskey v. Kemp: victim race 213–14
Machery, Edouard 26
maltreated children: and cognitive impairment 152; and epigenetics 98; and IQ 152, 153
maltreated females: hypercortisolism in 95
maltreatment: and antisocial behavior 95–6; and human brain development 91–3
Mao Zedong 28
marginalization: left realist criminology 132
marriage: and self-interest 35
Marx, Karl 26
Massey, Douglas:on emotions 17
mating effort 55; and cheater theory ("cad vs dad") 56; and criminal behavior 56–7
Mead, Margaret:on human nature 29
Mealey, Linda 56
Merton, Robert: anomie/strain theory 46, 147–8, 155
metaphysics 4; *see also* ontology
mind: as blank slate 28
Minneapolis: homicides 177
molecular genetics: heritability gap 69; trait variation 68
monoamine oxidase A (MAOA) gene: and allele gene 70; and antisocial behavior 70; GxE study 70
monozygotic (MZ) twins 63–4; and DZ twins, gene-environment correlation (rGE) 67; *see also* dizygotic (DZ) twins

Montagu, Ashley 89
mood regulation: norepinephrine (NE) 78
moral awareness: and IQ 143
moral codes 167
moral outrage: and cheaters 194
moral relativism 7–8; and immorality 8; and postmodernism 8
moral self-governance :and religion 160
murder: Burt on 127; of slave 127; as social construction 127; *see also* honor killings
Myrdal, Gunner: on ideology in social science 14

Nagel, Thomas 8
National Crime Victimization Survey (NCVS) 134
National Longitudinal Survey of Youth 149
natural selection: Darwin on 53; and human nature 27
nature: vs nurture 31, 62; seamlessness of 63; ubiquity of 26; *see also* human nature
Nettler, Gwynn 117
neuro-determinism: Crick on 39; experiments 40; *see also* determinism
neurobiology: and intelligence 139–41
neurotransmitters 77–8; *see also* gamma-aminobutyric acid; synaptogenesis
New Atheism movement: leading figures 161
New York City: homicides 177
Nietzsche, Friedrich: on belief in God 166
nominalism: definition 5; examples of 5; and radical/critical criminology 125; *see also* realism
non-belief: and antisocial behavior 166–7
norepinephrine (NE) 77–8; and criminal behavior 78; mood regulation 78
norms: moral 104, 120; prosocial 101, 104, 193; of reciprocal altruism 31, 35, 194; and social harmony 74
nurturing: and epigenetics 97

odds ratio 214
ontogeny 58
ontology: questions of 4
orbitofrontal cortex (OFC) 82; sex differences 108
orphanage-raised children: and epigenetics 97–8

parasympathetic system: autonomic nervous system (ANS) 102
parental input: socioeconomic status (SES) 147, 148, 149, 149–50
parenting effort 55; and non-crime behavior 56
Parieto-Frontal Integration Theory (P-FIT) 140
Park, Seunebae 7
Patterson, Orlando 21
peer influence: differential association theory (DAT) 114
Penrose, Roger 75
Personal Responsibility and Work Opportunity Reconciliation Act (PRWORA: 1996): criticisms of 158; positive effects 157–8
Peterson, Christopher 9–10
phenomenal/noumenal distinction: Kant 6
philosophy: and criminology 3, 4; of criminology, purpose 3; Einstein on 3; and science 3; scope 4; value of 3–4
Pinker, Steven 8
Plato: allegories 30; archetypal Forms 5; Aristotle, modes of thought 16, 18; chariot allegory 83; model of the soul (psyche) 83; Ring of Gyges allegory 34
Platonic Forms: and essentialism 11
Plomin, Robert 63
police: absence, and vigilantism 176; bias against 179; de-policing effects 176–7, 179; justified lethal force, use 182–3; lack of political support 178; low morale 178; proposals to abolish 173, 174–5; proposals to reduce in size 175–6; resignations 178; and reverse racism 183; shootings of Blacks 179–80; shootings by Black police officers 184–5; shootings of unarmed offenders 180–1; social functions 175; "war" on 177–8
police-community relations 133
policing: proactive 177
polymorphisms: serotonin, and criminal behavior 69–70; single-nucleotide (SNPs) 68; Val Met 68
postmodernism: and moral relativism 8
poverty: anti-poverty programs 157–8; causes of 154–5; and crime 155–6; definition 154; models of 154; and socioeconomic status (SES) 147, 154–5; "War on Poverty" (1964) 156–7; *see also* wealth and poverty

prefrontal cortex (PFC): role 76
Presentence Investigation Reports (PSIs) 206–8; defendant's access to 207–8; not mandatory 207; purpose 206–7
psychology: and biology 9
psychopaths: high-IQ people 146
Psychopathy Checklist Revised (PCL-R): Hare's 104–5
public opinion: and the death penalty 209–10
punishment: as altruism 190, 194; consequentialist view 186, 188; deterrence function 187, 194; Durkheim on 194–5; as evolutionary adaptation 192–3; moral justification for 186; public support for 190; rejection of 189–92; as retribution 188; Reznik on 189–90; and social learning theory (SLT) 116; *see also* retribution

race: criminal history as proxy 200; and criminal justice system 219; and the death penalty 211–13; and essentialism 11; and life without possibility of parole (LWOP) 218–20; and sentencing 197–9; *see also* victim race
radical/critical criminology: and nominalism 125; origins 124–5; and romanticizing of criminals 130–1; scope 124
rational choice theory: and agency 46
rationality: and criminal behavior 44, 45; definition 44; and emotion 16–17; and free will 43–6; instrumental 44; limits 45; and self-interest 44; and The Enlightenment 99–100; unintended outcomes 45; value-related 44; Weber on 44–5
Raven Standard Progressive Matrices test 138
realism: definition 5; *see also* critical realism; nominalism
recidivism: criminals 187, 188; risk assessments 204–5
reductionism: Dennett on 10; and determinism 8–9; eliminative 10; fear of 9; good 10
rehabilitation models: criminals 187
reinforcement sensitivity theory (RST) 82–6; definition 82
relative deprivation: left realist criminology 132
religion: and antisocial behavior 161–4; and crime prevention 164–7; Durant on 160; Luther King on 160; and moral self-governance 160; and self-control 167–9; as source of violence 161, 163; Tocqueville on 160; Washington on 159–60
retribution: and cheaters 194; as just deserts 189; Kant on 188–9; punishment as 188; rejection of 188; Zimmerman on 189; *see also* punishment
Reynolds, Barbara 174
Reznik, Rafi: on punishment 189–90
rGE *see* gene-environment correlation (rGE)
Ridley, Matt 10; on genes 63
risk-models: and sentencing guidelines 204
Rousseau, Jean-Jacques: Hobbes, comparison 34; on human nature 31
Russell, Bertrand 3

Sagan, Carl 28
Sartre, J.P. 37
SAT *see* Scholastic Aptitude Test (SAT)
Schlinger, Henry 136
Scholastic Aptitude Test (SAT): and IQ 151
Schopenhauer, Arthur: on free will 41
science: and philosophy 3; younger vs older science 9
Seattle: Capitol Hill Occupied Protest (CHOP) zone 176
self-control: and criminal behavior 121; and criminal opportunity 121; definition 120, 121; and effective parenting 120; and genetics 122–3; and guilt 120; low 120, 121; and religion 167–9; and serotonin 84
self-control theory 120–2; and child effects 122; as "T-Rex of criminology" 122
self-interest: and altruism 34–5; and behavior 43–4; and marriage 35; need for 33–4; and rationality 44; socially useful 34; Weber on 33–4; Wilson on 34, 35
selfishness: driver of good and evil 33–6
sentencing: Blacks 197–8; by Black judges 198; and criminal justice system 197, 201; and gender 201–3; and ideology 198; predictors of 199–200; and prior criminal

history 199–200; and race 197–9; as rationally-based sexism 201–2; research 198–9; serial killers 203; and Sixth Amendment violation 206; and victim characteristics 198; *see also* Presentence Investigation Reports (PSIs)
sentencing guidelines 203–6; and behavior prediction 204; contents 203; non-guideline states 205; purpose 203–4; and risk-models 204; and *United States v. Booker* 206; variations 206
September 11 (2001) events 161
serial killers; Blacks 181; gender distribution 202–3; high-IQ people 146; sentencing 203
serotonin (5-HT): brain function 70; and self-control 84
sex differences: criminality 107
sexuality: and criminality 54–6
Shafer, Stephen: on free will 37
Sharp, Boyd 19–20
Sixth Amendment violation: and sentencing 206
Skinner, B.E. 37
social ascription: socioeconomic status (SES) as 148
social bond theory 118; attachment 119; belief 119–20; commitment 119; involvement 119
social construction: human nature as 25, 30; murder as 127
social control 118
social harmony: norms 74
social instincts: Barkow on 31
social learning theory (SLT) 113, 115–16; differential reinforcement 116; discrimination 116; neglect of individual differences 117–18; and punishment 116; *see also* differential association theory (DAT)
socialization process 102
society: concept 6
socioeconomic status (SES): and genes 148–9; and IQ 148–50; parental input 147, 148, 149, 149–50; and poverty 147, 154–5; as social ascription 148; and temperament 153–4
sociogenomics 62
Sowell, Thomas: constrained/unconstrained visions 17–18
Spearman's *g*: intelligence measure 137
species: evolution of 27–8
Sperry, Roger 75
Spiro, Melford 30
square of crime: criminal justice systems in 133; definition 133; left realist criminology 133–5
staying alive hypothesis: Campbell 107–8
stress response: mediation of 95; value of 94–5
subculture: left realist criminology 132
Sun Tzu: *The Art of War* 30
Surratt, Mary 217
survival trait: criminal behavior as 54–5
Sutton, Willie 46–7
sympathetic system: autonomic nervous system (ANS) 102
synapses: elimination/retention 80
synaptogenesis: creation and elimination 79; in infancy 79

Teilhard de Chardin, Pierre: on evolutionary theory 60–1
temperament: and ideology 16–17; James on 16; and socioeconomic status (SES) 153–4
testosterone 80–1
Tinbergen, Nikolas: four questions 51
tit-for-tat reciprocity: and forgiveness 195–6
Tocqueville, Alexis de, on religion 160
trait variation: molecular genetics 68
triple imbalance hypothesis (TIH):and aggression 81–2
Turkheimer, E. 64–5
twins: adoption studies 63–5

uncertainty principle: Heisenberg 38
United States v. Booker: and sentencing guidelines 206
universals 5
USA: death penalty in 209–10, 211

vengeance *see* retribution
victim race: and death penalty 213–16; *McCleskey v. Kemp* 213–14
victimization: likely candidates 134–5
vigilantism: and police absence 176
violence: and evolutionary logic 59–60; female avoidance of 108; reasons for 56; religion as source of 161, 163
visions: constrained/unconstrained, Sowell on 17–18; *see also* constrained visionaries
Voltaire: on belief in God 166

Walsh, Denis 12
Walters, Glen 47
"War on Poverty": Johnson administration (1964) 156–7
Washington, George: on religion 159–60
wealth and poverty: liberalism-conservatism divide on 21–2
Weber, Max 38; on rationality 44–5; on self-interest 33–4
Wechsler, David 137
Whites: arrest rates 182; crime rates 182; death penalty, numbers 211–12; involvement in crime 180; *see also* Blacks
whore vs Madonna dichotomy 59
Wilson, Edward O. 9; on self-interest 34, 35
Wilson, James Q. 92, 186, 187
women: and the death penalty 217–18; on death row (2024) 217; homicides by 217; *see also* females
Woodger, Joseph 9

Young, Jock 46

Zack, Naoimi 11
zero-tolerance policing: crime prevention 134
Zimmerman, Michael: on retribution 189
Zuckerman, Phil 163

FSC
www.fsc.org
MIX
Papier | Fördert
gute Waldnutzung
FSC® C083411

Kolibri 360 GmbH
Ferdinand-Jühlke-Straße 7
99095 Erfurt, Deutschland
produktsicherheit@kolibri360.de